"This fascinating book fills a large gap, and provides an important corrective, showing Sabina Spielrein as an original and innovative psychoanalytic thinker in her own right, not as a minor or romantic character between Jung and Freud, nor as one who primarily borrowed from them and Piaget, for example. Cooper-White and Kelcourse, along with Harris and Naszkowska, give us Spielrein as one of the truly influential women in early psychoanalysis, despite erasure and non-citation. Accessible translations of her writings allow us to hear her own extraordinary voice."

– **Donna M. Orange, Ph.D., Psy.D.**, New York Postdoctoral Program in Psychotherapy and Psychoanalysis, New York, USA

Sabina Spielrein and the Beginnings of Psychoanalysis

Sabina Spielrein stands as both an important and tragic figure – misunderstood or underestimated by her fellow analysts (including Jung and Freud) and often erased in the annals of psychoanalytic history. Her story has not only been largely forgotten, but actively (though unconsciously) repressed as the figure who represented a trauma buried in the early history of psychoanalysis.

Sabina Spielrein and the Beginnings of Psychoanalysis joins the growing field of scholarship on Spielrein's distinctive and significant theoretical innovations at the foundations of psychoanalysis and serves as a new English language source for many of Spielrein's key works. The book includes:

- Four chapters by Felicity Brock Kelcourse, Pamela Cooper-White, Klara Naszkowska, and Adrienne Harris spanning Spielrein's life and exploring her works in depth, with new insights about her influence not only on Jung and Freud, but also on Piaget in Geneva and Vygotsky and Luria in Moscow.
- A timeline providing readers with important historical context including Spielrein, Freud, Jung, other theorists, and historical events in Europe (1850–1950).
- Twelve new translations of works by Spielrein, ten of which are the first ever translations into English from the original French, German, or Russian.

Spielrein's life and works are currently undergoing a serious and necessary critical reclamation, as the fascinating chapters in this book attest. *Sabina Spielrein and the Beginnings of Psychoanalysis* will be of great significance to all psychoanalysts, psychoanalytic psychotherapists, analytical psychologists, and scholars of psychoanalysis interested in Spielrein and the early development of the field.

Pamela Cooper-White is the Christiane Brooks Johnson Professor of Psychology and Religion, Union Theological Seminary, New York, and 2013–2014 Fulbright–Freud Scholar of Psychoanalysis, Vienna, Austria. She is the author of seven books including most recently *Old and Dirty Gods: Religion, Antisemitism, and the Origins of Psychoanalysis* (Routledge, 2017).

Felicity Brock Kelcourse is Associate Professor of Psychology of Religion and Pastoral Psychotherapy at Christian Theological Seminary in Indianapolis. Her most recent books include (as editor and contributor) *Human Development and Faith*, 2nd edition (Chalice, 2015) and *Transforming Wisdom: Pastoral Psychotherapy in Theological Perspective*, co-edited with K. Brynolf Lyon (Cascade, 2015).

The Relational Perspectives Book Series (RPBS) publishes books that grow out of or contribute to the relational tradition in contemporary psychoanalysis. The term *relational psychoanalysis* was first used by Greenberg and Mitchell[1] to bridge the traditions of interpersonal relations, as developed within interpersonal psychoanalysis and object relations, as developed within contemporary British theory. But, under the seminal work of the late Stephen A. Mitchell, the term *relational psychoanalysis* grew and began to accrue to itself many other influences and developments. Various tributaries – interpersonal psychoanalysis, object relations theory, self psychology, empirical infancy research, and elements of contemporary Freudian and Kleinian thought – flow into this tradition, which understands relational configurations between self and others, both real and fantasied, as the primary subject of psychoanalytic investigation.

We refer to the relational tradition, rather than to a relational school, to highlight that we are identifying a trend, a tendency within contemporary psychoanalysis, not a more formally organized or coherent school or system of beliefs. Our use of the term *relational* signifies a dimension of theory and practice that has become salient across the wide spectrum of contemporary psychoanalysis. Now under the editorial supervision of Lewis Aron, Adrienne Harris, Steven Kuchuck, and Eyal Rozmarin, the RPBS originated in 1990 under the editorial eye of the late Stephen A. Mitchell. Mitchell was the most prolific and influential of the originators of the relational tradition. Committed to dialogue among psychoanalysts, he abhorred the authoritarianism that dictated adherence to a rigid set of beliefs or technical restrictions. He championed open discussion and comparative and integrative approaches and he promoted new voices across the generations.

Included in the RPBS are authors and works that come from within the relational tradition and extend and develop that tradition, as well as works that critique relational approaches or compare and contrast them with alternative points of view. The series includes our most distinguished senior psychoanalysts, along with younger contributors who bring fresh vision. A full list of titles in this series is available at www.routledge.com/mentalhealth/series/LEARPBS.

Note

1 Greenberg, J. & Mitchell, S. (1983). *Object relations in psychoanalytic theory.* Cambridge, MA: Harvard University Press.

Sabina Spielrein and the Beginnings of Psychoanalysis

Image, Thought, and Language

Edited by Pamela Cooper-White and
Felicity Brock Kelcourse

LONDON AND NEW YORK

First published 2019
by Routledge
2 Park Square, Milton Park, Abingdon, Oxon OX14 4RN

and by Routledge
52 Vanderbilt Avenue, New York, NY 10017

Routledge is an imprint of the Taylor & Francis Group, an informa business

© 2019 selection and editorial matter, Pamela Cooper-White and Felicity Brock Kelcourse; individual chapters, the contributors

The right of the editors to be identified as the authors of the editorial material, and of the authors for their individual chapters, has been asserted in accordance with sections 77 and 78 of the Copyright, Designs and Patents Act 1988.

All rights reserved. No part of this book may be reprinted or reproduced or utilised in any form or by any electronic, mechanical, or other means, now known or hereafter invented, including photocopying and recording, or in any information storage or retrieval system, without permission in writing from the publishers.

Trademark notice: Product or corporate names may be trademarks or registered trademarks, and are used only for identification and explanation without intent to infringe.

British Library Cataloguing in Publication Data
A catalogue record for this book is available from the British Library

Library of Congress Cataloging in Publication Data
Names: Cooper-White, Pamela, 1955– editor. | Kelcourse, Felicity Brock, editor. | Spielrein, Sabina. Works. Selections. English.
Title: Sabina Spielrein and the beginnings of psychoanalysis : image, thought, and language / edited by Pamela Cooper-White and Felicity Brock Kelcourse.
Description: Abingdon, Oxon ; New York, NY : Routledge, 2019. | Includes bibliographical references and index.
Identifiers: LCCN 2018046086 (print) | LCCN 2018047071 (ebook) | ISBN 9781315104324 (e-Book) | ISBN 9781351597760 (Adobe) | ISBN 9781351597753 (ePub3) | ISBN 9781351597746 (Mobipocket) | ISBN 9781138098633 (hardback : alk. paper) | ISBN 9781138098657 (pbk. : alk. paper)
Subjects: LCSH: Spielrein, Sabina. | Psychoanalysts. | Psychoanalysis.
Classification: LCC BF109.S65 (ebook) |
LCC BF109.S65 S33 2019 (print) | DDC 616.89/17–dc23
LC record available at https://lccn.loc.gov/2018046086

ISBN: 978-1-138-09863-3 (hbk)
ISBN: 978-1-138-09865-7 (pbk)
ISBN: 978-1-315-10432-4 (ebk)

Typeset in Times New Roman
by Newgen Publishing UK

Printed and bound in Great Britain by
TJ International Ltd, Padstow, Cornwall

To our parents:
Tom and Connie,
Mitchell and Gioia

Contents

Contributors	xiii
Acknowledgments	xvii
Permissions	xix

Introduction   1
PAMELA COOPER-WHITE AND FELICITY BROCK KELCOURSE

PART I
Life and works – an overview   11

A comparative timeline: Spielrein, Freud, Jung, and other theorists, including key works and significant events within the history of psychoanalysis   13
PAMELA COOPER-WHITE, FELICITY BROCK KELCOURSE, AND ADRIENNE HARRIS

1 Sabina Spielrein from Rostov to Zürich: The making of an analyst   36
FELICITY BROCK KELCOURSE

2 From Zürich to Vienna: "The power that beautifies and destroys"   73
PAMELA COOPER-WHITE

3 Passions, politics, and drives: Sabina Spielrein in Soviet Russia   110
KLARA NASZKOWSKA

4 "Language is there to bewilder itself and others": Theoretical and clinical contributions of Sabina Spielrein   151
ADRIENNE HARRIS

PART II
Samples of Spielrein's writings – new translations in English — 195

5 On the Psychological Content of a Case of Schizophrenia (Dementia Praecox) (1911) (An Excerpt) — 197

6 Destruction as the Cause of Becoming (1912) — 209

7 Maternal Love (1913) — 254

8 The Forgotten Name (1914) — 256

9 Two Menstrual Dreams (1914) — 257

10 Russian Literature on Psychoanalysis (1921) — 261

11 Who Is the Guilty One? (1922) — 273

12 Time in Subliminal Psychic Life (1923) — 279

13 The Three Questions (1923) — 295

14 Some Analogies between Thinking in Children, Aphasia, and the Subconscious Mind (1923) — 301

15 Dr. Skalkovskiy's Report (1929) — 322

16 Children's Drawings with Eyes Open and Closed (1928/1931) — 330

Index — 367

Contributors

Pamela Cooper-White, PhD, is the Christiane Brooks Johnson Professor of Psychology and Religion at Union Theological Seminary, New York, and the 2013–2014 Fulbright–Freud Scholar of Psychoanalysis at the Sigmund Freud Museum and the University of Vienna. She is the author of seven books in the areas of pastoral/practical theology, feminist theory and violence against women, and the intersection of psychoanalysis and religion (history, theory, and clinical practice), including most recently *Old and Dirty Gods: Religion, Antisemitism, and the Origins of Psychoanalysis* (Routledge, 2017). Her current research includes a comparative study of Schönberg's Moses and Freud's Moses on a grant from the Arnold Schönberg Center, Vienna, and a book on memory and identity from a relational psychoanalytic and theological perspective.

Adrienne Harris, PhD, is Faculty and Supervisor at the New York University Postdoctoral Program in Psychotherapy and Psychoanalysis. She is on the faculty and is a supervisor at the Psychoanalytic Institute of Northern California. She established the Sandor Ferenczi Center at the New School University with Lewis Aron and Jeremy Safran in 2009. She coedits the Routledge book series "Relational Perspectives in Psychoanalysis" and is an editor of the International Psychoanalytic Association's e-journal (http://psychoanalysistoday.com). A relational analyst, she writes about gender and development, analytic subjectivity, ghosts, and the analysts developing and writing around the period of the First World War.

Felicity Brock Kelcourse, PhD, is Associate Professor of Psychology of Religion and Pastoral Psychotherapy and a core faculty member of the MA in Clinical Mental Health at Christian Theological Seminary, Indianapolis. She has authored numerous articles and edited or coedited four anthologies in the areas of pastoral theology and psychology and religion. Her most recent books include (as editor and contributor) *Human Development and Faith,* 2nd edition (Chalice, 2015) and *Transforming Wisdom: Pastoral Psychotherapy in Theological Perspective*, coedited with K. Brynolf Lyon (Cascade, 2015). A Diplomate pastoral psychotherapist in the American Association of Pastoral Counselors and a Marriage and Family Supervisor in continuous private practice since 1994, she is currently a post-Propaedeuticum candidate in the Inter-Regional Society of Jungian Analysts. Her research interests include the interaction of ego, psyche, and soul as they relate to discernment in religious experience and psychotherapy.

Klara Naszkowska, PhD, is a member of the Polish Centre for Holocaust Research/Polish Academy of Sciences in Warsaw, Poland, a 2019–2020 senior Fulbright exchange scholar to the USA, and the founding director of the International Association for Spielrein Studies. Having devoted her postdoctoral studies to Spielrein, she has authored a book and papers in English and Polish, given lectures, and served as a professional consultant on Spielrein for the Dramatic Theatre in Warsaw. On behalf of the Association, she is organizing the first international conference on Spielrein in Warsaw in April, 2020.

Translators and co-translators

Ekaterina Golynkina, PhD, is a Fellow of the British Psychoanalytical Society. She works for the British National Health Service as a Consultant Clinical Psychologist in the Complex Needs Service at Springfield University Hospital, London, as a Visiting Lecturer at the Tavistock Clinic, and as a psychoanalyst in private practice. She teaches the Introductory Lectures at the Institute of Psychoanalysis and internationally.

Judith Gresh, PhD, is a psychologist specializing in qualitative methods used in verbal discourse analysis. Her publications focus on applications examining the role of spirituality in psychiatric patients, the dynamics of personal habits in writing, and the concept of quality in scientometrics. She has held research and teaching positions at the University of Geneva and the University of Lausanne. She has worked extensively as a court translator in judicial proceedings. She is fluent in French, Hungarian, and Russian.

Robby Kongolo, MA Ed. in Language Education, is currently Head Lower Division French Teacher at St. Richard's Episcopal School, Indianapolis. He was the Director of the Language Program for Adult Language Learning at the Alliance Française of Indianapolis in 2014 and served as Language Interpreter for French, English, and Sango at Luna Language Services in 2015. His interests include linguistics and second language learning for young adults and adults.

Bettina Mathes, Dr. Phil., Habil., is a cultural historian, writer, and psychoanalyst in private practice. She is the author of three books on European cultural history, religion, and the visual arts, including the award-winning *Verschleierte Wirklichkeit: Die Frau, der Islam und der Westen* (cowritten with Christina von Braun, 2007/2017). Her essays on psychoanalysis, memory, art, film, and visual culture have appeared in *Third Text*; *FlashArt*; *Psychoanalysis, Culture & Society*; *Frauen und Film*, and *Chain* (among others). She writes regularly on film for the psychoanalytic quarterly *DIVISION/Review* (American Psychological Association, Div. 39), where she served as senior editor from 2015 to 2017. In 2009, she was invited to deliver the inaugural lecture of the series "Lecturas por la Paz" at the Instituto Euro-Arabe, Granada, Spain, where she lives and practices.

Jan Rehmann, PhD, is Visiting Professor for Critical Theory and Social Analysis, Director of the PhD program at Union Theological Seminary in New York City, and Privatdozent at the Free University in Berlin. He is the coeditor of the journal *Das Argument* and of the *Historical-Critical Dictionary of Marxism*. Selected publications include *Max Weber: Modernization as Passive Revolution. A Gramscian Analysis* (Haymarket Books, 2015); *Theories of Ideology. The Powers of Alienation and Subjection* (Haymarket Books, 2014); *Pedagogy of the Poor: Building a Movement to End Poverty* (Teachers

College Press, 2011, together with Willie Baptist); and *Postmoderner Links-Nietzscheanismus: Deleuze & Foucault. Eine Dekonstruktion* (Argument-Verlag, 2004).

Anatoli Samochornov, MA, MBA, is a translator, interpreter, and editor based in New York. He received his MA in linguistics from Nizhny Novgorod Institute of Foreign Languages in 1991 and an MBA from the University of Washington in 1994.

Sergey Trostyanskiy, PhD, is an Eastern Orthodox priest and scholar. He serves at St. Gregory the Theologian Church in New York City. He is the author of *St. Cyril of Alexandria's Metaphysics of the Incarnation* (Peter Lang, 2016) and has taught philosophy and patristics at Union Theological Seminary, New York; the General Theological Seminary, New York; and Marist College, Poughkeepsie, New York.

Acknowledgments

This project has been a labor of love for many years, and as such, we have many people to thank for their support! First and foremost, we thank Adrienne Harris, without whose generosity and collaboration this volume could not have been published. Thanks also go to Kate Hawes and Charles Bath at Routledge, and copy-editors John Stewart Marr and Céline Durassier, for bringing this project to fruition.

Our work has been enriched by many colleagues along the way. We are grateful to Isabelle Noth, whose collaboration resulted in the symposium on Spielrein in the Psychology, Culture and Religion Group of the American Academy of Religion in 2012, and to Lewis Rambo for publishing our initial foray into Spielrein's life and work in the journal *Pastoral Psychology* in 2015. Other scholars and organizations whose support has been invaluable include Daniela Finzi and the staff of the Sigmund Freud Museum, Vienna; the Jung Society of Atlanta; Ruth Cape; Sabrina Leroe; Henry Zvi Lothane; Peter Rudnytsky; Herman Westerink; and Jeanne Wolff-Bernstein. We also thank Klara Naszkowska, not only for her contribution to this volume, but also for her dedication in creating a new International Association for Spielrein Studies based in Warsaw, Poland (www.spielreinassociation.org).

Special thanks go to Spielrein biographer John Launer for his encouragement and consultation, and to the director of Spielrein's literary estate, Dr. Vladimir Shpilrain, for his permission to publish new English translations of Spielrein's work and support of our project overall.

We could not have completed this volume without the diligent work of our chief translators Judith Gresh and Bettina Mathes, and co-translators Ekaterina Golynkina, Robby Kongolo, Jan Rehmann,

Anatoli Samochornov, and Sergey Trostyanskiy. Thanks also to Jeremy Hultin for help with a passage in Greek, Alan Rhoda for his assistance in tracking down obscure translation references, and Mark Winborn for assistance with the chronology of Jung's works.

As always, we thank our families for their love and support.

With this project, we honor the memory of relational analyst Jeremy Safran, whose efforts to recover lost voices in the history of psychoanalysis remain an inspiration.

The editors

Permissions

Earlier versions of Chapters 1 and 2 appeared in 2015 in *Pastoral Psychology*, 64(2), 259–278. They are adapted for this book and reused by permission of Springer Publishing.

An earlier version of Chapter 4 appeared in 2015 in *Journal of the American Psychoanalytic Association*, 63(4), 727–768. Reprinted by permission of SAGE Publishing.

New translations are here published with kind permission from Vladimir Shpilrain, for the Spielrein literary estate.

Introduction

*Pamela Cooper-White and
Felicity Brock Kelcourse, editors*

Who was Sabina Spielrein (1885–1942)? In 1904, she was a brilliant 19-year-old Jewish girl who aspired to be a doctor, journeying from her home in Rostov-on-Don, Russia, to Zürich, Switzerland. There she was hospitalized at the Burghölzli hospital with a diagnosis of "hysteria," treated by Eugen Bleuler and Carl Jung, and was able, within less than a year, to begin her medical studies. Her diary entries from 1909–1912 (Carotenuto, 1982) reveal a young woman caught up in an intense transference toward her analyst, Jung, who nevertheless maintained her own sense of purpose and ambition, enabling her to become an analyst in her own right. This volume attempts to give Spielrein back her voice, emphasizing her development as the creative, pioneering analyst she was to become.

A glimpse into Spielrein's life and works

For the English-speaking public, Sabina Spielrein's name is now popularly best known, if at all, because of an American film, *A Dangerous Method* (Cronenberg, 2011), based on the eponymous book by historian John Kerr (1994), sensationalized for Hollywood audiences. The film itself focuses on Spielrein's young adulthood, from her admission to the Burghölzli to her graduation as a medical doctor and relocation from Zürich to Vienna, joining Freud's early circle of psychoanalysts. At the heart of this narrative is a trauma – Jung entered into a romantic relationship with Spielrein, which, as it began to come to light, threatened Jung's marriage and his reputation as a doctor. Freud became embroiled in attempting to put an end to the boundary violation, as both Jung's wife Emma, and Spielrein herself, warned him that more was going on than Jung had vaguely implied in previous letters. Freud was alarmed that such a scandal would destroy not only Jung, his hoped-for "crown prince" of psychoanalysis, but also could permanently tarnish the reputation of psychoanalysis itself. This worry prompted a series of technical papers by Freud that especially elucidate transference, countertransference, and the dynamics of the therapeutic relationship. Jung's relationship with Spielrein can also be understood as a catalyst for the flowering of ideas represented in *Symbols of Transformation* (1912/1956) and his *Red Book* (2009/1914–1930, 1952, 1957; see Chapters 1 and 2) and subsequent published writings (Jung, 1953–1979). In the aftermath, upon graduating with her medical degree, Spielrein moved to Vienna and joined Freud's own circle of analysts – at once declaring her independence from Jung and establishing herself in the font of psychoanalysis as an original thinker and analyst in her own right (Chapters 2–4).

This narrative, fairly well known in Jungian and some psychoanalytic circles, is now more accessible to a general audience thanks to John Launer's comprehensive 2015 biography *Sex versus Survival: The Life and Ideas of Sabina Spielrein* (Launer, 2015). No doubt it is impossible to consider Spielrein without also addressing the influence of Jung, Freud, Piaget, and other early developmental psychologists. However, a closer examination of her writings shows that she was a prolific and creative analyst and writer in her own right, and that her works are far from derivative. On the contrary, many of her writings propose ideas that were later accredited to other, more acclaimed theorists such as Melanie Klein, Anna Freud, Jean Piaget, Lev Vygotsky, and Alexander Luria (see Chapters 3 and 4). Her original works therefore deserve a fuller exposition in English than what is currently available.

Sources: recent recoveries

Spielrein's story might have been forgotten altogether if not for the discovery in 1977 of her diary from 1909 to 1912, as well as her correspondence with Jung and Freud, in the basement of the Palais Wilson in Geneva, Switzerland (formerly the Jean-Jacques Rousseau Institute of Psychology). Aldo Carotenuto's publication of these texts in Italian translation in 1980 was and remains the seminal source of information about Spielrein's subjective world, but, as evidenced by his book's title, *A Secret Symmetry: Sabina Spielrein between Freud and Jung* (Carotenuto, 1980,

1982), his focus was not on Spielrein's own contributions to psychoanalysis, but on the triangle of relationships between Spielrein and the two warring founders of psychoanalysis and analytical psychology.

In 1982, Carotenuto's text was translated into English. In the same year, another box of Spielrein documents was discovered in the family archive of the past director of the Rousseau Institute, and a revised version in German, which included previously unpublished letters from Jung to Spielrein, appeared in 1986 (Carotenuto, 1986). In 1994, John Kerr's *A Most Dangerous Method* (Kerr, 1994) based on both Carotenuto's sources and the Freud/Jung letters (McGuire, 1974), brought Spielrein's story to light for English-language readers, but again focused on the perils of early psychoanalysis as exemplified in the crisis of Spielrein's "wild analysis" with Jung and subsequent move to Vienna – and to Freud.[1] Also in 1994, the first translation into English of her early and best known paper, "Destruction as a Cause of Coming into Being" (Spielrein, 1994/1912), was published in the Jungian *Journal of Analytical Psychology*, and a second English translation followed soon after in the psychoanalytic journal *Psychoanalysis and Contemporary Thought* in 1995 (Spielrein, 1995/1912)[2] – demonstrating a renewal of interest in her work among both Jungian and classical analysts.

Spielrein gained further visibility, mainly in German-speaking countries, through the film *Ich hieß Sabina Spielrein* [My Name Was Sabina Spielrein] in 2002 (Márton, 2006). Unlike the more recent Hollywood film, this docudrama spans Spielrein's entire life and presents a compassionate portrait of a troubled but brilliant woman. Nevertheless, the film still tends to emphasize the drama of Spielrein's passionate longing for Jung and the turmoil of her early adult years. In 2003, a scholarly edited volume (Covington & Wharton, 2003, 2015) assembled English translations of previously unpublished letters between Spielrein and Jung, along with perceptive essays on various aspects of Spielrein's life and thought. The volume, written by and for psychoanalytic writers, is quite specialized, but offers important insights. A similar anthology, so far published only in German, presents six more essays on Spielrein's works (Karger & Weismüller, 2006). Spielrein's works began to be systematically translated and published in Russian in 1929 (Spielrein, 2008) and German in 1987 (Spielrein, 2002, 2006) but have remained mostly inaccessible until now in English and other languages.

The present volume had its genesis in 2012 as a session of the Psychology, Culture and Religion Group at the American Academy of Religion, with Pamela Cooper-White, Felicity Brock Kelcourse, and Isabelle Noth presenting a symposium on Spielrein's life and work (Cooper-White, 2015). This offering serves as a further – and hopefully interim – contribution toward the eventual goal of a critical edition of Spielrein's complete works in English.

The following is a summary of the contents of this volume.

Part I: Life and works – an overview

A Timeline: Spielrein's biography and publications are placed in historical context with Freud, Jung, Piaget, Vygotsky, Luria, and other prominent theorists of her era, in conjunction with specific events in the history of psychoanalysis.

Chapter 1

"Sabina Spielrein from Rostov to Zürich: the making of an analyst," by Felicity Brock Kelcourse, reviews Spielrein's life from birth through to 1911, the year in which she completed her medical studies in psychiatry and published her dissertation (with a newly translated excerpt presented in Chapter 5 of this volume). It focuses particularly on her own youthful transformation from hysterical patient to self-aware analyst in the context of her "wild analysis" with Jung.

Chapter 2

"From Zürich to Vienna: 'The power that beautifies and destroys'," by Pamela Cooper-White, focuses on the period of Spielrein's gradual shift in personal and professional allegiance from Jung to Freud, with a close reading of her best-known essay, "Destruction as the Cause of Becoming" (newly translated in Chapter 6 of this volume; cf., Spielrein 1994/1912).

Chapter 3

"Passions, politics, and drives: Sabina Spielrein in Soviet Russia," by Klara Naszkowska, covers the period in Spielrein's life from 1924, the year she left Geneva for Russia, until her untimely and brutal death at the hands of the Nazis in 1942. Spielrein played a prominent role in the development of psychoanalytic work in Russia, particularly in relation to early childhood development and education during the brief period of Trotsky's ascendency, and then the Stalinist era, when psychoanalysis was forced underground. During the Trotsky era, Spielrein was in close contact with Luria and Vygotsky, probably as their instructor (see also Chapter 4).

Chapter 4

"'Language is there to bewilder itself and others': theoretical and clinical contributions of Sabina Spielrein," by Adrienne Harris, offers a comprehensive analysis of the significance of Spielrein's work and her often-neglected influence on the work of Jung, Freud, Piaget, Vygotsky, Luria, Klein, and others. Harris's essay in particular makes clear why the current volume is so appropriate to Routledge's Relational Perspectives series. Spielrein's attention to multiplicity of the self and to the intersubjective, relational nature of development anticipated much of what characterizes contemporary relational psychoanalysis.

Part II: Sample writings – new translations in English

Chapter 5

This excerpt from "On the Psychological Content of a Case of Schizophrenia," Spielrein's 1911 dissertation, shows important themes already present in Spielrein's clinical work with a psychotic woman patient (and, as well, the origin of Spielrein's cryptic term "poetry").[3]

Chapter 6

"Destruction as the Cause of Becoming" (1912), Spielrein's best-known work, was the paper with which she made her scholarly "debut" at the Vienna Psychoanalytic Society in 1911. Steeped in symbolism, it represents her efforts to bridge her deep, mutually informed work with Jung together with Freudian psychoanalytic principles and, as well, her biological training as a physician. Following the dissertation, it establishes her lifelong commitment to detailed, empathic observation of her patients' and research subjects' modes of thinking. A highly original work, it offers a unique perspective on both women's sexual experience and the earliest known formulation of the death instinct, and represents the culmination of her early work most influenced by Jung (see Chapters 2 and 4).

Chapter 7

Maternal Love (1913) is a brief commentary on the impact of the primal experience of the mother on subsequent love relations.

Chapter 8

The Forgotten Name (1914) is a fragmentary clinical example of repression.

Chapter 9

Two Menstrual Dreams (1914) offers two brief dream analyses in which menstrual blood symbolically relates to both sexual and religious themes and the women dreamers' anxieties about love and childbirth.

Chapter 10

"Russian Literature on Psychoanalysis" (1921) is Spielrein's literature review of the first two decades of psychoanalysis in Russia. Writing from Geneva, Spielrein catalogues the works of Freud available in Russian at the time – a window into the genesis of Russian psychoanalytic thought – and offers authoritative critiques of her Russian colleagues' theory and practice.

Chapter 11

"Who Is the Guilty One?" (1922) responds to a symbolist play Spielrein saw performed in Geneva in the company of her colleague Édouard Claparède. In the play, a woman commits suicide after being subjected to a brutal "wild analysis" by her lover. Reading between the lines, echoes of Spielrein's unboundaried relationship with Jung reverberate.

Chapter 12

"Time in Subliminal Psychic Life" (1923) offers fascinating reflections on the idea of time both as experienced in dreams and through a multilingual analysis of the development of human language, where the future tense is derivative and subordinate to past and present, paralleling psychoanalytic insights about the primacy of the past. The structure of both language and dreams discloses the unconscious substrate of the mind where the past reigns and subconscious thought distills everything past, and everything desired, into an eternal present.

Chapter 13

"The Three Questions" (1923) represents Spielrein's emphasis in the 1920s on observational research (similar to Piaget and others at the Rousseau Institute in Geneva at the time) and is one of her last writings on explicitly existential, religious, and moral themes. She asked students to generate the three questions they would like to ask "God, Fate, or whatever you would like to call it," first with eyes open, and again with eyes closed. Analyzing and categorizing her data much as an ethnographer would today, the questions with eyes closed represented a much more narrow, self-conscious and social perspective, while with eyes open, students produced more consciously philosophical and intellectual questions.

Chapter 14

"Some Analogies between a Child's Thought, Aphasic Thought, and Subconscious Thought" (1923) offers detailed observations of a toddler's verbal expression to illustrate "crossing," or the persistence of subconscious thought in early speech, which Spielrein then compares to disturbances of adult vocalization in aphasia. In so doing, she illustrates the primacy of the symbolic unconscious substrate of conscious thought and makes the important claim: "It is only the collaboration of subconscious thought with conscious thought that can engender a creative work in this world; conscious thought must grasp what the unconscious offers it, and use it."

Chapter 15

"Dr. Skalkovskiy's Report" (1929), written after her return to Russia, offers Spielrein's considered opinion of the state of psychoanalysis and psychiatric treatment more generally, as observed from within the Russia of her period. It is a fascinating glimpse into contemporary issues in Russian psychoanalysis at its high-water mark, before the Stalinist purge.

Chapter 16

In "Children's Drawings with Eyes Open and Closed" (1931), Spielrein returns to her method of contrasting conscious and unconscious thought by observing both "normal" and clinically diagnosed child and adult subjects with open and closed eyes (cf. Chapter 13). She especially attends to the ways in which kinesthetic experience is mirrored in "blind" drawings. She analyzes her data with numerous case examples, concluding with twelve specific findings and recommendations that show how this method can be useful both in clinical diagnosis and in pedagogy.

The return of the repressed?

It has been suggested that Spielrein's full story was not only forgotten, but actively (though unconsciously) repressed as the figure who represented a trauma buried in the early history of psychoanalysis (Richebächer, 2003, pp. 208–209; see also Chapter 4) – her story was regarded as too "dangerous" to psychoanalysis itself as a theory and especially as a method and a profession. As many other traumatic stories related to the Holocaust are still just surfacing, her story as a Jewish woman analyst, who through her theoretical writings passionately hoped to create a bridge between the Jewish and "Aryan" races, is especially poignant (see Chapters 2 and 4). Sabina Spielrein stands as both an important and tragic figure – misunderstood or underestimated by her fellow analysts (including Jung and Freud), often erased in the annals of psychoanalytic history (see Chapter 4), and finally murdered in Rostov by the Nazis in 1942. Her life and works deserve a serious critical reclamation, as the following chapters – including twelve new English translations of Spielrein's works – attest.

Notes

1 Regarding the term "wild analysis," showing Freud's alarm at misuses of analytic technique around this time, see Freud (1957/1910).
2 Re-translated in Ch. 6, this volume, and again in Spielrein (2018), pp. 97–134.
3 The entire dissertation is now translated in Spielrein (2018), pp. 14–96.

References

Carotenuto, A. (1980). *Diario di una segreta simmetria: Sabina Spielrein tra Jung e Freud*. Rome: Astrolabio.
Carotenuto, A. (1982). *A secret symmetry: Sabina Spielrein between Freud and Jung*. A. Pomerans, J. Shepley, & K. Winston (Trans.). New York: Pantheon.
Carotenuto, A. (1986). *Tagebuch einer heimlichen Symmetrie: Sabina Spielrein zwischen Jung und Freud*. Freiburg: Kore.
Cooper-White, P. (2015). Introduction to Special Symposium: Beyond 'A Dangerous Method': Reclaiming Sabina Spielrein's voice in the field of psychology and religion. *Pastoral Psychology*, 64, 231–233.
Covington, C. & Wharton, B. (Eds.) (2003). *Sabina Spielrein: Forgotten pioneer of psychoanalysis*. New York: Brunner-Routledge
Covington, C. & Wharton, B. (Eds.) (2015). *Sabina Spielrein: Forgotten pioneer of psychoanalysis*, 2nd edn. New York: Routledge.
Cronenberg, D. (Director) (2011). *A dangerous method* (film). Los Angeles: Sony Pictures Classics.
Freud, S. (1957). "Wild" psychoanalysis. In J. Strachey (Ed.), *The standard edition of the complete psychological works of Sigmund Freud,* Vol. 11: 219–228. London: Hogarth. (Orig. publ. 1910.)
Jung, C.G. (1957–1979). *Collected works of C.G. Jung*. G. Adler (Ed.) R.F.C. Hull (Trans.) Princeton, NJ: Princeton University Press.
Jung, C.G. (2009). *The red book*. S. Shamdasani (Ed. & Trans.). New York: W. W. Norton. (Orig. unpubl. manuscript, 1914–1930, 1952, 1957.)
Karger, A. & Weismüller, C. (Eds.) (2006). *Ich hieß Sabina Spielrein: Von einer, die auszog, Heilung zu suchen*. Göttingen: Vandenhoeck & Ruprecht.
Kerr, J. (1994). *A most dangerous method: The story of Jung, Freud, and Sabina Spielrein*. New York: Vintage.
Launer, J. (2015). *Sex versus survival: The life and ideas of Sabina Spielrein*. New York: Overlook Duckworth.
Márton, E. (Director) (2006). *My name was Sabina Spielrein* (DVD). Chicago: Facets Video. (Orig. released as *Ich hieß Sabina Spielrein*, produced by Helgi Felix/Idé Film Felixson AB, 2002.)
McGuire, W. (Ed.) (1974). *The Freud/Jung letters: The correspondence between Sigmund Freud and C.G. Jung*. R. Hull & R. Manheim (Trans). Princeton, NJ: Princeton University Press.

Richebächer, S. (2003). "In league with the devil, and yet you fear fire?" Sabina Spielrein and C. G. Jung: A suppressed scandal from the early days of psychoanalysis. B. Wharton (Trans.). In C. Covington & B. Wharton (Eds.), *Sabina Spielrein: Forgotten pioneer of psychoanalysis* (pp. 227–249). New York: Brunner-Routledge.

Spielrein, S. (1912). Die Destruktion als Ursache des Werdens. [Destruction as the Cause of Becoming]. *Jahrbuch für psychoanalytische und psychopathologische Forschungen*, 4, 465–503. (Trans. this volume, Chapter 6.)

Spielrein, S. (1994). Destruction as a cause of coming into being. K. McCormick (Trans.). *Journal of Analytical Psychology*, 39, 155–186. (Orig. publ. 1912.)

Spielrein, S. (1995). Destruction as cause of becoming. S.K. Witt (Trans.), *Psychoanalysis and Contemporary Thought* 18, 85–118. (Orig. publ. 1912.)

Spielrein, S. (2002). *Sabina Spielrein: Sämtliche Schriften*, 2nd edn. T. Hensch (Ed.). Gießen: Psychosozial-Verlag/ Kore. (1st edn. 1987.)

Spielrein, S. (2006). *Nimm meine Seele: Tagebücher und Schriften* [*Take my soul: Diaries and writings*]. T. Hensch (Ed.). Freiburg: Freitag.

Spielrein, S. (2008). *Psychoanalyticheskie trudi* [*Psychoanalytic works*]. K. Sirotkin & E.C. Morozova (Eds.). Izhevsk: ERGO.

Spielrein, S. (2018). *The essential writings of Sabina Spielrein: Pioneer of psychoanalysis*. R. Cape & R. Burt (Eds. & Trans.). New York: Routledge.

Part I

Life and works – an overview

A comparative timeline
Spielrein, Freud, Jung, and other theorists, including key works and significant events within the history of psychoanalysis

Pamela Cooper-White, Felicity Brock Kelcourse, and Adrienne Harris[1]

	Freud (1856–1939)	Jung (1875–1961)	Spielrein (1885–1942)	Other theorists and events in Europe (1850–1950)
1842–1871				1842 – Josef **Breuer** born (d. 1925).
				1849 – Ivan **Pavlov** (d. 1936).
				1854 – Théodore **Flournoy** born (d. 1920).
	1856 – **Sigismund Freud** born in Freiberg, Moravia (now Příbor, Czech Republic) to Jacob Freud and Amalie Nathanson.			1856 – Emil **Kraepelin** born (d. 1926).
				1857 – Eugen **Bleuler** born (d. 1939).
	1858 – Brother Julius dies at seven months.			1858 – Wilhelm **Fliess** born (d. 1928).
	1860 – The Freud family moves to Vienna; Freud attends Gymnasium.			1860 – **Burghölzli** Mental Hospital established in Zürich.
			1861 – Nikolai (Naftal) Spielrein (father) born.	1861 – Lou **Andreas-Salomé** born (d. 1937).
			1863 – Eva Lubinskaya (mother) born.	
				1868 – Wilhelm **Stekel** born (d. 1940).
		1869 – Jung's parents Rev. Paul Jung (1842–1896) and Emily Preiswerk (1848–1923) marry.		1871 – Hermine **Hug-Hellmuth** born (d. 1924); Paul **Federn** born (d. 1950); Margarete **Hilferding** born (d. 1942).

1873–1881	Attends medical school, University of Vienna.	1870, 1872, 1873: Jung's parents suffer deaths of three infant children, two girls and a boy. 1873 – Édouard **Claparède** born (d. 1940); Oskar **Pfister** born (d. 1956). 1875 – Iran **Ermakov** (d. 1942). 1877 – Karl **Abraham** born (d. 1925). 1878 – Franz **Riklin** born (d. 1938). 1879 – Viktor **Tausk** born (d. 1919). 1879 – Auguste-Henri **Forel** (1848–1931) becomes director of the University of Zürich Psychiatric Hospital, the Burghölzli Asylum and establishes its international reputation for advanced treatment and research. 1875 – **Carl Gustav Jung** born in Kesswil, Thurgau, Switzerland. Family moves to Laufen, near Falls of the Rhine, when Jung is 6 months old. 1878 – Mother hospitalized. Jung, age 3, is ill, has dark-haired caregiver. First conscious trauma and "man-eater" dream before age 4. 1879 – Family moves to Klein-Huningen, near Basel.
1882–1886	1882 – Betrothed to Martha Bernays (1861–1951). 1883–1897 – Practices as a neurologist; collaborates with Breuer (until 1894).	1881 – Max **Eitingon** born (d. 1943); Ludwig **Binswanger** born (d. 1966). 1882 – Melanie **Klein** born (d. 1960); Alphonse **Maeder** born (d. 1971). 1883 – Pogroms against Jews in Rostov-on-Don. 1885 – **Spielrein** born in Rostov-on-Don to Nikolai Spielrein and Eva Lublinskaya. 1881 – Starts schooling in Basel, age 6, begins Latin lessons; aware mother has two personalities. 1882 – Emma **Rauschenbach** born in Schaffhausen, Switzerland. 1882–1884 – Jung, aged 7–9, fears inner split of self.

(continued)

	Freud (1856–1939)	Jung (1875–1961)	Spielrein (1885–1942)	Other theorists and events in Europe (1850–1950)
	1884–1885 – Experimental research on cocaine.	1884 – Sister Johanna Gertrud (Trudi) born (d. 1935).		1884 – Otto **Rank** born (d. 1939); Helene **Deutsch** born (d. 1982).
	1885 – Appointed (unpaid) *Privatdozent* at University of Vienna; studies with Jean-Martin **Charcot** in Paris (1825–1893).	1885 – Carves manikin as secret talisman (age 10).		1885 – Tatiana **Rosenthal** born (d. 1921).
	1886 – Opens private practice in Vienna; marries Martha Bernays.	1886 – Enters Basel Gymnasium.		
1887–1895	1887 – Mathilde, first child, born; five more children born: Martin (1889), Oliver (1891), Ernst (1892), Sophie (1893), and Anna (1895); Freud begins close friendship and correspondence with Fliess.	1887 – Begins to have fainting spells after fight with another boy.	1887 – Brother Jan born (d. 1938).	1888 – Toni **Wolff** born (d. 1953).
		1888 – Father begins service as chaplain of the Basel University mental hospital (Friedmatt), ending with his death in 1896.	1888–1889 – Psychosomatic symptoms begin.	1888 – Mary Esther **Harding** born (d. 1971).
		1891 – Jung (up to age 16) has two personalities (logical, compliant vs. secretly rebellious and mystical).	1890 – Spielrein, age 5, attends elite Fröbel school; can speak Russian, German, French, and English.	1890 – Jolande **Jacobi** born (d. 1973).
		1891–1894 – Growing interest in philosophy and science, alienated from his father's theology.	1891 – Brother Isaak born (d. 1937).	
			1892 – Age 7, spanked by father until age 11, symptoms of hysteria increase.	
	1895 – Publishes *Studies on Hysteria* with Breuer (includes case of "Anna O"); daughter Anna born; Martha's sister Minna Bernays joins household; begins work on *The Interpretation of Dreams*.	1895 – Begins studies in medicine at Basel; becomes fascinated with psychiatry/psychology.	1895 – Sister Emilia born; harsh household – father tyrannical and mother also beat the children; Spielrein begins diary.	1895 – **Anna Freud** born (d. 1982).

1896–1899	1896 – Freud's father Jacob dies; Freud recants "seduction [trauma] theory" of hysteria and breaks with Breuer; uses term "psychoanalysis" for the first time. 1897 – Freud begins self-analysis. 1899 – *Interpretation of Dreams* pre-published (including the topographical model of Conscious, Preconscious, and Unconscious); "strength to face a troubled life anew."	1896 – Jung's father Paul dies (Jung is 21). Five "Zofinga lectures" delivered while in medical school (1896–1899). 1898 – Begins investigation of occult phenomena by observing Helene **Preiswerk** (cousin, medium).	1899 – Brother Emil, last of five Spielrein children, born (d. 1938).	1896 – Lev **Vygotsky** born (d. 1934); Jean **Piaget** born (d. 1980). 1987 – Wilhelm **Reich** born (d. 1957). 1898 – Bleuler appointed professor of psychiatry at the Burghölzli Asylum.
1900–1903	1900 – *Interpretation of Dreams* official publication date. 1901 – Publishes *Psychopathology of Everyday Life*; *On Dreams*. 1902 – Named (unpaid) "Extraordinary" Professor at University of Vienna; begins "Wednesday Night Psychological Society"; Adler joins Freud's circle.	1900 – Jung completes medical studies, begins work at the Burghölzli under Bleuler. 1902 – Publishes medical thesis "On the Psychology and Pathology of the So-Called Occult Phenomena"; studies at Salpêtrière with Pierre **Janet**; begins word association research. 1903 – Marries Emma Rauschenbach, age 21; Bleuler and Jung increasingly interested in Freud's theories; publishes "On Manic Mood Disorder" and "On Simulated Insanity."	1901 – Sister Emilia dies at age 6; Spielrein's mental health symptoms increase; brilliant in school; decides on medicine as career; also studies Latin, piano, and voice. 1903 – Symptoms become more severe: deep depression, fits of crying, screaming.	1901 – Abraham joins Bleuler at the Burghölzli. 1902 – Alexander **Luria** (d. 1977). 1903 – Federn and Stekel begin practice of psychoanalysis; Paul **Schreber** (1842–1911) publishes *Memoirs of My Nervous Illness*.

(continued)

	Freud (1856–1939)	Jung (1875–1961)	Spielrein (1885–1942)	Other theorists and events in Europe (1850–1950)
1904	Freud ends correspondence with Fliess; Bleuler begins correspondence with Freud.	Age 29–30, first child, Agathe, is born; August 17 – First sees Spielrein as patient. Publishes "The Associations of Normal Subjects" with Franz Riklin (cousin); "On Hysterical Misreading."	Age 19; graduates from Gymnasium with honors; admitted to Burghölzli for "hysteria." Assists Jung with association experiments.	**Riklin** and Jung publish *The Associations of Normal Subjects*; **Russo–Japanese War**, 1904–1905.
1905	Publishes *Three Essays on Theory of Sexuality* (including infantile sexuality); *Jokes and Their Relation to the Unconscious*; "On Psychotherapy"; *Fragment of an Analysis* ["Dora"]; Rank joins circle.	Promoted to Senior Staff Physician; appointed Lecturer in Psychiatry at the University of Zürich. Eight publications, including "Cryptoamnesis," define the "unconscious" as "everything that is not represented in consciousness, whether momentarily or permanently."	Discharged from hospital; unpaid, informal analysis with Jung; enters University of Zürich as medical student.	
1906	Freud's first letter to Jung, thanking him for sending his *Diagnostic Association Studies*, which Freud had already acquired (1F 4/11²).	April – Correspondence with Freud begins. October 23 – "Difficult case of Russian girl [Spielrein]" (4J). Ten publications, including "Psychoanalysis and Association Experiments"; second child, Greta, born.		**Russian Revolution** (1905–1907); pogroms against Jews in Russia and Eastern Europe; Jones begins practice of psychoanalysis in London. Tatiana Rosenthal extols harmony between Freud and Marx.

1907	Receives visit from Jung, Binswanger, and Emma Jung; Publishes "Obsessive Actions and Religious Practices"; *Delusions and Dreams in Jensen's Gravida*.	March – Visits Freud, accompanied by Binswanger and Emma Jung; "The Freudian Theory of Hysteria" delivered as a lecture (published 1908), [Spielrein cited as a case] Jung: Nine publications including "The Psychology of Dementia Praecox."		Max Eitingon visits Freud. December – Abraham visits Freud and joins Freud's circle.
1908	March – Establishes *Jahrbuch* with Bleuler and Jung; publishes "Hysterical Phantasies and Their Relation to Bisexuality." September – Visits half-brothers in England and visits Jung at the Burghölzli for four days; Wednesday Night Society reconstituted as "Vienna Psychoanalytic Society."	Spring – Treats Otto Gross; at First International Congress becomes Freud's "heir apparent." December 3 – Franz born (first son, third of five children); thirteen publications including "The Content of the Psychoses."	Summer to November – Growing intimacy and secret meetings with Jung.	April – **First International Congress for Psychoanalysis ("Freudian Psychology"), Salzburg,** with Jung presiding. Bleuler publishes paper based on a study of 647 Burghölzli patients; Ferenczi joins Freud's circle; A.A. **Brill** and Jones visit Freud; Abraham founds Berlin Psychoanalytic Society.
1909	January – First letter from Pfister. February – Publishes *Analysis of a Phobia in a Five-Year-Old Boy* ["Little Hans"] in first edition of *Jahrbuch*; *Notes on a Case of Obsessional Neurosis* ["Wolf Man"]; correspondence with Jung and Spielrein.	January – Emma Jung writes to Spielrein's mother. March – Jung breaks off contact with Spielrein; second visit to Freud in Vienna; at first denies then in June confesses his "knavery" to Freud (133)]; eleven publications including "The Significance of the Father in the Destiny of the Individual"; "The Analysis of Dreams"; resigns from Burghölzli and opens private practice in Küsnacht.	February – Jung ends personal relationship and reestablishes fee for visits; Spielrein attacks him and runs out. June – Spielrein writes to Freud for consultation; confronts Jung, and they agree to a professional relationship.	Pfister visits Freud; Freud's books begin to be published in English, trans. by Brill: *Studies in Hysteria*, 1909; *Three Essays in Sexuality*, 1910; *The Interpretation of Dreams*, 1913. Osipov founds *Psychterapiya* in Russian, second psychoanalytic periodical after the *Jahrbuch*.

(continued)

	Freud (1856–1939)	Jung (1875–1961)	Spielrein (1885–1942)	Other theorists and events in Europe (1850–1950)
1910	August – Faints in Munich discussing peat bog mummies with Jung; trip to Clark University (only trip to USA) with Jung and Ferenczi, mutual dream analysis. September – Meets J.J. Putnam, William James, and Stanley Hall at Clark University. Publishes *Leonardo da Vinci and a Memory of his Childhood*; *Five Lectures on Psycho-Analysis*; "The Future Prospects of Psychoanalysis"; "A Special Type of Choice of Object Made by Men" (first use of term "Oedipus complex"); founds *Zentralblatt für Psychoanalyse*.	August – travels by sea to America with Freud and Ferenczi, loses respect for Freud's authority. Delivers lectures on "The Association Method" at Clark University; first recorded experiment with active imagination. Supervises Spielrein's dissertation, taking over from Bleuler at her request; first public formulation of his concept of the collective unconscious. Seventeen publications including "A Contribution to the Psychology of Rumour"; "On the Criticism of Psychoanalysis." September 20 – Wolff begins analysis with Jung.	Resumes contact with Jung, as dissertation advisor. November – Writes in diary she fears Jung will steal her ideas. December – Last "poetry" with Jung and farewell.	March – **Second International Congress, Nuremberg**, Jung serving as president; **International Psychoanalytical Association (IPA)** founded with Jung as president and Rank as secretary. April – Hilferding first woman admitted to Vienna Psychoanalytic Society.
1911	**Freud is 55** March – Presents Schreber Case to Third International Congress in Weimar; meets Andreas-Salomé.	**Jung is 36** Edits Spielrein's dissertation for *Jahrbuch*; eight publications including "A Criticism of Bleuler's Theory of Schizophrenic Negativism"; Wolff becomes Jung's research assistant.	**Spielrein is 26** January – Graduates from University of Zürich; dissertation "On the Psychological Content of a Case of Schizophrenia" published in *Jahrbuch, 3*; moves to Munich and then Vienna.	**Third International Congress of IPA, Weimar**, Jung as president; Bleuler publishes *Dementia Praecox, or the Group of Schizophrenias*; Brill founds **New York Psychoanalytic Society**; Jones founds **American Psychoanalytic Association**.

1912	October – Emma Jung writes to Freud with concern; Freud spends four days with Jung at Küsnacht.	Publishes *Symbols of Transformation* [*Wandlungen und Symbole der Libido*], Part I.	October 11 – Admitted to Vienna Psychoanalytic Society. November 29 – Reads from paper "Destruction as the Cause of Becoming" at Vienna Society meeting, anticipating Freud's "death drive" and Jung's views on "transformation."	October – Adler resigns from Vienna Society, founds "Society for Free Psychoanalysis"; Rosenthal returns to St. Petersburg to work as a neurologist at Vladimir **Bekhterev**'s Brain Institute. As head of the outpatient clinic, she treats neurotic patients there with psychoanalysis.
	March – writes to Jung about "epidemic of psychoanalysis" in Russia (306F). Founds *Imago* (journal for applied psychoanalysis); publishes "The Dynamics of Transference"; "On the Universal Tendency to Debasement in the Sphere of Love."	Publishes *Symbols of Transformation*, Part II in *Jahrbuch*, redefining libido as energy, not sexual drive; founds The Society for Psychoanalytic Endeavors; publishes "Concerning Psychoanalysis"; Seven publications in all.	Spielrein becomes friendly with Freud; "Destruction" paper published in *Jahrbuch* (edited by Jung); "On Transformation" in *Zentralblatt*, 2.	Claparède founds Jean Jacques Rousseau Institute.
	May – Travels to Kreuzlingen to see Binswanger, who is ill, and does not meet with Jung, who takes this as a dismissal ("the Kreuzlingen gesture").	Writes to Spielrein, telling her not to worry; uneasy truce with Freud in Munich.		June – Jones initiates a "Secret Committee" to ensure Freudian orthodoxy.
	November – Reconciliation with Jung in Munich, dealing with conflict among Viennese; Freud faints and Jung carries him out; Freud: "How sweet it must be to die!"	Fall – Lectures at Fordham University in New York City.	Marries Dr. Pavel Sheftel (June, Rostov); later declares disappointment and growing indifference toward marriage in letters to Freud.	October – Stekel resigns from Vienna Society.
	November–December – Acrimonious letters to Jung.	November–December – Acrimonious letters to Freud (338J, December 18, 1912); Jung begins to have vivid, catastrophic dreams and waking visions.	Lectures in Russia and works with Rosenthal and Abraham in Berlin.	

(*continued*)

	Freud (1856–1939)	Jung (1875–1961)	Spielrein (1885–1942)	Other theorists and events in Europe (1850–1950)
1913	**January 3 – Letter to Jung: "I propose we abandon our personal relations entirely."** Founds *Internationale Zeitschrift für Ärztliche Psychoanalyse* (IZP); publishes *Totem and Taboo*; numerous papers on technique (1911–1915). Writes to Abraham, "Jung is crazy," and writes to Spielrein, "We are and remain Jews. The others will only exploit us…" August – Visits statue of Moses in Rome; writes "The Moses of Michelangelo" (publ. 1914). At 4th International Congress in Munich, supports Jung's reelection as president.	**January 6 – Postal card to Freud: "I accede to your wish… 'the rest is silence'."** Begins intimate relationship with Wolff. Premonitions of World War I; intense preoccupation with images from the unconscious; seven publications including "General Aspects of Psychoanalysis"; "The Theory of Psychoanalysis"; "On the Doctrine of Complexes". Resigns as editor of *Jahrbuch*; resigns post at University of Zürich.	Publishes "Mother Love" in *Imago*, 2; "The Unconscious Phantasies in Kuprin's 'Duel'", *Imago*, 2; "The Mother-in-Law," *Imago*, 2; "The Dream from 'Pater Freudenreich'", (IZP, 1); "Self-Gratification with Foot Symbolism," *Zentralblatt*, 3. Begins specializing in child analysis; first child Irma Renate born December 17; considers separation and divorce. "Contributions to an Understanding of the Child's Mind" in *Zentralblatt*, 3. Father Nikolai urges Spielrein to return to Russia.	**September – 4th International Congress of IPA, Munich**, Jung as president. Vygotsky admitted to the Moscow University through a "Jewish Lottery"; Ferenczi founds **Hungarian Psychoanalytical Society**; Jones founds **London (later "British") Psychoanalytical Society**.
1914	Publishes "On Narcissism"; *On the History of the Psycho-analytic Movement*;	**Begins *The Red Book*** (1914–1930, 1952, 1957). **April – Resigns as president of IPA.**	Publishes "Two Menstrual Dreams," *IZP*, 2; "Animal Symbolism and a Boy's Phobia," *IZP*, 2; "The Forgotten Name."	5th International Congress on Care of Mental Illness in Russia, Moscow, (December 26–29, 1913; January 8–13, 1914).

1915	"Remembering, Repeating and Working-Through" (introduces "repetition neurosis"). Freud: **"The voice of Psychoanalysis is not heard in the world for the sound of cannons."**	Zürich group withdraws from IPA and forms independent Association for Analytical Psychology. **Final break with Freud.** Four publications including revision of "The Content of the Psychoses".	Husband Pavel is drafted into Russian army. Spielrein lives in Berlin, visits Munich to work on mythology, and studies musical composition; works in surgery while Renate is ill.	**July 28: World War I begins** – Germany invades France; Russia invades Germany. Jung from resigns IPA; Pfister remains loyal to Freud. September – Dresden Conference postponed.
	Publishes "Observations on Transference Love"; "Thoughts for the Times on War and Death"; *Instincts and Their Vicissitudes*; *Repression*; and *The Unconscious*.	No new publications. Wolff becomes "second wife" in Jung household. "On Psychological Understanding" and "The Theory of Psychoanalysis" published in English.	Publishes "An Unconscious Judgment," *IZP*, 3.	Marie-Louise **von Franz** born (d. 1998).
1916	Publishes "On Transience" and "A Connection between a Symbol and a Symptom." 1916–1917 – Freud gives last university lectures.	Publishes *VII Sermones ad Mortuos* (Seven Sermons to the Dead, 1925, in English); *Collected Papers on Analytical Psychology* (English translation); first use of terms "personal unconscious" and "individuation"; writes "The Transcendent Function" (first published 1957); "Psychic Conflicts in a Child," seven new works in all.		
1917	Publishes *Introductory Lectures on Psycho-Analysis*; "Mourning and Melancholia."	Publishes *On the Psychology of the Unconscious* (revised 1918, 1926, 1943).		Vygotsky graduates from Moscow University. **November 7 – Bolshevik "October" Revolution**, led by Vladimir **Lenin** with Leon **Trotsky**.

(continued)

	Freud (1856–1939)	Jung (1875–1961)	Spielrein (1885–1942)	Other theorists and events in Europe (1850–1950)
1918	Begins analysis of daughter Anna; publishes *From the History of an Infantile Neurosis* ["Wolf Man"].	January letter to Spielrein: "You are always trying to drag the Siegfried symbol back into reality…"; publishes "The Role of the Unconscious"; identifies the Self as the goal of psychic development for the first time.	Publishes "The Utterances of the Oedipus Complex in Childhood," *IZP*, 4. January – Letter to Jung, struggling with depression and Siegfried symbol; subsequent "profound and shattering" vision that "Siegfried is alive after all!"	**5th IPA congress in Budapest,** Karl Abraham as president. Piaget starts postdoctoral study in Zürich. **November 11 – World War I ends.** Some Germans blame Soviets, socialists, and Jews for Germany's defeat; extreme postwar poverty, hunger, and illness.
1919	Founds publishing house *Internationaler Psychoanalytisher Verlag*; publishes "A Child Is Being Beaten" and "The Uncanny."	Publishes in English "Instinct and the Unconscious," first use of term "archetype."	Correspondence with Jung ends.	Eitingon joins Secret Committee. Tausk commits suicide (age 40).
1920	Founds *International Journal of Psycho-Analysis*. Daughter Sophie dies in postwar flu epidemic. Publishes *Beyond the Pleasure Principle* (aggressive drive and the **"death drive"**), "The Case of Homosexuality in a Woman," and papers on telepathy.	Jung is 45; publishes "The Psychological Foundations of Belief in Spirits" (in English).	Speaks at 6th International Psychoanalytic Congress in The Hague on origins of child language. Publishes "On the Question of the Origin and Development of Speech," *IZP*, 6; "Renatchen's Theory of Creation," *IZP*, 6; "The Sense of Shame in Children," *IZP*, 6; "The Weak Woman," *IZP*, 6;	**6th IPA Congress at The Hague,** Ferenczi as president; Piaget, Anna Freud, and Melanie Klein present (40 attend); Hug-Hellmuth presents paper on child analysis. Piaget at Rousseau Institute, Geneva, 1920–1929.

1921	Publishes *Group Psychology and the Analysis of the Ego*.	Publishes *Psychological Types or the Psychology of Individuation* (1923, in English); identifies two "attitudes" (extraversion/introversion) and four "functions" (thinking/sensation, feeling/intuition). Identifies the "Self" as the goal of psychic development.	Researches Niebelungen and fairy tales. "Review: Isaak Spielrein, On Numbers That Are Difficult to Retain, and Calculation Tasks. A Comment on the Applied Science of Memory," *IZP*, 6; "Displaced Oral Eroticism," *IZP*, 6. Works at Rousseau Institute, Geneva.	Publishes "Russian Literature. Report on the Progress of Psychoanalysis in the years 1914–1919," *Beiheft der IZP*, 3; "Brief Analysis of a Child's Phobia," *IZP*, 7. Analyzes Piaget in Geneva for 8 months; he is "impervious to the theory."	February – Psychoanalytic Polyclinic founded in Berlin, using "Eitingon model" for training new analysts. Flournoy dies. **Russian Psychoanalytic Society** and Psychoanalytic Institute and Orphanage-Laboratory. Vygotsky publishes his first article on psychoanalysis. Luria founds Kazan Psychoanalytic circle. Piaget becomes director of the Rousseau Institute in Geneva. Rosenthal (age 36) commits suicide in Russia. Osipov, first proponent of Freud in Russia, is forced to escape. Hug-Hellmuth publishes "On the Technique of Child-analysis".
1922		Publishes "On the Relation of Analytical Psychology to Poetic Art" (1923, in English). Buys land near Bollingen.		Attends IPA Congress in Berlin (62 attend), where she delivers papers on time in the unconscious and paper on language and thought in children and aphasia; publishes "The Origin of the Child's Words 'Papa' and 'Mama'," *Imago*, 8; "Who Is the Guilty One?" *Journal de Genève*, 93;	**7th IPA Congress, Berlin,** Jones as president; Piaget presents a paper including work on children and aphasics. Anna Freud admitted to Vienna Society with paper "Beating Fantasies and Daydreams."

(continued)

	Freud (1856–1939)	Jung (1875–1961)	Spielrein (1885–1942)	Other theorists and events in Europe (1850–1950)
			"Switzerland: The Geneva Psychoanalytic Society," *IZP*, 8; "A Stamp Dream," *IZP*, 8; "Psychology of the Problem of Time; Report of the Seventh International Psychoanalytic Congress in Berlin," *IZP*, 8.	Andreas Salomé joins Vienna Society.
1923	Publishes *The Ego and the Id* (structural model). Diagnosed with cancer of the jaw, has radical surgery. Death of grandson Heinele.	Death of Jung's mother. Seminar, in English, on "Human Relationships in Relation to the Process of Individuation"; publishes "Child Development and Education" (in German). Continues work on Bollingen retreat.	Mother Eva dies. January – husband in Russia threatens divorce. Begins relationship with Dr. Olga Aksyuk. May, Spielrein is in financial difficulty in Geneva. **Returns to Russia (Moscow).** Publishes "Some Analogies between Thinking in Children, Aphasia, and the Subconscious Mind," *Archives de Psychologie*, 18; "Time in Subliminal Conscious Life," *Imago*, 9; "The Three Questions," *Imago*, 9; "A Dream and a Vision of Shooting Stars," *IJP*, 4; "The Motor Car as a Symbol of Male Power," *IJP*, 4; "A Spectator Type," *IZP*, 9; "The Train of Thought in a Two-and-a-Half-Year-Old Child, Session of the Swiss Psychoanalytical Association, January 13, 1923," *IZP*, 9.	Berlin Psychoanalytic Institute founded by Abraham, Eitingon, and others. Luria joins the Russian Psychoanalytic Society (RPS). 1923–1930: Freudo-Marxism discussed in Soviet journals.

1924	Publishes "The Economic Problem of Masochism"; *Collected Works* begun in German; honored as "Citizen of Vienna."	Visits USA and Pueblo Indians in New Mexico.	Chair of Department of Child Psychology, also employed part-time as a doctor. Teaches seminars on child development, unconscious thought, pursues interest in pedology. Works with children at Institute for Psychoanalysis in Moscow; joins Russian Psychoanalytic Society (RPS) in autumn. November – Presents "Aphasic and Infantile Thought" to RPS; likely teacher of Luria and Vygotsky. Spielrein named Chair of RPS. Daughter Nina Snetkova born to Sheftel and Aksyuk.	**8th IPA Congress, Salzburg,** Jones as president. January – Vygotsky participates in the Second All-Russian Psycho-neurological Congress, Leningrad, and is named a new member of the Russian Psychoanalytic Society; Luria publishes first psychoanalytic paper. Rank breaks with Freud. Hug-Hellmuth murdered by a nephew.

(continued)

	Freud (1856–1939)	Jung (1875–1961)	Spielrein (1885–1942)	Other theorists and events in Europe (1850–1950)
1925	Publishes *An Autobiographical Study*; writes *Inhibitions, Symptoms and Anxiety* (publ. 1926).	Lectures in Zürich on "Analytical Psychology"; lectures in England on "Dreams and Symbolism"; visits Elgonyi tribe during safari to Kenya. Publishes "Marriage as a Psychological Relationship." Increasing use of seminars. Publishes *Analytical Psychology: Notes of the Seminar given in Zurich* (in German) and *Dreams and Symbolism* (in English). Publishes (in English) "The Unconscious in the Normal and Pathological Mind" (revised in 1943 as "The Psychology of the Unconscious").	**Moves back to Rostov-on-Don.** Reunites with husband. Delivers lectures on reflexology and psychoanalysis to Society for Neurology and Psychiatry.	**9th IPA Congress, Bad Homburg**, Abraham and Eitingon presiding, Eitingon chairs new International Training Committee of the IPA. Anna Freud joins Secret Committee. Deutsch founds Vienna Psychoanalytic Institute. Abraham dies. Vygotsky collaborates with Luria to translate Freud, publishes six articles on development of thinking and language in children. Breuer dies.
1926	Freud is 70; publishes *The Question of Lay Analysis*; Einstein visits Freud in Berlin.	Returns from Africa via Egypt; growing interest in Western alchemy and Eastern religions.	Offers two courses on the significance of psychoanalysis for child studies. Eva, second daughter, born on June 18. Spielrein is sick with malaria and depressed.	1926–1928 – Piaget publishes five major books. In Russia, psychoanalysis is out of favor with Stalin.

1927	Publishes *The Future of an Illusion* (definitive declaration of atheism).	Publishes "Woman in Europe."	1927 – Publishes "Some Brief Comments on Childhood," *Zeitschrift für Psychoanalytische Pädagogik*, 2.	**10th IPA Congress, Innsbruck,** Eitingon as president. Trotsky expelled from the communist party. Bleuler resigns as Director of the Burghölzli. Pfister rebuts Freud with "The Illusion of a Future" in *Imago*.
1928		Publishes *Contributions to Analytical Psychology; Two Essays on Analytical Psychology* (in English) and, in German: "The Structure of the Psyche"; "The Spiritual Problem of Modern Man," ;"Psychoanalysis and the Cure of Souls," "The Relation between the Ego and the Unconscious," "On Psychic Energy," 13 German publications in all.	Sees patients in her home as the only trained analyst in Rostov-on-Don.	
1929		Publishes first essay on Western alchemy "Paracelsus," begins research collaboration with von Franz. Publishes "Freud and Jung: Contrasts"; "Commentary on *The Secret of the Golden Flower*"; "The Aims of Psychotherapy."	Publishes "Dr. Skalkovskiy's Report," Proceedings of the First Congress of Psychiatry and Neuropathology of the North Caucasus Region, Rostov-on-Don.	Joseph **Stalin** becomes dictator of Soviet Union. **11th IPA Congress, Oxford,** Eitingon as president. Ferenczi distances himself from Freud.

(continued)

	Freud (1856–1939)	Jung (1875–1961)	Spielrein (1885–1942)	Other theorists and events in Europe (1850–1950)
1930	Mother Amalie dies. Publishes *Civilization and Its Discontents*. Freud is awarded Goethe Prize for Literature.	Becomes vice-president of General Medical Society for Psychotherapy. Publishes "The Stages of Life"; "Psychology and Literature." *The Visions Seminars* (Zurich, 1930–1934).		Vygotsky publishes *Mind and Society*. Psychoanalysis condemned at first All-Union Congress on Human Behavior, Moscow.
1931	Freud celebrates 75th birthday.	Publishes (with Richard Wilhelm) "Basic Postulates of Analytical Psychotherapy."	Publishes "Children's Drawings with Eyes Open and Closed," *Imago*, 17. Likely attendee at conference of Isaak Spielrein's International Society of Industrial Psychology in Moscow.	Vygotsky's work attacked by **Stalinisty** and A.A. **Talanin**. Only Pavlov's psychology is state approved.
1932–1939	1933 – Publishes *New Introductory Lectures on Psychoanalysis*. "Why War?" with Einstein. 1936 – Freud is 80; cancer worsens; celebrates golden wedding anniversary. 1937 – Publishes *Analysis Terminable and Interminable*.	1932 – "Psychotherapists or the Clergy"; "Sigmund Freud in His Historical Setting"; "The Real and the Surreal"; *The Psychology of Kundalini Yoga*. 1933 – First "Eranos" meeting in Ascona, Switzerland; delivers paper on "A Study of the Individuation Process." Publishes *Modern Man in Search of a Soul* (in English).	1935 – Nicolai and Isaak Spielrein arrested. 1937 – Brother Isaak murdered by Stalin. 1937 – Husband Pavel dies of a heart attack.	1932 – **12th IPA Congress, Wiesbaden**, Eitingon as president. 1933 – **Hitler** elected Chancellor of Germany, Freud's books burned in Berlin; Ferenczi dies.

1934 – 13th IPA Congress, **Lucerne**, Jones as president; Lev Vygotsky dies (of tuberculosis); his *Thought and Language* published posthumously.			
1936 – Anna Freud publishes *The Ego and the Mechanisms of Defense*, 1st edn.			
1936 – 14th IPA Congress, **Marienbad**, Jones as president.			
1936 – Inauguration of the Analytical Psychology Club, New York.			
1936 – Pedology is banned in Russia; The Great Terror begins in Russia under Stalin.			
1936–1938 – Over 1 million Soviet citizens sent to gulags and murdered by the secret police.			
1938 – 15th IPA Congress, **Paris**, Jones as president; Hitler annexes Austria (the "*Anschluss*").	1938 – Hitler in Vienna; Gestapo arrests Anna; moves to London with help of Marie Bonaparte and Jones.	1934 – Founds and serves as first president for the International General Medical Society for Psychotherapy (charged with antisemitism for failing to resign). Publishes "A Review of Complex Theory"; "The Development of Personality."	
		1935 – Delivers Tavistock Lectures, London (publ. 1968 in English).	
		1936 – "The Concept of the Collective Unconscious"; *Dream Symbols of the Individuation Process*.	
		1937 – Delivers Terry Lectures at Yale University, published as *Psychology and Religion* (1938).	
		1938 – "On the *Rosarium Philsophorum*"; The Visions of Zosimos."	1938 – Father Nikolai dies. Brothers Jan and Emil executed by Stalin.
1939 – September 1, World War II begins; Rank dies; Bleuler dies.	1939 – Publishes *Moses and Monotheism*; brief writings on antisemitism (1938–1939); cancer inoperable.	1939 – Publishes *The Integration of the Personality* (recent articles published in English translation); "Psychological Aspects of the Mother Archetype.'" In Memory of Sigmund Freud"; "The Symbolic Life."	
1939 – Germany and the Soviet Union invade Poland.	September 23 – **Freud dies** (assisted suicide), London.		
		1941 – "The Psychology of the Child Archetype"; "A Psychological Approach to the Dogma of the Trinity"; "Transformation Symbolism in the Mass."	

(continued)

	Freud (1856–1939)	Jung (1875–1961)	Spielrein (1885–1942)	Other theorists and events in Europe (1850–1950)
1940–1949	1941 – Sister-in-law Minna Bernays dies, London.	1942 – Bollingen Foundation established to oversee publication of Jung's Collected Works. 1944 – Heart attack followed by a series of visions; *Psychology and Alchemy*. 1945 – "After the Catastrophe." 1946 – *The Psychology of the Transference*. 1947 – Publishes (in English) *Essays on Contemporary Events*; "On the Nature of the Psyche." 1948 – C. G. Jung Institute established, Zürich; publishes *On the Psychology of the Spirit* (in English); "Alchemy and Psychology," (in German). 1949 – *On the Psychology of Eastern Meditation* (in English).	First German occupation of Rostov-on Don. **1942, August – Nazis murder Spielrein and her two daughters, Renate and Eva, in mass shooting at Zmeyevsky gully in Rostov-on-Don.**	1941 – Anna Freud establishes Hampstead War Nurseries with Dorothy **Burlingham**, London. 1942 – Hilferding dies in Nazi concentration camp, Theresienstadt. 1943 – Max Eitingon dies, Jerusalem. **September 2 – World War II** ends. 1949 – **16th IPA Congress, Zürich**, Jones as president.
1950–1952	1951 – Wife Martha dies, London.	Publishes (in German): 1950 – *The Structure of the Unconscious*. 1951 – *Aion: Researches into the Phenomenology of the Self*; "On Synchronicity." 1952 – *Psychology and Alchemy* (1944 revision); *Symbols of Transformation* (1911, revised 1912, 1925, 1952). Revisits *The Red Book* briefly in 1952; continues working on *Memories, Dreams, Reflections*.		1951 – **17th IPA Congress, Amsterdam,** Leo **Bartemeier** as president. Hampstead Child Therapy Course and Clinic established in London (The Anna Freud Centre).

1953–1961

1953 – Wolff dies, Zürich. Publishes (all in English translation): 1953 – *The Spirit Mercury; Psychology and Alchemy; Two Essays on Analytical Psychology*.
1954 – *Spirit and Nature; The Symbolic Life; The Practice of Psychotherapy; The Development of Personality* (in English).
1955 – Wife Emma dies, Küsnacht (aged 73) *Mysterium Coniunctionis: ...Psychic Opposites in Alchemy;* "Mandalas."
1956 – *Symbols of Transformation* (in English).
1957 – *The Transcendent Function; Psychiatric Studies* (in English).
1957 – Adds final postscript to *The Red Book*.
1958 – *Psyche and Symbol; The Undiscovered Self; Psychology and Religion* (in English).
1959 – *The Archetypes of the Collective Unconscious; Aion* (in English).
1960 – *The Psychogenesis of Mental Disease; The Structure and Dynamics of the Psyche* (in English).
1961 – *Freud and Psychoanalysis*.
1961 – **Jung dies** of heart disease on June 6 (aged 85), Küsnacht, Switzerland.

1955 – **International Association of Analytical Psychology** founded, Zürich.

1956 – Pfister dies.

1962–1980s

1962 – *Memories, Dreams, Reflections* published posthumously in English.
1974 – *Freud/Jung Letters* first published (in German); 1979 in English).

1977 – Spielrein's diaries found in the basement of the Palais Wilson, Geneva.

1980 – Piaget dies in Geneva.
1982 – Deutsch dies; Anna Freud dies (October).

Notes

1 Adapted from Cooper-White (2015) and Harris (2015), with additional data supplied by Felicity Kelcourse and Klara Naszkowska. Timeline includes selected key events and publications. For more exhaustive histories and bibliographies, see Sources. Jung's early works, prior to 1919, are listed by date of publication in German, as listed in Vieljeux (1996) using titles as they appear in the English translation of the *Collected Works* (1957–1979). Selected later works, as found in Young-Eisendrath and Dawson (1997), may appear with first publications dates in German or English.
2 Abbreviations "F" and "J" designate letters from Freud to Jung, and Jung to Freud, in McGuire (1974).

References

[n.a.] (1907–1958). Chronik der DPG. Online at https://dpg-psa.de/Chronik_1907-1958.html. Accessed July 28, 2018.

Bair, D. (2003). *Jung: A biography*. New York: Back Bay Books/Little, Brown & Co.

Campbell, J. (Ed.) (1971). *The portable Jung*. R. F. C. Hull (Trans.). New York: Penguin.

Cooper-White, P. (2015). A comparative timeline: Spielrein, Freud, and Jung. *Pastoral Psychology*, 64(2), 235–240.

Freud, S. (1953–1974). *The standard edition of the complete psychological works of Sigmund Freud*, Vols. 1–24. J. Strachey (Ed.). London: Hogarth.

Gay, P. (2006). *Freud: A life for our time*. New York: W.W. Norton.

Gillespie, W.H. (2018). History of the IPA. (Orig. publ. 1982). Online at www.ipa.world/en/De/IPA1/ipa_history/history_of_the_ipa.aspx. Accessed July 28, 2018.

Ellenberger, H.F. (1970). *The discovery of the unconscious: The history and evolution of dynamic psychiatry*. New York: Basic Books.

Harris, A. (2015). Timeline: Sabina Spielrein, Jean Piaget, and Lev Vygotsky. In Harris, "Language is there to bewilder itself and others": Theoretical and clinical contributions of Sabina Spielrein. *Journal of the American Psychoanalytic Association*, 63(4), 767.

International Psychoanalytical Association (2018). Past IPA Congresses. Online at www.ipa.world/PastCongresses. Accessed November 6, 2018.

Jones, E. (1953–1957). *The life and work of Sigmund Freud* (Vol. 1–3). New York: Basic Books.

Jung, C.G. (1957–1979). *The collected works of C.G. Jung*. G. Adler & R.F.C. Hull (Eds.). Bollingen Series XX. Princeton, NJ: Princeton University Press.

Launer, J. (2015). *Sex versus survival: The life and ideas of Sabina Spielrein*. New York: Overlook Duckworth.

McGuire, W. (Ed.) (1974). *The Freud/Jung letters*. R. Hull & R. Manheim (Trans). Princeton, NJ: Princeton University Press.

Sigmund Freud Museum (n.d.). Sigmund Freud chronology. Online at www.freud-museum.at/online/freud/chronolg/chrnlg-e.htm. Accessed November 6, 2018.

Vieljeux, J. (1996). *Catalogue chronologique des écrits de Carl Gustav Jung*. Paris: Cahiers jungiens de psychanalyse.

Young-Eisendrath, P. & Dawson, T. (Eds.) (1997). The Cambridge companion to Jung. Cambridge, UK: Cambridge University Press.

Chapter 1

Sabina Spielrein from Rostov to Zürich
The making of an analyst[1]

Felicity Brock Kelcourse

> *I would like to create something great and good. Help me, Guardian Spirit!*
> *Help me, Fate. Show me the noble ideal that I should love...*
> (Spielrein, diary entry of December 8, 1910[2])

Introduction

After 100 years of psychoanalysis, how should we view Spielrein's fate? A rediscovered early pioneer of psychoanalytic thought (1885–1942), she was fortunate to be born to educated parents who encouraged her ambition, fortunate at 26 to publish a 1911 psychiatric dissertation on the treatment of schizophrenia mentored by Eugen Bleuler (1857–1939) and Carl Gustav Jung (1875–1961), and fortunate to have found the stamina and determination to publish 37 articles before her untimely, violent death (Spielrein, 2002; Launer, 2015, pp. 287–289). Much of her misfortune came at the hands of those who also cared for her – her emotionally distressed parents, the "wild analysis" she exchanged with Jung,[3] and the condescending advice she received from Freud, her husband Pavel, and perhaps, along the way, the colleagues with whom she exchanged ideas that were carefully cited by her but not, reciprocally, by them. And like so many of her generation, she was not spared from the destructive turmoil of revolution and war.

The familiar version of her story begins on the evening of August 17, 1904, when, as a 19-year-old girl, she was admitted to the Burghölzli hospital in Zürich in an agitated condition, diagnosed upon admission with "hysteria." In her admission records, the hometown was listed as Rostov (Russia), last residence Heller Sanatorium, Interlaken, religion "Israel" (Jewish). The recorded duration of her illness was two years, though in fact her symptoms had begun much earlier (Wharton, 2015a, p. 57). Less than ten months later, as of June 1, 1905, she had made sufficient progress to be discharged, having already enrolled at the Zürich University as a medical student. By the time this young woman was 26, she had completed her medical studies, including a dissertation on schizophrenia that was published in the third issue of the *Jahrbuch für Psychoanalytische und Psychopathologische Forschungen* (Spielrein, 1911), of which Carl Jung was the editor. Though she became a Shoah victim at age 57, when the Nazis invaded Russia, she had by then been a practicing analyst for nearly 30 years and published, under difficult circumstances, 37 journal articles in German, French, and Russian.

This brilliant woman was Sabina Spielrein (1885–1942). Her legacy has been overshadowed by the tumultuous collaboration of Freud and Jung between 1906 and 1913. From the perspective of English-language readers, Aldo Carotenuto (1982) and John Kerr (1994) lifted her name from obscurity only to have her original contributions to the early literature of psychoanalysis eclipsed by scandal, as sensationalized in the 2011 film *A Dangerous Method*.[4] With the hindsight of a century, many feel that it is time for Spielrein to reemerge from the shadows as a pioneering analyst in her own right.

My purpose in the present chapter is to focus on what we can glean or surmise about Spielrein's early development as an analyst, beginning with her childhood in a difficult family. It seems clear from the fact that she is cited twelve times in what is now known as *Symbols of Transformation* (Jung, 1967b/1911)[5] that her treatment and the subsequent elaboration of her thought had a profound influence on Jung, who was progressively her inpatient doctor, unpaid outpatient therapist, clinical supervisor, dissertation advisor, journal editor, and, somewhere along the way, her lover in "poetry," and she his muse (Carotenuto, 1982; Lothane, 2015; see also Chapter 2, this volume).[6] Clearly, she came to Jung as a wounded person, but he was wounded too, in ways that he was only beginning to discover. Their mutual influence on one other as an analytic pair, joined for a time by a powerful intersubjective bond, interests me far more than the opportunity to judge Jung from the moral high ground of twenty-first-century best therapeutic practice. I hope to present their relationship in a way that does justice to the struggles of both parties, from the standpoint of a psychoanalytically trained psychotherapist informed by postmodern family systems (McGoldrick et al., 2008), an intersubjective perspective (e.g., Atwood & Stolorow, 1993), and a phenomenological reading of Jung (Brooke, 2015).

Persons who are drawn to the helping professions disproportionately include those who, for reasons consciously known or unacknowledged, are in need of healing (Sedgwick, 1994). This includes individual trials suffered during the youthful stages of development (ages 0–25), such as life with addicted, neglectful, abusive, or emotionally unavailable parents (Miller, 2008).[7] It can also include intergenerational sources of suffering, as children unconsciously take on the wounds of prior generations and attempt to resolve them in their own lives (Wickes, 1988; McGoldrick et al., 2008).[8] Both Spielrein and Jung had intrapsychic and intergenerational challenges to overcome on their way to becoming creative, productive, and reasonably stable adults.

Sabina before Carl (1885–1904)

Spielrein was the first-born daughter of a well-to-do Jewish couple living in Rostov-on-Don near the eastern shores of the Black Sea in Tsarist Russia, southeast of modern-day Ukraine (Launer, 2015, pp. 12–13).[9] Her parents' marriage was apparently never happy. Both parents were university graduates, exceptional for that time and place. Her mother, Eva Lublinskaya, trained as a dentist and was the daughter and granddaughter of respected rabbis. Both Sabina's mother and her maternal grandfather, before marrying within their faith, had first loves who were Christians (ibid., pp. 15–16). Sabina's father, Nikolai, originally from Warsaw, prospered financially as a merchant during his children's formative years. Sabina's mother reportedly provoked him to rage and threats of suicide with lavish spending and threatened affairs. When Sabina was admitted to the Burghölzli hospital at the age of 19, parental strife and humiliating corporal punishment inflicted primarily by her father were cited as causes for what we would now consider post-traumatic stress. Under the heading "Family History of Illness," her hospital records list father as "Healthy, active, irritable, overwrought, neurasthenic, hot-tempered to the point of madness." Mother is identified as "Nervous (like patient) *hysterical!* Is a dentist. Has hysterical absences of a childish nature" (emphasis in original). Of her three younger brothers it was written that "1 brother has hysterical fits of weeping, another suffers from tics and is very hot-tempered, the third is melancholic, very hysterical, and even does wrong in order to suffer." The record also notes "1 sister – died of stomach ailment" (Wharton, 2015a, p. 58). The type of psychodynamic formulation we now consider standard for case conceptualization, including correlations between childhood events and later psychological disturbance, was still relatively novel in 1904.[10] In Spielrein's case, we are not limited to hospital records for insights into her early life, since her own diaries (Carotenuto, 1982, pp. 3–44; Spielrein, 2006, 2015), as yet only partially published or translated, date back to 1895 when she was ten years old (Spielrein, 2018/1913).

A precocious, sensitive child, Sabina attended a local Fröbel kindergarten with her brother, Yasha (aka Yakob, Jan), eighteen months her junior. It was a progressive school that reputedly accepted only the brightest children.[11] By as early as age three, she was reported to have begun a habit of encopresis, avoiding defecation as long as possible, which generally leads to inadvertent soiling. A generation later, Erik Erikson (1963) related the case of a little boy whose similar difficulties began when his beloved nurse left after becoming pregnant.[12] Sabina, as first-born, had two little brothers by the time she was five, and it may be that her parents were simply overwhelmed with caring for these younger siblings. We now know that punishing a child for symptoms similar to hers is counterproductive, but it would have been common for a child of that era to be spanked for such behavior, as Sabina reportedly was. A second daughter, Emilia, and third son Emil, were born in Sabina's tenth and fourteenth years. Fluent in German and French as well as Russian, since all three languages were spoken in her home, Sabina also studied biblical Hebrew. Her musical abilities included piano and voice as a child and later composition as an adult. In keeping with the Hasidic rabbis on her mother's side of the family, she had a mystical bent, believing that a Guardian Spirit spoke to her in German, telling her that she was destined for great things. By all reports, she was imaginative, with a rich inner life, and was apparently equally interested in the arts and in science (Launer, 2015).

With encouragement from her father, Sabina aspired to be a doctor, emulating her maternal and paternal uncles. Nevertheless, "my parents were proud of the 'purity' and 'naivety' of their daughter; or rather my mother was" (Spielrein 2018/1913, p.135).[13] Consider the possible motivation of a mother who distressed her husband with flirtations but also experienced "absences" (i.e., dissociative fugue states). It seems likely that some unspecified prior trauma motivated the mother to "protect" her daughter from any knowledge of sexuality, the very "Victorian-era" denial of sexuality that Freud's theories sought to dispel. When Spielrein later provoked her mother by confiding her feelings of love for Jung, her mother's advice was to keep him interested but to remain chaste.

Despite academic success, Sabina was afflicted with depression, nervous tics, compulsive masturbation, and psychosomatic ailments. Her mental health worsened at the age of sixteen when Emilia, age six, died from typhoid fever. Sabina then withdrew from friends and family, becoming increasingly agitated. Her symptoms included associating the sight of her father's hand (used for spanking) with defecation. When her mood and behavior failed to improve, her uncle – a doctor – took her to Switzerland for treatment, though her initial one-month hospitalization at the Heller Sanatorium was unsuccessful. At 10:30 pm on the night of August 17, 1904, she arrived at the Burghölzli mental hospital, made famous by August Forel (1848–1931) and Eugene Bleuler (1857–1939), who were respected throughout Europe (Covington, 2015).

Carl before Sabina

Spielrein's future mentor, Carl Gustav Jung (1875–1961), was born in Switzerland nineteen years after Freud's birth and ten years before Spielrein's. Jung's father studied ancient languages, completing a dissertation on the Song of Songs in Hebrew but, lacking money to continue his scholarship, became a country pastor by default (Ryce-Menuhin, 1994; Bair, 2003). Jung the son inherited both a penchant for multilingual scholarship and a concern for the mentally ill from his father, who served for many years as a chaplain for the Friedmatt, Basel University's mental hospital (Bair, 2003). Following the loss of three children who were born and died in 1870, 1872, and 1873, a healthy baby boy, Carl, was born in 1875. Parents frequently find it emotionally difficult to bond with a new baby following repeated losses, ambivalence that then becomes the basis for disorganized or reactive attachment in the child.[14] It was likely under the circumstances that Jung's early attachment to his parents would have been compromised, with implications for the stability of his relationships in later life. Like Spielrein, Jung (1989/1961) described his parents' marriage as troubled (p. 8).

Carl's mother, Emilie Preiswerk Jung, was the fourteenth and youngest child of Samuel Preiswerk, a minister who believed in the supernatural. All of Pastor Preiswerk's six sons followed him into ministry. Carl's cousin Helene (later the subject of his medical dissertation) was said to be a medium, and Carl described his mother as having a "number two" personality that was preternaturally knowing and uncanny (Jung, 1989/1961, p. 49). Jung's mother suffered from an unidentified mental illness, possibly hysteria; she was hospitalized for several months when Jung was three (ibid., p. 8). Reflecting on memories of his pre-oedipal experience toward the end of his life, Jung recalled strong impressions of two very different types of women who cared for him while he was separated from his mother. One was the family maid. "She had black hair and an olive complexion... This type of girl later became a component of my anima... From the period of my parents' separation I have another memory image: a young, very pretty and charming girl with blue eyes and fair hair... This girl later became my mother-in-law. She admired my father. I did not see her again until I was twenty-one years old"[15] (Jung, 1989/1961, pp. 8–9). D.W. Winnicott (1964), in a review of Jung's edited autobiography, *Memories, Dreams, Reflections*, suggested that Jung suffered from a childhood psychosis. This would not be inconsistent with the effect on a child of being raised by a mentally ill parent (Kelcourse, 1998).

As a schoolboy, Jung developed a fainting symptom with no discernible organic cause. This persisted until one day he overheard his father expressing the fear that his son might never be able to earn a living. Thereupon Carl was successfully able to will himself to stop fainting. And as we know from the letters Jung later wrote to Freud in 1907, young Carl was traumatized by a sexual predator: "... as a boy I was the victim of a sexual assault by a man I once worshipped," a trauma of unspecified date and duration (McGuire, 1974, p. 94). Despite these challenges to his development in childhood, at the age of 21, Jung found the ego strength to continue his studies and take responsibility for his mother and nine-year-old sister, Trudi, after his father's death.

Due in part to these familial influences, Jung maintained a lifelong interest in ancient languages, cultures, and religion, as well as the nonrational thought processes found in dreams, fantasies, psychoses, and religious experience. He excelled intellectually while repressing memories of childhood distress. Having earned his medical degree in 1900 at the age of twenty-five, Jung worked and lived for most of the next nine years at the Burghölzli psychiatric hospital of Zürich University, where he served first as a staff psychiatrist. There he developed his understanding of *complexes* (feeling-toned thought patterns) through his use of word association experiments that form the basis for our modern lie detector tests (Jung, 1973/1906).

When Sabina Spielrein arrived at the Burghölzli in 1904, Jung had served under Eugen Bleuler's leadership for four years, being expected to live and work there virtually day and night in what we might now call a residential therapeutic community (Graf-Nold, 2015, p. 88). When Jung first arrived in 1900, "only two experienced doctors (the director and the senior physician) and two inexperienced ones (an assistant and a trainee) had care of some 400 hospital patients" (ibid., p. 91). By 1902, Jung had completed his required medical dissertation "On the Psychology and Pathology of So-Called Occult Phenomena" (Jung, 1970/1902). In February 1902, after his engagement to Emma Rauschenbach (1882–1955), Jung tendered his resignation, hoping to take a position in Basel, which did not materialize (Graf-Nold, 2015 p. 92). At the end of 1902, he enjoyed a brief respite from hospital rounds by spending a winter semester in Paris to study theoretical psychopathology with Pierre Janet at the Salpêtrière, a hospital famous for treating hysteria. In February 1903, Jung married Emma, and by May 1903, he was back at the Burghölzli, moving the nineteen-year-old heiress into his doctor's hospital lodging, where she promptly became pregnant. Spielrein arrived the same year that the Jungs' first child, Agathe, was born.

The doctors had their own apartments on a separate floor, but often ate meals with patients and were on call as needed, twenty-four hours a day. The doctor's wives were also expected to take an active role in the community (Graf-Nold, 2015, p. 88). By October 1904, Jung was promoted to *Oberartz* (supervising physician), second to Bleuler, and then in December applied as a lecturer at Zürich University as well (ibid., p. 93).

Jung's supervisor, Eugen Bleuler, is remembered today for originating the term "schizophrenia" in a 1908 paper presented to the German Psychiatric Association in Berlin.[16] At that time, the differential diagnosis between schizophrenia-like symptoms resulting from post-traumatic stress, or "hysteria," and schizophrenia as a hereditary organic brain disorder may have been difficult to make initially, though both Bleuler and Jung were aware of the importance of this distinction with respect to both history and prognosis. Bleuler's approach to inpatient treatment was pragmatic, ego-supportive, and remarkably humane by the standards of his day (ibid.).

1904–1911: Spielrein and Jung in Zürich

In this section focusing on Spielrein's psychiatric treatment and subsequent development as an analyst, I have adopted the time frames suggested by Zvi Lothane (2015), which rely on previously unpublished letters between Spielrein and Jung to delineate four distinct phases of their relationship: (1) 1904–1905, Spielrein as inpatient; (2) 1905–1908, Spielrein as medical student protégé; (3) 1908–1910, Spielrein as analyst to her analyst; and (4) from 1911 on, Spielrein as an independent analyst and psychoanalytic theorist.[17]

Inpatient treatment (1904–1905)

Spielrein's case was diagnosed as hysteria upon admission by the twenty-nine-year-old Dr. Jung who, having been encouraged by Bleuler to read Freud's (1953b/1900) *Interpretation of Dreams*, began treating Spielrein using Freud's published descriptions of the then-novel psychoanalytic method (1955/1893–1895), despite his personal reservations about the sexual etiology of mental illness. Jung had been developing his ear for symbolic communication by conducting association experiments since 1901, and he proceeded to "analyze" Spielrein during episodic sessions, sometimes lasting three hours at a time, during which he attempted to understand her complexes (Launer, 2015, p. 46). Spielrein's initially disruptive behavior, eliciting negative attention by provoking staff, responded positively to treatment, with occasional setbacks when Dr. Jung was not available.[18] Prior to meeting Jung, Sabina had "fallen in love" first with an elderly uncle who was a doctor, then with an assistant at the Heller Sanatorium. Such intense admiration on the part of a young woman can be understood as a projection of her own desire to become a doctor. In this way, the attachment she felt to Jung during treatment was not unique; he simply became the focus of her hope for healing and a desired future.

Though Spielrein's sessions with Jung clearly helped to resolve many of her presenting symptoms, it is worth noting that the episodic frame for their inpatient work was very different from the consistent frame for outpatient treatment Freud had already established, typically consisting of six sessions a week at the same time of day for up to six months (Blanton, 1971). Even at this early stage in Spielrein's association with Jung, the professional context for the relationship was unclear, at least by modern standards. His initial interest in Spielrein was as a test case for Freud's methods; Jung later referenced Spielrein's case in "The Freudian Theory of Hysteria" (Jung, 1967a/1908).

Jung's treatment of Spielrein certainly seemed to confirm Freud's theories regarding the sexual etiology of hysteria. During their sessions, she was able to abreact humiliating memories of being spanked on her bare buttocks by her father while her brothers watched (hospital record from August 18, 1904 – Wharton, 2015a, p. 61). Violent arguments between her parents caused her to have unbearable pain in her feet (October 18, 1904 – ibid., p. 65). Meanwhile, Spielrein's own aptitude for psychiatry was evident early on: "Made a correct diagnosis of epilepsy from a letter handed out at the clinic and correctly supported her diagnosis" (November 4, 1904 – ibid., p. 67). By January 1905, she was gaining self-awareness and self-control: "Since the last abreaction substantial improvement. Still strongly emotional and unusually powerful expressions of feeling. At every stimulation of the complex she still reacts with her back, hands, tongue, and mouth, though significantly less so. She is now aware of it and hides her expressions of disgust behind her hands" (ibid., p. 70).

Following this objective observation, a curiously subjective entry in Jung's handwriting appears: "Yesterday at my evening visit, pat. was reclining on the sofa in her usual oriental, voluptuous manner, with a sensuous, dreamy expression on her face." Just before Jung entered the room, Spielrein had been reading Forel's *Hypnotism* and was reacting to a story of a boy being caned by other boys. "When Ref. opens the book to find the passage that triggered off the father complex, the pat. suddenly displays defensive movements and gestures of disgust" (ibid., p. 70). What is notable about this passage is that Jung's own perception of his patient seems to be colored by his experience of her as the dark-haired embodiment of what he would later identify as his "anima" type. Jung's description of her as "oriental, voluptuous... sensuous, dreamy" suggests that, by as early as January 1905, he was becoming attracted to her – "in love" with her, as she would later be with him. Spielrein was the exotic "other," the dark-haired Russian granddaughter of a rabbi, so different from Jung's wife, the respectable Swiss mother of his children.[19] Although Bleuler displayed interest in Freud's psychoanalytic method, one suspects that Jung would not have been comfortable sharing his personal feelings toward his patient with his scientifically minded supervisor. If he consciously noted an attraction to Spielrein, Jung apparently kept it to himself for the time being.

The Burghölzli of 1904 was a true "asylum" in the sense that patients whose mental illnesses were either hereditary or induced by addictions or abuse were to be treated with kindness and respect. Every patient capable of contributing through work was given a task. Both patients and staff were expected to attend psycho-educational sessions designed to help them understand the nature of mental illness. As Spielrein recovered, she assisted Jung and other doctors in ongoing association experiment research. By as early as September 26, 1904, Bleuler was able to write to Spielrein's father, "We have now happily succeeded in stimulating Miss Spielrein's interest in scientific pursuits, so that she can be distracted for hours at a time from her pathological obsessions" (Wharton, 2015a, p. 73). By April 1905, eight months after being admitted as an inpatient, she began to attend medical lectures at the university while still living at the hospital. On June 1, 1905, armed with a medical certificate from Bleuler stating that she was not mentally ill, only "nervous... with hysterical symptoms," she was discharged and began to live independently in Zürich while continuing her medical studies (ibid., p. 77).

Spielrein as medical student protégée (1905–1908)

In an April 25, 1905, journal entry, Spielrein reflected on her transition from patient to medical student:

> I have been afire with interest and now I have a contrary feeling that weighs heavily upon me! I feel isolated from the other students… I feel myself more thorough, serious, critically evolved, independent… To me, life without science is completely useless. What else is there for me if there is no science? Get married? But that thought fills me with dread… The price is subjugation of the personality… No! I do not want such love: *I want a good friend to whom I can bare my soul; I want the love of an older man so that he would love me the way parents love and understand their child (spiritual affinity)*… If only I were as wise a human being as my Junga! [Russian term of endearment]
> (Lothane, 2015, pp. 128–129, emphasis added)

The language here is not that of erotic desire, but rather the admiration of a patient for her doctor, a student for her mentor, the longing of a young woman alienated from her actual father hoping to find a father figure to rely on. Meanwhile, through her own treatment and her transition to treating patients as an analyst herself, she was beginning to develop the "observing ego" that every therapist needs to make effective use of supervision. Self-observant self-supervision is required to manage countertransference responses to patient material that can evoke painful associations and longings from the therapist's own experience (Sedgwick, 1994). The intersubjective field between Spielrein and Jung was ripe for this, as was the case Spielrein would later choose for her dissertation (see below and Chapter 5).

In the same passage, she goes on to lament, "How stupid that I am not a man; men have it easier with everything. It is a shame that everything in life goes their way. I do not want to be a slave!" (ibid., p. 129).[20] Spielrein may be reflecting on the fate of her mother, an intelligent, professionally trained woman who was nevertheless dependent on her husband for reasons of social propriety. In Zürich, Spielrein was fortunate that, as a foreigner, a Russian Jew, the rules of Swiss society did not apply to her. Respectable Swiss young ladies like Emma Jung, who would have liked to matriculate at the university, were forbidden by their parents to do so (Clay, 2016). Nevertheless, many did attend public lectures. Jung's university lectures were so popular that he had quite a following among the *Zürichberg Pelzmäntel*, "the 'fur-coat ladies' from the richest part of the city, dismissed by those who scorned both them and Jung as… 'sex-starved groupies or postmenopausal hysterics'" (Bair, 2003, p. 98, citing an anonymous local source).

If Spielrein wanted Jung's attention during her student years, she certainly had plenty of competition. From 1905 to 1909, while he was still living and working at the Burghölzli, Jung remained overworked with a crushing patient load, medical students to supervise in both patient care and thesis writing, lecturing up to twelve hours a week, and, as his own alliance with Freud intensified, taking on in 1908 editorial duties for a new psychoanalytic journal as well as the presidency of Freud's annual Psychoanalytic Congresses. Apparently, Jung did agree to meet with Spielrein once a week in an office at the hospital that was not a private setting, for fear that she might relapse if he withdrew his ongoing support (cf., June 4, 1909 – McGuire, 1974, pp. 228–230). And from her journal entries, it is clear that he continued to serve as an important "selfobject" in the course of her professional development (Kohut, 1971, 1984).[21] She wrote:

> I cannot bear even the smallest judgment of my personality, and even when given in the form of a simple instruction it can turn into a stinging sermon… it gets me into a rage (I do not know why this happens.) I can take anything only from Junga… To-morrow I am going to the medical library and will borrow Hartmann's '[Philosophy of] The Unconscious'… Since I saw his book at Junga's I believe it is worth reading.
> (Lothane, 2015, p. 129, diary entry June 8, 1905)

Here, in the midst of an ongoing idealization of her mentor Jung, she is also observing and questioning her own behavior. While it is not surprising that a previously traumatized person would be easily wounded and self-conscious, it is significant that Spielrein is curious about her own behavior rather than blaming others for causing her discomfort. Though Jung continued to see Spielrein on an unpaid outpatient basis during this period, the reality as seen by both Spielrein and Jung seems to have been more of a friendship than an ongoing "treatment" per se, though clearly Jung, as a lecturer at the university and supervisor of Spielrein's clinical work, was the senior partner in the relationship.

Contrary to the seductive secretiveness one might expect from someone intent on conducting a clandestine affair, Spielrein wrote quite openly to her mother about her feelings for Jung on August 26, 1905:

Dear Mamochka [Mummy],

… I am deliriously happy as never before in my life. At the same time it hurts and I would like to cry from happiness. You have probably guessed that the cause of all this is Junga. I visited him today. He comforted me about Remi [a woman patient at the Burghölzli under Spielrein's care]; in his opinion, he tells me, her condition has improved markedly… Junga told me that I should not be wearing a hat with holes in it and that I should also get my shoes mended. I replied that I had run out of money, but that I had already received so much that I could not ask my parents for more.
(Lothane, 2015, p. 130)

Jung then lends her money, knowing from his own relatively impoverished childhood how being the one without new clothes can damage a young person's self-esteem (Bair, 2003, p. 29n60).

Here, we have a former therapist acting *in loco parentis* as he occupies the roles of faculty mentor and supervisor for his former patient. Present-day professional boundaries that would avoid so many overlapping roles, especially with a former analyst of any description, were not in place in these early days of psychoanalysis, leading to confusion of rights and responsibilities. Eva Spielrein, alarmed to think that her daughter might not be safe in the context of this relationship, asked Jung for a referral.

Spielrein's successful recovery demonstrated the value of the psychoanalytic method. But the therapeutic confusion that followed was to have a profound effect on Spielrein, Jung, and Freud, influencing the course of psychoanalytic history. By as early as September 25, 1905, after Spielrein had been discharged but was still relying on Jung for unpaid emotional support, Jung prepared a "Report on Miss Spielrein to Professor Freud in Vienna, delivered to Mrs. Spielrein for use if the occasion arises," thereby referring Sabina to Freud's care in response to her mother's concern. The report begins as a standard case summary, but concludes:

> During treatment the patient had the misfortune to fall in love with me. She raves on to her mother about her love in an ostentatious manner, and a secret perverse enjoyment of her mother's dismay seems to play a not inconsiderable part. Now in this distressing situation the mother wants to place her elsewhere for treatment, with which I am naturally in agreement.
> (Wharton, 2015a, p. 78)

Jung's 1905 report was apparently never sent to Freud and in fact predates his first contact with Freud in 1906. It indicates that an intense transference (and countertransference) had developed in the course of inpatient treatment. Spielrein's letters to her mother stating her fondness for Jung caused her mother to be worried that Jung might take advantage of her daughter, but also provided a measure of safety by making her mother aware of the ongoing relationship as it evolved. Spielrein's subsequent diary entries indicate that, even though she began to fantasize about causing "her Junga" to leave his wife for her, her reality-testing ego functions were fully intact. As a student only recently discharged from the hospital with lingering symptoms, Spielrein was nevertheless fully cognizant of the potential negative consequences of consummating an affair, personally and professionally, for both Jung and herself. Jung, on the other hand, was finding it increasingly difficult to maintain his professional mien in the relationship, hence his willingness to hand Sabina off to Freud.

At the dawn of psychoanalysis, the importance of the analyst's own training analysis was not understood. Even today there are psychiatrists, psychologists, and master's-level therapists who do not undertake their own therapy as a training requirement. The value of a training analysis is that the therapist's own wounds and complexes can be explored though anamnesis, an exploration of one's past as it relates to current life concerns. Therapists in training invariably find that painful places in their own psyches are touched upon as they work with certain clients. When countertransference responses that might complicate a therapist's treatment of a case arise, the clinical supervisor can then encourage the supervisee to explore the personal basis for these responses in his or her own therapy (Kelcourse, 2010). It appears that as Jung continued to associate with Spielrein outside the bounds of the hospital setting, he found himself increasingly drawn to her, and she to him. Meanwhile, his young wife, only three years older than Sabina, was busy with babies one and two, and Bleuler, by all accounts a demanding taskmaster, was working Jung and all the doctors under his command to the bone.

From the beginning of the Freud/Jung correspondence in April 1906 until Spielrein left Zürich in 1911, Jung's attempts to cope with the intense countertransference he developed using Freud's psychoanalytic method resulted in requests for supervision. Jung mentioned Spielrein's case to Freud in his fourth letter, "disguising" the case by stating that the unnamed patient had an older brother, when in fact she herself was the oldest child: "First trauma between third and fourth year. Saw her father spanking her older brother on the bare bottom... couldn't help thinking afterwards that she had defecated on her father's hand" (October 23, 1906 – McGuire, 1974, p. 6). From this report and Jung's history, we can infer the interlocking nature of his countertransference to Spielrein, who had experienced early trauma and abuse of a sexually invasive nature, as he had.

What were some of the circumstances that caused Jung to reach out to Freud with this particular case after a six-year steady diet of schizophrenics, addicts, relatively few hysterics (Graf-Nold, 2015, p. 97),[22] and others who were generally more severely impaired in their daily functioning than the ambulatory neurotics seen by Freud? In addition to overwork and pressures on the domestic front, Jung's relationship with Bleuler as a father–mentor was strained, hence his need for an outside supervisor's perspective. Who better than the founder of psychoanalytic treatment? Jung may already have realized that he needed support not only for his relationship with his former patient, but also for himself.

Like Spielrein, Jung's childhood was marked by attachment injuries, parental conflict, sexual abuse in Jung's case, and repeated physical abuse in Spielrein's case. As yet unanalyzed regarding his own woundedness, the intensity of his analytic work with Spielrein and other patients with both hysterical and psychotic symptoms, coupled with grueling demands at the Burghölzli, to say nothing of married life in close quarters with infants, meant that Jung was increasingly unable to contain the flights of non-directed thinking that were to become *Symbols of Transformation* (Jung, 1967b/1911–1912).[23]

In March 1907, Jung visited Freud at his home in Vienna for the first time and, in addition to their intense thirteen-hour conversation, is said to have learned from Minna, Freud's sister-in-law, of her discomfort regarding her intimate relationship with Freud (Billinsky, 1969).[24] If this occurred, it would be notable as a suggestion that Freud himself shared Jung's "polygamous tendencies" (cf., McGuire, 1974, p. 207), which in Jung's case were a consequence of maternal absence coupled with childhood sexual abuse. In his letter of October 28, 1907, Jung wrote to Freud about his own woundedness:

> My veneration for you has something of the character of a "religious" crush… I still feel it is disgusting and ridiculous because of its undeniable erotic overtones. This abominable feeling comes from the fact that as a boy I was the victim of a sexual assault by a man I once worshipped.
>
> (ibid., p. 94)

It seems likely that Jung's work with Spielrein's psychosexual complexes had uncovered his own. From this point on, Jung's relationship with Freud was fraught with underlying tensions that were further exacerbated by their attempts to analyze each other as they traveled to the New World to speak at Clark University in 1909 (Jung, 1989/1961, p. 158).

Spielrein as analyst to her analyst (1908–1910)

In April 1908, the First Congress for Freudian Psychology was held in Salzburg. In May 1908, Spielrein passed her preliminary medical examination, the same month Otto Gross, a brilliant, addicted, mentally ill doctor, was referred to Jung for inpatient treatment. Gross had been Bleuler's patient in 1902 and 1904. This time, Gross's father, desperate for a cure, had attempted to refer him to Freud, who, claiming to be too busy, sent him on to Jung with the promise to take Gross on in October. Dealing with Gross was not good for Jung's own mental health, which was already strained. Based on his reported symptoms,

Gross was likely self-medicating with morphine, cocaine, and opium for bipolar disorder, with its attendant mania often manifesting as hypersexuality. Gross and his wife had recently participated in a free-love commune (Bair, 2003, p. 139), and Gross had earlier attempted to persuade Jung that "[t]he truly healthy state for the neurotic is sexual immorality" (McGuire, 1974, p. 89). Jung, the preacher's kid, husband of a respectable Swiss heiress, wrote to Freud objecting to Gross's immorality after first meeting Gross at a 1907 conference in Amsterdam. Gross eventually escaped from the Burghölzli against medical advice, but not before persuading Jung that they should "analyze" each other. Gross's influence only added to Jung's struggle with thoughts of polygamy that would entail unfaithfulness to his wife and risk social opprobrium if acted upon. On December 4, 1908, Jung wrote to Spielrein confessing the depths of his distress:

> My Dear,
>
> I regret so much; I regret my weakness and the curse of fate that is threatening me. I fear for my work, for my life's task… You will laugh when I tell you that recently *earlier and earlier childhood memories have been surfacing* from a time *(3–4th year)* when I often hurt myself badly, and when, for example, I was once only just rescued from certain death by a maid. My mind is torn to its very depths. I, who had to be a tower of strength for many weak people, am the weakest of all. Will you forgive me for being as I am? For offending you by being like this, and forgetting my duties as a doctor towards you? Will you understand that I am one of the weakest and most unstable of human beings? … Give me back now some of the love and patience and unselfishness which I was able to give you at the time of your illness. Now I am ill.
>
> (Wharton, 2015b, p. 34, emphasis original)

The year 1909 was a tumultuous one for both Jung and Spielrein as their relationship intensified under the influence of external and internal pressures. Since first contacting Freud in 1906, Jung had become reliant on him, to the exclusion of Bleuler, with the result that Bleuler was increasingly alienated from them both. Emma Jung, now with three young children in tow – Agathe, born 1904, age five;

Greta, born 1906, age three; and Franz, born 1908, still an infant – had been pressuring her husband since before Franz's birth to move out of the hospital into their own home. Rumors were flying about an affair, and not for the first time, Emma considered divorcing Jung (Bair, 2003, p. 114). Despite the split in his psyche Jung experienced as he was drawn to Spielrein (and later Maria Moltzer and Toni Wolfe),[25] he knew that he did not want to risk losing the emotional support and financial security he derived from his wife. By 1909, the Jungs had moved into what was to be their lifelong home in Küsnacht, south of Zürich on the Zürichsee. Jung then resigned from the Burghölzli. Now if Spielrein and Jung wanted to see each other, travel by ferry or train was required.

In March 1909, Jung attempted to break with Spielrein, believing that she was the source of scandalous gossip. The same day he tendered his resignation at the Burghölzli, the basis of his professional reputation to date, he wrote to Freud that:

> … a woman patient, whom years ago I pulled out of a very sticky neurosis with greatest devotion, has violated my confidence and my friendship in the most mortifying way imaginable. She has kicked up a vile scandal solely because I denied myself the pleasure of giving her a child.
> (March 7, 1909 – McGuire, 1974, p. 207)

In a subsequent letter, Jung finally names the woman he has been in contact with since her 1904 hospitalization:

> Spielrein is the person I wrote to you about… She was, so to speak, my test case, for which reason I remembered [sic] her with special gratitude and affection. Since I knew from experience that she would immediately relapse if I withdrew my support, I prolonged the relationship over the years and in the end found myself morally obliged, as it were, to devote a large measure of friendship to her, until I saw that an unintended wheel had started turning, whereupon I finally broke with her. She was, of course, systematically planning my seduction, which I considered inopportune. Now she is seeking revenge… I need hardly say that I have made a clean break. Like Gross, she is a case of fight-the-father, which

in the name of all that's wonderful I was trying to cure *gratissime* (!) ... During the whole business Gross's notions flitted about a bit too much in my head... Gross and Spielrein are bitter experiences.
(June 4, 1909 – ibid., p. 228)

Comparing Spielrein, who by all accounts had made an excellent recovery, to Gross, who was spiraling out of control, is clearly an injustice to Spielrein. As for "fight-the-father" authority issues, Jung's conflicts with Bleuler and, increasingly, with Freud suggest that his perception of Spielrein in this regard was in part his own projection, especially given her later attempts at reconciliation between Freud and Jung. Spielrein eventually persuaded both Jung and Freud that she was not the source of the rumor.

The following excerpts are taken from Spielrein's diary entries beginning August, 1909. Here we have an opportunity to witness the further development of her observing ego, the quality of "psychological mindedness" and self-awareness so necessary for the analyst, as she notes the conflict between her modesty (as emphasized by her mother) and wanting to be admired as a twenty-four-year-old woman in the bloom of youth. While staying in a hotel in Berlin (August 27–28, 1909), she records her response to being observed dressing in her room by men whose windows faced hers across a courtyard:

> If one wants to be completely honest – one must also be able to note things down which give a little insight in to the psychology of so-called modest girls, to which category I also belong... I noticed that a nice young gentleman was gazing into my room; I felt myself blushing deeply, and this mild manifestation of the unconscious, which I noted quite objectively, pleased me very much. For a moment I hesitated. Modesty won out, and I hid behind the curtain... A little later an older gentleman looked out of the upper building and... how wonderful! A wave of deep disgust washed over [me].
> (Carotenuto, 1982, p. 4)

What significance might this instance of self-awareness have for Spielrein? It shows that, despite the psychic conflicts around sexuality and attachment that brought her into treatment as a nineteen-year-old girl, she is now able to experience the enjoyment of being seen and admired by a young person of her own age that would naturally belong to this stage of young adulthood. The fact that she registers disgust at the sight of the older gentleman, in the absence of any more troubling symptoms, is also a sign of health for a girl whose erotic fantasies had previously been colonized by the comingled emotions of anger and arousal at the thought of her father's hand. In this same diary entry, she imagines herself as a great teacher, surrounded by her disciples: "Great love is what I would wish to teach my disciples. Is there Someone who knows this? ... I could not express the main thing, and that is that my friend loves me" (ibid., p. 5). Here, she claims Jung as the "Someone" who loves her in the role of an ego-ideal, one who inspires her to greatness as her guardian angel did in her youth.

The next entry is from September 21, 1909, from Kolberg, where she was staying with her family on holiday. Apparently, on this trip, Spielrein continued to confide her feelings for Jung to her mother.

> Mother says it is impossible for my friend and me to remain friends once we have given each other our love… Dear Fate, allow us, my friend and me, to be exceptions, allow us to meet each other always radiant with pleasure, to support each other in joy and sorrow, to form one soul, even at a distance, to reach out our hands to each other in the search for the "higher, farther, wider" or, as my friend says, "the good and the beautiful" that we may be a support to many who are weak. Allow me to be his guardian angel, his spirit of inspiration, always spurring him to new and greater things. Do I perhaps ask too much? If it is too much, well, it need not always persist with the same intensity, but at least until I find someone who will take his place, someone whom I can call my husband in highest bliss. … Guardian Spirit, allow there to be a pure, noble friendship between us, in the sense in which I understand the word, allow this feeling to satisfy me completely and to become a ray of light to my solitude!
>
> (ibid., p. 6)

On this same family vacation, Spielrein's mother told her the story of her own first love. His Christian parents were opposed because she was Jewish.

> They told the bridegroom all sorts of tales about his bride. The latter was too proud to defend herself. He hurt her feelings with his ridiculous suspicions... Thus the break came about. My mother felt her life was ruined; the world had lost its color for her, a new love seemed impossible.

She then met Spielrein's father, who proposed four times until she finally said yes. "They became a couple. One could hardly imagine two more different people" (ibid., p. 7).

Here we have the basis for a thrice-repeated intergenerational pattern: Spielrein in love with a Christian who cannot fully return her love (in this case because he is married), with the expectation that, just like her mother and grandfather before her, she must eventually face the need to marry someone from within her own culture, her own faith.

The next entry, written when she is back in Zürich, demonstrates an awareness of her dreams and their implications for her waking life, understood from a symbolic perspective. She is distressed because, though Bleuler is her thesis advisor, he has yet to read the thesis she has submitted for completion of her medical degree requirements:

> As soon as Prof. Bleuler left... I wept in torrents... I was supposed to hear about my dissertation, I was hopelessly depressed: I feared the worst. I begged my guardian spirit to preserve me from losing my wits, and the very night before the fateful event I had a dream that I was with Father and Mother and heard my father say that I had come into the world to accomplish something great; I should just continue to work calmly and patiently... upon waking... I got up and continued with my work, as if I had never been tortured by doubts. Only later did I find anything remarkable in this seamless transition between dream and reality, and even conscious consideration of the phenomenon could not destroy my calm. The father represents the ancestor component in a person, a component that is often clairvoyant, in any case means much more for the fate of the individual than any momentary conscious attitude...
>
> (ibid., pp. 7–8, September 23, 1909)

On the basis of this dream, which she is clearly interpreting from a teleological, archetypal Jungian standpoint, rather than from a Freudian perspective, which would emphasize oedipal dynamics, she decides to risk once again asking Jung for support:

> Despair gave me courage. I ran to my friend, with whom I had not wanted to speak for a long time. For a good while I found no words, until I was finally able to tell him of my desperate situation and ask him to read my dissertation, if for no other reason than that he figures in it. He laughed at *Prof. Bleuler* as an analyst and said surely I had not come to make fun of a person whom I liked so much. We arranged that in September I would ask for my dissertation back from *Prof. Bleuler* and send it to my friend. This perfidy toward my old professor tormented me constantly. Later I would confess it to him, but that will not make him feel any less wronged by his triumphant rival, who only ten years ago was his humble student and now, as a "scientific giant," as Prof. Bleuler himself calls him, derides his old teacher.
>
> (ibid., p. 8, emphasis in original)

Here, Spielrein finds herself triangulated between warring authority figures, as in her family of origin. Only the year before, at the First International Congress for Psychoanalysis in Salzburg (April 27, 1908), Freud had conspired, excluding his Jewish Viennese colleagues by meeting secretly with the Swiss analysts, to found the *Jahrbuch für Psychoanalytische und Psychopathologische Forschungen* with Freud and Eugen Bleuler as "co-directors" and Jung as editor. But in the interim, Jung had repeatedly bypassed Bleuler by going directly to Freud, as their letters from this period indicate (McGuire, 1974; Bair, 2003). Since June 1909, Jung had already moved his wife and three children into their own home in Küsnacht, withdrawing from his administrative responsibilities at the outpatient clinic and devoting himself to private practice. By September 1909, relations between Bleuler and Jung had reached a low ebb.

Spielrein's diary entry from September 23, 1909, does not indicate where her meeting with Jung took place. If she met him in his own home, as on subsequent occasions, the response from Jung she documents is all the more surprising:

> The most important outcome of our discussion was that we both loved each other fervently again. My friend said we would always have to be careful not to fall in love again; we would always be dangerous to each other… At the beginning he was annoyed that I had not sent my paper to him long before, that I did not trust him, etc. Then he became more and more intense. At the end he pressed my hands to his heart several times and said this should mark the beginning of a new era. What could he have meant by that? Will we see each other or not? I am much too proud to go to him, and he cannot come to me… How will things develop?
> (Carotenuto, 1982, pp. 8–9)

Here we see several dimensions of Spielrein's inner dialogue. On the one hand, she is leery of burning her bridges with Bleuler, her dissertation advisor of record, whom she had continued to rely on during her break with Jung. On the other hand, mindful of the acrimony between Bleuler and Jung, and knowing that Jung is referenced in her dissertation, *Über den Psychologischen Inhalt eines Falles von Schizophrenie (Dementia Praecox)* [*On the Psychological Content of a Case of Schizophrenia*] (Spielrein, 1911), she risks her own chances for degree completion if Bleuler does not approve of her work. Then, as now, it was perilous for an aspiring scholar to subject her thesis to review by professors with opposing views.

Her tone with regard to Jung's passionate gesture of pressing her hands to his chest is dispassionate, quizzical: "… a new era. What could he have meant by that?" A careful reading of Spielrein's diary strongly suggests that her relationship with Jung never included intercourse, but rather embraces of the "everything but" variety, with all the passion of an unrequited longing, sometimes mutual, sometimes not (Lothane, 2015). Spielrein was too proud and too ambitious to become a mere mistress, the plaything of a great man. Her dreams of greatness indicate that she wanted to be known as a scholar in her own right and also to attain social respectability as a wife and mother.

Prior to completing her medical school examinations in 1910, she remained in touch with Jung. An alternative reading of their interaction from Spielrein's point of view portrays him as the would-be seducer and her as an aspiring analyst doubtless flattered by his attention, but also resolute in maintaining a firm grip on her own personal and professional goals:

> Tomorrow I have my first final examination. I have already abreacted all my grand emotions by playing the piano… My whole being is suffused with love. I would like to create something great and good. Help me, Guardian Spirit! Help me, Fate. Show me the noble ideal that I should love… What still torments me is that I cannot give my father the love he deserves and therefore am partly passive toward him, and partly express my feelings in a negative way, but fundamentally I feel that I have an unusually good, wholly unselfish father, to whom I owe much gratitude… I see myself being swept away in the grand ballroom in the arms of my beloved. Who might this beloved be? That I do not know! I am afraid to think of it. Do what you will, Fate. My first goal is to do well on my examination… My friend and I had the tenderest "poetry" last Wednesday. What will come of that? Make something good of it, Fate, and let me love him nobly. A long, ecstatic kiss in parting, my beloved little son!
> (Carotenuto, 1982, p. 37, December 8, 1910)

Several days later, she reports the following encounter with Jung:

> Instead of showing me calm love, he fell back into the "Don Juan role," which I find so repellent in him. Although he considers me honest in love, he said I ought to belong to that category of women made not for motherhood but for free love. What should I say? I blush deeply as I recall it. I was profoundly depressed and said many foolish things. Do not let me perish Guardian Spirit! I want to love someone with all my soul, someone who can return my feeling with all the strength of youth; I want to be a wife and mother, not just a diversion. I want him to see what I am capable of, what I am worth. I want him to love me madly and want to be able to defy him. I want him to see how I am capable of loving and how I can rise above the feeling. But I do want to love someone! Where is the man I could love?
> (ibid., p. 38, December 21, 1910)

As Pamela Cooper-White notes in her analysis of Spielrein's best-known paper, "Destruction as the Cause of Becoming" (this volume, Chapter 2; Spielrein, 1912, trans. this volume, Chapter 6), completed the year after Spielrein's graduation from medical school, the Siegfried legend served as a transitional object for Jung and Spielrein:

> [Spielrein] wrote to Jung when sending him the first draft of the paper, "Receive now the product of our love, the project which is your little son Siegfried" (Carotenuto, 1982, p. 48). In her own fantasy, Siegfried not only represented a child to bind Jung to her permanently, but a deed of cosmic significance – to "give birth to 'a great Aryan-Semitic hero' who would unite these different and warring races forever."
>
> (Cooper-White, Ch. 2 this volume, p. 85, citing Covington & Wharton, 2015, p. 5)

In the myth of Siegfried, Brünhilde is both lover and mother to the hero. Given the unboundaried nature of their "wild analysis," especially during the years 1909–1910 when Jung had broken with his own father–mentor, Bleuler, and was soon to break with Freud as well, Spielrein functioned as both mother and lover to Jung. Knowing that she would ultimately not agree to be his mistress, Jung could nonetheless bask in the glow of her admiration. Siegfried, a fantasy of shared greatness, served as a bridge or "transitional object" (Winnicott, 1971) during what was, for both of them, a liminal time of transition. In this way, Siegfried was part of their "poetry" as surely as any physical touch. In sharing this symbol, they sought to be healed by each other.

Spielrein's dissertation, now available in translation (Spielrein, 2018),[26] reads as an interesting mixture of early Freudian and Jungian theory. Like Jung, she paid careful attention to all the seemingly illogical non sequiturs of her patient, seeking out the thought correspondences that would make what others heard as word salad intelligible. Spielrein is not cited with Jung in Downing and Mills' *Outpatient Treatment of Psychosis: Psychodynamic Approaches to Evidence Based Practice* (2017), yet Jung's references to her work in *Wandlungen und Symbole der Libido,* also published in 1911 (Part 1), make it clear that they shared a similar view of the symbolic underpinnings of conscious thought. Spielrein was also careful to relate her patients' psychotic complexes back to specific sexual traumas, as opposed to developmental traumas such as parental abuse and emotional neglect that we might understand primarily as attachment injuries from the standpoint of relational psychoanalysis.

Spielrein and her patient had a lot in common. One imagines that it was not difficult for Spielrein to empathize with this woman's plight despite the difference in their ages, having been hospitalized herself (for hysteria) only seven years earlier. The except included in Chapter 5 includes the anamnesis of the case, though Spielrein is careful to note at the outset that she avoided reading the case history in advance so that she could approach the case "without taking into account established scientific opinion, with the unique intention to gain a deeper understanding of these patients' mental processes (Ch. 5, p. 197)." In other words, she is choosing to take an essentially phenomenological approach, assuming that through careful listening she would be able to enter into the vocabulary of the patient's experience, just as we do today when we ask for the associations to a dream. It is clear that she is paying close attention to what she would later identify as linkages and "crossing" between associations (cf., Spielrein, 1923b; Chapter 14), focusing on "immediate, spontaneous information from the patient" (Ch. 5, p. 197) as in her work with children's language and motor aphasia.

From the anamnesis, we learn that the case includes religious symbolism and that the patient is musical, well-read, intellectual, married to a professor, sexually repressed, and traumatized by history, both in childhood and in the course of her marriage. Like Spielrein, she began masturbating in childhood after being beaten by her father. Today, we would understand this as a compulsive attempt at self-soothing. Pediatricians note that "Excessive masturbation may be a symptom of emotional deprivation and may develop subsequent to actual or perceived withdrawal of parental affection" (Leung & Robson, 1993, p. 238). Spielrein may have gained insight into traumas from her own childhood, despite the fact that her transient symptoms of hysteria were not comparable to the full-blown schizophrenic symptoms of her patient. She finds ample coded allusions to the patient's traumatic second experience of giving birth, followed by a spontaneous abortion at two months that left the patient hospitalized for three months. Two years later, the patient became increasingly agitated, accusing her husband of not being sufficiently religious. He was suspected of having an affair and giving the patient syphilis, which in her mind may have caused the abortion. The patient is Protestant while her husband is Catholic. From Part 1 of the dissertation under the heading "Catholicizing," we read:

> ... the patient says a lot about the fact that, here in the hospital, she was "catholicized." Question: [from Spielrein] "What do you mean by 'catholicizing'?" Answer: "The history of art is in contact with Michelangelo, Sistine art, and the Madonna... Sistine art gives rise to sexual art: through the beautiful image one can be transformed into poetry, [and] perhaps forget obligations."
>
> (Ch. 5, p. 201)

Spielrein unravels the patient's meaning as follows:

> "Sistine art" (chapel), and the Catholic religion (Art = "poetry"), respectively, are linked with beauty (Madonna, Raphael, Michelangelo)... With the phrase "forget obligations," delivered from the mouth of a married woman, "poetry" is viewed as an explicit erotic element, so that we can compare "poetry" = "amorousness."
>
> (ibid.)

Carotenuto, Kerr, and others, in reading Spielrein's references to "poetry" in her diaries, have assumed that the word appeared as a code for Spielrein's erotic attraction to Jung, and his to her. That element is here, but there is more. This "poetry" is ambivalent because Spielrein goes on to write:

> ... the patient confirms that her husband was delighted with beauty and forgot about his responsibilities in relation to his wife and children [by having an affair with his student]. [The patient continues:] "The psychology of vanity is not related to the psychology of motherhood... I have no respect for the soul who promotes beauty [here equated with lust] over internal purity."
>
> (ibid.)

The patient feels polluted by her husband's infidelity and blames him for the death of their child. Spielrein certainly would have met Emma Jung and perhaps her two oldest daughters since the Jungs lived in the hospital a few floors above the patients until they moved to Küsnacht in 1909. To give in to Jung's suggestion that she be a "free" woman, unbound by obligations, would have violated her own religious aspirations to purity. Freud later commented to Jung after meeting Spielrein in person that she appeared "uncommonly ambivalent" (March 21, 1912 – McGuire 1974, p. 494), and with good reason. What Spielrein aspired to above all was to accomplish something great and good in her life. She looked to Jung to be her good father and hoped to provide for him some of the mother love that was lacking during his own period of childhood psychosis (Winnicott, 1964; Covington, 2015, p. 168). Her truest passion was for the work they shared, the meeting of their minds as they explored the symbolic meanings of their patients.

Spielrein quotes Jung nineteen times in her dissertation, Freud six times, Pfister, Bleuler, Stekel, and Schreber two times, while Abraham, Rank, Riklin, and Maeder are each cited once. Between the Introduction and Conclusion, the dissertation is divided into nine sections. The first seven are based on the patient's words, thoughts, and associations: I. "Catholizing"; II. "Psycho-Sistine Experiments"; III. Histology and its Treatment; IV. The Industrial or Economic Question; V. Poetry of the Tropics and Water Symbolism; VI. Iron, Fire, and War; VII. Poverty Complex and Garment Symbolism. In section VIII, "Discourses from Medical History," Spielrein adds "several statements from the patient's medical history, in order to show that she [the patient] also uses analogous chains of associations when talking with persons; furthermore that one may apply the same analytical approach to those statements that have nothing to do with me" (or her potential personal influence). In section IX, "Childhood Impressions, Ideas on Transformation, Dreams," Spielrein notes that, like herself, the patient "possessed the 'ability to dream' (Spielrein 2018/1911, p. 70)." Like Spielrein's father, the patient's father was good to her at times, but later became abusive as an alcoholic, establishing similarly painfully ambivalent feelings of longing toward her father as those Spielrein experienced. In this section, commenting on the patient's dream that she was killed and woke up as a horse, Spielrein notes that, "Here, too, death is connected with sexual fantasies. The ideas on transformation (which are present in the mythology of each people), seek to find support in Darwin's theory in a way that is quite logical to the unconscious" (ibid., p. 76).

Further on, Spielrein notes that "the patient herself explains quite correctly what a symbol is: it is an object into which one projects one's own being (= love) and that acts in the same way in which one would act oneself" (Spielrein 2018/1911, p. 79). From this we can infer that the meaning of Siegfried was not primarily a physical child, as Jung must have known despite his disparaging comments about Spielrein to Freud (see above). For Spielrein, it was her own vision of a great work that she and Jung would share in a dual unity pre-oedipal transference/countertransference as opposed to the explicit eroticism of an oedipal intersubjectivity.

It is poignant to note, in the dissertation and also in later articles translated in Part II of this volume, hints of a future book on the importance of symbolic thought in the unconscious (cf., Spielrein 1923a, 1923b; Chapters 12 and 14). Sadly, it was not Spielrein's fate to complete this envisioned work.

Spielrein as an independent analyst and psychoanalytic theorist (1911 onwards)

Spielrein was important to Freud and Jung, not only as the test case that brought them together as collaborators, but also as the first psychiatrist to publish a dissertation referencing Freud's psychoanalytic methods in conjunction with Jung's phenomenological approach to treatment. Despite the condescending tone of the letters that Freud and Jung exchanged about her, Freud cited her work four times and Jung twelve times in *Symbols of Transformation* alone. Though Freud thought that marrying a nice Jewish doctor would cure her of her Aryan fantasies, Spielrein continued to correspond with Jung until 1918, alluding to the mystical and ambiguous Siegfried symbol they shared, and corresponded with Freud until 1923. She not only attempted to bridge the differences between the two through her own understanding of symbols, but, according to Launer (2015), she was ahead of her time by attempting to provide a biological basis for psychoanalytic thinking (pp. 72–74 et passim). This was a theoretical vein that both Freud and Jung resisted, while Spielrein presaged the focus of subsequent theorists on the innate importance of attachment (Bowlby, 1969; Stern, 1985).

Jung is credited with the "anima/animus" concept that developed in the context of his relationship with Spielrein, and Freud subsequently acknowledged in a footnote that a version of a "death instinct" appeared in Spielrein's "Destruction" paper (Freud, 1955/1920, p. 55n2; see Chapters 2 and 4, this volume). Others see Spielrein's influence in Jung's theory of individuation as a process of transformation in which creating the new requires embracing destruction and change (Jantzen, 2009). Melanie Klein is known for her psychoanalytic work on representations of the breast in infancy, which may well have been influenced by Spielrein's paper "The Origin and Development of Spoken Speech" delivered at the 6th International Psychoanalytic Conference in The Hague (1920), which Klein attended. Anticipating Winnicott's understanding of transitional phenomena, Spielrein recognized the infantile origins of speech arising "in an intermediate zone between the pleasure and reality principles" (Spielrein, 1922; Kerr 1994, p. 493). Anna Freud is recognized as a founder of child analysis education, while Spielrein's earlier work in this area in Geneva and later in her native Russia have remained, until recently, largely unknown.

Following the 1920 conference, Spielrein moved to Geneva and was delegated to the Institute Rousseau as an evangelist for psychoanalysis. She conducted a "didactic" analysis with Piaget that, according to him, left him "impervious to theory" (Noth, 2015, p. 284; cf., Chapters 3 and 4, this volume). In 1924, she moved to Moscow, establishing early childhood care based on psychodynamic principles, and then returned to her birthplace where, following the rise of Stalin and his banishing of psychoanalysis, she was killed with her two daughters when the Nazis invaded Rostov-on-Don for the second time in 1942. Whether she was too idealistic to believe that Germans who spoke the language of her Guardian Spirit could be butchers, or simply too depressed following the deaths of her brother Isaak (1937), father Nikolai, husband Pavel, and brothers Jan and Emil, all of whom died in 1938 (Launer, 2015, p. 256), she resisted those who urged her to flee. Her life was cut short at the age of fifty-seven. Had Aldo Carotenuto not published her diaries, Spielrein's work might well have remained forgotten.

Spielrein was also influential as an early psychoanalytic patient. What "Anna O" (Bertha Pappenheim) and "Dora" (Ida Bauer) were for Breuer (Freud & Breuer, 1955/1893–1895) and Freud (1953a/1905) – foundational cases for the practice of psychoanalysis – Spielrein was for analytical (Jungian) psychology. Arriving as an inpatient at the Burghölzli in 1904, hers was the first case Jung attempted to treat using Freud's psychoanalytic method. The treatment was both a success and a disaster: a success because Spielrein went on to train as a psychiatrist, publishing articles in German, French, and Russian; and a disaster because she was in some respects betrayed by both Jung and Freud, left unhealed. What Jung and Freud learned from her about transference and countertransference and what subsequent analysts can glean from her treatment inform understandings of therapeutic transformation, individuation, boundaries, and frame identified as best practices today (Sedgwick, 1994).

Jung's "wild analysis" with Spielrein served, among other sources of psychological stress, to precipitate his own period of "creative illness" from 1913 to 1919, as revealed in *The Red Book* (Jung, 2009), following his break with Freud. In moral terms, Jung's psychological vulnerability at this stage in his career does not excuse his "use" of Spielrein, Toni Wolff, and others in transgressing therapeutic boundaries. These are the potential perils of intense countertransference that have served to establish the emphasis on the "temenos," the inviolate container required for therapeutic transformation that is the norm for analysts today (Cwik, 2010, p. 174).[27] Only the unambiguous "poetry" of true intersubjectivity can serve our deepest longing for transformation.

Perhaps it is most compassionate to allow these three pioneers of depth psychology – Spielrein, Freud, and Jung – to have the last word:

One loves one's ideal in the other.[28]

(Spielrein, c. 1906)

Essentially, one might say, the cure is effected by love.[29]

(Freud, December 6, 1906)

The love of S. for J. made the latter aware of something he had previously only vaguely suspected, namely of a power in the unconscious which shapes our destiny.[30]

(Jung, September 1, 1919)

Notes

1 An earlier version of this essay appeared in *Pastoral Psychology*, 64(2), 241–258.
2 Carotenuto (1982, p. 36) – Spielrein diary entry December 8, 1910.
3 Regarding the unbounadried "wild analysis" that was regularly practiced during the early days of depth psychology before transference-countertransference dynamics were fully understood, see examples in Falzeder's *Psychoanalytic Filiations: Mapping the Psychoanalytic Movement* (2015), pp. 38–45, 98–99; see also this volume, p. 9n1.

4 Cronenberg (2011) – film based on the eponymous book by John Kerr (1994).
5 Spielrein is also cited seven times in volumes 3, 4, 7, 11, and 13 of Jung's (1957–1979) *Collected Works*.
6 Spielrein refers to "poetry" in her dissertation (Spielrein, 1911, 2018; also see Ch. 5 below).
7 For an introductory review of the "good-enough" conditions for "normal" development, see Kelcourse (2015, Part 1).
8 Genograms for both Jung and Freud can be found in McGoldrick, Gerson, and Petry (2008), [n.p.], Color Figures 7, 28.
9 For further biographical details, see Launer (2015). Portions of Spielrein's early history are also summarized in Kelcourse (2014).
10 Covington (2015) notes that "Bleuler protects Sabina from contact with her father… he can see how destructive this relationship is…" (p. 121).
11 Friedrich Fröbel (1782–1852) was a German educator specializing in early childhood development. He coined the term "Kindergarten" and also created educational toys. Note that Sabina's parents did not send her away to school, as sources prior to Launer (2015) had reported, and clearly wanted the best education for their gifted daughter. Spielrein may have developed her own professional interest in early childhood development as the beneficiary of this progressive education.
12 The case of four-year-old Peter is reported in "The Theory of Infantile Sexuality" (Erikson, 1963, pp. 53–58).
13 Bair, p. 681n33, cites Spielrein's (1913) publication *"Beiträge zur Kenntnis der kindlichen Seele"* ["Contributions to an Understanding of the Child's Mind"] as evidence for Spielrein's mother's inconsistent attitude toward sexuality, based also on the letters mother and daughter later exchanged.
14 For example, Heller and Zeanah (1999) observed mothers who had delivered a child within nineteen months after a perinatal loss. When the child was a year old, the researchers assessed the mother–child attachment relationships and found that 45% of the infants had disorganized attachments to their mothers. A study conducted by Hughes et al. (2001) also found evidence of disorganized attachment behavior in infants born subsequent to stillbirth.
15 In Jung's theory, the "anima" is the inner feminine component of a man's psyche. In *Psychological Types,* Jung (1971) writes, "The inborn mode of *acting* has long been known as *instinct*, and for the inborn mode of psychic apprehension I have proposed the term *archetype*" (p. 376, emphasis in original). When the anima archetype or "soul-image" for a man becomes associated with an actual person, "[T]his person is the object of intense love or equally intense hate (or fear). The influence of such a person is immediate and absolutely compelling, because it always provokes an affective response" (pp. 470–471, 1971/1921). For Jung, this archetype, or "pattern of psychic perception and understanding common to all human

beings" (Hopcke, 1989, p. 13), has the role of guide to the unconscious, "a mediatrix between one's ego and one's inner life" (p. 91).
16 Moskowitz and Heim (2011).
17 While the time frames are adopted from Lothane (2015), the designations are mine.
18 Details about Spielrein's clearly disturbed and disruptive behavior can be found in Wharton (2015, "Burghölzli Hospital Records of Sabina Spielrein," pp. 57–82).
19 In the course of his life, Jung came to a fully intersubjective perspective on the countertransference with the understanding that the client has as much impact on the therapist as the reverse. But the Jung of 1904, though quickly promoted to leadership positions at the Burghölzli, was still young in the practice of his craft. Modern Jungians appreciate the ways that the therapist's own wounds can benefit the patient, given adequate self-awareness on the part of the therapist (cf., Sedgwick, 1994).
20 Lothane is drawing his citations from two previously unpublished sources that cause him to view the Carotenuto's and Kerr's readings of Spielrein's relationship with Jung as incorrect.
21 Kohut's (1971, 1984) term *selfobject* refers to the way another person, and/or the functions provided by another person, can be experienced as part of the self. In a *selfobject transference* or, by extension, countertransference, the patient experiences the analyst as part of him or herself and vice versa.
22 Graf-Nold (2015) notes that while hysteria was at that time "the main paradigm for clinical psychiatric research" (p. 97), these cases were rarely seen at the Zürich clinic.
23 In the foreword to the fourth (Swiss) edition, Jung wrote "The whole thing came upon me like a landslide... it was the explosion of all those psychic contents which could find no room, no breathing-space in the constricting atmosphere of Freudian psychology..." (p. xxiii).
24 Note that there is no agreement among scholars as to whether the relationship was actually incestuous or merely familial, with Minna as a younger traveling companion interested in his work, as was his daughter Anna.
25 On Jung's relationship with Maria Moltzer, see Shamdasani (1998) and Healy (2017).
26 References to Spielrein's dissertation beyond the pages excerpted in Chapter 5 of this volume are taken from the dissertation translation supplied by Ruth I. Cape and Raymond Burt (Spielrein, 2018).
27 Regarding ethics in Jungian analysis, see also Merkur (2017).
28 Undated dairy entry (Moll, 2015, p. 21).
29 Freud to Jung, quoted in McGuire (1974, pp. 12–13).
30 Jung to Spielrein, September 1, 1919, quoted in Wharton (2015, p. 51).

References

Atwood, G., & Stolorow, R. (1993). *Faces in a cloud: Intersubjectivity in personality theory.* Northvale, NJ: Jason Aronson. (Orig. publ. 1979.)
Bair, D. (2003). *Jung: A biography.* New York: Little Brown.
Blanton, S. (1971). *Diary of my analysis with Sigmund Freud.* New York: Hawthorn Books.
Billinsky, J.M. (1969). Jung and Freud: The end of a romance. *Andover Newton Quarterly*, 10, 30–43.
Bowlby, J. (1969). *Attachment and loss, vol. 1: Attachment.* New York: Basic Books.
Brooke, R. (2015). *Jung and phenomenology.* New York: Routledge.
Clay, C. (2016). *Labyrinths: Emma Jung, her marriage to Carl, and the early years of psychoanalysis.* New York: Harper.
Carotenuto, A. (1982). *A secret symmetry: Sabina Spielrein between Jung and Freud.* New York: Pantheon.
Covington, C. (2015). Comments on Burghölzli hospital records. In C. Covington & B. Wharton (Eds.). *Sabina Spielrein: Forgotten pioneer of psychoanalysis*, 2nd edn. (pp. 114–125). New York: Routledge.
Covington, C. & Wharton, B. (Eds.) (2015). *Sabina Spielrein: Forgotten pioneer of psychoanalysis*, 2nd edn. New York: Routledge.
Cronenberg, D. (Director) (2011). *A dangerous method* (film). Berlin: Lago Film.
Cwik, A. (2010). From frame through holding to container. In M. Stein (Ed.). *Jungian psychoanalysis: Working in the spirit of C.G. Jung* (pp. 169–178). Chicago: Open Court.
Downing, D. & Mills, J. (2017). *Outpatient treatment of psychosis: Psychodynamic approaches to evidence-based practice.* London: Karnac.
Erikson, E. (1963). *Childhood and society.* New York: Norton. (Orig. publ. 1950.)
Falzeder, E. (2015). *Psychoanalytic filiations: Mapping the psychoanalytic movement.* London: Karnac.
Freud, S. (1953a). Fragment of an analysis of a case of hysteria ["Dora"]. In J. Strachey (Trans.). *The standard edition of the complete psychological works of Sigmund Freud* (hereafter *SE*). Vol. 7 (pp. 1–123). London: Hogarth. (Orig. publ. 1905.)
Freud, S. (1953b). The interpretation of dreams. *SE* (4–5 entire). (Orig. publ. 1900 [1899].)
Freud, S. (1955). Beyond the pleasure principle. *SE* 18, 1–63. (Orig. publ. 1920.)
Freud, S. & Breuer, J. (1955). Studies on hysteria. *SE* 2 (entire). (Orig. publ. 1893–1895.)
Graf-Nold, A. (2015). The Zürich school of psychiatry in theory and practice: Sabina Spielrein's treatment at the Burghölzli clinic in Zürich. In C.

Covington & B. Wharton (eds.). *Sabina Spielrein: Forgotten pioneer of psychoanalysis*, 2nd edn. (pp. 83–113). New York: Routledge.

Healy, N.S. (2017). *Toni Wolff and C.G. Jung: A collaboration*. Los Angeles: Tiberius.

Heller, S.S. & Zeanah, C.H. (1999). Attachment disturbances in infants born subsequent to perinatal loss: A pilot study. *Infant Mental Health Journal*, 20, 188–199.

Hopcke, R. (1989). A guided tour of the *collected works* of C.G. Jung. Boulder, CO: Shambala.

Hughes P, Turton P, Hopper E, McGauley G.A., & Fonagy P., (2001). Disorganised attachment behaviour among infants born subsequent to stillbirth. *Journal of Child Psychology and Psychiatry and Related Disciplines*, 42(6), 791–801.

Jantzen, G., (Ed.) (2009). *Redeeming the present*. Burlington, VT: Ashgate.

Jung, C.G. (1957–1979). *The collected works of C.G. Jung*. G. Adler & R.F.C. Hull (Eds.). Bollingen Series XX. Princeton, NJ: Princeton University Press. (Hereafter *CW*.)

Jung, C.G. (1967a). The Freudian theory of hysteria. *CW* 4, 10–24. Princeton, NJ: Princeton University Press. (Orig. publ. 1908.)

Jung, C.G. (1967b). Symbols of transformation. *CW* 5 (entire). (Orig. publ. 1911–12, rev. ed. 1952.)

Jung, C.G. (1970). On the psychology and pathology of so-called occult phenomena. *CW* 1, 3–17. (Orig. publ. 1902.)

Jung, C.G. (1971). Psychological types. *CW* 6 (entire). (Orig. publ. 1921.)

Jung, C.G. (1973). The psychopathological significance of the association experiment. *CW* 2, 408–425. (Orig. publ. 1906.)

Jung, C.G. (1989). *Memories, dreams, reflections*. A. Jaffé (Ed.), R. Winston & C. Winston (Trans.). New York: Vintage/Random House. (Orig. publ. 1961.)

Jung, C.G. (2009). *The red book*. S. Shamdasani (Ed. & Trans.). New York: W.W. Norton. (Orig. unpubl. manuscript, 1914–1930, 1952, 1957.)

Kerr, J. (1994). *A most dangerous method: The story of Jung, Freud, and Sabina Spielrein*. New York: Random House.

Kelcourse, F. (1998). Discernment: The art of attention in religious experience and psychotherapy. *Dissertation Abstracts International*, 59, 2472.

Kelcourse, F. (2010). Intersubjective and theological contexts of pastoral counseling supervision: Self, psyche and soul. In W.R. DeLong (Ed.), *Courageous conversations: The teaching and learning of pastoral supervision* (pp. 243–266). Lanham, MD: University Press of America.

Kelcourse, F. (Ed.) (2015). *Human development and faith: Life-cycle stages of body, mind and soul*, 2nd edn. St. Louis: Chalice Press.

Kelcourse, F. (2014). Spielrein. In D.A. Leeming (Ed.), *Encyclopedia of psychology and religion*, 2nd edn., Vol. 1. (pp. 1706–1710). New York: Springer.

Kohut, H. (1971). *The analysis of the self*. Madison, CT: International University Press.

Kohut, H. (1984). *How does analysis cure?* Chicago: University of Chicago Press.

Launer, J. (2015). *Sex versus survival: The life and ideas of Sabina Spielrein.* New York, Overlook Duckworth.

Leung, A. & Robson, L. (1993). Childhood masturbation. *Clinical Pediatrics,* 32(4), 238–241.

Lothane, Z. (2015). Tender love and transference: Unpublished letters of C. G. Jung and Sabina Spielrein. In C. Covington & B. Wharton (Eds.), *Sabina Spielrein: Forgotten pioneer of psychoanalysis,* 2nd edn. (pp. 126–157). New York: Brunner-Routledge.

McGoldrick, M., Gerson R., & Petry, S. (2008). *Genograms: Assessment and intervention.* 3rd edn. New York: W. W. Norton.

McGuire, W. (Ed.) (1974). *The Freud/Jung letters.* R. Hull & R. Manheim (Trans.). Princeton, NJ: Princeton University Press.

Merkur, D. (2017). *Jung's ethics: Moral psychology and his cure of souls.* J. Mills (Ed.). New York: Routledge.

Miller, A. (2008). *The drama of the gifted child.* New York: Basic Books. (Orig. publ. 1979).

Moll, J. (2015). Unedited extracts from a diary. In C. Covington & B. Wharton (Eds.). *Sabina Spielrein: Forgotten pioneer of psychoanalysis,* 2nd edn. (pp. 14–29). New York: Routledge.

Moskowitz, A & Heim, G. (2011). Eugen Bleuler's Dementia Praecox or the group of schizophrenias (1911): A centenary appreciation and reconsideration. *Schizophrenia Bulletin,* 37(3), 471–479.

Noth, I. (2015). Beyond Freud and Jung: Sabina Spielrein's contribution to child psychoanalysis and developmental psychology. *Pastoral Psychology,* 64, 279–286.

Ryce-Menuhin, J. (1994). Jung's father, Paul Achilles Jung, and the Song of Songs: An introduction. In *Jung and the monotheisms: Judaism, Christianity and Islam* (pp. 233–240). New York: Routledge.

Sedgwick, D. (1994). *The wounded healer: Countertransference from a Jungian perspective.* New York: Routledge.

Shamdasani, S. (1998). The lost contributions of Maria Moltzer to analytical psychology. *Spring: A Journal of Archetype and Culture,* 64, 103–120.

Spielrein, S. (1911). Über den psychologischen Inhalt eines Falles von Schizophrenie (Dementia Praecox) [On the psychological content of a case of schizophrenia]. *Jahrbuch für Psychoanalytische und Psychopathologische Forschungen,* 3, 329–400. (Excerpt trans. this volume, Chapter 5; full trans. in Spielrein, 2018, pp. 14–96.)

Spielrein, S. (1912). Die Destruktion als Ursache des Werdens. [Destruction as the cause of Becoming]. *Jahrbuch für Psychoanalytische und Psychopathologische Forschungen,* 4, 465–503. (Trans. this volume, Chapter 6.)

Spielrein, S. (1913). Beiträge zur Kenntnis der Kindlichen Seele. [Contributions to an understanding of the child's mind.] *Zentralblatt für Psychoanalyse und Psychotherapie,* 3, 57–72. (Trans. in Spielrein, 2018, pp. 135–154.)

Spielrein, S. (1922). Die Entstehung der kindlichen Worte Papa und Mama. *Imago*, 8, 345–367. [trans. in Covington & Wharton, 2015, pp. 233–248.]

Spielrein, S. (1923a). Die Zeit im unterschwelligen Seelenleben. Imago, 9, 300–317. (See Chapter 12, this volume.)

Spielrein, S. (1923b). Quelques analogies entre la pensée de l'enfant, celle de l'aphasique et la pensée subconsciente. *Archives de Psychologie*, 18, 305–322. (See Chapter 14, this volume.)

Spielrein, S. (2002). *Sabina Spielrein: Sämtliche Schriften [Collected works]*, 2nd edn. T. Hensch (Ed.). Giesen: Psychosozial-Verlag/Kore. (1st edn. 1987.)

Spielrein, S. (2006). *Nimm meine Seele: Tagebücher und Schriften [Take my soul: Diaries and writings]*. T. Hensch (Trans.). Freiburg: Freitag.

Spielrein, S. (2015). Unedited extracts from a diary (with a prologue by Jeanne Moll.) J. Moll, P. Bennett & B. Wharton (Trans.). In C. Covington & B. Wharton (Eds.). *Sabina Spielrein: Forgotten pioneer of psychoanalysis*, 2nd edn. (pp. 14–29). New York: Routledge. (Orig. unpubl. manuscript, c. 1906–1907.)

Spielrein, S. (2018). *The essential writings of Sabina Spielrein: Pioneer of psychoanalysis*. R. Cape & R. Burt (Eds. & Trans.). New York: Routledge.

Stern, D.N. (1985). *The interpersonal world of the infant*. New York: Basic Books.

Wharton, B. (2015a). Burghölzli Hospital Records of Sabina Spielrein. In C. Covington & B. Wharton (Eds.). *Sabina Spielrein: Forgotten pioneer of psychoanalysis*, 2nd edn. (pp. 57–82). New York: Routledge.

Wharton, B. (Trans.) (2015b). Letters of C.G. Jung to Sabina Spielrein. In C. Covington & B. Wharton (Eds.). *Sabina Spielrein: Forgotten pioneer of psychoanalysis*, 2nd edn. (pp. 30–56). New York: Routledge.

Wickes, F. (1988). *The inner world of childhood.* Boston, MA: Sigo. (Orig. publ. 1927.)

Winnicott, D.W. (1964). Memories, dreams, reflections: By C.G. Jung [book review]. *International Journal of Psychoanalysis*, 45, 450–455.

Winnicott, D.W. (1971). Transitional objects and transitional phenomena. In *Playing and reality* (pp. 1–25). New York: Routledge. (Orig. publ. 1953.)

Chapter 2

From Zürich to Vienna
"The power that beautifies and destroys"

Pamela Cooper-White

Introduction

Sabina Spielrein's theoretical imagination was in full flower when she presented the opening section of her first professional paper to Freud's circle in Vienna on November 29, 1911 (Nunberg & Federn, 1974, pp. 329–335), just six weeks after she "turned up unexpectedly" at the Vienna Society and was voted into membership (McGuire, 1974, p. 447; Nunberg & Federn, 1974, p. 280).[1] The paper was entitled "Die Destruktion als Ursache des Werdens" ["Destruction as the Cause of Becoming"] and was published in the *Jahrbuch* in the following year (Spielrein, 1912, 1994, 1995; see new translation in this volume, Chapter 6).[2] In 1910, she had completed her doctoral dissertation entitled "On the Psychological Content of a Case of Schizophrenia" (Spielrein, 1911; excerpt trans. in this volume, Chapter 5; for full trans., see Spielrein, 2018, pp. 14–96) at the University of Zürich under the supervision of C.G. Jung – who had also been her doctor and psychoanalyst at the Burghölzli hospital beginning in 1904 when she was nineteen years old and diagnosed (by Jung himself) with "hysteria" (Wharton, 2015, p. 57).

The "Destruction" paper represents some of Spielrein's most innovative contributions to psychoanalysis at a time of particular creativity and ferment in the newly forming field. While Spielrein's later works increasingly came to explore problems associated with child analysis and childhood development, especially after the birth of her first daughter, Renate, in 1913 (Noth, 2015), this paper is especially important because it stands at a crucial crossroads in Spielrein's claiming of her own authority as an analyst and a theorist drawing from a wide range of sources: biological, psychological, mythological, and religious. In many ways, her ease in exploring mythological, archetypal themes reveals Spielrein's passionate attachment to Jung as analyst and intellectual mentor – even her *Doktorvater*[3] – and also the love of her life. It reflects the Wagnerian/mythological theme of Brünhilde and Siegfried's love and sacrifice, which provided romantic and mystical fodder for both Jung and Spielrein during their period of intense closeness in 1909–1910.

At the same time, her focus on libido, neurosis born of repression, and countervailing forces of death and destruction show her intellectual allegiance – as well, perhaps, as a growing erotic/oedipal transference – toward Freud (which she confessed in a self-analysis in her diary in 1912: "Now Prof. Freud is the one who causes me to glow; ... Dr. J.['s]... love would leave one cold") (Carotenuto, 1982, p. 43). She worked on this paper in Munich, where she moved immediately upon completing her medical degree with honors in Zürich, and she completed it after moving again within the year to Vienna. John Kerr (1994) has suggested that the paper, whose circulation coincided with the widening and increasingly public break between Spielrein and Jung, "reads like nothing so much as an attempt to mediate between the two theoretical worlds of Zürich and Vienna" (Kerr, 1994, p. 396). This effort was doomed to fail, however, as the rift between Freud and Jung was widening. Jung was editing Spielrein's paper for the *Jahrbuch* (the fledgling International Psychoanalytical Association's official scientific journal), even while bringing his work on Part 2 of *Transformations and Symbols of the Libido* (*Wandlungen und Symbole der Libido*, 1912), which we now know through its revised title *Symbols of Transformation* (Jung, 1967a/1911–12, 1952), to a conclusion. This was the work Jung foresaw would cost him his friendship with Freud once and for all. It was certainly at the very least fuel for the funeral pyre of their relationship (Kerr, 1994, p. 399; Bair, 2003, pp. 217–240; Gay, 2006, pp. 230–243; Cooper-White, 2017, pp. 34–40).

Born out of this turbulent history, Spielrein's paper represents her first independent work as a doctor and psychoanalyst, and it stands at the crossroads of her journey both intellectually and literally from Jung to Freud. Her ideas for the paper were already percolating by as early as 1909, as revealed in diary entries and letter drafts (Carotenuto, 1982, pp. 107–108). What follows here is a summary of Spielrein's paper, situating the work in her biography along the way. I hope to show how her paper represents a significant, if emotionally ambivalent, turning point in her life – as well as a bridge between Jung and Freud in the years immediately preceding their dramatic break.

It should be said, perhaps, at the outset of this summary that the paper is dense, rambling, and at times reads more like stream of consciousness than a doctoral-level paper. At the same time, the flow of associations she presents is not unlike Jung's (1912; 1967a/1911–12, 1952) own explosion of ideas and images in Part 2 of *Transformations and Symbols of the Libido*, which he struggled mightily to organize into a coherent work (Homans, 1979, pp. 65–66; Kerr, 1994, p. 329).

Spielrein's writing also more generally reflects the almost feverish productivity of this period of early psychoanalytic theorizing. The somewhat inchoate nature of the paper mirrors the fecundity of ideas within analytic circles at the time. No single idea had quite yet achieved the status of canon, except some of Freud's most basic "discoveries," such as the unconscious itself and the topographical model, the libido as the central motivating force or "drive" (*Trieb*) of human life, the genesis of neurosis in repression of sexual wishes, and early formulations of the Oedipus complex.

Freud's *Interpretation of Dreams* (1953a/1900) and *Three Essays on the Theory of Sexuality* (1953b/1905) were foundational texts, and Freud had been theorizing about the Oedipus complex for almost a decade, with references to Oedipus by as early as 1900 in *The Interpretation of Dreams*, with its first elaboration in print appearing at around this same period, in 1910.[4] Freud and Jung were developing parallel but different concepts about the workings of the mind, with Freud's (1955a/1912) "Two Principles of Mental Functioning" (the pleasure principle and the reality principle) claiming priority over Jung's "Two Kinds of Thinking" (the rational and the symbolic) – an idea already in print in *Transformations and Symbols of the Libido*, Part 1 (Jung, 1911 and Kerr, 1994, pp. 335–337). Freud's fully psychodynamic structural model of ego, id, and superego did not appear until over a decade later in 1923 with *The Ego and the Id* (Freud, 1961/1923.)

Freud's (1955a/1920) "Beyond the Pleasure Principle," in which he introduced aggression as a second drive alongside the libido and his own version of "the death instinct," did not appear until 1919 in manuscript form and was only published, in revised form, in 1920 after the death of his daughter, Sophie, from the Spanish Flu that swept through Europe in the wake of World War I. Thus, many of the ideas Spielrein explored in her paper on destruction predated those of Freud's and belong to a period of unsettled theoretical creativity – and also rivalry – among the growing circle of practitioners of this new science (and art) of psychoanalysis.

Summary of the paper

Spielrein's paper begins with a seemingly straightforward psychoanalytic problem – to tackle the question of the relationship between sex and death/destruction: "why this most powerful drive, the reproductive drive, houses within itself, besides the a priori to be expected positive feelings, negative ones such as anxiety and disgust, the latter of which ought to be overcome in order to arrive at positive activity?" Her paper begins in a resolutely Freudian vein, referencing Freud and the neurotogenic effects of repressive, moralistic child-rearing. She then immediately quotes Jung's (1911) *Transformations and Symbols of the Libido* (Part 1) (which first appeared alongside her dissertation in the *Jahrbuch*; cf., Jung, 1967a/1911–12, 1952). This is the Jung who is still under the sway of Freudian ideas about the centrality of sexuality, but also the Jung who is moving toward a dialecticism of his own in which every important phenomenon also bears its own opposite:

> The passionate longing, i.e., *the libido, has two sides: it is the power which beautifies everything and, under certain circumstances, destroys everything.* One often pretends to not quite understand what the destroying quality of the creative power could possibly be. A woman who abandons herself to her passions, especially under today's cultural circumstances, experiences the destructive quality only too soon. One must take one's thoughts a little outside the realm of bourgeois morality in order to understand the feeling of boundless insecurity that overcomes the human being who surrenders to fate unconditionally. To be fruitful – that in itself is self-destruction, for with the birth of the next generation the previous one has passed its peak. And so our descendants become our most dangerous enemies, with whom we cannot come to terms, for they will outlive us and take the power from our enfeebled hands. This fear of erotic fate is entirely understandable, for there is something

entirely unforeseeable in it. Fate generally holds unknown dangers, and the continual reluctance of neurotics to take a chance on life is explained by the wish to be permitted to stand aside, in order not to have to wrestle in the dangerous struggle of life. Those who forgo the venture of experiencing [life] must stifle the wish for it, i.e., commit a kind of suicide. This explains the death fantasies that so readily accompany the renunciation of the erotic wish.
(Spielrein, 1911; see Ch. 6, pp. 209–210, emphasis added)

On the other hand, it is clear in this first quotation that Spielrein's project, like much compelling research, is also autobiographical. The dialectic of passion and destruction certainly characterized much of what she experienced in her own passionate desire for Jung, both while it was (quasi?-)consummated (designated only by the obscure term "poetry"[5] in Spielrein's diary – borrowed, as it turns out, from her schizophrenic patient; Spielrein, 1911) and again while Jung was struggling to regain his professional composure and putting her off. The quote describes Jung's own ambivalence as well, in somewhat self-serving terms – one either gives in to the passionate libido in a heroic surrender to Fate (as he did with Spielrein) or one neurotically cowers under the repression of bourgeois propriety (as he did only briefly, once after the birth of his first son and again after Spielrein's departure, before taking up a long-term sexual relationship with another young patient, Toni Wolff).[6] There is perhaps even a sense in which Spielrein, with her newly minted doctorate, is throwing Jung's words back at him, showing him his hypocrisy in the form of a scientific paper that would be her ticket to Freud's inner circle.

Following the introduction, Spielrein continues her paper by recruiting facts and sources of evidence for her thesis. She does not clearly state this thesis at the outset, but it is helpful to summarize it here from the very end of the paper:

... to prove, respectively, the existence of the destructive element of sexuality, both in recent psychological phenomena, and, as well, in mythological formations... that psychologically, and congruent with biological facts, the reproductive drive consists of two antagonistic components, therefore both a drive for Becoming and a drive for Destruction.
(Ch. 6, p. 246)

As noted in this final sentence, she investigates three areas to support her argument: (1) biological facts; (2) individual psychological observations; and (3) life and death in mythology.

The biological section

The first section of the paper is quite brief, likely shortened for publication based on Freud's critique that the paper was too biologically reductionist[7] (McGuire, 1974, p. 469). Spielrein notes that many species such as the mayfly forfeit their lives during procreation. Further, "Due to the fusion of sexual cells, what happens during copulation is the most intimate union of two individuals: one pushing forth into the other." In order for fertilization to occur, she writes, a "transformation affects the whole organism: destruction and restoration – which are always part of the organism's general functioning – now occur abruptly." Rather than ascribing resistance, anxiety, or disgust to the proximity of excreta to the genitals, as some Freudians had claimed, she asserted that joy is mixed with anxiety and disgust because the sexual partners are sensing "the destructive component of the sexual instinct" (and here it seems she is referring especially to women's experience, as she describes how the ovum is invaded by the sperm and the female is invaded by the male) (Ch. 6, p. 211).

Individual psychological observations

Moving on to psychological observations in the second section of her paper, Spielrein jumps to a reassertion of Freud's premise that nothing is affectively charged in the present without a re-experiencing of "feeling-toned contents (experiences) that lie hidden in the unconscious" (p. 212). She gives several examples, such as a girl's fantasy of being a witch as a displacement of identification with her mother, but then moves more in the direction of Jung and the collective unconscious by describing how in dream images, sea and earth represent not only the individual mother, but the "Ur-mother both in the conscious and unconscious idea of all peoples" (p. 213). She then takes an unexpected turn and identifies Becoming as much more than biological birth and maturation or psychological ego development. Echoing Jung's idea of individuation as transformation through tapping into both the personal and the collective unconscious, she states that "world-weariness [*Weltschmerz*]" results when "each particle of our being yearns to return to its original state from which, in turn, a new Becoming will emerge" (p. 213).

Here, Spielrein directly contests Freud's pleasure principle and his location of adult pleasure solely in infantile sexuality, stating that "we might just as well derive everything from the drive for food [*Nahrungstrieb*]" (p. 213). Anticipating Anna Freud's later articulation of a developmental line of "rational eating" (A. Freud, 1981), Spielrein argues for nurturing and self-preservation through eating as an equal and at times interchangeable motivating force with sexual desire. She then goes on, following that line of argument, to propose that pleasure resides primarily in the ego, but:

> ... I must emphatically contend that the ego-psyche [*Ichpsyche*], conscious and unconscious, is governed by impulses that lie still deeper and that do not concern themselves at all with our emotional reactions to the demands made by said impulses. Pleasure is nothing but the ego's affirmative response when confronted with these demands that spring from deep down below. We can derive pleasure from unpleasure, and pleasure from pain… There is thus something deep inside us which, as paradoxical as it may sound, wants, even desires, this self-damage, for the ego responds to it with pleasure. The wish to put oneself in harm's way, the pleasure in pain, is, however, completely incomprehensible if all we consider is the pleasure-seeking life of the ego.
>
> (p. 215)

While this appears to be an overly simplistic reading of Freud, even in 1912, it reflects Freud's (1955a/1920) later ruminations in *Beyond the Pleasure Principle* – his own impetus for considering a death instinct and an aggressive drive – that there were post-traumatic phenomena such as the "repetition compulsion" that resisted explanation by the pleasure principle alone. It is, as well, no doubt born of Spielrein's own personal experience, having uncovered a masochistic tendency through her own analysis with Jung, possibly accompanied by a less well-analyzed but consciously retrieved experience of shameful erotic pleasure from physical abuse by her father (Kerr, 1994, p. 33; Launer, 2015, p. 17). This writing also foreshadows object relations theory's concept of a coexistence of love and hate, aggression and reparation beginning in infancy and the pre-oedipal period, especially as articulated by Melanie Klein and D.W. Winnicott.[8]

Ascribing multiple motives for "our entire psychic life," anticipating both Freud's structural model with its dynamic conflict among ego, id, and superego, as well as Jung's concept of complexes, she goes on to assert:

> [T]the psyche... consists of numerous individual beings [*Einzelwesen*]. It is Jung who speaks of the autonomy of complexes, which means – according to Jung – that we do not have an undivided I within us but rather various complexes competing for predominance.
>
> (p. 215)

She gives a case example and then continues:

> I was led to believe that the main characteristic of the individual consists in being a "dividual" [*ein Dividuum*]. The closer we get to conscious thinking, the more differentiated our mental representations; the deeper we enter into the unconscious, the more general, more [arche]typal[9] they become. The depth of our psyche knows no "I," it only knows its summation, the "We"; or the current I, viewed as an object, becomes subordinate to other similar objects.
>
> (p. 216)

For those of us who now work out of a more postmodern relational-psychoanalytic paradigm, these ideas offer a very early precursor of our contemporary turn toward multiplicity and intersubjectivity (e.g., Flax, 1993; Bromberg, 1994, 2001; Davies, 1996; Harris, 1996; Cooper-White, 2007, 2011).

Spielrein then goes on to give further case examples. Drawing on her treatment of schizophrenic patients, she points to the importance of symbolic expression (e.g., Spielrein, 1911; Chapter 5 this volume). While hysteria causes what she calls a "a hypertrophic ego" and a corresponding "increased sensitivity," she says that in dementia praecox (schizophrenia) there is a further diminishment of ego activity, through which one can see a much greater dissolution of the personal psyche, as "[t]he collective psyche strives to turn the ego-psyche into an impersonal, [arche]typal one" (p. 217).

How she brings this back to the theme of destruction as an intrinsic aspect of creativity is a bit tortured, and her argument meanders through this contest between the individual ego-organized psyche and the collective psyche. The ego seeks self-preservation, while the collective psyche desires dissolution of the individual into a recreated ego – "the drowned ego-particle surfaces richer than before, adorned with new representations" (p. 219). The artist walks this tightrope, she asserts, in which the (arche-)typal is projected into a work of art that taps the collective unconscious. Thus, the new creation – whether artistic or procreative – results in the death of the old "ego-particle" alongside the birth of "a new, perhaps more beautiful form... [that] returns as an Other that came into being at the expense of that particle." Such creative dissolution and "unconscious processing" is required for relationship, she says, because "the purely personal can never be understood by others" (p. 220).

Taking yet another turn, she asserts that love itself is dangerous and destructive because rather than allowing for sublimation of the "[arche]typal" in the expression of images, in the actual consummation of love

> ... [a]s soon as reality claims its rights, as soon as the word becomes deed, the group of mental representations that correspond to this reality dissolves and produces a blissful feeling of relaxation; at that moment we are completely unproductive psychically. Every representation reaches its maximum life when it most intensely awaits its transformation into reality: its realization is its destruction.
>
> (p. 221)

However, she goes on, one experience of love (i.e., one expression of a complex) is only one among many avenues by which the unconscious may emerge. All sublimated products will be expressed either through abreaction or art. And the highest symbols of "primal experience," which bear elevated mythological or religious status – such as the Sun, Nature, or Christ – "remain in the psyche in the form of a most intense longing for a return to the original source, specifically to dissolve oneself in the progenitors." This explains, she says, "why religion, the most elevated, so readily becomes a symbol of the lowest, i.e., sexual activity" (pp. 221–222).

From this she turns again to elements of destruction in sexual life, citing wartime neurosis and violence stirred up by "disturbances of sexual life" and noting how:

> ... in times of war representations of destruction stir up precisely those representations that are connected to the destructive element of the reproductive drive. These latter representations can spoil Being [*Dasein*][10] even for normal people, and they are all the more damaging for the neurotic, in whom the mental representation of Destruction outweighs that of Becoming [*Werden*], and who is waiting for suitable symbols that may represent this destruction fantasy.
>
> (p. 223)

She uses the Christian imagery of Christ's resurrection to argue for the close association among symbols of death, birth, and rebirth. Similarly, the snake, the horse, and every sexual symbol in a dream, as in mythology, simultaneously represents both a "life- and death-bringing god."

At this point, she goes into a long, rather purple-prose excursus based on Nietzsche's *Also Sprach Zarathustra*, in which she asserts:

> For Nietzsche, both love and knowledge consist in sucking in the depth of the sea, like the sun. Thus, for Nietzsche knowledge is nothing other than a desire for love, for creation. The glowing sun suckles at the sea like a lover, and the wildly heaving sea rises with a thousand breasts toward the sun, hungry for kisses like an enraptured woman. ... If mother is his own depth, the union with mother has an autoerotic meaning, i.e., it is a union with himself.
>
> (p. 225)

She brings this back to the intertwining of love and death with a quote from Nietzsche: "Loving and perishing: these have gone together since the beginning of time. Will to love: that is also being willing for death" (p. 226). Both the image of swallowing the sun and the image of the sea as both mother and collective unconscious correspond directly to visions that Jung had in December 1913, well after the publication of this paper, which were subsequently painted in his *Red Book* (e.g., Jung, 2009/1914–1930, 1952, 1957, image 119). For Jung, the imagery of the mother was becoming increasingly ambivalent – not only the romantic, life-giving "eternal feminine" (*das ewig Weibliche* of romanticism), but also terrible and destructive (cf., Kerr, 1994, p. 331). For Spielrein, however, destruction remains transformational only through surrender to love and passion.[11]

Spielrein then takes an interesting excursus into describing how one loves and is loved as both subject and object, and how the woman, because of her more passive role in sexuality, comes more readily to identify with the man's view of her as beloved, transforming this into a "wish-personality" (p. 224) with which she may auto-erotically engage. She ends this section with the argument that the destructive component of the sexual instinct may thereby lead to sadistic or masochistic identifications and, further, that "the boundary is not that sharply drawn, firstly because all humans are bisexual." From here, she returns to her primary thesis by stating, "These [masochistic acts] are merely different forms and degrees of self-annihilation. The procreative act itself is self-annihilation" (p. 228). Echoing Jung's fascination with the archetype of Phanes, the orphic child-god (e.g., in *The Red Book*, Jung, 2009/1914–1930, 1952, 1957, image 113, and later carvings at Bollingen), she writes in a Nietzschean/Jungian liturgical tone: "You have to learn to overcome (destroy) yourself. How else would you create the higher, the child?" (p. 228)

She concludes this section with the following summary statement:

> The drive for self-preservation is a simple drive consisting only of a positive [tendency]; the drive for the preservation of the species, whose task it is to dissolve the old in order for the new to be created, has both a positive and a negative element, i.e., the drive for the preservation of the species is ambivalent in its nature. This is why arousing the positive element always also provokes the arousal of the negative element, and vice versa. Inasmuch as the *self*-preservation drive strives to protect the *individual* from foreign influences, it is a "static" drive. The drive for the preservation of the *species* however is a "dynamic" drive, aiming at the transformation, the "resurrection" of the individual in a new form. Without the destruction of the old state, change cannot and will not happen.
> (p. 234, emphasis added)

Thus, in this central portion of the paper, Spielrein posits a death instinct, but one very different from what either Freud or Jung would eventually propose.[12] Rather than setting libido and aggression/death as opposing internal forces (as Freud does) or relegating the death instinct to a problematic dimension of mental life such as "introversion"[13] (as Jung does), she places destruction *within* the libido, as inextricably interwoven with a cosmic demand that, for life to come into being, life-as-it-is must die. Both physiologically and in the psyche, the transformation that leads to newness of life – whether literal birth or psychic birth/individuation – requires the death of the old and the relinquishment of the self-preserving status quo, or the ego, to the primal, untamed force of Life itself – a theme that Jung would also eventually develop in *The Red Book* (2009/1914–1930, 1952, 1957).

Life and death in mythology

In the final section of the paper, Spielrein further illustrates this assertion with imagery drawn from religion and mythology. In a kind of stream of consciousness conflating numerous sources – similar to other writings of the time such as Frazer's expanded edition of *The Golden Bough* (2012/1911–15) and many of Jung's later writings on myth and symbolism – she attempts to show how life and death are frequently merged in symbolic images. She cites the Tree of Life in the bible, and from other religious cults, as bearing both death (often as punishment for sexual activity), but also resurrection to new life. This is echoed in Christ's crucifixion on the tree of the cross, resulting in redemption and new life for humankind; the legend of Adam being revived by his son, Seth, by planting three apple seeds in Adam's mouth (Spielrein notes here "Freud's displacement upward"); and the twig as a phallic symbol of life and sexual potency (p. 236).

"What role does Christ, God's son, play in this? How does he redeem humankind?" (p. 236) Spielrein inquires. She makes a leap to the myth of the Nibelungen, from which Wagner derived his Ring Cycle. "The hibernating Brünhilde (earth)," she writes,

> is saved by Siegfried's victorious light (sun), who cuts through her suit of armor (ice-crust) with his sword, thereby impregnating her. As opposed to the sagas, in *The Nibelungenlied*, the process is not described as an act of fertilization or impregnation, as with sun and earth, but it is represented as a cutting-through; its erotic significance is emphasized by a kiss. What is important is that, through Brünhilde, Siegfried impregnates his mother. True, Siegfried's mother is Sieglinde but Brünhilde is her sister; she loves whomever

Sieglinde loves, namely Siegmund. She feels herself into Sieglinde's role, and this way Sieglinde becomes her wish-personality, her sexual personality [*Sexualpersönlichkeit*], respectively. By saving Siegfried, she saves her own wish, her own child.

(p. 237)

This passage would seem to be wildly off the rails of Spielrein's argument if it were not for the association she reveals in her letters and diaries – that, in fact, she even thought of the relationship between herself and Jung as the relationship between Brünhilde and Siegfried, and perhaps in line with this regarded Jung himself as her "beloved little son"[14] (Spielrein's diary, December 8, 1910, cited in Carotenuto, 1982, p. 37). Going even further, she wrote to Jung when sending him the first draft of the paper, "Receive now the product of our love, the project which is your little son Siegfried" (ibid., p. 48).[15] In her own fantasy, Siegfried not only represented a child to bind Jung to her permanently, but a deed of cosmic significance – to "give birth to 'a great Aryan-Semitic hero' who would unite these different and warring races forever" (Covington, 2015, p. 5; cf., Chapters 3 and 4 in this volume). Although she declared this fantasy "vanquished" when her daughter, Renate, was born (Carotenuto, 1982, p. 87), nearly seven years later, Spielrein would write to Jung of her "profound and shattering" realization that "he is alive after all, her Siegfried!" (letter from January 28, 1918, in ibid., p. 88).

However, she ended up presenting this paper in a state of self-banishment from Jung's inner circle. Perhaps she was reflecting in the Brünhilde–Siegfried passages on this self-imposed exile from Zürich as a kind of deathlike sleep, from which Siegfried – the product of her love for Jung – might still revive her. (In the meantime, Jung was busy killing off the Siegfried hero within himself and getting closer and closer to his own creative madness, leading to his surrender during Christmas 1913 to the visions that would become the kernel of *The Red Book*.)

"Like Eve," Spielrein goes on in the "Destruction" paper,

Brünhilde violates the father's commandment and is banished from the kingdom of the gods, just as Eve is banished from Paradise. This violation (the defense of her wish-personality whose sins she takes upon herself, as it were) brings a death-like sleep upon Brünhilde from which the spring sun Siegfried awakens her.

(p. 237)

Longing ambivalently for both Jung and Freud at this juncture in her life and career, she states: "Very often, for example in Wagner's [*Götterdämmerung*], the yearning for death is a yearning for *Liebestod*, for dying while consummating love." Brunhilde dies in the fire (love-fire) joined with her horse, and in dying calls out: "In fiery glory/Blazes your lord,/Siegfried, my hero and love ... Siegfried! Siegfried! Blessed is my greeting to you!" (pp. 237–238).

She interprets:

> Here, death is a victorious song [*Siegeslied*] of love! Brünhilde, as it were, passes away in Siegfried: Siegfried is the fire, the redemption that comes from the sun's blazing heat. In this primal progenitor [*Urerzeuger*], Brünhilde dissolves, becoming fire herself. In Wagner's oeuvre death is often nothing other than the destructive component of the instinct to become [*Werdeinstinkt*].
>
> (p. 238)

This, she states, is Freud's "rescue motif" (*Rettertypus*), also seen in Wagner's opera *The Flying Dutchman*. Wagnerian lovers

> sacrifice themselves for their love, and die. The similarity between the Nordic Siegfried and the oriental Christ are remarkable. Christ too is a Savior type [*Rettertypus*] who sacrifices himself for humankind. Siegfried is the sun god and his beloved is mother earth; Christ is also a sun god. Christ dies at the Tree of Life; he is fastened to it as though he were its fruit. Like the fruit, Christ perishes and enters Mother Earth as seed. The fertilization leads to the formation of new life, to the resurrection of the dead. Through Christ's death and resurrection Adam's guilt is paid.
>
> (p. 239)

Spielrein goes on to discuss sacrifice for sin in both Christian and Jewish sources, as well as ancient Persian and Greek mythology.

It is striking that Spielrein, a Jew, returns again and again to the symbolism of Christ's sacrifice. However, this can be explained both by her absorption of Jung's own exploration of Christ as an archetypal figure and by her sense of a heroic calling to create a rapprochement between Aryans and Jews – a view that Freud did not share. After his break with Jung, Freud warned against her idealism as naive and dangerous, writing to her in the summer of 1913:

> I am, as you know, cured of the last shred of my predilection for the Aryan cause, and would like to take it that if [your] child turns out to be a boy he will develop into a stalwart Zionist... We are and remain Jews. The others will only exploit us and will never understand or appreciate us.
>
> (Carotenuto, 1982, pp. 120–121)

That Spielrein herself identified with the hero as well as with an "eternal feminine" – and perhaps identified even with Christ's sacrifice – is revealed in a letter to Jung written later, in 1918:

> According to Freud, the Siegfried fantasy is merely wish fulfillment. I have always objected to this merely. I told myself I was slated for something great, I had to perform a heroic deed: if analysis now reveals that my love for X was not perfectly platonic; as I was convinced it was and wanted it to be – why should I resist and not view it as my heroic deed to sacrifice myself after all for this sacred love and create a hero?
>
> (Carotenuto, 1982, p. 80)

At the very conclusion of her paper, she introduces a further caution into the symbolism of life, death, and eternal life. Eternal life, she says, is dangerous, just as, paradoxically, "Death in itself is pure horror; death in the service of the sexual instinct, i.e., its destructive element which leads to Becoming, is salutary and health-giving" (pp. 244–245). Eternal life is like the life of the walking dead, like the Flying Dutchman who is condemned to endless voyaging from place to place, "long[ing] for a suitable object he cannot attain." The Dutchman can only be saved from his eternal curse of wandering the earth by the true love of a (mortal) woman (named Senta in the legend). Spielrein interprets:

> ... the Flying Dutchman shows us that what we long for is erotic death, i.e., a death that leads to new Becoming – Senta and the Dutchman rise from the waves in an intimate embrace... The world can only be saved when life returns to its primal source ...
>
> (pp. 245–246)

With this final argument, Spielrein is perhaps simultaneously chiding Jung for retreating from the erotic embrace of sacrificial passion and having her revenge by asserting her allegiance once again to Freud's theory of the centrality of sexuality.

Following this final statement, she recapitulates her thesis, which by the end of the paper seems weighted down with all the theoretical and symbolic fruit she has laid on it. Lapsing once more into a tone of objective dissertation-ese, she concludes, "I do believe… that my examples sufficiently show that psychologically, and congruent with biological facts, the reproductive drive consists of two antagonistic components, therefore both a drive for Becoming and a drive for Destruction" (p. 246).

Love and death, publication, and reviews

By the time she presented her paper, she had become a full participant in the Vienna Society's Wednesday night deliberations. After Spielrein had remained quiet during her first few meetings, Freud wrote her an encouraging note in late October:

> Dear Frau Doktor, As a woman you have the prerogative of observing things more accurately and of assessing emotions more closely than others… I fully appreciate your attitude and look confidently to the future. I have been doing that, after all, for many years and under much more difficult circumstances. I hope that you will feel quite at home in our circle. With cordial greetings, Freud.
> (Carotenuto, 1982, p. 115; Lothane, 2015, p. 146)

Otto Rank reported in his minutes of the Wednesday night meeting of November 8 that Spielrein spoke up, made some good theoretical points, and was acknowledged in further comments by several other members and by Freud himself. As noted above, she even asserted her own priority of ideas regarding the link between sex and death (Nunberg & E. Federn, 1974, p. 316). Freud was now taking Spielrein seriously, both agreeing and debating with various elements of her own thinking (cf., Kerr, 1994, pp. 359–360), as he did with all of the members of the Society.

Spielrein presented a portion of her paper on "Transformation" to the Vienna colleagues on November 29, 1911. Rank recorded in the minutes that Tausk found her view "valuable." But other than that, the discussion became a voluble debate, with (Paul) Federn, Rosenstein, Rheinhold, Stekel, and Friedjung all taking turns to reassert the primacy of their own theories of life and death. The only other woman present, Frau Dr. Stegmann, offered the most understanding interpretation: "The fear of love is fear of the death of one's own personality. Love is indeed to be regarded as a transition from the small individual to the great cosmic life" (Nunberg & E. Federn, 1974, p. 334). Freud fairly sidestepped the debate about love and death in his concluding remarks, preferring to use Spielrein's paper as a springboard to make a methodological critique of Jung's uncritical use of mythology (ibid., p. 335). Spielrein ended up by expressing regret at being misunderstood and attempting clarification of her own point of view, but the simmering feud between Freud and Jung claimed the circle's attention (ibid.).

The following day, Freud wrote to Jung, capitalizing on the moment to convey criticism of Jung's own methods, using Spielrein's paper as the proxy for his critique:

> Fräulein Spielrein read a chapter from her paper yesterday. (I almost wrote the *ihrer* [her] with a capital "i" [= your])... I have hit on a few objections to your [*Ihrer*] (this time I mean it) method of dealing with mythology, and I brought them up in the discussion with the little girl... What troubles me most is that Fräulein Spielrein wants to subordinate the psychological material to *bio*logical considerations; this dependency is no more acceptable than a dependency on philosophy, physiology or brain anatomy. ΨA *farà da se* [goes by itself].
> (McGuire, 1974, p. 469, emphasis in original)

Freud's slip of the pen showed the extent to which he perceived – and disapproved of – Jung's influence on Spielrein's thinking.

As Jung and Spielrein had been mutually exploring the ideas of love, death, and sacrifice during the height of their personal relationship, Spielrein privately worried while still in Zürich that Jung "would simply borrow the whole development of the idea" of a death instinct without giving her the credit (diary entry, November 1910, in Carotenuto, 1982, p. 35). She wrestled with these suspicions, and her self-assurances are riddled with her own ambivalence and guilt for having ambition in her own right – yet her self-assertion also peeks through her self-blame and idealization:

> Is this another case of unfounded distrust on my part? I wish so fervently that it might be so, for my second study [the "Destruction" paper] will be dedicated to my most esteemed teacher, etc. How could I esteem a person who lied, who stole my ideas, who was not my friend but a petty, scheming rival? And love him? I do love him, after all. My work ought to be permeated with love! I love him and hate him, because he is not mine. It would be unbearable for me to appear a silly goose in his eyes. No, noble, proud, respected by all! I must be worthy of him, and the idea I gave birth to should also appear under my name.
>
> (ibid.; Covington, 2015, p. 3)

In August 1911, Jung received Spielrein's first draft of the paper in his role as editor of the *Jahrbuch*, two months before her first appearance at the Vienna Psychoanalytic Society. Her singular devotion to her work while in Munich had yielded a significant and expansive piece of work. Jung's reply about publishing in the *Jahrbuch* was equivocal, swinging from praise to appropriation of her ideas for himself, and betraying his ambivalence about both its publication and her growing attraction to Freud and Vienna:

> I have not yet been able to finish reading your comprehensive study… I have read so far with care that I can permit myself a provisional judgment. I am surprised at the abundance of excellent thoughts which anticipate various ideas of my own. But it is good that others see things the same way as I do. Your thinking is bold, far-reaching, and philosophical. Hence the *Jahrbuch* will hardly be the right place for its publication. Either you can make a small independent book of it, or we could try to include your work in Freud's "*Schriften zur angewandten Seelenkunde*" (papers on applied psychology). That would be the right place. Various points of detail still need to be filled out. I hope grandfather Freud

will have the same joy as I have over this fruit of your spirit. Your stay in Munich does now seem to have been satisfactory in every respect. Meanwhile I congratulate you most heartily on your paper. With affectionate greetings, yours very sincerely, Dr. Jung.

(Jung, 2015, p. 37)

Once he learned that Spielrein was preparing to formally present her paper to the Vienna Society, he wrote in a more placating tone in early November:

In these circumstances I must send you the [Destruction] paper back immediately; I am sorry about it, since I have not finished it yet. In fact I was detailed to an exercise in the mountains so that I lost all the time I had set aside for your work. *Please send me back your paper immediately*, when you have made the necessary use of it. I must certainly study it thoroughly, because there are so many important thoughts in it. I must be completely quiet in order to understand it all properly. Until now I have not had a moment's peace. My dear, you are not to think that I retain any hard feelings towards you. I am just waiting for a few days' peace in order to read your work again *at one sitting*. If I am disturbed once more in the middle of it, I shall never reach a clear and conclusive understanding. I am sorry that you have been worried unnecessarily. I beg your forgiveness. Your work is on its way to you registered as a valuable package by immediate post. Your news from Vienna is interesting – and distressing[16]... Apart from Freud, Rank and Sachs there is little there that is serious. Please don't betray me. Your ever devoted friend.

(ibid., pp. 38–39, emphasis in original)

The last sentence, "Please don't betray me," reveals the depth of his fear that Freud would reject him and he would lose Spielrein to his father–rival as well. About a week later, he begged again for her paper, with assurances that he would not steal her ideas without attribution, but would cite her work fairly:

I would ask you again to send me the paper back straight away. In Part 2 of my work [*Transformations and Symbols*]... I have made frequent references to your ideas. I should like to do so with your new paper too. *So that we are in harmony*. With affectionate greetings and apologies, your very devoted friend.

(ibid., p. 39, emphasis added)

Two weeks after her presentation to the Vienna Society, likely in response to Spielrein's dejection over the mixed reception of her paper by Freud and his circle, Jung wrote, "My Dear, Don't be so downcast. Your paper will go into the *Jahrbuch* if Prof. Freud wishes it. *I heartily congratulate you on your success…* Freud has told me some very good things about you" (ibid., p. 40, emphasis in original). But Jung was still keeping his finger in the wind, to see which way Freud's opinion was blowing. The note "if Prof. Freud wishes it" placed the onus of accepting the piece back on Freud and the Viennese – absolving himself of responsibility for the negative responses. In that light, his congratulations seem premature and disingenuous.

Spielrein was perhaps not above manipulating Jung either to ensure the paper's publication. She wrote to Jung in January 1912 that "Prof. Freud, of whom I have become very fond, thinks highly of me and tells everyone about my 'magnificent article', and he is also very sweet to me personally" (Carotenuto, 1982, p. 41). As she was no doubt well aware, Freud's praise of her work would fuel Jung's determination to keep her on board – and to remain on board with her if her own ship began to sail. But the journey to publication was not an easy one, in no small part because the paper, like Spielrein herself, had become a pawn in Jung's and Freud's own growing rivalry. If it had not been for Jung's inner conflict in this period about challenging Freud's authority while maintaining his respect, as well as his fear of reprisals if his "piece of knavery" with Spielrein (McGuire, 1974, p. 236) should be fully revealed, Spielrein's serious work might never have seen the light of day.[17]

Rivalry and conflict over priority of ideas was not only between Freud and Jung, but was a growing issue among Freud's followers in general (Cooper-White, 2017, pp. 27–32), and had seeped like a poison into the relationship between Jung and Spielrein as well. Freud, for his part, wrote to Jung the following March, "She is very bright and well organized; there is meaning in everything she says" (McGuire, 1974, p. 494). But in the next breath, he also made conspiratorial gestures toward Jung by criticizing her: "... her destructive drive is not much to my liking, because I believe it is personally conditioned. She seems abnormally ambivalent" (ibid.). Either Spielrein had overestimated or misrepresented Freud as friendlier toward her ideas than he truly was or his opinion of the paper had cooled considerably. Freud's view would not have been helped by the fact that when it was published in the *Jahrbuch*, it appeared alongside Jung's (1912) *Transformations and Symbols of the Libido*, Part 2, which was Jung's strongest assertion to date of his rejection of Freud's definition of the libido as entirely sexual.

Certain similarities between the two massive papers, both in style and content, would have been obvious to everyone. After Spielrein first submitted her paper to him, however, Jung began to conceive of a "death tendency" as an element of "introversion" (his term both for retreat into fantasy and regression into "primitive" human experience as symbolized in mythology). In a letter written on March 25, 1912, he again assured Spielrein that he would credit her work, as he was struggling to articulate his own tortuous explication of a death instinct in Part 2 of *Transformations and Symbols*.[18] In response to her ongoing concern that he might not be giving her fair attribution for her ideas about the death instinct, he perhaps protested too much. He invoked their mutual exchange of ideas in past years – and even an interpenetration of their souls:

> My Dear, You are upsetting yourself unnecessarily again. When I said there were "uncanny" similarities, you again took that much too literally. I was intending it much more as a compliment to you. Your study is extraordinarily intelligent and contains splendid ideas *whose priority I am happy to acknowledge as yours. The death tendency or death wish was clear to you before it was to me, understandably!* ... I express myself so differently from you in my work that no one could imagine that you had borrowed in any way from me. There is no question of it at all. With regard to the hidden interpenetration of thought, there are more lofty questions here which do not come into consideration in public life and of which, in any case, we know too little to be able to reckon seriously with them. *Perhaps I borrowed from you too; certainly I have unwittingly absorbed a part of your soul, as you doubtless have of mine.* What matters is what each of us has made of it. And you have made

something good. I am glad that you are representing me in Vienna. The new work will *certainly* be misunderstood. I hope you will be able to represent my new ideas. With affectionate greetings, your friend.

(Jung, 2015, p. 42, emphasis in original)

As Coline Covington (2015) suggests, Jung's letter "reads like a sleight of hand" (p. 4) – with its patronizing tone, he suggests that the implication might be that she had borrowed from him and not the other way around. He then dismisses the concern altogether by assigning the "uncanny similarities" to a romantic merger of souls and alluding to the possibility of a more cosmic sort of unspoken communion. If Spielrein were to trust her own suspicions, she certainly would have had reason to do so upon reading the kicker at the end of the letter: that she is to represent *his* new ideas in Vienna – where, on the contrary, she traveled to assert her independence and advance her own career at the center of Freud's circle.

While attempting to soothe Spielrein's doubts with evocations of their former closeness, he wrote treacherously to Freud behind her back on April 1, 1912:

> I was working on Spielrein's paper just before my departure. One must say: *desinat* [sic] *in piscem mulier formosa superne*. ["What at the top is a lovely woman ends below in a fish" – Horace]. After a very promising start the continuation and end trail off dismally. Particularly the "Life and Death in Mythology" chapter needed extensive cutting as it contained gross errors and, worse still, faulty, one-sided interpretations. She has read too little and has fallen flat in this paper because it is not thorough enough. One must say by way of excuse that she has brought her problem to bear on an aspect of mythology that bristles with riddles. Besides that her paper is heavily overweighted with her own complexes. My criticism should be administered to the little authoress *in refracta dosi* only, please, if at all. I shall be writing to her myself before long.
> (McGuire, 1974, p. 498; see also Kerr, 1994, p. 406)

The two men had found a temporary truce in a shared pathologizing of the "little authoress."

Three weeks later, however, the tide had turned again, and Freud's tone had changed. Freud wrote to Jung cryptically and perhaps a bit ominously, "Spielrein, to whom I was glad not to mention your criticism, came to say good-bye a few days ago and discussed *certain intimate matters with me*" (McGuire, 1974, p. 499, emphasis added). Kerr (1994) reads this as a veiled warning that Spielrein had disclosed more about her relationship with Jung and requested to begin analysis with Freud, in Freud's own words in his letter to her on June 14, "to break your dependency on Jung" (Carotenuto, 1982, p. 116). Jung, perhaps recalling his narrow escape from public scandal in the earlier years when both his wife and Spielrein's mother were seeking Freud's intervention, would have been put on notice that he was again under scrutiny; perhaps Freud's sympathy for Spielrein and her feelings of betrayal by Jung had then been rekindled. At the same time, Freud endeavored in his letter to Spielrein to enlist her help in holding on to his tenuous relationship with Jung, writing, "I am most grateful for your clever words to Jung, there is no lack of others who are at pains to widen these chinks into a breach" (ibid.).

Spielrein had apparently also consulted Freud about her priority of ideas and her fear of plagiarism. Freud wrote to Spielrein in the same June letter:

> Since our conversation on the subject I have come to share your views of the priority problem. The germ of this idea may certainly be found in our earlier work. Indeed, if one wants to be precise, the clear expression of the same idea may be found in Abraham's "Dream and Myth," p. 70. Jung must have forgotten this passage when he dictated the words in question to you, and so did I when I wrote that note in *Imago*. Elsewhere, I shall have to amend my praises of Jung in your and A[braham]'s favor.
>
> (ibid.)

Perhaps hearkening back to the early days when the Vienna Society had held an ideal of "intellectual communism" (although it had been a point of contention from the beginning), Freud concluded with a verbal wave of his hand, "On the whole, however, this priority question is not very important" (Nunberg & Federn, 1962, pp. 299–303).

In any case, unbeknownst to Freud until later that summer, Spielrein had already found a new way out of her infatuation with Jung, as well as the triangle with her two warring mentors. On June 1, 1912, Spielrein, "hungry for a man" (Márton, 2006a), and likely allowing her parents to find a suitable partner following the Russian Jewish tradition (Launer, 2015, p. 156), suddenly married an observant Jewish medical doctor, Pavel Sheftel. Freud subsequently declined to analyze her, not wishing to interfere with the budding relationship with her new husband (Carotenuto, 1982, p. 117).

Meanwhile, the next six months saw the final dissolution of Jung's and Freud's relationship, as they waged an increasingly acrimonious war of letters, competing publications,[19] and collegial backstabbing. In close-volleying letters at the beginning of January 1913, Freud proposed that they end their personal relationship, and Jung replied on January 6 with a terse typewritten postcard that read, "I accede to your wish that we abandon our personal relations, for I never thrust my friendship on anyone. You yourself are the best judge of what this moment means to you. 'The rest is silence'" (McGuire, 1974, p. 540). Tellingly, the final quote is Hamlet's dying words to Horatio.

Just two weeks after the decisive rupture with Jung, on January 20, 1913, Freud wrote to Spielrein warning her that a negative review was forthcoming in the first issue of the Vienna Society's new and rival journal, the *Zeitschrift für Psychoanalyse*. Evading direct responsibility for the review, Freud had assigned it to another member of the Vienna Society, Paul Federn (who at times during the Society's discussions came across as more "Freudian" than Freud himself). Freud wrote:

> The first issue of the *Zeitschrift*, a fair proof of which lies before me already, carries a review of your last great contribution. We have taken the liberty of criticizing it freely, because the Zürich people have asked us expressly to do so. Don't be angry, and read it through with indulgence.
>
> (Carotenuto, 1982, p. 118)

The letter perhaps reveals Freud's continuing wish to keep Spielrein on his side, by blaming "the Zürich people" (Jung's crowd) for any harshness in the review – even though he had assigned it to one of his own closest adherents.

Federn's (1913) review, in fact, was mixed. In the pages of the minutes of the Vienna Psychoanalytic Society (Nunberg & E. Federn, 1974), Federn appears to be a thoughtful but narrowly loyal adherent to Freud's core principles. He would not have been very likely to appreciate Spielrein's more "mystical" (i.e., Jungian) explorations. Different readers have drawn different conclusions about the quality of the review, however. Kerr (1994) states, "It would have taken more than 'indulgence' for Spielrein to get through Paul Federn's review. One can scarcely imagine a more condescending or profoundly wrongheaded reading of her work" (p. 448). In Kerr's view, Federn oversimplified her argument as a justification of sadomasochism and asserted that while women may be concerned with the propagation of the species, men are not. On the other hand, Launer (2015) presents the review as "mainly sympathetic" (p. 138). The review ended with a surprisingly positive note toward Zürich, as well as a bow to a (stereotypical) preference of women for emotionality. Federn wrote: "Disregarding its objective truth, the paper seems to me, thanks to the author's sensitivity for emotional relationships, a contribution as well to the analysis of the mystical modality of thought that is so significant for humanity" (trans. Kerr, 1994, p. 449).

Jung did make good on his promise, and in the end cited Spielrein sixteen times in *Symbols of Transformation* (Jung, 1912, 1967a/1952). The last published mention of Spielrein's "Destruction" paper (until the recent revival of interest in her work) came in the form of a footnote in Freud's *Beyond the Pleasure Principle* in 1920. Freud wrote:

> A considerable portion of these speculations have been anticipated by Sabina Spielrein (1912) in an interesting and instructive paper which, however, is unfortunately not entirely clear to me; she there describes the sadistic components of the sexual instinct as "destructive."
>
> (Freud, 1955a/1920, 55n2)

The legacy of Spielrein's theory was mainly remembered for many decades as merely a footnote to one of Jung's earliest major works and to Freud's oft-quoted and debated theory about aggression and the death instinct. It should be noted, however, that neither man handed out footnotes lightly, and their citations of Spielrein's work were not quite as faint praise as Kerr (1994) suggests (p. 502; cf., Wolff-Bernstein, 2014).

Spielrein's contribution to the death instinct

In spite of the prominence of a number of early women analysts, including both Anna Freud and Melanie Klein, and in spite of Spielrein's prolific publication record spanning two decades, Spielrein was denied credit as one of the pioneers of psychoanalysis. Although Spielrein's writing and admission to Freud's Vienna circle predated Anna Freud's by eleven years, it is Anna who is generally regarded as the founder of child analysis (Richebächer, 2003, p. 209). Spielrein was not mentioned in Ernest Jones's standard biography of 1953, and is mentioned only once in relation to Freud's footnote in Peter Gay's (2006) biography (pp. 396, 396–397n). She is also mentioned only in passing in Paul Roazen's (1975) *Freud and His Followers* (p. 282). It was not until the publication of Carotenuto's (1982) *Secret Symmetry* that interest in Spielrein was revived – and then under the whiff of scandal and pathology. In Carotenuto's book, dredging up Jung's own self-serving account of Spielrein's "case" at a congress in 1907, Carotenuto, Bruno Bettelheim, and Max Day have characterized her in terms of psychosis, severe hysteria with schizoid characteristics, and borderline personality, respectively (Richebächer, 2003, p. 247).

As Swiss analyst, Sabine Richebächer, observed:

> The question of repression can also be applied to the history of psychoanalysis itself. We could say: first Sabina Spielrein was forgotten. There were reasons enough for that. Her person, her name, undoubtedly recalled the break between Freud and Jung in 1913 which was so traumatic for the psychoanalytic movement. Spielrein was moreover an independent person and someone with a will of her own who would not allow herself to be slotted into the interests of the psychoanalytic movement as a mere apparatchik. In the patriarchal structures of psychoanalysis she caused offence again and again; Ernest Jones, the one-time President of the International Psychoanalytic Association, could not stand her… Thus we are faced with the strange finding that, of all disciplines, psychoanalysis, which is founded on a belief in the healing power

of memory, stubbornly resists its own history. And the handing down of a false diagnosis – which Sabina Spielrein was given retrospectively – ensures that nothing changes.

(Richebächer, 2003, pp. 246–247)

Was Spielrein's "Destruction" paper a unique contribution to psychoanalysis? The "Destruction" paper has mostly been known, when referenced at all, as perhaps the earliest published theory of the death instinct. Did Spielrein originate the idea? Kerr (1994) dates the idea of a "death instinct" per se almost a decade earlier, in a 1903 book entitled *Rhythm of Life* by Pasteur Institute director, Élie Metchnikoff (p. 499). Even more generally, the idea of an "indissoluble connection between sex and death," using Freud's words in a letter to the Swiss pastor and psychoanalyst, Oskar Pfister, early in 1909 (Freud & Meng, 1963, p. 20; Noth, 2014, p. 45), was a familiar nineteenth century Romantic idea; in music, the famous *Liebestod* ("Love Death") from the opera *Tristan und Isolde* by Jung's and Spielrein's favorite composer, Richard Wagner, was of course already well-known, having been premiered in 1865. Wagner's music was ascendant in these years, embraced both by pan-German anti-Semites *and* by many Jewish composers and music lovers who (naively) forgave him his anti-Semitism due to their appreciation of his musical genius ([n.a.], 2013–2014).

Fritz Wittels, a prickly member of both Freud's society and Karl Kraus's circle, stated flatly during a meeting of the Wednesday Night Psychoanalytic Society in April 1907, "that the death instinct appears in association with love is as old as the world" (Nunberg & Federn, 1962, p. 179). As Spielrein mentions in a footnote, Wilhelm Stekel, another member of Freud's Wednesday Night Society, had also been writing along Freudian lines about "the wish to die… contrary to the nature of the sexual instinct underlying the wish to live" (Spielrein, 1912, p. 465n1). Theodor Reik read a paper to their Vienna group on a similar theme just two weeks before Spielrein's presentation in 1911 (Nunberg & Federn, 1974, pp. 310–319). Just a month after her admission to the group, she was bold enough to note the similarity between Reik's paper and her own completed work (ibid., p. 316). In the discussion that followed Reik's presentation, the entire group in fact appears to have taken this linking of sex and death for granted.[20] Moreover, as much as this eventually became a bone of contention between them,

Jung and Spielrein were both discussing and writing about the idea of a death instinct – as well as a theory of symbolic communication beyond sexual wish fulfillment and the idea of the collective unconscious – at the same time. The idea, then, had already been in the air for some time. Spielrein *cannot* be credited with the entire concept of a death instinct, as Kerr and others have suggested.

On the other hand, Spielrein's rendering of a "death instinct" was unique in its formulation, and merited Freud's (albeit somewhat confused) footnote when he finally published on the subject in 1920 in *Beyond the Pleasure Principle*. Spielrein's articulation of a death instinct, as we have seen, is quite different from Freud's. Freud adopts aggression and the death instinct as two versions of a drive placed in direct opposition to the libido, continuing his approach to the mind as a hydraulic system of opposing forces or a battle between instinctual life and accommodation of the ego to civilization. Spielrein, on the other hand, makes no such concession to civilization. She locates generativity primarily in the wildness of the collective, primal life force, which must overrun the socially tamed ego in order that new life can emerge, both biologically and in the psyche. While Freud's logic eventually brought him to the assertion that "where id was, ego shall be" (Freud, 1964, p. 80) – a triumph of the rational – Spielrein argues in this paper for the necessity of allowing ego to dissolve in the primal forces of life, even sacrificially, in the service of growth and transformation. In Spielrein's own pithy formulation, "where love reigns, the ego, that sinister despot, dies" (Ch. 6, p. 234).

For Spielrein, death and destruction are not opposed to life, but are inherent in both sexual pleasure and (although she continually nods to Freud's primacy of the sexual drive) in all psychic growth and development. It is not in the rational individual's self-mastery or in the neurotic's ambivalent resistance as discussed by Freud, but in Spielrein's female psychotic patients' dissolution of the ego that she finds compelling evidence of a deeper layer of vitality that, through sublimation – *not* hyper-rationality – can be made available to everyone.

Spielrein's clinical examples and frequent references to women's experience also suggest a counter-narrative to the largely male-dominated world of early psychoanalysis. Although we might disagree especially with her romanticization of masochism, she was claiming feminine modes of experience – as she herself defined them – as authoritative sources for her argumentation, including passivity, masochism, and exalted sacrifice, but also autoeroticism and bisexuality. In these ways, Spielrein's essay stands on its own as a distinctive contribution to psychoanalysis, including but also moving beyond the concept of the "death instinct" per se.

Idealism, romanticism, and the denial of destruction

In a tragic paradox, Spielrein's ability to probe the "Shadow side" of sexuality and to assert that destruction was inherent in the life force did not aid her in viewing the approaching Nazi threat with life-saving clarity. She had returned to Russia in 1923 and initially found meaningful work as a psychoanalyst in Moscow. She reunited with her husband and gave birth to a second daughter, Eva, in 1926. However, the political winds were shifting, and by the 1930s her life was a series of losses and deaths. Her husband and father had both died, and friends warned her that it was unsafe to remain in Russia. By the time the Nazis first occupied Rostov-on-Don, her three brothers, all scientists, had already been executed or deported during Stalin's reign of terror, psychoanalysis had been banned, and she had lost her job (Richebächer, 2003, p. 245). Freud's books had been burned in Germany in 1933. Five years later, Hitler was in Vienna, and the Freud family fled to London. Whether or not escape might have been possible for her, Spielrein remained in Russia, in her hometown of Rostov.

The same romantic idealism that was a source of creative explorations into the realms of love, heroism, and the deep truths available in myth and symbol appear to have served in the end to blind her to her own peril. She could not view Siegfried as evil, even though his legend had been appropriated as a symbol of the Aryan *Übermensch* in the twisted ideology of Nazism, when he had borne such tender and heroic personal meaning in her own life. She loved Wagner and German culture, and German was the chosen language of much of her scholarship. Her niece, Menicha, said, "She could not believe that the Germans could do such terrible things" (Márton, 2006a, p. 11). Margarita Khatyaturyan, a classmate and friend of Sabina's younger daughter, Eva, said in an interview, "People said they should leave the city. But Sabina Nikolajewna told me: 'I studied in Germany. I know the Germans very well. They are not able to act like that. They would never kill us'" (ibid.).

In spite of their sometimes less-than-friendly motives, perhaps both Freud and Jung perceived something cautionary in their assessments of Spielrein, which they shared both with her and with one another. Freud's description of her as "abnormally ambivalent" may have been picking up on some splitting that no doubt did contribute to her ability to idealize external (male) heroes while sinking into self-blame and depression. Her history of physical punishment at the hands and strap of her father may have instilled a tendency – noted in contemporary accounts of her dress and behavior – to ward off humiliation by assuming a posture of humility. Covington reports:

> … during this period of her life Spielrein was described by relatives as a solitary figure, intense, serious, working long hours and puritanical in dress, wearing old clothes, some of them torn, so as not to spend money on herself. Her idealisation of self-sacrifice seems to have resulted in self-deprivation.
> (Covington, 2015, p. 12)

Jung had warned her, in an ambiguous expression of self-interest, but also, perhaps, some genuine concern:

> You are always trying to drag the Siegfried symbol back into reality, whereas in fact it is the bridge to your individual development. Human beings do not stand in one world only but between two worlds and must distinguish themselves from their functions in both worlds. That is individuation. You are rejecting dreams and seeking action. Then the dreams come and thwart your actions. The dreams are a world, and the real is a world. You have to stand between them and regulate the traffic in both worlds, just as Siegfried stands between the gods and men.
> (Jung, 2015, p. 49)

Perhaps the tragedy is that while Spielrein could identify the link between Destruction and Becoming, she was never able to give up her longing for the Siegfried hero to manifest literally in her life. And when the devil came in the disguise of her beloved hero, she could not recognize him. On July 27, 1942, eyewitnesses observed Spielrein and her daughters being marched by the Nazis to the Zmeyevsky gully on the outskirts of Rostov, where they were shot and killed along with 10,000 other civilians.

In her paper, Spielrein wrote, "[Christ's] burial is a re-implantation into Mother Earth. Resurrection is rebirth." It is impossible to reconcile this idealized vision of death and resurrection with the image of Spielrein and her daughters thrown into a mass grave in a ravine. But perhaps by remembering Spielrein's story whole – not just as a lurid sex scandal or a cautionary tale of "a dangerous method," but as a narrative of a woman's brilliance and determination in the midst of perpetual opposition – we can participate in the healing memory of one trauma at the heart of psychoanalysis and restore Spielrein to her proper place as a pioneer of psychoanalysis and a creator of ideas about love and death that continue to challenge and disturb us to this day.

Notes

1 Freud wrote to Jung the next day, suggesting a certain social awkwardness and disconcerting frankness on Spielrein's part: "She said I didn't look malicious, as she had imagined I would" (McGuire, 1974, p. 447).
2 The *Jahrbuch* was founded in 1908 by Freud in a secret meeting with the Swiss analysts at the First International Congress for Psychoanalysis in Salzburg, with Freud and Eugen Bleuler as "co-directors" and Jung as editor. This meeting was an attempt on Freud's part to recruit support from the Zürich psychoanalytic faction, in part to expand psychoanalysis beyond its Viennese (and Jewish) origins. The Viennese had been deliberately excluded for the time being – the only member of Freud's Vienna Psychoanalytic Society included in the founding of the *Jahrbuch* was Otto Rank.
3 German term for dissertation advisor, but implying a stronger personal mentorship – literally, "doctoral father."
4 Freud alluded to oedipal dynamics in 1909 with the case of "Little Hans" (Freud, 1955b/1909) and first used the term in *A Special Type of Choice of Object Made by Men* (Freud, 1957/1910) the following year. By 1913, he had applied the theory to the evolution of civilization in *Totem and Taboo* (Freud, 1955c/1913).
5 In her dissertation (excerpt trans. in this volume, Chapter 5; see also Chapter 1), she interprets her patient's use of the word "poetry" as "an explicit erotic element, so that we can compare 'poetry' [*'poesie'*] =

'amorousness'." In my view, there has been enough voyeuristic speculation about salacious details (further exaggerated by Cronenberg's 2011 film). Perhaps it is enough to say that Spielrein was savvy, idealistic, and/or principled enough not to allow the risk of pregnancy to interrupt her career.

6 For a detailed history of Wolff's and Jung's relationship and Wolff's important contributions to analytical psychology and to Jung's own theoretical formulations, see Healy (2017). Nowhere in this formulation of Jung's is the possibility (which Freud did recognize, fearing for the reputation of an already embattled profession) that passion could also lead to unprofessional behavior and the exploitation of a patient's vulnerability.

7 This may at first seem ironic, since Freud is often accused of a biological reductionism of his own in his insistence on the centrality of sexuality in human motivation. However, Freud was clearly attempting to distinguish himself from his contemporaries who believed all mental phenomena were the products of genetic or physiological "degeneracy." For Freud, the libido was a *psycho*-physiological drive, which was better treated verbally in an appeal to the patient's mental contents and not purely through electromagnetic or other physiological means used at the time (thanks to Hermann Westerink, 2014, for this clarification). Launer (2015) emphasizes that Spielrein's interest in biology and the role of evolutionary adaptation, following Darwin, represented yet a third, fairly independent strand of thought from Jung and Freud, derived from her medical training (pp. 73, 144, et passim).

8 Covington (2015) suggests that this line of thought "seems to predict here what might be considered an object relations approach to instinct, in that the 'nurturing instinct' necessarily entails and is reliant upon the primary relationship between mother and infant. In this formulation, Spielrein locates the destructive drive not simply within the reproductive drive but more fundamentally within the 'nurturing instinct' as the first experience of pleasure. In this sense, the destructive drive is traced to its pre-Oedipal roots. The regressive pull towards loss of self within the other, as can be experienced within the sexual act, is therefore present in its precursor image of the suckling of the infant at the breast, i.e., of the experience of being at one with the world" (pp. 7–8). Covington also interprets Spielrein's Brünhilde–Siegfried fantasy about Jung as an intensely pre-oedipal erotic transference, and the theory of a destructive drive as a sublimation of "the destructive impulses and phantasies that arose as a result of the intolerable frustration she seems to have continued to experience in her love relations" (pp. 11–12).

9 As noted in Chapter 6, Spielrein uses the term "*typisch*" throughout this paper in a way that suggests that she is referring to Jung's theory of archetypes. We therefore chose in this volume to translate "*typisch*" as

"[arche]typal" rather than the more literal "typical," which does not convey an archaic, collective meaning.

10 Spielrein continues to use this term in a philosophical sense in her later writings, even before Heidegger's elaboration on the concept was well developed (see Spielrein, 1923, trans. in this volume, Chapter 12, n xii).

11 Kerr (1994) asserts: "There was indeed a personal, and quite contemporary, reason why Jung's reverie [in Part 2 of *Transformations and Symbols of the Libido* (i.e., Jung, 1912; 1967a/1911–12, 1952)] did not escape the overexcited Underworld ruled by the 'destructive mother'. Let us look at that reverie one last time. He descends into an Underworld of fantasy and there finds himself confronted by a woman who would hold him fast if she could, a woman who confronts him maliciously with exquisitely regressive temptations, a woman with ready access to his own fantasy life, a woman who is as comfortable being his fantasied mother as being his eternal consort, a woman who can experience him both as lover and as the son he would sire in her, a woman who tells him that all sexual attraction involves destruction, a woman who in the end positively dares him to be 'Siegfried'. Behind the image of the 'destructive mother' of Jung's reverie, I submit, stands the unabashed authoress [sic] of 'Destruction as a Cause of Coming into Being'" (p. 333).

12 For a discussion of the similarities and differences among these theories and their interlocking historical development, see Chambrier (2006).

13 This is Jung's term both for retreat into fantasy and regression into "primitive" human experience as symbolized in mythology, introduced in Jung (1967a/1912) (Kerr, 1994, pp. 327–328).

14 Ironically, even as Spielrein and Jung played out a mother–son fantasy of mythical proportions, Freud and Jung were enacting an increasingly toxic oedipal struggle of father vs. son and king vs. rebellious crown prince.

15 Carotenuto (1982) dates this letter as "probably written during the early months in 1912," but Jung's letter to Spielrein on August 8, 1911 (Jung, 2015, p. 37), suggests that she sent the paper for the first time even before presenting it to the Vienna Society – corrected in Carotenuto (1986, p. 138) to the beginning of August 1911.

16 Presumably referring to the contentious October 11 meeting, in which the "Adler gang" was ejected from the Vienna Society, and not a controversy regarding her own work. For more detail, see Cooper-White (2017, pp. 33–34, 190).

17 For more details on these shifting sands, see Kerr (1994, pp. 352–357).

18 For more on Jung's struggle with this paper, see Homans (1979, pp. 27–28, 58–73, et passim); and regarding its connection to Spielrein's work, see also Kerr (1994, pp. 322–334). For Jung, the death instinct belonged to the domain of introversion (fantasy and dreams) and was not inherent in all sexuality as Spielrein was proposing (Cf., Jung's later revisions in Jung, 1967a/1911–12, 1952).

19 Ironically, this conflict included their own mutual suspicions of plagiarism and a race to preempt one another's theories, played out in their race to publish alternative versions of two modes of thought – Jung's (1967b/1912) "two ways of thinking" as rational and symbolic vs. Freud's (1958/1911) "two principles of mental functioning" as the pleasure principle and the reality principle. For more on this rivalry see Kerr (1994, pp. 276, 336).
20 Hans Sachs cited further examples in the literature, including Milton's *Paradise Lost*, Schnitzler's *Der Weg ins Freie* (The Path to Freedom), and Shakespeare's *Hamlet*, to which Sadger added Schnitzler's *The Veil of Beatrice* (Nunberg & Federn, 1974, pp. 314–315).

References

[n.a.] (2013–2014). *Euphorie und Unbehagen – Das Jüdische Wien und Richard Wagner*. Exhibit at the Jüdisches Museum Wien, September 24, 2013–March 16, 2014, Vienna, Austria.
Bair, D. (2003). *Jung: A biography*. New York: Back Bay Books/Little, Brown & Co.
Bromberg, P. (1994). "Speak! That I may see you": Some reflections on dissociation, reality, and psychoanalytic listening. *Psychoanalytic Dialogues*, 4(4), 517–547.
Bromberg, P. (2001). *Standing in the spaces: Essays on clinical process, trauma, and dissociation*. Hillsdale, NJ: Analytic Press.
Carotenuto, A. (1982). *A secret symmetry: Sabina Spielrein between Freud and Jung*. A. Pomerans (Trans.). New York: Pantheon.
Carotenuto, A. (1986). *Tagebuche einer heimlichen Symmetrie: Sabina Spielrein zwischen Jung und Freud*. Freiburg: Kore.
Chambrier, J. (2006). Sabina Spielrein (1912): Die Destruktion als Ursache des Werdens. In A. Karger, & C. Weismüller (Eds.), *Ich hieß Sabina Spielrein: Von einer, die auszog, Heilung zu suchen* (pp. 85–98). Göttingen: Vandenhoeck & Ruprecht.
Cooper-White, P. (2007). *Many voices: Pastoral psychotherapy in relational and theological perspective*. Minneapolis, MN: Fortress Press.
Cooper-White, P. (2011). *Braided selves: Collected essays on multiplicity, God, and persons*. Eugene, OR: Cascade.
Cooper-White, P. (2014). Beyond "A dangerous method": Sabina Spielrein and the "death instinct." Fulbright lecture presented at the Sigmund Freud Museum, Vienna, January 17.
Cooper-White, P. (2017). *Old and dirty gods: Religion, antisemitism, and the origins of psychoanalysis*. London & New York: Routledge.
Covington, C. (2015). Introduction. In C. Covington & B. Wharton (Eds.), *Sabina Spielrein: Forgotten pioneer of psychoanalysis* (pp. 1–13). New York: Routledge.

Cronenberg, D. (Director) (2011). A dangerous method (film). Los Angeles: Sony Pictures Classics.

Davies, J.M. (1996). Dissociation, repression, and reality testing in the countertransference: false memory in the psychoanalytic treatment of adult survivors of childhood sexual abuse. *Psychoanalytic Dialogues*, 6(2), 197.

Federn, P. (1913). Sabina Spielrein: Die Destruktion als Ursache des Werdens. *Internationale Zeitschrift für Ärtzliche Psychoanalyse*, 1, 92–93.

Flax, J. (1993). Multiples: On the contemporary politics of subjectivity. In J. Flax (Ed.), *Disputed subjects: Essays on psychoanalysis, politics and philosophy* (pp. 92–110). New York: Routledge.

Frazer, C. (2012). *The golden bough*. 3rd edn., 12 vols. Cambridge, UK: Cambridge University Press. (Orig. publ. 1911–1915; 1st edn. 1890.)

Freud, A. (1981). The concept of developmental lines. *Psychoanalytic Study of the Child*, 36, 129–136.

Freud, E. & Meng, H. (Eds.) (1963). *Psycho-analysis and faith: The letters of Sigmund Freud and Oskar Pfister*. New York: Basic Books.

Freud, S. (1953a). The interpretation of dreams. In J. Strachey (Ed.), *The standard edition of the complete psychological works of Sigmund Freud* (hereafter *SE*), 4–5 (entire). London: Hogarth. (Orig. publ. 1900.)

Freud, S. (1953b). Three essays on the theory of sexuality. *SE* 7, 125–248. (Orig. publ. 1905.)

Freud, S. (1955a). Beyond the pleasure principle. *SE* 18: 1–64. (Orig. publ. 1920.)

Freud, (1955b). Analysis of a phobia in a five-year-old boy ["Little Hans"]. *SE* 10, 3–152. (Orig. publ. 1909.)

Freud, S. (1955c). Totem and taboo. *SE* 13, ix–164. (Orig. publ. 1913.)

Freud, S. (1957). A special type of choice of object made by men. *SE* 11, 163–176. (Orig. publ. 1910.)

Freud, S. (1958). Two principles of mental functioning. *SE* 12, 213–226. (Orig. publ. 1911.)

Freud, S. (1961). The ego and the id. *SE* 19, 1–66. (Orig. publ. 1923.)

Freud, S. (1964). The dissection of the psychical personality. Lecture 31 in *New introductory lectures on psychoanalysis*. *SE* 22: 57–80. (Orig. publ. 1933.)

Gay, P. (2006). Freud: A life for our time. New York: W.W. Norton.

Harris, A. (1996). False memory? False memory syndrome? The so-called False Memory Syndrome? *Psychoanalytic Dialogues*, 6(2), 155–188.

Healy, N. S. (2017). *Toni Wolff and C.G. Jung: A collaboration*. Los Angeles: Tiberius Press.

Homans, P. (1979). *Jung in context: Modernity and the making of a psychology*. Chicago, IL: University of Chicago Press.

Jung, C.G. (1911). Wandlungen und Symbole der Libido: Beiträge zur Entwicklungsgeschichte des Denkens, Erster Teil. [Transformations and symbols of the libido: Contributions to the history of the development of thought, Part 1.] *Jahrbuch für Psychoanalytische und Psychopathologische Forschungen*, 3(1):120–227.

Jung, C.G. (1912). Wandlungen und Symbole der Libido: Beiträge zur Entwicklungsgeschichte des Denkens, Zweiter Teil. [Transformations and symbols of the libido: Contributions to the history of the development of thought, Part 2.] *Jahrbuch für Psychoanalytische und Psychopathologische Forschungen*, 4(1):162–464.

Jung, C.G. (1967a). Symbols of transformation, Parts I & II. R.F.C. Hull (Trans.). In *The collected works of C.G. Jung* (hereafter CW). Vol. 5 (entire). Bollingen Series XX. Princeton, NJ: Princeton University Press. (Orig. publ. Jung, 1911–1912 – see Jung, 1911, 1912 above; 2nd expanded edn. publ. 1952.)

Jung. C.G. (1967b). Two kinds of thinking. *CW* 5, 7–33. (Orig. publ. Jung, 1912.)

Jung, C.G. (2009). *The red book*. S. Shamdasani (Ed. & Trans.). New York: W.W. Norton. (Orig. unpubl. manuscript, 1914–1930, 1952, 1957.)

Jung, C.G. (2015). The letters of C. G. Jung to Sabina Spielrein. B. Wharton (Trans.). In C. Covington & B. Wharton, B. (Eds.), *Sabina Spielrein: Forgotten pioneer of psychoanalysis*, 2nd edn. (pp. 33–62). New York: Brunner-Routledge.

Kerr, J. (1994). *A most dangerous method: The story of Jung, Freud, and Sabina Spielrein*. New York: Vintage.

Launer, J. (2015). *Sex versus survival: The life and ideas of Sabina Spielrein*. New York: Overlook Duckworth.

Lothane, H.Z. (2015), Tender love and transference: Unpublished letters of C. G. Jung and Sabina Spielrein (with an addendum/discussion). In C. Covington & B. Wharton (Eds.), *Sabina Spielrein: Forgotten pioneer of psychoanalysis,* 2nd edn. (pp. 126–157.) New York: Routledge.

Márton, E. (2006a). Interviews with Sabina Spielrein's family and friends. In Cine-Notes to E. Márton (Director), *My name was Sabina Spielrein* (DVD) (pp. 10–11). Chicago, IL: Facets Video.

Márton, E. (Director) (2006b). *My name was Sabina Spielrein* (DVD). Chicago, IL: Facets Video. (Orig. released as *Ich hieß Sabina Spielrein*, produced by Helgi Felix/Idé Film Felixson AB, 2002.)

McGuire, W. (Ed.) (1974). *The Freud/Jung letters*. R. Hull & R. Manheim (Trans.). Princeton, NJ: Princeton University Press.

Noth, I. (2015). "Beyond Freud and Jung": Sabina Spielrein's contribution to child psychoanalysis and developmental psychology. *Pastoral Psychology*, 64(2), 279–286.

Noth, I. (2014). *Sigmund Freud – Oskar Pfister Briefwechsel 1909–1939*. Zürich: Theologischer Verlag.

Nunberg, H. & Federn, E. (Eds.) (1962). *Minutes of the Vienna Psychoanalytic Society, Vol. 1: 1906–1908*. M. Nunberg (Trans.). New York: International Universities Press.

Nunberg, H. & Federn, E. (Eds.) (1974). *Minutes of the Vienna Psychoanalytic Society, Vol. 3:1910–1911*. M. Nunberg (Trans.). New York: International Universities Press.

Richebächer, S. (2003). "In league with the devil, and yet you fear fire?" Sabina Spielrein and C. G. Jung: A suppressed scandal from the early days of psychoanalysis. B. Wharton (Trans.). In C. Covington & B. Wharton (Eds.), *Sabina Spielrein: Forgotten pioneer of psychoanalysis* (pp. 227–249). New York: Brunner-Routledge.

Roazen, P. (1975). *Freud and his followers*. New York: Alfred Knopf.

Spielrein, S. (1911). Über den psychologischen Inhalt eines Falles von Schizophrenie (Dementia Praecox) [On the psychological content of a case of schizophrenia (Dementia Praecox)]. *Jahrbuch für psychoanalytische und psychopathologische Forschungen*, 3, 329–400. (Excerpt trans. in this volume, Chapter 5; for full English transl., see Spielrein, 2018, pp. 14–96.)

Spielrein, S. (1912). Die Destruktion als Ursache des Werdens. [Destruction as the cause of becoming]. *Jahrbuch für psychoanalytische und psychopathologische Forschungen*, 4, 465–503. (Trans. in this volume, Chapter 6.)

Spielrein, S. (1994). Destruction as a cause of coming into being. K. McCormick (Trans.). *Journal of Analytical Psychology*, 39, 155–186. (Orig. publ. 1912.)

Spielrein, S. (1995). Destruction as cause of becoming. S.K. Witt (Trans.) *Psychoanalysis and Contemporary Thought*, 18, 85–118. (Orig. publ. 1912.)

Spielrein, S. (2018). *The essential writings of Sabina Spielrein: Pioneer of psychoanalysis*. R. Cape & R. Burt (Eds. & Trans.). New York: Routledge.

Westerink, H. (2014). Response to Cooper-White, P. (2014). Beyond "A dangerous method": Sabina Spielrein and the "death instinct." Fulbright lecture presented at the Sigmund Freud Museum, Vienna, January 17.

Wharton, B. (Trans.) (2015). Burghölzli Hospital Records of Sabina Spielrein. In C. Covington & B. Wharton (Eds.), *Sabina Spielrein: Forgotten pioneer of psychoanalysis* (pp. 57–82). New York: Routledge.

Wolff-Bernstein, J. (2014). Response to Cooper-White, P. (2014). Beyond "A dangerous method": Sabina Spielrein and the "death instinct." Fulbright lecture presented at the Sigmund Freud Museum, Vienna, January 17.

Chapter 3

Passions, politics, and drives
Sabina Spielrein in Soviet Russia

Klara Naszkowska

> I think that I was born for this job, that it is my calling.
> My life would have no meaning without it.
> (Sabina Spielrein, employee questionnaire, 1923)

> To me, life without science is completely senseless.
> What else is there for me if there is no science?
> Get married? But that thought fills me with dread.
> …
> [H]ow stupid that I am not a man: men have it easier with everything.
> It is a shame that everything in life goes their way.
> I do not want to be a slave!
> (Sabina Spielrein, diary entry, 1905[1])

Introduction

In May 1923, Sabina Spielrein packed her intimate diaries, correspondence, and other documents into a chest. She left them with her colleague Édouard Claparède, the renowned psychiatrist and the founder of the Jean-Jacques Rousseau Institute, a school of educational science in Geneva, where she worked, before setting off for Moscow.[2] As the official account has it, the documents were "accidentally" discovered in October 1977 in the basement of the Palais Wilson, which had housed the Rousseau Institute from 1937, and were turned over to the Jungian analyst, Aldo Carotenuto.[3] His (1980) volume *Diario di una Segreta Simmetria. Sabina Spielrein tra Jung e Freud* (Carotenuto, 1980; translated in Carotenuto, 1982 as *A Secret Symmetry: Sabina Spielrein between Jung and Freud*) presented a selection of Spielrein's diary entries from 1909 to 1912

(Carotenuto, 1982, pp. 3–44), letters to Carl Jung from 1911 to 1918 (ibid., pp. 45–90)[4], letters to Sigmund Freud from 1909 to 1914 (ibid., pp. 91–112), letters from Freud from 1909 to 1923 (ibid., pp. 113–127), and a confabulatory essay "The Story of Sabina Spielrein" penned by Carotenuto (ibid., pp. 129–214). His "Story" was a typical example of history distorting "herstory." Carotenuto recognized the historical significance of the unearthed documents in relation to Freud and Jung, but failed to acknowledge Spielrein's intellectual significance. The discovery did not lead him or others at the time to read Spielrein's own work, even though it was easily available in journals. He minimized Spielrein's professional accomplishments by shifting the focus from her contributions to the development of Jung's theories and to her private life (her adolescent illness and her relationship with Jung) and whitewashed Jung.[5] The publication of *A Secret Symmetry* caused a massive upsurge of interest in Spielrein's life and work.[6] Unfortunately, in the first years that followed Carotenuto's publication, many scholars, myself included, unintentionally repeated and consolidated his false assumptions and confabulations.

The objective of this chapter is to present a fuller picture of the least recognized, least analyzed, and most undervalued period in Spielrein's life and work – namely, her time in Soviet Russia – and to dispel the misconception that it was not a fruitful and productive time. I am greatly indebted to the scholars who discovered and brought to light the following materials: Spielrein's Burghölzli hospital records, diary extracts, correspondence with Sigmund Freud, Carl Jung, her mother, father, friends, colleagues, and others, as well as thirty-three scholarly papers Spielrein wrote between 1912 and 1931 (Brinkmann & Bose, 1986; Wackenhut & Willke, 1994; Cifali, 2001; Covington & Wharton, 2003, 2015; Richebächer, 2005, 2016; Spielrein, 2006; this volume).[7] Additionally, I am indebted to the academics who interviewed the survivors of the Stalinist purges and the Holocaust and contributed to our understanding of Soviet and Stalinist Russia. Most importantly, my gratitude goes to Spielrein's German biographer, Sabine Richebächer (2003, 2005, 2016), as well as Alexander Etkind (1994a, 1997), Magnus Ljunggren (2001, 2011), Victor Ovcharenko (1995, 1999a), Elisabeth Márton (2006), Coline Covington (2004, 2015), Martin Miller (1985, 1990, 1998), and James Rice (1982a, 1982b).

Furthermore, I have been greatly inspired by the scholars who have reinterpreted material that was initially presented in a selective, speculative, biased manner by Carotenuto and many subsequent scholars and authors (e.g., Kerr, 1994; Hampton, 2002; Faenza, 2003; Cronenberg, 2011) – most importantly, I thank Spielrein's British biographer, John Launer (2015a, 2015b), as well as Henry Zvi Lothane (2007, 2012, 2015), Adrienne Harris (2015, 2016), Pamela Cooper-White (2015a, 2015b, 2015c, 2017), and Felicity Kelcourse (2015).

We are still facing blank spots, gaps, and unclear moments in Spielrein's story, despite the discoveries of materials pertaining to her and the acquired testimonies of the survivors of the Stalinist purges and the Holocaust. Much of Spielrein's rediscovered archive, however, remains in a private collection in Switzerland and has not been published or systematically studied. My aim is to fill in those gaps as adequately as possible by considering the available archival and testimonial data against the rapidly changing social and political climate of Soviet Russia, as well as the fate of psychoanalysis enmeshed with the politics and terror of the Stalinist regime.

Life in Geneva

Why did Spielrein decide to move back to Russia? She didn't. She intended to return to Geneva, where she lived and worked, after two months. Furthermore, in her application for a short-term visa to Russia, she emphatically stated, "I do not wish to remain there under any circumstances" (Geneva immigration police dossier, Richebächer, 2005, p. 250).

In the early months of 1923, Spielrein had slipped into serious financial troubles. She had always struggled to support her family. In Berlin, where she stayed between 1912 and 1914 with her husband, Pavel Sheftel, and their sickly little daughter, Renate (Irma Renate), Sheftel did not have a job. Afterwards, at the outbreak of the First World War, he was drafted into the Russian Army to serve as a military doctor and left Spielrein alone with Renate. She moved to Geneva hoping to change her financial situation and improve her daughter's health, but still could not afford membership fees for professional organizations, so Freud paid for her fees to the Psychoanalytical Society in Vienna, and her membership in the Swiss Psychoanalytic Society was paid for by one of its wealthy founders, Emil Oberholzer. When the war ended, Sheftel did not return from Russia and Spielrein continued the life of a single mother in Geneva. Then, in 1923, Spielrein's earnings from the Rousseau Institute and her private practice couldn't cover the rent. According to Sheftel, she was living like a refugee and a beggar. He worried that their daughter, then eight years old, would be forced to cease being a child and act like an adult when living with her mother under these conditions, without her father and her grandparents (undated letter, Richebächer, 2005, p. 242). Spielrein must have felt very lonely in Geneva.

Spielrein's entire family was encouraging her to return to her hometown, Rostov-on-Don. By as early as 1913, her father, Nikolai Arkadyevich, had urged her to "[b]ring light to the Russian darkness" (Spielrein, 2006, p. 154). Russia, after the October Revolution in 1917 and the Bolshevik Red Army victory in the civil war (1918–1922), was in chaos, suffering from hyperinflation, poverty, famine, and epidemics. The official ideology of dialectical and historical materialism had already begun to dominate science (cf., Stalin, 2013/1938). According to historian René van der Veer (1990), "it had become virtually impossible to occupy an important position in the scientific world without being a convinced (or declared) communist" (p. 206). Persecutions had already begun: psychiatrist Nikolai Osipov – the self-proclaimed first proponent of Freud in Russia – was forced to escape in 1921; Freud's close colleague, Lou Andreas-Salomé, had been deprived of her fortune and was living on charity. The Spielrein family had survived the civil war, but their possessions and money were confiscated, and the Communists ordered them to share their rococo palace at 37 Pushkinskaya (Pushkin Street) in Rostov-on-Don with other families. Sabina's old bedroom became shared by her mother, Eva Lublinskaya, her brother, Emil, his wife, Fanya Burnstein, and their son, Mark. Adding to the turmoil was Eva's declining health – she suffered from arthritis and angina (cf., medical report from August 29, 1918, Richebächer, 2005, p. 218).

Nevertheless, Spielrein's father, Nikolai, and her brothers, Emil and Isaak, all believed that the newly formed USSR would welcome Sabina with open arms, and that in Moscow her career would resume at full speed (letters from Nikolai, Emil, and Isaak Spielrein, Richebächer, 2005, p. 237). At that time, the budding Soviet Union seemed welcoming of nonobservant, educated Jews working in the sciences.[8] Spielrein's well-educated brothers had become successful scientists in the USSR. Isaak was head of the entire field of industrial psychology in Moscow; Emil was a professor of biology and zoology in Rostov.[9] Many leaders of the Bolshevik movement were Jewish or part Jewish, including Leon Trotsky, who was also a supporter of psychoanalysis, or "Freudism," as the new theories were named in the USSR (cf., Etkind, 1994b). Many nonreligious Jews, including Isaak and Nikolai, identified with socialist or communist ideas.

In a letter dated January 17, 1923, Sheftel presented his wife with an ultimatum. He ordered her to make a clear-cut decision: give their family a chance or divorce him (Richebächer, 2005, p. 248).

I would argue that Spielrein was not tempted by the idea of being closer to her birth family. A family photograph from 1909 springs to mind. It was taken during Spielrein's visit from Zürich: Eva, Sabina, Nikolai, Emil, Isaak, and Jan (another brother of Sabina's) are gathered around the table, with Sabina sitting, leaning away from her family and looking intently at a book on the table (Carotenuto, 1982, p. xiv). During her time in the West, Spielrein maintained only sporadic contact with her family – according to Richebächer (2005), only sixteen letters were exchanged with her family members between 1921 and 1923. Spielrein did not visit her dying mother in 1922 or attend her funeral (Eva died on March 25, 1922). Also, her personal relationship with her brother, Isaak, was practically nonexistent, and there is no evidence of a professional collaboration despite the fact that they specialized in similar fields and worked in the same institutions. Isaak's daughter, Menikha Spielrein, stated that she saw Sabina only three times in her life (Covington, 2004). John Launer (2015b), British psychotherapist and author of *Sex versus Survival*, has put forward the idea that childhood traumas must have strained the relationship between Sabina and Isaak. I would add that it also weakened her bond with her mother and the other two brothers, Emil and Jan. In keeping distance from her family, Spielrein seemed to have followed the advice of her former doctor from the Burghölzli clinic and director of the institution, Eugen Bleuler, for whom she had immense respect. Hospital records attest to the fact that, during treatment in her adolescent and later years, Spielrein's mental condition suffered considerably from contact with her family. Bleuler persistently recommended that

Spielrein's father not visit her daughter in the hospital and urged her to convince her brothers not to move to Zürich while Sabina received mental treatment there (Wharton, 2015, pp. 81–109).

Freud initially advised Spielrein to move back to Berlin, a vibrant center for psychoanalysis. The cost of living was lower and she could find work there with an array of Russian publishing houses. Later, in a letter dated February 9, 1923, Freud approved of her decision to move to her motherland (Carotenuto, 1982, p. 127). It was an important destination on the psychoanalytical map, and Freud was very interested in spreading his school of thought there. Many of his patients came from pre-Soviet Russia, including the famous Wolf Man, and from other Central and Eastern European countries, such as Poland, Romania, and Hungary (cf., Jones, 1961, p. 14). Freud developed professional and private relations with numerous Russians, most importantly with Andreas-Salomé, Spielrein, Nikolai Osipov, and Max Eitingon, later a member of Freud's secret inner circle.

In the first decade of the 1900s, Russia had accepted psychoanalysis before many Western countries did, partially because of a large contingent of Russian medical students studying at European intellectual centers, most importantly Zürich, Vienna, Berlin, and Leipzig. At the same time that Spielrein was training at the world-famous Burghölzli clinic, four other Jews from southwestern Russia were completing internships there: Eitingon, Tatiana Rosenthal, Fanya Chalevsky, and Esther Aptekmann. Other prominent Russians to study medicine in the West included Osipov, Moshe Wulff, and Ivan D. Ermakov (cf., Rice, 1982a; Etkind, 1997). All of the above returned to Russia at some point to work in the field of psychoanalysis, with the exception of Eitingon, who moved from Zürich to Berlin and later to Israel. Upon his return to Moscow, Osipov began publishing articles on psychoanalysis (Osipov, 1908a, 1908b) and established a weekly psychoanalytical circle called "Little Fridays." In 1909, Osipov and one of the members of the circle, Nikolai A. Vyrubov, founded a bimonthly journal, *Psychoterapiya* (*Psychotherapy*), the first periodical in the world devoted to psychoanalysis after the *Jahrbuch für Psychoanalyse* (cf., Joravsky, 1978; Lobner & Levitin, 1978; Young, 1979; Miller, 1985, 1990, 1998; van der Veer, 1990, 2011; Etkind, 1994a, 1997; Ovcharenko, 1999b). The first issue of the journal from February 1910 appeared six months before Freud's own journal *Zentralblatt für Psychoanalyse* (cf., Ljunggren, 2014). On March 21, 1912, Freud famously wrote to Jung, "In Russia (Odessa) there seems to be a local epidemic of psychoanalysis" (McGuire, 1974, p. 495).

The eruption of the October Revolution and the Russian Civil War delayed the development of psychoanalysis in Russia, but in the early 1920s, it seemed to be flourishing in Soviet Russia (particularly when perceived from a distance). The Russian Psychoanalytic Society was established in Moscow in 1921, with Ermakov as its first president.[10] There were five centers for psychoanalysis – in Moscow, Petrograd, Kiev, Odessa, and Rostov-on-Don – with about thirty listed members (cf., Marti, 1976). A state-supported Psychoanalytic Institute (also headed by Ermakov) and an Orphanage-Laboratory (*Kinderheim-Laboratorium*) were opened in Moscow in 1921. A state-owned publishing house was issuing translations of all of Freud's books almost immediately after their original publication. The institute, the nursery, and the publishing house were located in a Ryabushinsky Mansion (now the Maxim Gorky Literary and Memorial Museum) at 6/2 Malaya Nikitskaya. It is a classic art nouveau house designed by renowned architect Fyodor Shekhtel and built between 1900 and 1903 for Stepan Pavlovich Ryabushinsky, a billionaire banker. After the October Revolution, the mansion was appropriated by the Bolsheviks. In addition, private practices were being opened: Osipov's in Saint Petersburg, Wulff's in Moscow, and Leonid Drosnes's in Odessa. In general, psychoanalysis was receiving broad attention in Soviet Russia.

Moscow: The first step toward the east

Spielrein did not give in to her husband's ultimatum. She chose better professional prospects in Moscow and wouldn't reunite with Sheftel in Rostov just yet. Throughout her life, she remained focused on her work, driven by professional goals and ambitions. In a letter to Spielrein, Sheftel called his wife's dedication "an almost cruel love for science" (Richebächer, 2005, p. 237). It may be distressing to recognize in hindsight that it was trivial factors such as financial troubles that pushed her toward the east, suffering, and death. But Spielrein's time in Soviet Russia was very prolific and would prove monumental in shaping her legacy.

After the Russian Civil War, however, Russian society's approach toward psychoanalysis changed. First, during the Cultural Revolution and the sociopolitical transformations happening with the birth of the USSR, psychoanalysis served as a political–ideological tool. In the first years following the civil war, the Bolshevik Party was in transition, internally divided, and led by an unstable leadership. This situation resulted in the increased interest in psychoanalysis among higher-ranking members of the party. Second, Freudism was a short-term craze, "a popular fad" – in Lenin's words (Zetkin, 1929, p. 44) – that attracted nonprofessionals: philosophers, writers, and artists. Between 1923 and 1930, in Soviet journals began a semiprofessional discussion on the compatibility of Freudism and Marxism, the usefulness of Freud's doctrine to Marxism, and the possibility of creating Freudo-Marxism (Bykhovsky, 1923; Reisner, 1924; Trotsky, 1960/1924). However, the discussion did not result in any real impact on political opinion. As Etkind (1997) argued, "The future… was decided in the end by people who had trouble understanding not only Freud but even Marx" (p. 225). The debate was terminated as soon as Joseph Stalin, an unpredictable, paranoiac tyrant, came to power between 1926 and 1927 (cf., Miller, 1985, 1998).

The first to discuss the correspondence between Freudism and Marxism, albeit not in writing, were members of the Kazan psychoanalytic circle established by Aleksander Luria (a future student and colleague of Spielrein) in the summer of 1922, with the official approval of Freud and Ernest Jones, then president of the International Psychoanalytical Association. In articles that followed, Luria (1925a, cf., 1926), initially an ardent supporter of psychoanalysis, attempted to work Freudism into the new methodology of Marxism. He believed (1925a) that, on the one hand, psychoanalysis "follows" Marxism in its intention to study the entire human personality, and, on the other, it "has laid the first solid foundation (together with the theory of human responses and reflexes) for a materialist, monistic psychology that takes a positive approach to the mind of the whole person" (pp. 15, 34). Luria presented Freudism as materialist (an analytical, objective study of "true" things) and monistic (perceiving the world as "a single system of material processes"). In his view (1925a), man was whole, and the human mind was part of the world outside, "a product of the activity of the brain and, in the final analysis, of the effects of the social environment and the class relations and conditions of production underlying it on the brain and on each individual human being" (pp. 8–9). Luria argued that Freudism and the budding Marxist psychology shared a dialectical approach based on the assumption that material conditions are changing constantly, dynamically. In his attempt to adapt Freudism to the present moment (1925a), he forced upon it the label of a "positive science of man as a social or, more precisely, a class being" (p. 10).

Another psychoanalyst who attempted to create a socialist version of psychoanalysis was Tatiana Rosenthal. Her exclamation from 1906 – "What a harmony we might have with the combination of Freud and Marx!" – can be considered the first association of Marxism and psychoanalysis (quoted in Neiditsch & Osipov, 1922, p. 517). Rosenthal's biography shows similarities between her life and Spielrein's. Both were Jewesses born in Russia in 1884, patients at the Burghölzli, and studied medicine in Zürich in the first decade of the 1900s. Both became members of the Vienna Psychoanalytic Society, attended the Wednesday meetings (Rosenthal from 1912), and worked in Berlin alongside Karl Abraham. Rosenthal returned to Russia before Spielrein did, at the outbreak of the First World War, to become the director of the polyclinic for the treatment of psychoneuroses, which was attached to the Brain Pathology Research Institute in her birth town, Saint Petersburg. Subsequently, she became head of the psychoanalytical nursery school predating the famous Orphanage-Laboratory directed by Vera Schmidt. Rosenthal committed suicide in 1921 (cf., Rice, 1982a).

In response to papers by Bykhovsky, Reisner, Trotsky, Luria, and others, a potent counterattack was mounted. In general, the response associated Freudism with bourgeois ideology, decadence, destruction, and irrationalism. When Luria (1932a) turned away from psychoanalysis in the early 1930s, he chose the same rhetoric (cf., Miller, 1985, 1998).

Lev Semyonovich Vygotsky chose not to participate in that debate. In his 1927 essay on the historical meaning of the crisis in psychology (Vygotsky, 2004/1927), he stated that supporters of Freudo-Marxism misrepresent psychoanalysis by forcing onto it labels of materialism and monism, and that Freudism and Marxism don't have much in common; but Vygotsky decided not to release it. The paper was first published posthumously in 1982 (ibid.). Vygotsky's earlier lecture on reflexology and psychoanalysis (1987/1926) was in harmony with Freudo-Marxism.[11] Like most practicing psychoanalysts in Russia, Spielrein avoided participating in this debate, which was semiprofessional and underlain with politics.

Passion for science

Little information is available concerning Spielrein's private life in Moscow. She was still a hardworking single mother with financial worries. Devoted to her professional work, she struggled with domestic chores and motherhood. According to the testimony of some school friends of Spielrein's second daughter, Eva (born in Russia eleven years after Renate's birth), Spielrein "didn't care very much about what she looked like, and was filled with a passion for science and for her work. She was not at all practical when it came to household matters, for example she hardly ever cooked" (Covington, 2004, p. 436). Renate, a beautiful girl with dark, curly hair, often stayed with Isaak, his wife, Rakhil, and their daughter, Menikha. According to Menikha, Rakhil thought of Renate as troubled – she was strange, she lied frequently, and she lived too much in her own imaginary world (Covington, 2004, p. 437). Spielrein, a brilliant psychoanalyst and doctor, must have struggled with raising her elder daughter. This is not unusual. Her colleague and fellow psychoanalyst, Hermine Hug-Hellmuth, stated:

> I consider it impossible for anyone to analyze properly his own child. This is so… because in this case the analyst is often driven to re-construct too freely, and also because the narcissism of the parents would make it almost unbearable to hear from their own child the psycho-analytic revelations.
> (Hug-Hellmuth, 1921, pp. 304–305)

Hug-Hellmuth did not have children of her own, but she attempted to treat her deeply troubled nephew, Rudolph (Rolf) Otto Hug, who was in her unofficial care since the death of his mother (Hug-Hellmuth, 1986/1911). Rudolph later claimed that she had psychoanalyzed him without his permission, and he murdered her in 1924 (cf., MacLean & Rappen, 1991; Geissmann, 2005). Similarly, Melanie Klein's daughter and psychoanalyst, Melitta Schmideberg, disowned her, and Klein's son was said to have committed suicide (cf., Grosskurth, 1986).

Upon her arrival in the USSR in 1923, Spielrein was a member of an international intellectual elite that included eminent thinkers of the century: Bleuler, Jung, Freud, Claparède, and Piaget. She had worked alongside them, collaborated with them, inspired many of them, and influenced their views while working in influential intellectual centers from Zürich and Vienna to Berlin and Geneva. In 1923, she was one of the most educated scientists in Soviet Russia and only the second analyst in the country who was sanctioned by the International Psychoanalytical Association (after Wulff). It is likely that her notably less educated and less experienced Moscow colleagues received her with envy and kept their distance.

Spielrein joined the Russian Psychoanalytic Society in the autumn of 1923 (Luria joined at the same time). The following year, she became chair of the society. From September 1923, she was employed at the State Psychoanalytical Institute, the Orphanage-Laboratory, the First Moscow University as chair of the Department of Child Psychology, and as a doctor for the association Third International in a suburb of Moscow. Unfortunately, we only know about her work at the institute and the nursery.

Initially, it seemed that she made a wise choice in coming to Moscow. She could further pursue her transdisciplinary interests and her open approach to science. The character and scope of the institute allowed her to continue her work across the fields of psychoanalysis, psychology, psychiatry, child development, biology, mythology, history of arts, literature, and musicology, and to combine research, teaching, and clinical work. Spielrein's interest in biology (particularly Mendel's work) and evolution (the work of Darwin and Weismann) – one of the most original traits in her approach to psychoanalysis – was in line with Marxist psychology, which believed that science should be rooted in biology. When Spielrein worked at the Ryabushinsky Mansion, it housed a laboratory, a library, an outpatient department, a publishing house, and the *Kinderheim-Laboratorium*. As Launer (2015b) has pointed out:

> In some ways [the institute] resembled the Rousseau Institute in Geneva, with its combination of an experimental school with a training and research centre. It also tried to emulate the institute

that Abraham set up in Berlin in the same year. It was certainly more substantial than anything Freud had succeeded in setting up in Vienna, or Jung in Zürich.

(p. 218)

At the institute, Spielrein held seminars on child development and the psychology of unconscious thought and delivered lectures, all of which were extremely popular among students. In November 1923, she delivered the presentation "Aphasic and Infantile Thought" during one of the meetings of the Russian Psychoanalytic Society (Spielrein, 1923a). Additionally, she examined children and treated patients at the polyclinic. She explored the new field of pedology (alternatively labeled "pedagogical psychology" or "experimental pedagogy"), a comprehensive, transdisciplinary study of children's behavior and development that became very popular in the Soviet Union, Poland, and Ukraine in the 1920s and 1930s and was precisely in line with Spielrein's eclectic interests.

Politics and other people's dreams of success

We may reasonably assume that two Moscow students, Aleksander Luria and Lev Vygotsky, attended Spielrein's lectures and seminars devoted to child analysis, the field in which they would both later be recognized as experts. Furthermore, Luria was employed at the State Psychoanalytical Institute at the same time as Spielrein, and Vygotsky was a close colleague of Isaak Spielrein. By 1923, Spielrein was a senior scholar of worldwide reputation, having almost thirty publications in the field. Luria, very resourceful and productive, was only twenty-one at the time, and Vygotsky, educated as a lawyer and philologist, didn't publish his first psychoanalytical paper until 1924. While both men would go on to enjoy extremely successful careers, both failed to acknowledge Spielrein's influence or to pay tribute to her (cf., Vygotsky, 1962/1934).

Luria adopted Spielrein's eclectic approach to child analysis and combined subjective and objective data. The scope of his work lay at the intersection of psychoanalysis and neurology, or "mind" and "brain." It is simply shocking that in Luria's discussion (1925a) of the theory of drives and the erogenous organs, such as the description "the mother's breast [that] touches the infant's mouth and stimulates the oral mucosa" (p. 31), he failed to mention Spielrein, his colleague and compatriot, in either the main text or one of 120 references. He continued to omit her name throughout his life, not mentioning it even once in his autobiography, *The Making of Mind* (Luria, 1979).

Vygotsky, previously a literary scholar based in Gomel (in the southeast of present-day Belarus), shifted his focus from the analysis of novels and plays to child analysis as soon as he moved to Moscow and became a student at the University of Moscow.[12] That same year – 1924 – he published six psychoanalytical papers (1924a, 1924c, 1924d, 1982/1924, 1983a/1924, 1983b/1924); became an editor of a book (1924b) on "defectology" – training for teachers of disabled children; and delivered four lectures. At the second All-Russian Congress on Psychoneurology in Leningrad,[13] Vygotsky (1987/1926) presented his first paper, a critique of reflexology (proposed by Vladimir Bekhterev and Ivan Pavlov) and in harmony with Konstanty Kornilov's reactology. After the lecture, Kornilov invited Vygotsky to join the Institute of Experimental Psychology in Moscow, which Kornilov had been in charge of since 1923.[14] In the other two papers Vygotsky presented during the Congress on Psychoneurology, he discussed the methodology of teaching psychology (personal communication from Gita Vygotsky, cited by van der Veer & Valsiner, 1993, p. 41).[15] Vygotsky's fourth lecture (1999/1925) delivered that year was given at the Institute of Experimental Psychology and was devoted to the problem of consciousness. In the following years, Vygotsky made a swift and definite transition from literary analysis to psychological empirical research. He focused on the same subject as Spielrein: the relationship between language, speaking, and thought in children. In his textbook (1926) on pedagogical psychology, he discussed three stages in the development of language and children. Like his colleague Luria, Vygotsky also failed to acknowledge Spielrein's impact on the development of his theories. Etkind (1997) draws a parallel between Vygotsky and Jean Piaget in reference to Spielrein's impact on their professional contributions. They both launched their careers in child analysis immediately after meeting her – Piaget in Geneva and Vygotsky in Moscow. The scope of their interests was closely aligned with Spielrein's (cf., Piaget, 1923a, 1923b; Radzikhovskii & Khomskaya, 1981).[16]

Vygotsky and Luria (1994/1925) cowrote an introduction for the Russian translation of Freud's (1955/1920) *Beyond the Pleasure Principle*. Again, they made not a single reference to Spielrein, despite the fact that Freud had named her as a contributor to the development of his theory of drives. While Spielrein was essentially erased from history for over thirty-five years, Luria and Vygotsky became internationally renowned as a neuropsychologist and a developmental psychologist, respectively. Why was there such a discrepancy in their destinies?

First, the unfortunate fate of Russian psychoanalysis and psychoanalysts was closely associated with the political events in Soviet Russia. As soon as Stalin won the battle for power in the Kremlin, he began to eliminate his enemies outside and, subsequently, inside the Communist Party. It didn't take much to be labeled an enemy of the state. As historian Robert Conquest (1968) estimates, between a million and a million and a half Soviet citizens were murdered from 1936 to 1938 by the Soviet secret police – the NKVD, precursors of the KGB (cf., Snyder, 2010, 2015). The USSR was becoming a very dangerous place to live – and to practice psychoanalysis. The welcoming face of Soviet Russia that Spielrein's family depicted soon proved a fragile, temporary illusion.

The second reason Spielrein's legacy remained buried while her colleagues prospered was that Luria decided to play politics. A social and political climber, and a conformist, Luria demonstrated a good understanding of the political demands of the time. The year he arrived in Moscow (1921), he joined a very tight circle of figures in charge of Russian psychoanalysis – including Ermakov, Wulff, and the Schmidts – and became the long-standing "scientific secretary" of the Institute for Psychoanalysis. He initially supported psychoanalysis in the public debate, but he quickly changed sides and joined the attack on Freud when Stalin came to power. Thus, the impact of psychoanalysis in the USSR was sharply diminished. Luria was one of the very few Soviet psychoanalysts who survived the Stalinist purges, the Holocaust, and the Second World War.[17]

Vygotsky – in Luria's words (1979), "the leading Marxist theoretician" (p. 43) – plainly expressed his support of Marxism. In his then-unpublished paper from 1927, Vygotsky (2004/1927) stated, "Marxist psychology is not a school amidst schools, but the only genuine psychology as a science. A psychology other than this cannot exist" (p. 343). As his biographers van der Veer and Valsiner (1993) have determined, "Vygotsky sincerely believed the utopian statements of leading Soviet ideologists and politicians about the future communist state" and was "carried away by the prevailing ideology and the revolutionary zeal of the time" (pp. 55, 56).

Spielrein, on the other hand, was shy, short, with a soft voice and a powerful mind. She did not maneuver between political factions or express interest in success as defined by others' appraisal. She could have acted on her reputation as a sophisticated intellectual from the West with impressive personal connections to Freud, Jung, Abraham, Claparède, Bleuler, and others, but she chose not to. She was driven by dreams different from many of those who would survive Stalin's regime, including Luria and, for example, Aron Zalkind.[18]

The Orphanage-Laboratory connected to the State Psychoanalytic Institute opened on August 19, 1921, and was unofficially run by Vera Schmidt. Luria's (1925b) description of the institution, published in Germany in 1925, might have inspired Anna Freud to set up the Hampstead Child Therapy Course and Clinic in 1951 (later becoming the Anna Freud Centre), a center for treatment, research, and training located in London.[19] Unfortunately, since Vera Schmidt had no analytical education, the Orphanage-Laboratory was mismanaged and strongly influenced by politics. Despite its name, it was not a research center and did not house a laboratory. In reality, it was a boarding school for children of party officials, such as Stalin and the Schmidts.

When Spielrein had arrived in Soviet Russia, the Orphanage-Laboratory was on probation. The Ministry of Education was concerned with ethical and professional standards at the institution and designated a committee to supervise the Institute for Psychoanalysis, its nursery, and the Russian Psychoanalytic Society – a move that might have been purely political. Spielrein and Luria were appointed as consultants to an inspection scheduled for September 17, 1923. The committee, however, annulled the inspection that same day. The nursery was given the prerogative of complying with Marxist ideology. Etkind (1997) speculates that the only person powerful enough to have passed such a resolution was Trotsky.

The following year, the teachers protested against poor working conditions and the "unbelievably difficult atmosphere." They lacked psychoanalytic training and were receiving no support from Ermakov. They wanted "someone with more social and educational experience" to manage the institution. Spielrein reported that "she felt it necessary that her workload be lightened, that she be given more independence and be allowed to have students." In addition, she was dissatisfied that the State Psychoanalytic Institute was not providing her the opportunity to observe children "in person" (Central State Archives of Russia, fund 2307, section 23, file 13, pp. 19–20, cited by Etkind, 1997, pp. 171–172). She must have been very dissatisfied and disappointed with the nursery's unprofessionalism and political inclinations. "The nightmarish conditions of the home, with its desperate and untrained teachers, all trying to cope with the disturbed offspring of communist party bosses, must have seemed like some grotesque antitype of the Burghölzli" (Launer, 2015b p. 222).

Spielrein didn't publish any papers during her stay in Moscow, but we know of her future plans for publications.[20] Swedish journalist Magnus Ljunggren (2001) observed, "There is much to suggest that she was planning a major study based on her work with children that would rival research being done in the West by Melanie Klein and Anna Freud" (personal communication from Ovcharenko, p. 90).

Rostov-on-Don: Moving farther east

Spielrein left Moscow for Rostov-on-Don in the last months of 1924 or at the beginning of 1925. Again, why did she decide to move even farther east, deeper into Soviet Russia? Did she believe that she could escape the Stalinist regime by being over a thousand kilometers from the capital? And why did she finally decide to return to her hometown after more than twenty years? Launer (2015, p. 226) suggests that Spielrein decided to reunite with her husband who had stayed in Rostov since his return from service in the Russian Army during the First World War. When Sheftel received no response from Spielrein to his ultimatum in January 1923, he began a romantic relationship with a non-Jewish doctor from Ukraine, Olga Aksyuk. Their daughter, Nina Snetkova, was born on August 18, 1924. It appears to me that the dissolution of her marriage did not trouble Sabina Spielrein. By as early as 1912, she had declared dissatisfaction, disappointment, and growing indifference toward marriage in her letters to Freud (cf., Carotenuto, 1982, p. 117), her father (Spielrein, 2006, p. 154), and her friend, Rebecca Ter-Oganessian (Richebächer, 2005, p. 195) (Spielrein and Sheftel married in June 1912). She had considered separation and divorce as early as in 1913 (Richebächer, 2005, p. 198). I believe that the birth of Nina might have finally prompted her to return to Rostov. Possibly, it revoked the fantasy of Siegfried, a real/imaginary "spiritual child" she once desired to have with Carl Jung, "an Aryan–Semitic hero" to bridge the theories of Jung and Freud, a fantasy that was (at least temporarily) "vanquished" with the birth of Renate (cf., Carotenuto, 1982, p. 87; Covington, 2015, p. 5; Chapters 1 and 4 in this volume).

Rostov-on-Don was destroyed in large part during the Russian Civil War. As soon as Spielrein arrived, her husband returned to her, and they moved together to a three-room apartment in an old yard that was converted from stables (her official address was 33 Dmitrievskaya).[21] As far as we know, they did not reunite entirely. Sheftel stayed in a separate room with his name on the door, while Spielrein and Renate shared a bedroom. They spent most of their days apart. Their relationship did not improve with time – it was still rather unhappy. Sheftel was intellectually Spielrein's inferior, and, as their acquaintances reported, they were both conscious of that fact (personal communication from Valeria Él'vova, cited by Ljunggren, 2001, p. 91). It is impossible not to compare Spielrein's dissatisfying marriage to Sheftel with her relationship with Jung. Elisabeth Márton may be right to interpret the two relationships in the following way:

> I think what Sabina missed in her relationship with her husband she found in her relationship with Jung – all this inspiration, all this dialogue. She and Jung could talk about music, philosophy, literature, and their poetry. She missed having an intellectual partner with whom she could share ideas. And, of course, there was the love she felt for Jung. I am convinced that she missed all of that very much… In her husband she never found the intellectual partner she needed.
>
> (Covington, 2004, p. 436)

Indeed, in her letter to Eitingon from August 1927, Spielrein expressed deep loneliness caused by isolation from the West and her former colleagues: "I am longing to get together with all of you" (Richebächer, 2016, p. 127). However, there is no indication that she had Jung in mind in particular, and, actually, there is no evidence of Spielrein's ever mentioning Jung again after their correspondence ended in 1919.

Additionally, Sheftel was not easy to live with: he had depressive tendencies and mood swings and would often lose his temper. In these ways, he was like Nikolai, Spielrein's father (cf., Covington, 2015, pp. 117–119; Wharton, 2015, p. 61). Launer (2015b) suggested that Sheftel was also a victim of an unsuitable arranged marriage, was separated from his wife and daughter for almost ten years against his wishes, and might have been traumatized by his experiences as a military doctor (Launer, 2017). The time in Rostov must have also been difficult for Renate, who barely knew Russia or Sheftel, and was about to begin high school.

Marital difficulties notwithstanding, Eva, their second daughter, was born on June 18, 1926. That the newborn was named after Spielrein's mother is unexpected, as Spielrein was distant from her mother. It might have been Sheftel's decision: he maintained a close relationship with his mother-in-law, visiting her almost daily in the 1920s. When the elder Eva fell ill, she moved in with Sheftel's sister, and after Eva's death he sent many emotional letters to Nikolai and Spielrein, calling Eva "Mother Earth" (letter from Sheftel to Spielrein, May 4, 1922, Richebächer, 2005, p. 246).

Spielrein was "suffering badly from malaria and could not trust [herself] to take anything on," and then, in 1926, she was "too hopelessly depressed" to take on any professional responsibilities (Spielrein's letter to Eitingon, Richebächer 2016, pp. 125, 126). Spielrein connected her depression with malaria; however, the fact that she has just become a mother suggests that she was likely suffering from postpartum depression.

With Stalin's political triumph over Trotsky, Freudism lost its protection, and the movement began to gradually dissolve. In August 1925, the State Psychoanalytic Institute and the Orphanage-Laboratory ceased to exist. The children's home was closed after a scandal, when one of the commissions reported children to exhibit "bad sexual behavior" (Etkind, 1997, p. 214). Journals were being closed down, and many psychoanalysts emigrated, left psychoanalysis, or were murdered. In his attack on Freudism in 1924, Vladimir Jurinets (1924) mentioned two psychoanalysts by name: Freud and Sabina Spielrein, which clearly suggests both Spielrein's prominence and her political vulnerability at the time.

In 1927, Vladimir Bekhterev, neurologist and founder of objective psychology (reflexology) and pedology in pre-Soviet Russia, was invited to conduct a neurological assessment of Stalin and diagnosed him with acute paranoia. Bekhterev was poisoned the next day and replaced by Zalkind. Trotsky was expelled from the Communist Party in November 1927 and from the USSR in February 1929. The same year, a Russian sociologist and party official, Isaij Sapir (1929–1930), condemned psychoanalysis and announced the end of the movement in the USSR. Vera Schmidt's last report from the meeting of the Russian Psychoanalytic Society appeared in 1930 and covered the period between January and March. The Society was officially dissolved in 1933. All psychoanalytic books had been withdrawn from bookshops and libraries. In his report on the fate of psychoanalysis in USSR, psychiatrist Elias Perepel (1939) confirmed that the school officially ceased to exist in the early 1930s. In 1931, Stalin named Ivan Pavlov's experimental psychology the only state-approved theory of human behavior and shut down the debate on Freudism. Terms such as "Freudism," "Freud," and "psychoanalysis" were prohibited (cf., Kozulin, 1984).

Stalinism was also gradually clamping down on other fields that had enjoyed the privilege of not being intervened in, including industrial psychology, which Isaak Spielrein founded, and pedology. The latter was banned on July 4, 1936, through the special decree "On the Pedological Perversions," issued by the Ministry of Education. With it, all pedological writings disappeared from public access for several decades, including those penned by Vygotsky, a supporter of the discipline.

Work, work, work

In Rostov-on-Don, Spielrein – "still the only trained analyst" there as of 1927 (Spielrein's letter to Eitingon, Richebächer, 2016, p. 125) – initially worked in the Rostov's school preventive outpatient clinic as a pedologist and treated children and adults in a psychiatric polyclinic. Then, after 1936, she worked as a part-time school physician. We may assume that she maintained a private practice at home and was working in deep secrecy, as she had "a room that was totally empty except for a huge, lonely sofa" (Etkind, 1997, p. 176). This room had no windows.[22] Thus, we are forced to stitch together bits and pieces of information available from extant documents and testimonies to establish what she was actually doing. Sheftel was chief pediatrician in the children's clinic. He might have also seen patients at home. Nonetheless, financial worries persisted. Their daughters began to contribute: Renate returned to Rostov from the Moscow music conservatory for the summer holidays on June 22, 1941 – the day of the German invasion of the USSR – and took up work at a nursery, and both daughters occasionally earned money playing music. They were reportedly both brilliant musicians, Renate a cellist and Eva a violinist (Covington, 2004; Richebächer, 2005). Spielrein cared deeply for her daughters. She supported their musical education and accompanied them to concerts (cf., Covington, 2004, pp. 436–437).

Contrary to popular opinion (Carotenuto, 1982; Kerr, 1994; Hampton, 2002; Faenza, 2003; Cronenberg, 2011), Spielrein's time in Rostov-on-Don was fruitful and productive. She continued to work at the intersection of the fields of child analysis, developmental psychology, and pediatrics. In my opinion, her innovative transdisciplinary approach, exhibited as early as in her best-recognized paper on love and destruction (Spielrein, 1912), is by no means her most astonishing accomplishment. She summarized her cross-disciplinary interests in 1923 in a requisite questionnaire for immigrants to Russia:

> I worked in the Zürich Psychiatric Clinic (with Professor Bleuler) and in a domestic clinic (with Professor Eichhorst) but when I don't recall. I began to do research early on, partly on topics I chose myself, partly on the topics proposed by Profs. Bleuler and Jung. Apart from my own work, I worked in a psychiatric clinic with Professor Bleuler, in a psychoneurological clinic with Professor Bornhöffer (Berlin) and on psychoanalysis with Doctor Jung in Zürich and Professor Freud in Vienna. In Munich I worked on mythology, and the history of arts, and as a teaching-doctor in psychology in the Rousseau Institute of Professor Claparède in

Geneva. I researched source material for the Niebelungenlied and other folktales.

> (Central State Archives of Russia, fund 2307, section 23, file 13, pp. 19–20, cited by Ovcharenko, 1999a, p. 365)

In Rostov-on-Don, Spielrein continued to focus on the subject of speech development. Her approach was rooted in psychoanalysis. She would complement case material with clinical observations of infants and children during play. Spielrein believed that by giving children a lot of space and watching them carefully and meticulously, without interruptions or haste, an analyst would be able to elicit their true emotions and feelings. Spielrein and Hermine Hug-Hellmuth, another pioneer of psychoanalysis, were the first to set up the method of play therapy in the 1910s. Spielrein (1929) – unlike many of her colleagues, including Melanie Klein and Anna Freud – acknowledged Hug-Hellmuth and attributed the first description of the method of play therapy to her. Hug-Hellmuth (1919/1912) discussed the importance of observing one's own children – she had observed and analyzed her nephew, Rudolph Otto Hug. She presented her landmark paper (1921) on play technique during the Sixth International Psychoanalytical Congress at The Hague in September 1920. Spielrein first identified play therapy as a method in "Contributions to an Understanding a Child's Mind" (1913, 2018), the first psychoanalytic essay on children's fantasies. Following Renate's birth on December 17, 1913, she drew considerable inspiration from closely watching her daughter. In her Rostov paper "Some Brief Comments on Childhood" (1928), Spielrein presented results of an observation of children with emotional ailments. Without comments or interruptions, she watched them display their predicaments during play. Her former colleague from Geneva, Jean Piaget, subsequently adopted the method of clinical observation and employed it in his work (cf., Vidal, 2001; Santiago-DelaFosse & DelaFosse, 2002; Harris, 2015; Launer, 2015a).

Between 1925 and 1927, Spielrein delivered two lectures in Soviet Russia: one on reflexotherapy and psychoanalysis to the Society for Neurology and Psychiatry and one titled "The Results of an Investigation into the Animistic Ideas of Children from 3 to 14 Years Old in Moscow and Rostov-on-Don" to the Pedagogical Society of the North Caucasus University in Rostov. In the winter of 1926, she offered two courses on "The Significance of Psychoanalysis for Child Studies" to kindergarten and school doctors. They comprised a six-hour theoretical part and a practical part for Spielrein's demonstration of how to carry out psychological tests on children in kindergartens, schools, and hospitals. In a 1927 letter to Eitingon, she expressed interest in dreams with manifestations of the representations of car, airplane, sun, stars, weather, spiders, shoes, telephone, telegraph, radio, hat, thread, and stitching (Richebächer, 2016). In the winter of 1928, Spielrein gave a lecture entitled "Children's Drawings with Open and Closed Eyes" (1931/1928) to the Pedological Society on the outcome of her experiment with drawing children.[23] Spielrein repeated an experiment she conducted previously with her students in Geneva (1923b, trans. in this volume, Chapter 16), but this time, the majority of the subjects under observation were children suffering from a variety of impairments, disabilities, neuroses, and other mental problems. Spielrein scrutinized several hundreds of drawings created with children's eyes open and closed. The lecture focused on the emergence of autistic and social speech associated with the three-stage model of development of language and thought, first formulated by Spielrein (1920) in her presentation delivered at The Hague, then further expanded in a number of papers (Spielrein, 2015a/1922, 1923a, 1923b, 1931). The core of the argument she presented in 1928 (1931) was that drawings made with closed eyes were more primitive, intimate, emotional, and associated with corporality in comparison to drawings made with eyes open.

A (proto-)feminist

Note that Spielrein's model of development of language and thought comprised three stages – Autistic (the term "autistic" was borrowed from Bleuler; cf., Bleuler, 1924/1916, 1950/1911), Magical, and Social – and anticipated by thirty years Jacques Lacan's concept of the three orders (Real, Imaginary, and Symbolic), associated with stages of child development and also relevant through the entire life (Lacan, 1953, 1986, 2008). The Autistic stage in Spielrein's model and the Real order in Lacan's poststructuralist rereading of Freud draw on Freud's undifferentiated pre-oedipal stage. Then, a child believes itself to be a part of the mother. There is no external world apart from the two of them remaining in a dyadic unity; there is no lack, no unconscious, and no sexual difference. According to Spielrein (2015a/1922), in the second, Magical stage, a child begins to have "a vague idea" of an outer world. It sets about to separate itself from the mother. Spielrein's Magical stage resembles Lacan's Mirror stage, when a child differentiates itself from the mother (m/other) upon recognizing its coherent image in the figurative or metaphorical mirror (that is, of its mother's eyes), identifies with it, and enters the Imaginary realm (Lacan, 1986, 2008). In Spielrein's Social as well as Lacan's Symbolic stages, when "[t]he child learns only slowly to draw a sufficiently clear line between itself and the external world to enable it to see itself from the point of view of its fellow human beings," it acquires "optional," "social language intended for fellow human beings" (Spielrein, 2015a/1922, pp. 302, 301).

The fundamental difference between Spielrein's model of language and thought development and Lacan's notion of the three orders rests in the understanding of when language originates. In Lacan's terms, the first two realms associated with the mother (or the mother-figure) – the Real and the Imaginary – are pre-verbal, pre-linguistic, and pre-cultural. The mother is linked with silence, non-subjectivity, deficiency, and negativity (for Lacan, the first two orders are problematic). Entrance into social and cultural structures and acquisition of language require abandonment of the mother. In the Mirror stage, when a child realizes that the mother turns her loving gaze away from it and toward the father (or the father-figure), the latter separates a child from its mother. Moreover, he forbids further incestuous relations with the mother and forces a child to repress its desire for it. Lacan rewrote the Oedipus complex as a Symbolic structure: a child acquires the notion of self and becomes a subject in language, society, law, and culture on behalf of its father. There is no place for feminine discourse within the Symbolic language.

Differently from Lacan, Spielrein (2015a/1922) recognized the non-verbal, primitive sounds of the Autistic stage as the first language. In her account, it derives from the intimate, carnal contact with the mother: the oral experience of pleasurable suckling, feeding on the mother's breast, touching her breasts with the mouth, and touching her body.

Th[e] expression [of thought] or language should not necessarily be a language of words. Thought can be translated into a melody, into movements (gestures for example), into images, etc. The language expressing our thoughts may be intended to us, as in dreams, what we call autistic language, or it may be intended to others, and is socialized language.

(Spielrein, 1923a; trans. in this volume, Chapter 14)

The autistic language is built with the "sensations of bodies" (Spielrein, 1931/1928), "quite vague sensations of *warmth*, of *softness* (in contact with the mother's body), of *liquid*, of fullness, etc. The baby will naturally always want to repeat these sensations; so it will instinctively bring its mouth into a position, which produces the sounds" (Spielrein, 2015a/1922, p. 297, emphasis added). In contrast to the socialized speech directed at others, the autistic speech exists for its own sake – the sole purpose of pleasure and self-enjoyment.

Spielrein's concept of the primitive, "kinesthetic" autistic language associated with the mother also brings to mind the theories of Hélène Cixous (1976, 1981, 1986/1975) and Luce Irigaray (1980, 1985, 1992, 1999), who argue with the Freudo-Lacanian perspective and postulate a non-Symbolic feminine language (*écriture féminine*) associated with the mother, corporality, and feminine *jouissance*. In their description of autistic or feminine language, Spielrein (2015a/1922) and Cixous (1976), respectively, employ an almost identical set of symbols and associations: mother's body, breasts, womb, mouth, fluid (in Cixous: fetal waters and milk), music, melody, rhythm, tone, pitch, and touch. The "words" of the autistic language are images, music. Cixous (1986/1975) places an emphasis on the voice of the mother belonging to the pre-oedipal stage, heard before the acquisition of the Symbolic paternal language. In Spielrein, the autistic language is linked with a "deep-rooted knowledge, originating long before birth," felt "already in the womb" (Spielrein, 1931/1928; trans. in this volume, Chapter 16). Cixous (1976) differentiates the feminine pre-verbal, semiconscious, and instinctual language of the mother from the official paternal Symbolic language, and postulates feminine creativity, the intangible "writing through the body," "writing in white ink" (mother's milk) (p. 881). Irigaray (1985, 1992, 1999) proposes a language capable of expressing feminine desire – the intangible *le parler-femme*, "speaking (as) woman," or "womanspeak" founded on touch – in response to the Freudo-Lacanian dominance of sight. Spielrein also recognized the parallel existence of the subconscious autistic language of the mother and the conscious symbolic language of the father:

> Our conscious thought is primarily a verbal thought; our subconscious thought has retained the primitive character in the sense that it's mainly kinesthetic-visual thought. Our conscious thought is always accompanied by a parallel organic, hallucinatory thought, translating conscious thought in images; this parallel thought is the subconscious mind/thought.
> (Spielrein, 1923a, trans. in this volume, Chapter 14)

The above argument proves Spielrein to be a pioneering feminist thinker.

Strong convictions

Sabina Spielrein (1929) presented her last known work during the proceedings of the First Congress of Psychiatry and Neuropathology of the North Caucasus Region, held in Rostov-on-Don in 1929. It was a potent defense of Freud and his teaching, delivered during a very turbulent and dangerous time in the USSR, when psychoanalysts feared for their lives. As far as we know, "[i]t may well have been the last time anyone spoke publicly in support of psychoanalysis in the Soviet Union for the next fifty years" (Launer, 2015b, p. 225). This does not come as a surprise. Spielrein was a courageous and free-thinking person. As Launer (2015b) describes:

> Her voice was clear and authoritative. The lecture does not suggest she made any attempt to conceal her past connections. It shows no evidence that she was intellectually dulled, or politically cowed, or that she had stopped seeing herself as part of the movement in which she had played a central formative role.
> (p. 225)

Only a few months later, in January 1930, psychoanalysis was condemned during the First All-Union Congress on Human Behavior in Moscow. Spielrein's last known publication appeared one year later, in 1931, in the leading European scientific journal *Imago*.

As mentioned, Spielrein did not participate in public political discussions. However, I believe she did make some political statements. First, in her private letter to Eitingon from August 24, 1927, Spielrein commented on the association between psychoanalysis and Marxism: "the teaching of Freud and Marx do not need to exclude each other and can co-exist perfectly well" (Richebächer, 2016, p. 123). She was also planning on writing an article on the psychology of Marxism (cf., Launer, 2015b, p. 218). Second, given the political climate of the time, her defense of Freudism from 1929 onward could also be considered a very courageous political statement (Spielrein, 1929; trans. in this volume, Chapter 15). Finally, Spielrein had possibly sided with the protest of teachers employed at the Orphanage-Laboratory and even helped them frame their letter to Ermakov in 1924 (Launer, 2017).

In the period leading up to the Great Terror, on January 25, 1935, the NKVD arrested Nikolai and Isaak Spielrein. Sabina's father and brother were both stripped of their property and tortured. The secret police later released Nikolai, but charged Isaak with espionage and sent him to the gulags. When the Great Terror reached its peak in 1937, scientists, wealthier citizens, and everyone suspected of disloyalty to Stalin could have been easily declared enemies of the state and murdered. Hundreds of thousands were, including Spielrein's three brothers: firing squads executed Isaak on December 26, 1937, Jan in January 1938, and Emil in June 1938. Pavel Sheftel died of a heart attack in 1937; Nikolai died "shaken to the core" in mid-1938 (Ovcharenko, 1999a, p. 367).

According to Menikha Spielrein, Nina Snetkova, Sverlana Konyaeva, Valeria Él'vova, and Eva's school friends, Sabina Spielrein was exhausted, bent, and broken (cf., Etkind, 1997; Ljunggren, 2001; Covington, 2004; Richebächer, 2005). She looked much older than her age and dressed in dark, old-fashioned, worn-out clothes. She was "out of step with the times, almost helpless in everyday Soviet life" (personal communication from Menikha Spielrein, cited by Ljunggren, 2011, p. 44). But she was also remembered as "well mannered, friendly, and gentle" (letter from Menihka Spielrein, Lothane, 2007, p. 84).

Six months after Sheftel's death, Spielrein visited Olga Snetkova in Krasnodar with the proposition that they share responsibility for Eva and Nina should Spielrein herself or Snetkova come to harm under the reign of the Terror. Snetkova agreed, and they spent New Year's Eve of 1937 together at Spielrein's home.

Why did Spielrein decide to stay in Rostov-on-Don? According to her niece, Menikha, Spielrein refused to believe the information on German crimes reported by the Russian media (letter from Menihka Spielrein, Lothane, 2007, p. 84). I personally find her hesitation understandable, having been raised in post-Communist Poland – Spielrein knew that state media controlled by Stalin couldn't be trusted, and any information it provided could easily have been Communist propaganda. The party was a massive propaganda apparatus. Valeria Él'vova stated, "Sabina claimed she knew German culture and had nothing to fear" (personal communication, cited by Ljunggren, 2001, p. 93). Freud also believed in the civility of the Germans and almost missed his chance to escape from Vienna, delaying any action until June 1938, after the *Anschluss*. At the time, European Jews were commonly immersed in German culture, arts, and sciences, and they trusted Germans and regarded the anti-Semitic activities of the 1930s as episodic violent displays of the rabble that would soon dissipate (cf., Trepp, 2001).

However, Spielrein also didn't trust firsthand information about German crimes that Menikha recounted having heard from her teachers who emigrated from Germany to the German department of the Foreign Languages Training Center in Moscow. Menikha recalled Spielrein "was tough as far as her convictions were concerned – she could not be convinced of the contrary" (letter from Menihka Spielrein, Lothane, 2007, p. 84).

I would like to suggest that Spielrein perceived the German-speaking world and the German language as a refuge. She wrote in her diary in 1910, "I don't want to go to Russia! The German language, which I have adopted for my journal, clearly shows that I want to stay as far away from Russia as possible. Yes, I want to be free!" (Carotenuto, 1982, p. 35). In Zürich, as a teenager, she had regained mental health after escaping her family's dysfunctional emotional violence and the suffocating limitations she faced in Russia (cf., Chapter 1, this volume). In Switzerland, she was able to fulfill her wish of becoming a doctor, an aspiration she could not have achieved in Tsarist Russia, which excluded women from higher education and greatly discriminated against Jews in accordance with the *Numerus Clausus* from 1887. It was no coincidence that Zürich was considered a haven for female Russian students (cf., Weizmann, 1949). As Launer (2015b) has pointed out, the struggles Spielrein had experienced in Europe were not comparable to those she would face in the USSR. In German-speaking cities – Zürich, Vienna, and Berlin – she suffered a broken heart, poverty, and health issues; in Soviet Russia, she lived in an atmosphere of omnipresent suffering and death – repressions, purges, the gulags. I find it easier to understand Spielrein's decision not to escape the approaching German army when I consider these circumstances.

Germany invaded western Poland on September 1, 1939, and two weeks later, the Soviet Union invaded Poland's eastern regions. In the summer of 1940, Hitler began preparation for an offensive on the USSR; on June 22, 1941, he launched Operation Barbarossa, thus smashing the political pact between the two nations. The first German occupation of Rostov-on-Don began on November 21, 1941. Spielrein's house was destroyed during an air raid, and she moved to a communal basement with her two daughters along with Olga Aksyuk and Nina Snetkova.[24] Eight days later, the Red Army forced the Germans to retreat to the outskirts of the city. Rostov was subjected to continual bombardment. At that time, there were approximately 40,000 Jews in the city. Around a half of them fled before the second German invasion, as did Aksyuk and Snetkova, who escaped through Chechnya to Dagestan. As far as we know, Spielrein had several opportunities to flee. According to Nina (Spielrein's stepdaughter), Olga Aksyuk wanted to take Eva and Renate with her (Richebächer, 2005, p. 293). Spielrein refused. She must have been exhausted, starving, confused. Perhaps she wanted Germany to take Rostov, as she valued Germany more than Stalinist Russia. Perhaps she still refused to believe that the German policy against Jews was true.

On July 27, the Germans retook Rostov-on-Don. A special detachment, Sonderkommando 10A, commanded by Heinrich Seetzen, entered the city to round up and murder Jews, Communists, and psychiatric patients. They persuaded leaders of the Jewish community that Jews would remain unharmed provided they registered and then assembled at designated points when the time was announced. Those leaders called on Jewish citizens to comply. Some recognized the ploy and committed suicide or barricaded themselves at home, but most Rostov Jews, including Spielrein, believed their community leaders. At 8 a.m. on August 11, 1942, they began to assemble, with Spielrein and her daughters gathering at a designated point on Sozialisticheskaya Street. Her non-Jewish friends watched the gathering of Rostov Jews.

> The last time [Spielrein] was seen was in the summer of 1942, in a column of Jews, destined for annihilation, whom the Nazis were driving in the direction of the Zmeyevsky gully... Poorly dressed, mortally tired and occupied with thoughts known only to herself, Sabina Spielrein shuffled along in the column together with her daughters.
> (personal communication from Nina Snetkova, cited by Ovcharenko, 1999a, p. 368)

She was squeezed into one of the trucks and taken to the immense Zmeyevsky (Snake) Ravine three miles outside of town. According to Leo Maar, a German translator present during the events, Jews were told to strip and leave their clothes and personal belongings in a house near the ravine. They were still being deceived – their executioners assured them they would receive new clothes and travel to a work camp. At the same time, other prisoners were digging mass graves for them (Maar's testimony from an investigation into Heinz Seetzen, Federal Archive, Ludwigsburg, cited by Richebächer, 2005, pp. 298–299). We may assume that the Germans continued as usual: they lined Jews up in front of the graves and shot them. That day, 13,000 Jews were murdered; over the following days, another 3000–5000 were shot at the Jewish cemetery. In total, approximately 27,000 people were murdered in Rostov-on-Don by the Germans: Jews, Communists, psychiatric patients, and others.

Life after death

With every article and book published on the subject, we are discovering and simultaneously "inventing" Sabina Spielrein, as Nicolle Kress-Rosen (2003) put it. This chapter is another piece in a puzzle that is the reconstruction of Spielrein's life, work, and legacy, a puzzle that has yet to be fully reassembled. A notable portion of the relevant documents (mainly correspondence and diaries) remains in the private possession of the de Morsier family (heirs of Édouard

Claparède), yet to be examined, catalogued, and published. Hopefully, we will soon receive access to these documents, and the data they provide will allow us to fill in the blanks. We still have an eleven-year gap to fill with information, between Spielrein's last publication (1931) and her death (1942). For myself, I am very excited to learn what Spielrein was working on in deep secrecy during her final years (for she must have been working!), what her state of mind was, and about the nature of her involvement in politics.

Notes

1 The first quotation is from a ministry of education employee questionnaire Spielrein filed out in September 1923 (Central State Archives of Russia, fund 2307, section 23, file 13, pp. 19–20, cited by Etkind, 1997, p. 172). The second and third quotations are diary entries from April 25, 1905 (cited by Brinkmann & Bose, 1986, pp. 215–216).
2 I would like to express my gratitude to Dr. Alexandra Smith, my PhD supervisor at the University of Edinburgh, for bringing Sabina Spielrein to my attention. I would also like to thank John Launer and Alan Lockwood for their input and guidance.
3 Note the unusual circumstances of the acquisition of the documents, as described by Carotenuto: after Carotenuto's book on Jung/Freud correspondence that mentioned Spielrein's name was released in February 1977, he was contacted by his colleague, Carlo Trombetta, "a close student of the thought of Claparède [who] was much taken with what I [Carotenuto] had written, and the reference to Sabina Spielrein reminded him that he had come across the name in the past, in the course of his historical researches on Claparède. Trombetta later spoke of my [Carotenuto's] book to Professor Georges de Morsier of Geneva, whose memory had miraculously preserved that references made in the text to the subject of Jung and Sabina Spielrein. In October 1977 Carlo Trombetta received a telephone call from de Morsier, who informed him that some documents had been found in the cellars of the Palais Wilson… Would Carotenuto perhaps be interested?" (Carotenuto, 1982, pp. xlii–xliii).
4 Jung's letters to Spielrein were later published by Covington and Wharton (2015, pp. 30–56).
5 The English version was published in 1982.
6 The publication of the Freud/Jung letters in 1974 caused the first – and far less significant – wave of interest in Spielrein. The importance of the volume took some years to percolate through.
7 Diary extracts 1897–1912 (Spielrein, 2006), diary extracts 1906/1907? (Spielrein 2015b/1906–1907), childhood Russian diaries, German student diaries (Wackenhut & Willke, 1994), excerpts from Spielrein's Russian

diary (Lothane, 2015), hospital records (Spielrein, 2006; Wharton, 2015), and family letters (Wackenhut & Willke, 1994; Lothane, 2003; Spielrein, 2006). In 1986, the Jung Estate lifted the initial embargo and released Jung's 1908–1919 letters to Spielrein (Carotenuto, 1986; Covington & Wharton, 2015). As with every researcher writing about Spielrein, I am greatly indebted to those researchers who gathered, scrutinized, and interpreted the discovered material, most importantly to Minder (2001a, 2001b), Covington and Wharton (2015), Graf-Nold (2015), Lothane (2007, 2012, 2015), and Vidal (2001).

8 Religious Jews were in a completely different situation. Jewish religious institutions were shut down, many violent anti-Semitic attacks occurred, and Jews were fleeing to North America and Palestine. Russia had been hostile toward Jews for centuries. First, it refused to admit Jews into its borders. Then, as a result of the Three Partitions of the Polish–Lithuanian Commonwealth (in 1722, 1793, and 1795), "Russia found itself with the largest Jewish population of the world" (Trepp, 2001, p. 195). The policy of the successive Russian tsars and tsarinas was to convert Jews to Catholicism, force them to emigrate, or murder them. In 1791, Empress Catherine II (the Great) established a territorial prison, dubbed a "Pale of Settlement" and limited to the territory of former Poland, very small parts of Ukraine, and the shore of the Black Sea (including Rostov-on-Don). It existed with varying borders until 1917. In the 1880s, Tsar Alexander III instigated pogroms against Jews. Nicholas II followed suit. Although he was executed during the October Revolution of 1917, this did not end the persecution of Jews (cf. Trepp, 2001).

9 Her third brother, Jan, returned to the USSR after Sabina's homecoming. He was a professor of physics.

10 Before the First World War, the Society acted within the Russian Union of Neuropathologists and Psychiatrists, elected in 1911.

11 Vladimir Bekhterev, a neurologist, created reflexology around 1918 as an objective study of physiological reflexes (e.g., gestures, behaviors). It did not study psychic objects; however, it was called the first Marxist psychology and became the dominant school in the Soviet psychology of the 1920s, until it came to be considered incompatible with Marxism in 1929 and was discontinued shortly afterward. Reactology substituted reflexology in an attempt to harmonize with Marxism. It was created around 1930 by Konstantin Kornilov, the contemporary director of the Institute of Experimental Psychology in Moscow. Reactology studied human behavior as an array of reactions (biological and introspective). In 1931, a communist cell of the Moscow Institute of Psychology concluded that Kornilov's theory was anti-Marxist (cf., Pavón-Cuéllar, 2017; Riegel & Meacham, 2017).

12 Vygotsky was admitted to the university via casting of lots. The *Numerus Clausus*, enforced in 1887, set a Jewish educational quota at 10% in cities

within the Pale of Settlement, 5% in cities outside the Pale, and 3% in Moscow and Saint Petersburg (then Leningrad).
13 The name Saint Petersburg was changed to Petrograd in 1914, to Leningrad in 1924, and back to Saint Petersburg in 1991.
14 Psychologist Georgii Ivanovich Chelpanov founded the Moscow Institute of Psychology in 1912 and became head of the institution. In 1923, following a heated discussion, Chelpanov was replaced by his former student, Kornilov. The institute's personnel were replaced with young, eager, often inexperienced Communists, and the name was changed to the Institute of Experimental Psychology (cf., Daniels, Cole, & Wertsch, 2007, pp. 25–41).
15 Gita Vygotsky (Russian: Vygotskaja) was a daughter of Lev Vygostky.
16 Van der Veer and Valsiner (1993) provide a different account of Vygotsky's entrance into psychology. They argue that "Vygotsky's shift in interest towards problems of psychology, pedology, and education was a very gradual one, but one that had taken place to a considerable extent before he started working at Kornilov's Institute of Experimental Psychology in Moscow... [T]he Gomel period marks the origin of Vygotsky's psychological thinking. It was in Gomel that he performed his first psychological experiments and gave his first talks on subjects related to education and psychology. It also was in Gomel that Vygotsky started to absorb the available psychological, educational, and pedological literature" (p. 12).
17 Vygotsky fell ill in the fall of 1925 and died of tuberculosis in 1934.
18 Zalkind was one of the first supporters of Freud in the Soviet Union and one of the first to experiment with psychoanalysis. However, as soon as he climbed the ladder and became important in the Communist Academy, an organ of the party's Central Committee, he joined the attack on Freud (in 1924). Nonetheless, his career came to grief with the banishment of pedology.
19 Four years earlier, Anna Freud founded the Hampstead Child Therapy Course.
20 In an employee questionnaire, Spielrein stated that she planned to publish two new papers on symbolic thought (Central State Archives of Russia, fund 2307, section 23, file 13, pp. 19–20, cf., Etkind 1997, p. 171). Her article "The Problem of the Unconscious in Contemporary Psychology and Marxism" was listed in a prospective contents list for the second volume of the periodical *Psychology and Marxism*, edited by Luria. It was never published. The draft is in Luria's personal collection (cf., Etkind, 1997, p. 172).
21 Aksyuk moved with Nina to Krasnodar. Sheftel visited them regularly (personal conversation with A. Zhuravlyov, cited by Launer, 2015b, pp. 226, 282n2).
22 Covington (2004) compares the room to a womb, a safe place for her patients, but also poses a question about its reflection on Spielrein's state

of mind (p. 436). But let's remember that the room was located in a former stable and that Spielrein was forced to conduct sessions in secrecy, given the political climate. I also disagree with Covington's suggestion that Spielrein's masochistic nature stopped her from fleeing Rostov-on-Don and contributed to her death.

23 Interestingly, Spielrein's father, Nikolai, who was living in Rostov-on-Don at that time, translated the Russian paper into German. Of course, Spielrein could have translated the essay herself. It seems that, despite her traumatic childhood experiences and her difficult relationship with her father, Spielrein remained on good terms with him.

24 The vast majority of information we have concerning Spielrein's life and work during the war years was collected by Sabine Richebächer during archival research and interviews with Nina Snetkova. Richebächer discovered a secret report to Rostov Regional Communist Party Secretary Dvinski from August 24–25, 1943, that included witness testimonials (cf. Richebächer, 2005, pp. 294–302). A copy of that report remains in the archives at Yad Vashem, Jerusalem.

References

Bleuler, E. (1924). *Textbook of psychiatry*. (A.A. Brill, (Trans.). New York: Macmillan. (Orig. publ. 1916.)

Bleuler, E. (1950). *Dementia praecox; or, the group of schizophrenias* J. Zinkin, (Trans.). New York: International Universities Press. (Orig. publ. 1911.)

Brinkmann, E. & Bose, G. (Eds.) (1986). *Sabina Spielrein: Ausgabe in 2 Bänden, Bd. 2: Ausgewählte Schriften*. [*Sabina Spielrein: Issue in 2 volumes, Vol. 2: Selected writings.*] Freiburg: Kore.

Bykhovsky, B. (1923). O metodologicheskikh osnovaniiakh psychoanalitischeskogo uchenia Freida. [On the methodological foundations of Freud's psychoanalytic theory.] *Pod Znamenem Marksizma* [*Under the banner of Marxism*], 11–12, 158–177.

Carotenuto, A. (1980). *Diario di una segreta simmetria: Sabina Spielrein tra Jung e Freud*. [*Diary of a secret symmetry: Sabina Spielrein between Jung and Freud.*] Rome: Astrolabio.

Carotenuto, A. (1982). *A secret symmetry: Sabina Spielrein between Jung and Freud*. A. Pomerans (Trans.). New York: Pantheon.

Carotenuto, A. (1986). *Tagebuch einer heimlichen Symmetrie. Sabina Spielrein zwischen Jung und Freud*. [*Diary of a secret symmetry: Sabina Spielrein between Jung and Freud.*] Freiburg: Kore.

Cifali, M. (2001). Sabina Spielrein: A woman in psychoanalysis, another picture. P. Bennett (Trans.). *Journal of Analytical Psychology*, 46, 129–138.

Cixous, H. (1976). The laugh of the Medusa. K. Cohen & P. Cohen (Trans.). *Signs*, 1(4), 875–893.

Cixous, H. (1981). Castration or decapitation? A. Kuhn (Trans.). *Signs*, 7(1), 41–55.

Cixous, H. (1986). Sorties: Out and out: Attacks/ways out/forays. B. Wing (Trans.). In H. Cixous & C. Clément (Eds.), *The newly born woman* (pp. 63–130). Minneapolis, MN: University of Minnesota Press. (Orig. publ. 1975.)

Conquest, R. (1968). *The great terror: Stalin's purge of the thirties*. New York: Macmillan Company.

Cooper-White, P. (2015a). A comparative timeline: Spielrein, Freud, and Jung. *Pastoral Psychology*, 64, 235–240.

Cooper-White, P. (2015b). Introduction to special symposium: Beyond "A dangerous method": reclaiming Sabina Spielrein's voice in the field of psychology and religion. *Pastoral Psychology*, 64, 231–233.

Cooper-White, P. (2015c). The power that beautifies and destroys: Sabina Spielrein and "Destruction as a cause of coming into being." *Pastoral Psychology*, 64, 259–278.

Cooper-White, P. (2017). *Old and dirty gods. Religion, antisemitism, and the origins of psychoanalysis*. New York: Routledge.

Covington, C. (2004). An interview with Elisabeth Márton. *Journal of Analytical Psychology*, 49, 435–441.

Covington, C. (2015). Comments on the Burghölzli hospital records of Sabina Spielrein. In C. Covington & B. Wharton (Eds.), *Sabina Spielrein: Forgotten pioneer of psychoanalysis*, 2nd edn. (pp. 114–125). New York: Routledge.

Covington, C. & Wharton, B. (Eds.) (2003). *Sabina Spielrein: Forgotten pioneer of psychoanalysis*. New York: Brunner-Routledge.

Covington, C. & Wharton, B. (Eds.) (2015). *Sabina Spielrein: Forgotten pioneer of psychoanalysis*, 2nd edn. New York: Routledge.

Cronenberg, D. (Director) (2011). *A dangerous method* (film). Los Angeles: Sony Pictures Classics.

Daniels, H., Cole, M., & Wertsch, J.V. (Ed.) (2007). *The Cambridge companion to Vygotsky*. Cambridge, UK: Cambridge University Press.

Etkind, A. (1994a). How psychoanalysis was received in Russia, 1906–1936. *Journal of Analytical Psychology*, 39, 191–202.

Etkind, A. (1994b). Trotsky and psychoanalysis. *Parisian Review*, 61, 303–308.

Etkind, A. (1997). *Eros of the impossible: The history of psychoanalysis in Russia*. Boulder, CO: Westview Press.

Faenza, R. (Director) (2003). *Prendimi l'anima*. [Take my soul.] (film). Rome: Medusa Film.

Freud, S. (1955). *Beyond the pleasure principle*. In J. Strachey (Ed.), *The standard edition of the complete psychological works of Sigmund Freud*, Vol. 18, 1–64. London: Hogarth. (Orig. publ. 1920.)

Geissmann, C. (2005). *A history of child psychoanalysis*. London & New York: Routledge. (Orig. publ. 1992.)

Graf-Nold, A. (2015). The Zürich school of psychiatry in theory and practice: Sabina Spielrein's treatment at the Burghölzli clinic in Zürich. In C. Covington & B. Wharton (Eds.), *Sabina Spielrein: Forgotten pioneer of psychoanalysis*, 2nd edn. (pp. 83–113). New York: Routledge.

Grosskurth, P. (1986). *Melanie Klein: Her world and her work.* New York: Knopf.

Hampton, C. (2002). *The talking cure* (play). London: Faber.

Harris, A. (2015). "Language is there to bewilder itself and others": Theoretical and clinical contributions of Sabina Spielrein. *Journal of the American Psychoanalytic Association*, 63(4), 727–767.

Harris, A. (2016). The ghost behind the ghost. In A. Harris, M. Kalb, & S. Klebanoff (Eds.), *Ghosts in the consulting room: Echoes of trauma in psychoanalysis* (pp. 115–120). New York: Routledge.

Hug-Hellmuth, H. (1919). *A study of the mental life of the child.* J.J. Putnam & M. Stevens (Trans.). Washington, DC: Nervous & Mental Disease Publishing. (Orig. MS 1912.)

Hug-Hellmuth, H. (1921). On the technique of child-analysis. *International Journal of Psychoanalysis*, 2, 287–305.

Hug-Hellmuth, H. (1986). Analysis of a dream of a 5 ½ year-old boy. G. Maclean (Trans.). *Psychiatric Journal of the University of Ottawa*, 11(1), 1–5. (Orig. publ. 1911.)

Irigaray, L. (1980). When our lips speak together. C. Burke, (Trans.). *Signs*, 6(1), 69–79.

Irigaray, L. (1985). This sex which is not one. C. Porter & C. Burke (Trans.). In L. Irigaray (Ed.), *This sex which is not one*. (pp. 23–33). Ithaca, NY: Cornell University.

Irigaray, L. (1992). *Speculum of the other woman.* G.C. Gill (Trans.). Ithaca, NY: Cornell University Press.

Irigaray, L. (1999). The bodily encounter with the mother. D. Macey (Trans.). In M. Whitford (Ed.), *The Irigaray reader* (pp. 34–46). Oxford: Blackwell.

Jones, E. (1961). *The life and work of Sigmund Freud.* New York: Basic Books.

Joravsky, D. (1978). The construction of the Stalinist psyche. In S. Fitzpatrick (Ed.), *Cultural revolution in Russia, 1928–1931* (pp. 105–128). Bloomington, IN: Indiana University Press.

Jurinets, V. (1924). Frejdizm i marksizm. [Freudism and Marxism.] *Pod Znamenem Marksizma* [*Under the banner of Marxism*], 8/9, 51–93.

Kelcourse, F. (2015). Sabina Spielrein from Rostov to Zürich: The making of an analyst. *Pastoral Psychology*, 64, 241–258.

Kerr, J. (1994). *A most dangerous method. The story of Jung, Freud, and Sabina Spielrein.* New York: Vintage.

Kozulin, A. (1984). *Psychology in utopia: Toward a social history of Soviet psychology.* Cambridge, MA: MIT Press.

Kress-Rosen, N. (2003). Kindred spirits. B. Wharton (Trans.). In C. Covington & B. Wharton (Eds.), *Sabina Spielrein: Forgotten pioneer of psychoanalysis* (pp. 251–270). New York: Brunner-Routledge.

Lacan, J. (1953). Some reflections on the ego. *International Journal of Psychoanalysis*, 34, 11–17.

Lacan, J. (1986). *The four fundamental concepts of psycho–analysis*. A. Sheridan, (Trans.). London: Penguin/Peregrine.

Lacan, J. (2008). *The mirror stage as formative of the function of the I in écrits: A selection*. A. Sheridan (Trans.) (pp. 1–8.) London & New York: Routledge Classics.

Launer, J. (2015a). Carl Jung's relationship with Sabina Spielrein: A reassessment. *International Journal of Jungian Studies*, 7, 179–193.

Launer, J. (2015b). *Sex versus survival: The life and ideas of Sabina Spielrein.* London: Overlook Duckworth.

Launer, J. (2017). Personal communication, July 8.

Ljunggren, M. (2001). Sabina and Isaak Spielrein. C. Rongle (Trans.). *Slavica Lundensia*, 21, 79–95.

Ljunggren, M. (2011). Memories of a land in stagnation. *Baltic Worlds*, 3, 42–46.

Ljunggren, M. (2014). *Poetry and psychiatry: Essays on early twentieth-century Russian symbolist culture*. C. Rougle (Trans.). Boston, MA: Academic Studies Press.

Lobner, H. & Levitin, V. (1978). A short account of Freudism: Notes on the history of psychoanalysis in the USSR. *Sigmund Freud House Bulletin*, 2(1), 28–29.

Lothane, H.Z. (2007). The snares of seduction in life and in therapy, or what do young Jewish girls (Spielrein) seek in their Aryan heroes (Jung), and vice versa? *International Forum of Psychoanalysis, 16*:12–27, 81–94.

Lothane, H.Z. (2012). Sabina Spielrein between Carl Gustav Jung and Sigmund Freud: The naked truth vs. salacious scandals. *Off the Couch: The Ezine of Psychoanalysis and Culture*, 2(1), 8–15. Online at http://internationalpsychoanalysis.net/wp-content/uploads/2012/05/OffTheCouchV2N1a.pdf. Accessed July 30, 2018.

Lothane, [H.]Z. (2015). Tender love and transference: Unpublished letters of C. G. Jung and Sabina Spielrein. In C. Covington & B. Wharton (Eds.), *Sabina Spielrein: Forgotten pioneer of psychoanalysis* (pp. 126–157). New York: Routledge.

Luria, A.R. (1925a). Psychoanalysis as a system of monistic psychology. *Soviet Psychology*, 16(2), 7–45.

Luria, A.R. (1925b). Russische psychoanalytische Vereinigung. [The Russian Psychoanalytic Association.] *Internationale Zzeitschrift für Psychoanalyse*, 11, 136–137.

Luria, A.R. (1926). Die moderne russische Physiologie und die Psychoanalyse. [The modern Russian physiology and psychoanalysis.] *Internationale Zeitschrift für Psychoanalyse*, 12(1), 40–53.

Luria, A.R. (1932a). Krizis burzhuaznoi psychologii. [The crisis of bourgeois psychology.] *Psychologiia*, 102, 63–88.

Luria, A.R. (1979). *The making of mind: A personal account of Soviet psychology*. M. Cole & S. Cole (Eds.). Cambridge, MA: Harvard University Press. (Orig. unpubl. MS 1976.)

MacLean, G. & Rappen, U. (1991). *Hermine Hug-Hellmuth: Her life and work*. New York: Routledge.

Marti, J. (1976). La psychoanalyse en Russie et en Union Soviétique de 1909 à 1930. [Psychoanalysis in Russia and in the Soviet Union from 1909 to 1930.] *Critique*, 32(346), 199–236.

Márton, E. (Director) (2006). *My name was Sabina Spielrein* (DVD). Chicago, IL: Facets Video. (Orig. released as *Ich hieß Sabina Spielrein*, produced by Helgi Felix/Idé Film Felixson AB, 2002.)

McGuire, W. (Ed.) (1974). *The Freud/Jung letters*. Princeton, NJ: Princeton University Press.

Miller, M.A. (1985). Freudian theory under Bolshevik rule: The theoretical controversy during the 1920s. *Slavic Review*, 44(4), 625–646.

Miller, M.A. (1990). The reception of psychoanalysis and the problem of the unconscious in Russia. *Social Research*, 57(4), 875–888.

Miller, M.A. (1998). *Freud and the Bolsheviks: Psychoanalysis in imperial Russia and the Soviet Union*. New Haven, CT: Yale University Press.

Minder, B. (2001a). Sabina Spielrein: Jung's patient at the Burghölzli. *Journal of Analytical Psychology*, 46, 43–66.

Minder, B. (2001b). A document. Jung to Freud 1905: "A report on Sabina Spielrein." *Journal of Analytical Psychology*, 46, 67–72.

Neiditsch, S. & Osipov, N.E. (1922). Psycho-analysis in Russia. F. Newman & L. Holzman (Trans.). *The International Journal of Psychoanalysis*, 3(4), 514–518. Online at https://archive.org/stream/TheInternationalJournalOfPsychoanalysisIii1922Part4/J_III_1922_Part4_djvu.txt. Accessed July 30, 2018.

Osipov, N.E. (1908a). Psychologicheskie i pskihopatologicheskie vzgliady Sigmunda Freud'a v nemetskoi literature 1907 goda. [Sigmund Freud's psychological and psychopathological views on German literature in 1907.]. *Zhurnal nevropatologii i psikhiatrii* [*Journal of Neuropathology and Psychiatry*], 3–4, 564–584.

Osipov, N.E. (1908b). Psychologiia kompleksov i assotsiativnyi eksperiment po rabotam Tsiurikhskoi kliniki. [The psychology of complexes and the association experiment in the Zürich clinic.]. *Zhurnal nevropatologii i psikhiatrii* [*Journal of Neuropathology and Psychiatry*], 6, 1021–1074.

Ovcharenko, V. (1995). Le destin de Sabina Spielrein. [The fate of Sabina Spielrein.] *L'Évolution Psychiatrique*, 60(1), 115–122.

Ovcharenko, V. (1999a). Love, psychoanalysis and destruction. C.J. Wharton, (Trans.) *Journal of Analytical Psychology*, 44, 355–373.

Ovcharenko, V. (1999b). The history of Russian psychoanalysis and the problem of periodisation. C.J. Wharton (Trans.) *Journal of Analytical Psychology*, 44, 341–352.

Pavón-Cuéllar, D. (2017). *Marxism and psychoanalysis: In or against psychology?* P. Kersey & D. Pavón-Cuéllar (Trans.). New York: Routledge.

Perepel, E. (1939). The psychoanalytic movement in the USSR. *Psychoanalytic Review*, 26, 299–300.

Piaget, J. (1923a). *Le langue et la pensée chez l'enfant* [The language and thought of the child.] Neuchâtel: Delachaux et Niestlé.

Piaget, J. (1923b). La pensée symbolique et la pensée de l'enfant. [Symbolic thought and the thought of the child.] *Archives de Psychologie*, 18(72), 273–303.

Radzikhovskii, L.A. & Khomskaya, E.D. (Eds.) (1981). A. R. Luria and L. S. Vygotsky: Early years of their collaboration. *Soviet Review*, 20(1), 3–21.

Reisner, M.A. (1924). Freid i ego shkola o religii. [Freud and his school on religion.] *Pechat' i revoliutsiia* [Press and revolution], 1, 40–60 & 3, 81–106.

Rice, J.L. (1982a). *Freud's Russia: National identity in the evolution of psychoanalysis.* Piscataway, NJ: Transaction Publishers.

Rice, J.L. (1982b). Russian stereotypes in the Freud–Jung correspondence. *Slavic Review*, 41(1), 19–34.

Richebächer, S. (2003). "In league with the devil, and yet you fear fire?" Sabina Spielrein and C. G. Jung: A suppressed scandal from the early days of psychoanalysis. B. Wharton (Trans.). In C. Covington & B. Wharton (Eds.), *Sabina Spielrein: Forgotten pioneer of psychoanalysis* (pp. 227–249). New York: Brunner-Routledge.

Richebächer, S. (2005). *Sabina Spielrein: Eine fast grausame Liebe zur Wissenschaft. Biographie.* [Sabina Spielrein – An almost cruel love of science. Biography.] Zürich: Dörlemann.

Richebächer, S. (2016). "I long to get together with all of you...": A letter of Sabina Spielrein-Sheftel (Rostov-on-Don) to Max Eitingon, 24 August 1927. M. Molnar (Trans.). *Psychoanalysis and History*, 18, 119–133.

Riegel, K.F. & Meacham J.A. (2017). *The developing individual in a changing world.* New York: Routledge.

Santiago-Delafosse, M.J. & Delafosse, O.J.M. (2002). Spielrein, Piaget and Vygotsky: Three positions on child thought and child language. *Theory and Psychology*, 12(6), 723–747.

Sapir, I. (1929–1930). Freudismus, soziologie, psychologie. [Freudianism, sociology, psychology.] *Pod znamenem marksizma,* [Under the banner of Marxism], (1929) 6, 937–952 & (1930) 1, 123–147.

Snyder, T. (2010). *Bloodlands: Europe between Hitler and Stalin.* New York: Basic Books.

Snyder, T. (2015). *Black earth: The Holocaust as history and warning.* New York: Tim Duggan Books.

Spielrein, S. (1912). Die Destruktion als Ursache des Werdens. [Destruction as the cause of Becoming]. *Jahrbuch für psychoanalytische und psychopathologische Forschungen*, 4, 465–503. (Trans. this volume, Chapter 6.)

Spielrein, S. (1913). Beiträge zur Kenntnis der Kindlichen Seele. [Contributions to an understanding of the child's mind.] *Zentralblatt für Psychoanalyse und Psychotherapie*, 3, 57–72. (Trans. in Spielrein, 2018, pp. 135–154.)

Spielrein, S. (1920). On the question of origin and development of speech. *International Journal of Psychoanalysis*, 1, 359–360.

Spielrein, S. (1923a). Quelques analogies entre la pensée de l'enfant, celle de l'aphasique et la pensée subconsciente. [Some similarities between thinking in children, aphasia, and the subconscious mind.] *Archives de Psychologie*, 18, 305–322. (Trans. this volume, Chapter 14.)

Spielrein, S. (1923b). Die drei Fragen. [The three questions]. *Imago*, 9, 260–263. (Trans. this volume, Chapter 13.)

Spielrein, S. (1928) Einige kleine Mitteilungen aus dem Kinderleben. [Some brief comments on childhood.] *Zeitschrift für Psychoanalytische Pädagogik*, 2, 95–99.

Spielrein, S. (1929). Dr. Skalkovskiy's report. (Trans. this volume, Chapter 15.)

Spielrein, S. (1931). Kinderzeichnungen bei offenen und geschlossenen Augen. [Children's drawings with eyes open and closed.] A. Spielrein (Trans. from Russian). *Imago*, 17, 359–391. Orig. lecture "*Detskie risunki pri otkrytyx i zakrytyx glazax,*" Rostov-on-Don, Russia, 1928. (Trans. this volume, Chapter 16.)

Spielrein, S. (2006). *Nimm meine Seele: Tagebücher und Schriften* [*Take my soul: Diaries and writings*]. T. Hensch (Trans.). Freiburg: Freitag.

Spielrein, S. (2015a). The origin of the child's words Papa and Mama: Some observations on the different stages in language development. B. Wharton (Trans.). In C. Covington & B. Wharton (Eds.), *Sabina Spielrein: Forgotten pioneer of psychoanalysis*, 2nd edn. (pp. 233–248). New York: Routledge. (Orig. publ. 1922.)

Spielrein, S. (2015b). Unedited extracts from a diary (with a prologue by Jeanne Moll.). J. Moll, P. Bennett & B. Wharton (Trans.). In C. Covington & B. Wharton (Eds.), *Sabina Spielrein: Forgotten pioneer of psychoanalysis*, 2nd edn. (pp. 14–29). New York: Routledge. (Orig. unpubl. MS c. 1906–1907.)

Spielrein, S. (2018). *The essential writings of Sabina Spielrein: Pioneer of psychoanalysis*. R. Cape & R. Burt (Eds. & Trans.). New York: Routledge.

Stalin, J.V. (2013). *Dialectical and historical materialism*. New York: Prism Key Press. (Orig. publ. 1938.)

Trepp, L. (2001). *A history of the Jewish experience*. Springfield, NJ: Behrman House.

Trotsky, L. (1960). *Literature and revolution*. R. Strunsky (Trans.). Ann Arbor, MI: University of Michigan Press. (Orig. publ. 1924.)

Van der Veer, R. (1990). The reform of Soviet psychology: A historical perspective. *Studies in Soviet Thought*, 40(1), 205–221.

Van der Veer, R. (2011). Tatyana on the couch: The vicissitudes of psychoanalysis in Russia. In S. Salvatore & T. Zittoun (Eds.), *Cultural*

psychology and psychoanalysis: Pathways to synthesis (pp. 49–65). Charlotte, NC: Information Age Publishing.
Van der Veer, R. & Valsiner, J. (1993). *Understanding Vygotsky: A quest for synthesis.* Cambridge, UK: Wiley-Blackwell.
Vidal, F. (2001). Sabina Spielrein, Jean Piaget: Going their own ways. P. Bennett, (Trans.). *Journal of Analytical Psychology*, 46, 139–153.
Vygotsky, L.S. (1924a). Foreword. In A.F. Lazursky (Ed.), *Psychologija obshchaja i eksperimental'naja* (pp. 5–23). [*General and experimental psychology.*] Leningrad: Gosudarstvennoe Izadatel'stvo.
Vygotsky, L.S. (Ed.) (1924b). *Voprosy vospitanija slepykh glukhonemykh i umstvenno oststalykh detej.* [*The issues of education of blind, deaf and mute children.*] Moscow: Izdatel'stvo SPON NKP.
Vygotsky, L.S. (1924c). Foreword. In *Voprosy vospitanija slepykh, glukhonemykh i umstvenno oststalykh detej* (pp. 3–4). [The issues of education of blind, deaf and mute children.] Moscow: Izdatel'stvo SPON NKP.
Vygotsky, L.S. (1924d). K psychologii i pedagogike detskoj defektivnosti. [Towards the psychology and pedagogy of defectiveness in children.] In *Voprosy vospitanija slepykh glukhonemykh i umstvenno oststalykh detej* (pp. 5–30). [The issues of education of blind, deaf and mute children.] Moscow: Izdatel'stvo SPON NKP.
Vygotsky, L.S. (1926). *Pedagogicheskaya psychologiya: Kratkii kurs.* [*Pedagogical psychology: A short course.*] Moscow: Izdatel'stvo Rabotnik Prosveshcheniya.
Vygotsky, L.S. (1962). *Thought and language.* A. Kozulin (Trans.). Cambridge, MA: MIT Press. (Orig. publ. 1934.)
Vygotsky, L.S. (1982). Foreword. In *Sobranie sochinenij: Vol. 1. Voprosy teorii i istorii psychologii* (pp. 63–277). [*Collected works, Vol. 1. The problems of the theory and history of psychology.*] (hereafter CW.) Moscow: Pedagogika. (Orig. publ. 1924.)
Vygotsky, L.S. (1983a). Defekt i kompensacija [Defect and compensation]. In *Sobranie sochinenij: Vol. 5. Osnovy defektologii* (pp. 34–49). [CW, Vol. 5. The fundamentals of defectology.] Moscow: Pedagogika. (Orig. publ. 1924.)
Vygotsky, L.S. (1983b). Slepoj rebenok [A blind child]. *Sobranie sochinenij: Vol. 5, Osnovy defektologii* (pp. 86–100). [CW, Vol. 5. The fundamentals of defectology.] Moscow: Pedagogika. (Orig. publ. 1924.).
Vygotsky, L.S. (1987). The methods of reflexological and psychological investigation. R. Van Der Veer (Trans.). *CW, Vol. 3. Problems of the theory and history of psychology* (pp. 35–49). New York & London: Plenum. (Orig. publ. 1926.)
Vygotsky, L.S. (1999). Consciousness as a problem in the psychology of behavior. N. Veresov (Trans.). *Undiscovered Vygotsky: Études on the prehistory of cultural-historical psychology* (pp. 251–281). Frankfurt am Main: Peter Lang. (Orig. publ. 1925.)

Vygotsky, L.S. (2004). The historical meaning of the crisis in psychology: A methodological investigation. R. Van Der Veer (Trans.). In R.W. Rieber & D.K. Robinson (Eds.), *The essential Vygotsky* (pp. 227–343). New York: Kluwer Academic/Plenum. (Orig. unpubl. MS 1927; 1st publ. 1982.)

Vygotsky, L.S. & Luria, A. (1994). Introduction to the Russian translation of Freud's 'Beyond the pleasure principle'. In R. van der Veer & J. Valsiner (Eds.), *The Vygotsky reader* (pp. 10–18). Oxford, UK: Blackwell. (Orig. publ. 1925.)

Wackenhut, C.V. & Willke, A. (1994). *Sabina Spielrein. Missbrauchsüberlebende und Psychoanalytikerin.* [*Sabina Spielrein: Abuse survivor and psychoanalyst.*] Unpubl. diss., Hannover, Germany.

Weizmann, C. (1949). *Trial and error: The autobiography of Chaim Weizmann.* London: Hamish Hamilton.

Wharton, B. (Trans.) (2015). Burghölzli hospital records of Sabina Spielrein. In C. Covington & B. Wharton (Eds.), *Sabina Spielrein: Forgotten pioneer of psychoanalysis*, 2nd edn. (pp. 57–82). New York: Routledge.

Young, D. (1979). Ermakov and psychoanalytic criticism in Russia. *Slavic and East European Journal*, 23, 72–86.

Zetkin, K. (1929). *Reminiscences of Lenin. Dealing with Lenin's views on the position of woman and other questions.* London: Modern Books.

Chapter 4

"Language is there to bewilder itself and others"
Theoretical and clinical contributions of Sabina Spielrein[1]

Adrienne Harris

Introduction

There are many ways to begin this story. On August 18, 1904, a young Russian woman (she is nineteen) is admitted to the Burghölzli hospital. She is described as disturbed, hysterical, psychotic, volatile. She is Jung's first patient and her transference to him is almost immediately passionate and highly erotized. Later, she is caught up in the conflicts and breakdown of the relationship of Freud and Jung.

We know this version of Sabina Spielrein's entrance into the medical and psychoanalytic worlds of Europe from films and some early biographies, from her letters and diaries written in the period 1906–1907 (Spielrein, 2015b/1906–1907), and even from her psychiatric records (Covington & Wharton, 2015, pp. 57–82). Spielrein has been cast as a young madwomen, later involved in a boundary violation, precocious and brilliant, but sexually transgressive. In this version, she is often weighed down by a masochistic character that is used to explain her marriage, her relationships, her work choices, and indeed all of the events right up to her doom in 1942 when Germans invaded her town of Rostov-on-Don.

My commitment to writing about Spielrein's intellectual and clinical life, which had been entirely erased for half a century, began in the mix of distress and irritation I felt at this version of her story. In focusing on the more salacious accounts of the fought-over child/woman caught between the two big Others, Freud and Jung, Spielrein reappears, but too much as a kind of pornographic caricature. Just as she resurfaces, we are in danger of losing this interesting thinker again.[2]

So I am beginning the story another way. Sabina Spielrein, like many young Russian women of her class and generation (she was born in

1885), comes to Europe hungry for education. By all accounts, she is a particularly brilliant student. Switzerland was a kind of Mecca for young, often Jewish, Russian women, a place finally to grow and thrive intellectually and professionally.[3] Chaim Weizman, the first president of Israel, marries a girl from Rostov. He and his wife are in Switzerland contemporaneously with Spielrein.

> This group of girls from Rostov differed significantly from ordinary Jewish girls in university in Switzerland at that time – in their appearance, manners and views. They were much more attractive than girls of their age from the Pale of Settlement, who looked, for the most part, nervous, disillusioned, exhausted and hungry.
> (Etkind, 1997, p. 133)

Spielrein arrives in Switzerland in a state of breakdown and eventually becomes a patient at the Burghölzli hospital. She is discharged after nine months, and at the end of that period, Eugen Bleuler, the hospital head, recommends that she begin medical school. John Launer's (2015) biography of Spielrein notes that by the second half of her stay at the hospital, she is engaged in scientific studies, assisting in research, including some of Jung's work on word associations, and she seems markedly better (p. 34).

Rightly, we see Spielrein (and her Russian contemporaries like Max Eitingon, Lou Andreas-Salomé, and Moishe Wulff) as grounded both in European and Russian philosophy and cultural thought and at the forefront of the analytic communities developing in Europe and later in Russia (Miller, 1986, 1998; Etkind, 1997; see also Chapter 3 in this volume). Throughout her working and writing life, Spielrein was anchored in Freudian and Jungian theory. By the 1920s and after her medical training, one sees her deep engagement with psychology, and with more specialized disciplines like physiology, linguistics, and child development.

Spielrein qualifies as a doctor, writes a dissertation on schizophrenia, likely the first psychoanalytic dissertation[4] (Spielrein, 1911, excerpt in this volume; for a full translation, see Spielrein, 2018). Late in 1911, Spielrein gives a paper at the Wednesday night meeting of the Vienna Psychoanalytic Society (Nunberg & Federn, 1974, pp. 329–335),[5] about a month after being voted into membership (ibid., p. 280). She would have been twenty-six years old and only the second woman admitted to the Society. Her trajectory after Vienna is complex and includes marriage and a child, as well as work in Berlin, Zürich, Lausanne, and finally Geneva for a period of productive writing and thinking. She has over thirty publications; many are significant, all are interesting.

A later move to Moscow in 1923 brings her to the newly formed Soviet Union during a period there in which psychoanalysis is very much in the ascendant. At that time and in that place, Spielrein would have been one of the most senior figures in psychoanalysis in its period of great creativity. It was a brief optimistic historical moment in which, in many areas in the arts, sciences, and social theory, there were great hopes for the integration of political thought, psychoanalysis, and social science. Spielrein is doomed finally by the tragic, not to say vicious destruction of psychoanalysis in the Soviet Union in the late 1920s. She returns to her husband in the context of moving from Moscow back to Rostov and has another child. In 1942, in Rostov, she is murdered, with both her children, by advancing German troops.

Each of these stories carries something of her extraordinary and extraordinarily tragic history. The quote in this essay's title is one of Sabina Spielrein's many enigmatic statements, almost buried in her powerful and difficult paper, "Destruction as the Cause of Becoming" (trans. this volume, Chapter 6; see also Chapter 2; cf., Spielrein, 1912; 1994/1912, 1995/1912). By all accounts, this essay, presented at that Wednesday night meeting, had, from the beginning, a difficult reception.[6] Otto Rank's minutes on the presentation attest to challenges and incomprehension, along with fascination. The minutes were recorded by Rank, but compiled and translated decades later by Nunberg and Federn (1974, pp. 329–335). In his report, Rank notes that Spielrein herself felt that the group had not understood, nor had she fully explained, her focus on transformation. Creation and destruction are entwined in the project of transformation and growth. This dialectic is one to which she is attuned for the rest of her writing and working career.

However difficult and challenging that paper may be, I would argue that it rightly belongs in the psychoanalytic canon. Yet, as we know, Spielrein herself, and much of her subsequent work, vanished, disappearing for much of the rest of the century. We know of her paper on sexuality and destruction probably only because of Freud's reference to it in his paper on the death instinct, *Beyond the Pleasure*

Principle (Freud, 1955/1920, p. 55n2). Her paper was not available in English until the 1980s. But she has many publications scattered across several different languages and collected only in German and Russian editions, although an English edition is underway.

She is linked to five of the most significant intellectual figures in the first half of the twentieth century: Freud, Jung, Jean Piaget, Aleksander Luria, and Lev Vygotsky. In their time, these latter two were spoken of, respectively, as the Beethoven and the Mozart of Russian psychology. Spielrein is a few years younger than her Russian colleague, Max Eitingon, ten years older than Vygotsky and Piaget, and twenty years older than Luria. That Spielrein appears only as a footnote in *Beyond the Pleasure Principle* (ibid.) and another footnote in his essay on Schreber (Freud, 1958/1911:79) seems almost incomprehensible.

In the two decades since the astonishing, almost random recovery of her letters, diaries, and papers, a devoted and increasingly active international network of scholars working on Spielrein has been developing. I write this chapter deeply indebted to this very interdisciplinary group.[7]

I am aware of the dangers in this reconstructive project. Seeing Spielrein's intellectual and professional life silenced both in its time and for decades afterwards, I run the risk of a repolarizing reversal, making Spielrein the mothership from which all interesting ideas, classical, postmodern, and relational, flow. I am hoping to restrain that impulse enough to help you encounter a deep and original thinker, contributing clinical and theoretical work in some very hot spots, key locations at a time of intellectual and cultural synergy in the period from roughly 1911 to 1928, an important period in the history of psychoanalysis and a seedbed for the study of child development.

My approach has been both to do historiography and to make speculative links across theory and practice and across historical periods. I can locate Spielrein in her intellectual and cultural milieu and in the potent moments in psychoanalytic history in the 1920s. I have also felt free to associate Spielrein's ideas, her preoccupations, and her strategies and methods to other figures in psychoanalysis, spread across the past century. I can find echoes of and affinities with Spielrein in Loewald (1980a, 1980b), in Ferenczi (1989/1924), in Matte-Blanco (1975, 2005), in the new focus on reverie (Ogden, 1997; Ferro, 2005), and in the renewed attention to the complexities of representation and unrepresentable experience (Botella & Botella, 2005; Ferro, 2005; Levine et al., 2013).[8] She can also be seen in the context of the unfolding discourse on sexuality, regression, and excess from the 1920s onward (Muller, 1932; Lampl-de Groot, 1933; Ferenczi, 1989/1924; Stein, 1998; Laplanche, 1999, 2016; Dimen, 2003; Saketopoulou, 2015).

It is not that Spielrein foresees and forecasts all of these developments, only that the deep interests she pursued over her career take her into waters we are still exploring and into ways of thinking that we continue to evolve and practice. There is above all and continuously Spielrein's deep devotion and commitment to psychoanalytic ideas and practices, a devotion that by the end of her life would have become profoundly dangerous. There is her attention to bridging and transdisciplinary work. There is much evidence of her attunement to patients and her interest in clinical nuances and in forms of interpretation that remain subtle and deliberately un-intrusive. There is her great talent for child observation, evidenced in research and in treatment. I am intrigued by her unfolding work on sexuality, on mind and mind's otherness, and on the unconscious underpinnings of thinking and speaking. I consider that the placement of Spielrein in the genealogy of psychoanalysis, in its lineage (perhaps more simply in the conversation), to be a matter of ethics, as well as of intellectual interest and utility.

Another danger in this pursuit of Spielrein is that in focusing on her theoretical and clinical contributions I might lose her voice and her individuality and might minimize the questions that initiated this project. What happened? Is this a story about the fate of women or outliers in psychoanalysis, the propensity for eclipse and erasure that "disappeared" a number of figures, perhaps most significantly Ferenczi? Is it the conforming and not the maverick woman who stays in view in this field? Do Spielrein's work and reputation continue to be filtered through the anxieties about her relationship with Jung, the hovering suspicions around boundary violations that so often impugn the reputation of the victim? There is also the effect of an often crushing triangulation as Spielrein is caught up in the conflict between Jung and Freud.

It is not always easy to locate Spielrein's character and sensibility, or even her idiom as a writer and thinker. Nicole Kress-Rosen (2003) makes two important comments: "We are discovering [Spielrein] and inventing her at the same time" (p. 251), and, most tellingly, that in reading Spielrein in her own language, in the texts as she constructed them, the affects that most emerge are "sadness" and "loneliness" (p. 252).

There are larger political issues that play a part as well. Regarding her work in Moscow, we could ask if Spielrein's life and her work are collateral damage when psychoanalysis, all of its institutions, and many of its adherents are destroyed in the Soviet Union during the 1930s. The murder of Trotsky and the ascendency of Stalin doomed many revolutionary projects, psychoanalysis among them. It is hard not to wonder about the ways her fate and the importance of her work were inevitable casualties, on the one hand, of the ideological shifts in the Soviet Union, and, on the other, of the severing of cognitive studies from clinical and psychoanalytic ideas in the post-World War I period.

Spielrein's psychoanalytic perspective, which was lifelong and unwavering, would have been very dangerous in the Soviet Union, but also unwelcome in the postwar West, where the cognitive revolution was underway, engendering experimental and theoretical work focused on logical thinking, mastery of language, symbolization, and abstraction. These postwar developments are periods of expansive power for Piaget (1923, 2001/1926) and Vygotsky (1962/1934, 1978, 1987). Along with all of these changes, psychoanalysis loses its presence in these transdisciplinary ventures. Thus, Spielrein's work disappears as well. These losses, very much linked, are a central theme of this chapter.

My project began with a quite general agenda: turning a ghost into an ancestor. Rather quickly and surprisingly, it morphed into something more: a focused exploration into two key moments in transdisciplinary work. Here, I am focusing on the interactive development of psychoanalysis, child analysis, and child development studies at an interface at which, I believe, Spielrein is an important interlocutor. The two periods – one in Western Europe, most notably in Geneva between 1913 and 1923, and the other in Moscow from 1923 to the early 1930s – launched theories and methods regarding both research and clinical treatment that remain very much alive in both psychoanalysis and developmental psychology.

For about eight months, Spielrein was Piaget's analyst. To a modern reader, this does not appear to have been a long treatment, although in that period, it was perhaps a more typical length. Piaget certainly sought to distance himself from the treatment with Spielrein and from psychoanalysis more generally. But we might keep the question of transference (and countertransference) as a subtext of their collaborations and professional encounters. It appears that Piaget was present at the International Psychoanalytical Association (IPA) Congress in 1920 at The Hague, where Spielrein presented a paper on language and thought of the child, a paper that includes a model of stages in language development proceeding from what she termed "autistic" or private speech, through stages of magical speech and then social speech.

A few years later, Piaget published a book with a nearly identical title and a comparable model of speech development (Piaget, 2001/1923). These ideas appear in other publications (Piaget, 1923, 1927, 2013/1932). Similarly, around the same time, between 1924 and 1926, Vygotsky published a series of articles on language and thought and on the relation of inner speech to social communication (Vygotsky, 1987). There is much to be said and much already written about where these three theorists overlap and where they differ and part company (Vidal, 2001; Santiago-DelaFosse & DelaFosse, 2002), but I am addressing a particular moment when a number of shared ideas, models, and methodologies emerged, overlapping and complementing one other. It is a potent emergent moment for theory and practice, and one person goes missing.

It is this conundrum of distinction and erasure that pressures one to overwrite her story. So my effort here is to keep us attentive to her biography and to the question of what happened, even as we explore an increasingly mature, multiply skilled, always scholarly and rigorous thinker, practicing an imaginative and creative mixture of psychoanalytic work, theory building, research, and teaching.

When I began reading about Spielrein's years in Geneva, a door blew open in my mind and, in an unexpected way, two stages in my intellectual and professional life linked together (Harris, 1976). As a developmental psychologist immersed in Piaget, Vygotsky, and psycholinguistics, I had read all of these texts without ever seeing the psychoanalytic ideas that undergirded them. As I now reread early Piaget, Vygotsky, and Luria, the DNA of psychoanalysis, and therefore of Spielrein, is everywhere, hidden in plain sight.

Piaget speaks of child thought as "like a nest of tangled threads which may break at any moment." Spielrein talks of the "stickiness" of thought, the complex "crossings" and splitting of ideas and verbal associations and play (Spielrein, 1923c, trans. this volume, Chapter 14). Children's minds, Piaget says, "are woven on two different looms, one above the other." The lower loom he assigns to Freud. Indeed, Spielrein was always attentive to the subconscious aspects of speech, the primitive cast of mind that will be bridged to symbolic language.

Both in Geneva and in Moscow, Spielrein would have been part of two projects Freud was very concerned with. First and most prominently, Freud was deeply engaged in the task of internationalizing psychoanalysis. Spielrein was certainly a participant in the efforts in Geneva to establish various centers of training. This was, for Freud and others, a project in which Russia, Russian patients, and Russian institutes were crucial. Spielrein is known to have been active at the Hague Congress in 1920, where discussions and planning for the development of psychoanalysis in Russia were underway.

The second project involved Freud's interest in interdisciplinary efforts in the service of psychoanalysis as a branch of general psychology. Spielrein's work, spanning disciplines, research, and practice, could be viewed in the light of Freud's explicit agenda to embed psychoanalysis within a general theory of psychology, indebted to various disciplines, including philosophical reflections on mind:

> In an 1896 letter to Fliess, Freud wrote: "I am continually occupied with psychology – really metapsychology; Taine's book *L'intelligence* suits me extraordinarily well." In August of 1898 Freud wrote Fliess about another psychological philosopher [Lipps] who had caught his interest: "I have set myself the task of building a bridge between my germinating metapsychology and that contained in the literature."
>
> (Makari, 1994, pp. 564–565)

Freud saw his metapsychology (which we should note he calls meta*psychology* not meta*psychoanalysis*) in a lineage from philosophy as well as experimental psychology. In looking at Spielrein's work and its influences, I think one can track movement both from philosophy and physiology, but also in the opposite direction; that is, from psychoanalysis into psychology, particularly developmental psychology. At this historical juncture, Spielrein is the linchpin and central engine in this migration of psychoanalytic methods and ideas into child psychology, particularly the area of embodiedness and symbolization in the unfolding of speech and thought, and in the study of levels of consciousness. I am going to argue that the shattering of these collective moments of work severed cognitive studies from its important roots in psychoanalysis. The loss of these transdisciplinary possibilities – with their scientific, clinical, and aesthetic elements – is significant.

I have characterized the periods, first in Geneva and then in Moscow, as moments of cultural synergy, two "hot spots" between which Spielrein is the common thread. What emerges in each of these cities is a unique collaborative community that arises and fosters the emergence of powerful new ideas for forms of work. The intellectual products of these hot spots are made from the interweaving of persons, ideas, philosophical underpinnings, and methodologies. There are perhaps many examples of this kind of synergy. I am thinking of the postwar collaborations of Klein, Bion, Rosenthal, and Segal as they worked out issues of projection and of transference phenomena generally, leading to insights into projective identification and its role in communication.[9] The collaborative work and the individual writings might be best thought of as a field in which the gestalt is more than the elements and where the intellectual outcome is emergent.

Throughout my intellectual and professional life, I have found myself drawn to a place of work and theory development that is primarily transdisciplinary. I am interested in a location where movements across intellectual worlds – psychology, psychoanalysis, epistemology, child development – find a moment of intersection and interaction. Spielrein's work sits at just such an intersection. She bridges these worlds, a project and practice that marks her as very contemporary (Fonagy, 1995). Chaos theory (Freeman, 1990; Harris, 2005) applies the term "strange attractor" to situations and structures where elements unpredictably interact such that new forms of thinking and working can emerge. One might certainly argue that this was Freud's vision, one spoiled by various movements of sectarian exclusion.

After months of reading and preparing this chapter, I can summarize what I think Spielrein's theoretical contributions are and how significant the loss of this person and her work is. I will then spend the rest of the essay exploring in more detail the scope and reach of her ideas, while also keeping our attention on her life trajectory and forces in the field and in history. I will start with my conclusions and then, in later sections, try to show you how I got there.

First, Spielrein brings to developmental psychology the method of observation, which she would have learned in the context of child analytic work. Hermine Hug-Hellmuth (1919/1912), in her seminal *Mental Life of the Child*, notes the origins of child psychoanalysis in the analyst's observation of their own children. Hug-Hellmuth has suffered an eclipse not unlike Spielrein's.[10] By 1913, Spielrein had published a paper on children's playful and erotic investment in speech games through observations of her first daughter, Renate (Spielrein, 1913a, 2018, pp. 135–154), and later a paper on a boy's phobic response to certain emotionally loaded words and symbols (2001a/ 1913a). These works, and Spielrein's work on child language, all antedate similar work by Melanie Klein and Anna Freud, yet most histories of child psychoanalysis start with those two figures.

Launer (2015, pp. 190, 200) notes that Abraham, Klein, Anna Freud, Ferenczi, and Hug-Hellmuth were present at the Congress at The Hague where Spielrein delivered her paper on language and thought, complete with a stage theory, clinical data, and a focus on the unconscious in infantile life (summarized in Spielrein, 1920d), a topic she later pursued in conjunction with Piaget.[11] With only forty attendees at that congress, it would seem very likely that all of these figures had exposure to Spielrein's ideas and work. Examining Klein's early papers on child analysis (1926, 1932), one sees that she cites Abraham, Ferenczi, Gross, and Groddeck, along with Freud. Except for a single footnote in Klein's 1926 paper (p. 56), Spielrein goes unmentioned.

Perhaps our field has built a canonical story, as many empires do, upon the disappearance of indigenous people – many, though not all of them, women. Why does this matter? Klein and Anna Freud are great creative forces in psychoanalysis. As Isaac Newton famously remarked, "If I have seen a little further it is by standing on the shoulders of giants." This notion dates back to the twelfth century and has found expression ever since. The idea reflects a feeling among many intellectual communities that lineage matters, that it is an ethical matter to acknowledge what comes before, and also that this care with genealogy creates a richer, deeper account of ideas and concepts as they unfold.

Second, Spielrein holds a very dialectical theory of developmental change, of the transactions between internal and external worlds in which affect, social interaction, and evolving intention are all present. She was, from the outset of her working life, interested in transformation. She was engaged in a project – still unfolding in psychoanalysis today – to find ways of modeling mutative action and psychic change. These dialectical features are present in both psychoanalytic theory and developmental theory. These principles were carried forward in developmental psychology via Piaget and Vygotsky, but we need to remember that Spielrein was the senior psychoanalytic figure working and theorizing in the intellectual community in which each of them worked. It was a *clinical* methodology that launched child experimental psychology, an endeavor quite different from the more experience-distant, structured experimental work of Claparède (e.g., 1923), in whose institute Spielrein and Piaget once worked.

Think of the dominant models of change in both of these fields. From psychoanalysis, there is the encircling transaction of projection and introjection. From Piaget (Piaget, 1923; Flavell, 1963), there is the conjoint activity of assimilation and accommodation, his account of genetic epistemology. From Vygotsky (1962/1934), there is the concept of the zone of proximal development and the dialectic of thought and speech. In Vygotsky's model, change *emerges* from dialogue, the back-and-forth of conversation, the transformation of thinking and speaking that bounces between the social field and the internal world.

All of these developmental models of mutative action share a common process: the transactions that transform internal experience through action/thought/fantasy that, in turn, is externalized to transform the external world. Change comes through disequilibration and reintegration, through destruction and reformation. Spielrein, an early and powerful contributor to this model, thinks and writes about these ideas for the length of her visible professional career (1911–1928). For Spielrein, transformations arise in a dialectical process of creativity and destruction, a format we encounter again in nonlinear dynamic systems (Freeman, 1990; Harris, 2005).

Third, she develops a model of language and speech in development that interweaves with both Piaget's and Vygotsky's. All three are two-function, three-stage models for the evolution of language and thought. As these three figures diverge in their interests over time,

Spielrein continues to see the evolution of speaking and thinking through a psychoanalytic lens. What this means for her work is that levels of representation, the power of unconscious forces in speaking, and the role of affect and of relatedness in the evolution of speaking and thinking predominate. For Spielrein, there is an overriding function of verbal play that can be seen in the revelation of internal worlds, desires, and aggressions that appear disguised and displayed in wordplay. Her ideas, always rooted in psychoanalysis, also contain an unwavering commitment to the social and unconscious roots of the child's mind and speech. Given our contemporary interest in unrepresented experience, in figurability, mentalization, and the like (Botella & Botella, 2005; Levine, Reed, & Scarfone, 2013), Spielrein's papers on speech and thought, and on time and subliminal process, make fascinating reading. Her papers on speech and thought provide a window into the psychoanalytic base that informs developmental psychology and developmental psycholinguistics.

Fourth, Spielrein produced original and highly creative work on the development of consciousness and on the child's experience of space, temporality, and intentionality, concepts that were of significant interest to Piaget. In a format that Vygotsky would later use, Spielrein explored concepts of time, space, and causality at the levels of consciousness at which these concepts are expressed by children and by aphasics (e.g., Spielrein, 1923c, trans. this volume, Chapter 14). She is interested in the play of association and dissociation in wordplay, in the presence of temporality and intentionality, in unconscious experience, and in the evolution and dissolution of patterns of thought and speech in conditions of developmental difficulty or psychotic functioning. For Spielrein, unconscious thought is figurative, oddly patterned with adhesions and dissociations, but it is the bedrock on which all higher functions sit.

Finally, there is her contribution to female sexuality. In her great early paper – "Destruction as the Cause of Becoming" (1912; Chapter 6, this volume) – she explores mind through exploring sexuality, and vice versa. Transformation, she believed, was at the heart both of sexuality and mental life, with creation and destruction always moving in dialectical tension. It is perhaps ironic, given her turbulent life, that it is central to Spielrein's method and her theoretical approach that immersion in bewilderment, destructiveness, and chaos can lead to new understanding.

Sexuality, creativity, destruction: body and mind

Perhaps tellingly, in "Destruction as the Cause of Becoming," (1912) Spielrein launches her idea about the proximity of desire and deathly preoccupations, the intertwining of disgust and ecstasy, with a quote from Jung: "The passionate longing, i.e., the libido, has two sides. It is the power that beautifies everything and, under certain circumstances, destroys everything" (Ch. 6, p. 209).

Then she finds her own voice:

> From my experiences with girls I can say that anxiety is the feeling that normally moves to the forefront… when, for the first time, the fulfillment of the wish seems possible. … [O]ne feels the enemy within oneself; it is one's own ardor which compels one with iron necessity to what one does not want. One feels the end, the passing away, from which one wants to escape into unknown distant lands.
>
> (p. 210)

Spielrein begins with an experience-near account of sexuality and a quite revolutionary account of female sexuality in particular. Her rendering of sexuality centers on extremes of action and excess while retaining a commitment to the elements of enigma and uncertainty endemic in sexual life. Drawing on biology and on individual psychology, Spielrein notes the close links in sexuality of life and death, making and destroying, excitement and disgust, pleasure and pain (see also Chapter 2, this volume):

> [W]hat happens during copulation is the most intimate union of two individuals: one pushing forth into the other. The difference is merely quantitative: it is not the whole individual that is being sucked in, but only a part of it – a part, however, which at that moment represents the value of the whole organism. The male part dissolves into the female, the female part, stirred into restlessness, receives a new form from the foreign intruder.
>
> (p. 211)

For Spielrein, destruction and regeneration always commingle. Ecstasy, anxiety, and disgust coexist as elements of sexuality.

Here, I want to introduce Etkind's (1997) idea that the work of Russian symbolism (late nineteenth- and early twentieth-century writers and philosophers) was a powerful influence on Spielrein's generation. There are striking parallels between symbolist thought and psychoanalysis. Both systems stress the levels of reality, the power of hidden depths of feeling and sensibility, the uncanny force of unconscious life. Add Nietzsche to this mix and we are squarely in a world of ideas in which love and destructiveness are deeply intermingled, where death wishes and "gender mix" are in play. Etkind stresses the intense preoccupation within Russian symbolism of Dionysian ideas and forces, elements that appear in this paper and others throughout Spielrein's writing career.

It is known – indeed, it was acknowledged by Freud – that Spielrein's paper on creativity and destruction was a significant force in Freud's (1955/1920) work in *Beyond the Pleasure Principle*.[12] Despite the difficulty in the initial reception of Spielrein's paper, I think one can track some points of influence or inspiration in addition to Freud's. I see her ideas surfacing in Tausk's (1933) paper on the influencing machine. Otto Gross (2012/1913) very explicitly draws on Spielrein in his essay "On the Symbolism of Destruction." He had noticed the physical and sexualized violence in the play of a psychotic boy, and linked his observations to Spielrein's ideas about the inherent presence of destructiveness in psychic life.

I want to trace a lineage in Spielrein's work in relation to sexuality and activity as aspects of gender. Spielrein's interest in activity as a source and support of desire might lead us to the 1920s and to some of the women who, as the immediate followers of Freud, were apparently supposed to accept his ideas about passivity and receptivity and to ground femininity and female desire in internalization and receptivity. Significantly, Lampl-de Groot (1933), Muller (1932), and others follow another path. It is a path Spielrein had already trod. A dominant characteristic of this work in the 1920s is that incorporation was seen not simply as passive and receptive, but as active and transformative. In this sense, work on sexuality and work on the mental activities of internalization are cast by Spielrein in quite similar terms.

What is interesting about these figures from the 1920s is that their ideas are much closer to Spielrein than to Freud, but closer also to Ferenczi's *Thalassa: A Theory of Genitality* (1989/1924). In that book, Ferenczi focuses on two phenomena: first, the evolution of sexuality as an experience of admixture, not renunciation and rupture; and second, the regressive nature in excitement, the longing for undoing, the mixture of states of being, excitation and terror, pain and pleasure (see Bonomi, 2014). Like Ferenczi, Spielrein seems to have seen incorporation or internalization as a highly active and expansive process, a way of conceptualizing mental activity that we might note echoing again in Bion on the function of the container, and in both Piaget and Vygotsky on the power of assimilation and the dialectical transformation of word and concept.

Of course, we need to question the line of influence. How much did Spielrein's ideas have an effect, subtle or overt, on the evolution of such concepts as destruction and the death drive, as well as in the area of sexuality? Was she picking up the zeitgeist or was she charting new ground? Or was it some of both? Did her ideas enter, in a very underground way, people's ruminations on the phenomena of sexuality, particularly female sexuality?

In a certain moment in "Destruction as the Cause of Becoming," as she is interpreting a passage from Faust, she says this:

> Being extended into the dark sea corresponds with entering into the dark problem. The fusion of air and water, the blurring of above and below may symbolize that in the realm of the mother… all times and places melt into one another; that there are no boundaries between "above" and "below…"

She goes on to claim the power of infantile sexuality as an aspect of adult sexual life:

> Freud detects our adult love impulses [*Liebesregungen*], be they straightforward or sublimated, in the infantile age where we experienced the first pleasurable sensations, brought about by the persons who took care of us. Later we seek to re-experience these sensations of pleasure [*Lustempfindungen*]. And even when consciousness has long worked out a normal sexual aim, the unconscious is occupied with those representations that gave us pleasure in earliest infancy.

These ideas dominate her thinking and are a deep part of how she thought of body, mind, and speech.

Loewald (1988) explores some of these ideas at the end of a short essay on metapsychology: "Sexuality and aggression, in this philosophical shift harking back to pre-Socratic philosophy, are projected into nature – not a projection 'into the blue' but the rediscovery of an original correspondence and lasting affinity" (p. 54). He goes on to mention Jung as an originator of these ideas. Although Spielrein has again been "disappeared," we know that these ideas passed between her and Jung in letters and appeared in her diaries. It is necessary, I feel, to see that she is, at least, an interlocutor.

We might see that Spielrein is writing about what modern theorists like Bersani (2010) or Butler (2004) and psychoanalytic writers like Stein (1998), Dimen (2003), and Saketopoulou (2015) might speak of as the shattering of the self in the experience of excitement. Spielrein is insistent that we see these phenomena – destruction, creativity, excitement, disgust – as aspects not of morality, but of emergent and transformative psychic life. It is actually a curious hybrid concept, linked to Freud's death instinct, as he has suggested in his footnote, but linked also to a modern nonlinear dynamic systems theories, including chaos theory. One can notice as well the presence in Laplanche's model of sexuality as excess. Perhaps one can hear echoes of Spielrein in Laplanche's idea that transformation and retranscription of desires that arise intersubjectively. It is in these intrapsychically, and in the transformations that subjectivity and unconscious experience are constituted. My point is not to make Spielrein the Big Mother who dominates all creation, but only to ask, and to ask very frequently, why she is not included in the lineage of these ideas. Why, for example, does Laplanche (2002) engage both critically and integratively with Ferenczi but not Spielrein, even as he is speaking of the "destructuring and 'loosening' aspects of sexuality itself" (p. 38)?

To me, what is fascinating in "Destruction as the Cause of Becoming" is the clear link Spielrein makes between the experience of sexual life and the experience of mental life. She moves from concerns about sexuality as an experience of bodies inside other bodies, from questions of pleasure and pain, of many different ways of having the experience of taking a part of another's body into one's own, and then applies this directly to mental experience:

> Pleasure is nothing but the ego's affirmative response when confronted with these demands that spring from deep down below.

> We can derive pleasure from unpleasure, and pleasure from pain – pain that in itself is deeply tinged with unpleasure… There is thus something deep inside us which, as paradoxical as it may sound, wants, even desires, this self-damage, for the ego responds to it with pleasure.
>
> (Ch. 6, p. 215)

As she pursues these thoughts, she notes that they take her to an inevitable conclusion: the I, the individual, is always already divided. Differentiation is a feature of conscious life, merger and fusion a feature of the unconscious: "The closer we get to conscious thinking, the more differentiated our mental representations; the deeper we enter into the unconscious, the more general, more [arche]typal they become" (p. 216). Later in the essay, she states that "Freud showed that every dream image always, already, and at the same time, means its opposite… Bleuler's notion of ambivalence and Stekel's concept of bipolarity suggest that within us every positive drive coexists with a negative one" (p. 233).

Differentiation, the idea that there is a dawning awareness of an other inside the self, is, for Spielrein, a parallel to having another's body inside one's own. Minds, too, can be penetrated, carrying what Spielrein came to call "ego-psyche" (p. 215) and "we-psyche."[13] Hers is a metapsychology in which "otherness," splits in the self, and multiplicity are core concepts, all functioning at different levels of consciousness. The awareness of an internal presence of the "other" is an aspect of constituting the self, but it arises first in embodiment.

Spielrein's (1911) dissertation drew on a case of schizophrenia (see Chapter 1; excerpt trans. this volume, Chapter 5; Spielrein, 2018, pp. 14–96), and that work in concert with her (1912a) "Destruction" essay contains the genesis of her ideas about psychotic disturbances to mental life. When Freud (1958/1911) references the dissertation in his postscript to the Schreber case (p. 79), he does so in proposing that more interpretive material would be gathered from considering the "symbolic content of the phantasies and delusions" (p. 80), precisely Spielrein's focus. In the dissertation, she outlines and draws from clinical material the linkages between dream states and psychotic processes and productions. She is, in relation to the speech of the psychotic, always interested in the motor action, the sounds, and the collapse of symbolization.

Spielrein's ideas about psychosis are intriguing:

> In my opinion, it is a battle between the two antagonistic currents: the species-psyche versus the ego-psyche. ... [T]his insight is forced upon me: "I am a stranger to myself." Thoughts become depersonalized, they are "made," not thought, because they emerge from depths outside of the ego, from depths that turn the "me" [*ich*] into "we" or rather "they."
>
> (as trans. this volume, Ch. 6, p. 218)

What is in character for Spielrein, in this perspective, is her interest in the place of the individual and of the social in mental phenomena. She terms these the ego-type and the collective-type, the place of otherness in mental experience, the divisions of self in that metapsychology. And she tracks the movement of not-I and many I's and I-ness in the verbal play of a mother and child.

The psychotic, she notes, has become alienated from his or her own mind with the transposition of personal and unconsciously driven material – ego-psyche into the more collective "we-psyche" of the individual. These terms are designed to describe two (for Spielrein) distinct aspects of mental life. The ego-psyche reflects the more indigenous aspects of subjectivity, the part of self that we might term "intrapsychic," and here she is always encompassing unconscious phenomena. In the we-psyche, she theorizes those aspects of mental life that feel internalized from elsewhere, the presence of the other in the mind and being of any individual. This is the part of subjectivity that feels forcing, alien, implanted, split from the aspects of psyche that feel more individual and emergent. These distinctions about mental, personal, and bodily life, the presence of splits and divisions in the self, are central to Spielrein's view of psychotic process. There is, she felt, urgency in this alienation of personally meaningful experience into collective symbols. The problem is that the mind becomes littered with alien objects – "we" or "they": "Thoughts become depersonalized." Desire emerges from the experience of I. From the "we-psyche" state, the person lives as a spectator, observing self and other in some degree of alienation. In describing the patient in her thesis, Spielrein notes the woman's disinterest in her own internal world, the collapsing of the ego-psyche. She is close here, I would say, to an account of dissociative states.

The dissertation contains some interesting speculations about the distortions of temporality in psychotic thought: "*Das Unbewußte löst die Gegenwart in der Vergangenheit auf* [The unconscious dissolves the present into the past]" (Spielrein, 1911, p. 399). The unconscious will also immerse the future in the past. Throughout her writing and clinical life, she sees the power of regression and unconscious atemporality not only in sexual life, but in primitive forms of mental life and higher forms of representation as well. Again, I want to note the early date (1911–1912) at which Spielrein's ideas about psychosis and primitive states appear in psychoanalytic literatures.

Using words carries one away from self and individuality. But staying in the world of I-ness threatens dissolution and death. There is the beautiful sentence: "Language is there to bewilder itself and others" (Spielrein, 1912a, p. 477). From there it is not a great leap to her focus on symbolization and meaning in children's thought processes. These preoccupations and the papers she wrote after leaving Vienna led her by 1920 to the mature phase of her career: the work in Geneva.

Geneva: mind and words

After a period of change and movement (Lausanne, Zürich, Berlin), Spielrein settles in Geneva. Her period there begins in 1920 and lasts until she moves to Moscow in 1923. As in so many of the vicissitudes or turns in her life, personal and professional interests intersect. At this time, she has married and has a child. Perhaps she needed some distance from the fallout from the conflicts and final rupture between Freud and Jung. Perhaps she wanted a place to have an adult authority, and perhaps then she wanted freedom from the place of sexualized child figure in Jung's history and her reputation. Perhaps this was a bid for freedom, not an endlessly masochistic cycling through worlds. Perhaps these are my wishes and projections for her. This period of turmoil and productivity continues the enduring puzzle of how to situate Spielrein both in her own life and in the context of the professional fields in which she functioned.

In the period before Geneva, from 1912 to 1920 – a period of frequent moves and transitions – Spielrein produces some short papers, clinical communications, or research studies in which she is honing her ideas about speech and pleasure, speech, thought, and unconscious process. There is a short clinical account bearing on the question of sexuality in which the chief subject is the matter of envy and regression (Spielrein, 2001c/1913). This intrigued me, as I think envy is a deep dynamic issue, particularly for women (Harris, 1997), one not often taken up theoretically outside the Kleinian tradition. The paper is wittily titled "The Mother-in-Law."

In this short contribution, Spielrein examines a dynamic triangle that reverses oedipal life and convention. Turning the tables, and perhaps following a Ferenczian interest in early traumatic object relations, Spielrein puts into play the muddle between the wife's mother's attachment to her daughter and the competitive envy that surfaces in relation to her daughter's husband. Most particularly, she sees in the power and projection of mother into daughter signs of envy (of youthfulness, of sexuality). In a modern context, what we might call intersubjectivity lives in the mix of power and destructiveness in this early dyad. What is intriguing in this paper is Spielrein's argument that women's actual constrictions and limits in the world, particularly regarding opportunities for achievement, made identifications much more significant. Annie Reich (1953) explores a similar train of thought in looking at object choice in women. So projection and an inhabiting of the life and psyche of powerful figures might be said to operate with great intensity for many women, providing an intergenerational space in which to manage and sublimate envy.

Many of these shorter papers pursue her ideas about sexuality and female sexuality in particular (Spielrein, 1914, 1920b, 1920c, 1920d, 1923b, 1923d, 2001a/1914, 2001c/1913). The themes echo both her creativity/destruction paper and her dissertation, reflecting on the place and range of female sexuality (the place of culture and sanctions, but also of the destructiveness inherent in all creative and libidinous life). She contributes to a series of discussions on masturbation held at the Vienna Psychoanalytic Society (Nunberg & Federn, 1974, pp. 320–367, 1979, pp. 20–96), in which she has a number of interesting things to say about the transformation of guilt into excitement and destructive feelings and the cycling of arousal, guilt, and masochism, and from there a return to arousal. Focused particularly on masturbation in women, she notes the power of the maternal erotic, the mother's erotic links to her child (see also Spielrein, 1913b, trans. this volume, Chapter 7).

When she turns more directly to development in Geneva after 1920, one sees that she conceives of the emergence of symbolization from embodied, kinesthetic, vocal, and motoric experience, which are inherent to both unconscious and preconscious life. Representation, for Spielrein, is on a continuum: "As concerns the controversy regarding the role of sexuality, I was told that provided one has the will to do so, we might just as well derive everything from the drive for food [*Nahrungstrieb*]" (Spielrein, 1912a, p. 270). This almost throwaway line is part of her powerful commitment to regressive experience as constitutive of elaborated adult experience. But the line that comes just before situates her in more conventional aspects of sexual development: "the infantile sources of pleasure are the germs of sexual pleasure in the adult," and all of these sources for Spielrein arise in unconscious forms and in relatedness, or, as she puts it, "the caring hand of the nurse" (ibid.; Ch. 6, p. 214).

As seems often the case with Spielrein, reports about her impact were very mixed. The encounter of psychoanalysis and developmental psychology, fraught with politics and paranoia in all directions, was not easy, but there is a consensus that Spielrein's teaching was illuminating. We might reexamine Piagetian theory for its two-person-ness, its use of introjection and projection as basic models of mental action. And as in Ferenczi's theoretical innovations in this topic, internalization and introjection are seen as expansions of functioning and less as passive receptive movements.

Spielrein worked in Claparède's Institute Jean Jacques Rousseau, which he had formed in 1912. There she treated children, worked on psychoanalytic culture and institutions in the emerging Swiss analytic communities, and engaged both in pedagogy and research. The years of overlap with Piaget are approximately 1920–1923, years of productivity for Spielrein and an explosive beginning for Piaget, her analysand for about eight months during that time. This only deepens the complexity of their shared projects, the quite symmetrical interests, and often shared terminology, and yet the asymmetry of their fates and reputations (see also Chapter 3, this volume). Piaget (2001/1926) speaks of Spielrein in his book *The Language and Thought of the Child* (p. 2), but diminishes her importance, placing her interests in early childhood, a placement with a decided gender twist. In their overlapping lives and careers in Geneva, one can see reciprocal influences. Spielrein's interest in egocentrism is both similar and different from

Piaget's. She was perhaps more interested in individuality, in the unique character of children's thinking, its links to the body and to unconscious reverie. Exploring many of the topics Piaget was to take up in great detail, she was interested in the evolution in development of the child's experiences of temporality, causality, and space and a gradual mental orientation and relation to reality.

Her interests, both psychoanalytic and developmental, led her to look at the links between speech and shame (Spielrein, 1920c, 1920d). She examined the gender differences in presentations of shame regarding the body and regarding desire in the communications of two four-year-olds, noting the diffuseness of girl's shame.[14] Given the age range (two to four or five) of many of her research and clinical subjects, we would be talking about toddler shame, a subject deeply addressed by Alan Schore (2003). I found myself trying to think through this process via Spielrein's ideas about speech as a carrier of pleasure and reality and about shame induction being a moment when pleasure is met by reality and the system crashes. It looks like a conversation, but two extremely conflictual states mismatch. Expecting *jouissance*, the child/patient/analyst is met with prohibition, limit. Spielrein is interested in how these complex rivers of feeling and regulation intersect in conversation, in acts of misrecognition as well as acts of linking.

Several of Spielrein's papers focus on language and thought in the child, with interesting speculations on temporality and spatiality as these support speech and thought (Spielrein, 1920a, 1920d, 1921). It is all very phenomenological, in that complex mental life grows out of embodiment, out of the erotic body handled and reacted to, with vocalization, speech, and its music carrying unconscious process as a substrate of advanced mental function.

Spielrein was quite explicit about the importance of listening and holding with a light hand and with interpretations that were subtle and not invasive. This is of course good clinical listening, but it is also a crucial principle of doing research. Spielrein's training in psychoanalysis produced a deep encounter with the nature of thought and language, a training she used creatively and productively in research. Spielrein, as in all of her work, remained committed to the interpenetration of motor bodily experience and symbolization or word use. In looking at aphasia, speech, and a sample of child speech (Spielrein, 1923c), she comes to an astonishing and modern conclusion: "*Ce qui fait persister un groupe d'idées dans la pensée spontanée est le mouvement affectif* [What allows a group of ideas to persist in spontaneous thought is the movement of emotion]" (p. 315, my translation). Follow the affect if you want to understand the child/patient, an idea continuously being developed by psychoanalysts.

Spielrein pursued a kind of metapsychology in which the mind is characterized in relation to temporality and splitting (divided self-states, multiplicity). So from questions of sexuality to mind and symbolization, Spielrein traverses some interesting ideas, which in part she credits to Jung. Multiplicity and multiple states are characteristic of minds. Internal divisions in the self and splitting are usual forms of mental action. These are ideas Spielrein often returned to; they dominate her thinking in the "Destruction" paper. Again, I wish to point out that these ideas were emerging in her thought in 1911–1912.

Spielrein was interested in mental life as lived often at the edge between differentiation and union, difference and merger. In a way now familiar from the formalist thinkers in Italian psychoanalysis (with influences on figures like Antonino Ferro, 2005), as the levels deepen to increasingly unconscious forms of mental being, states of regression and merger come to predominate. One finds this spelled out in a highly formal theory by the Italian Matte-Blanco (1975), Segal (1957), and others (e.g., Fonagy, 1995). Fonagy, for example, writes of the state of "psychic equivalence," where fantasy and reality are not differentiated in the unconscious. Thinking of differentiation as an aspect of the conscious and preconscious mind takes Spielrein to the question of words as the site of otherness: the ego-psyche and the we-psyche; bewilderment by language. Using words carries one away from self and individuality. But staying in the world of I-ness threatens dissolution and death. Interestingly, desire emerges from the experience of I. From the "we" state, the person lives as a spectator, observing self and other in some degree of alienation.

Spielrein's theorizing easily and powerfully links psychoanalytic ideas to the emerging field of child psychology, seeing the onset of speech as carrying the regressive oral experience of feeding, nursing, and babbling. Speech arises in the embodied and intentional motive to link and find another, which then become routed through the forms of language (rules, meanings, etc.). We might see the evolution and appearance of these ideas in Loewald's work on primary and secondary process in language and symbolization (Loewald, 1980a).

In a paper on dream images of shooting stars (Spielrein, 2001b/1923), Spielrein identifies the interplay of memory and desire, what she terms the "crossing" of desire and disappointment in the mix of starry explosion and dark, watery fading. In 1913, in a short paper published in *Imago* (Spielrein, 2001d/1913), she analyzes an element in a Russian short story where a young man's anxiety arises in response to a triggering event (a train whistle). In the paper, Spielrein clearly talks about this event as trauma-driven and as the piercing of conscious reflection with split-off unconscious material, evolving a state of pervasive disquiet in the patient. Spielrein (1922) viewed time as a property of space and saw mind and consciousness as always constructed through the reverberations of temporality – meaning made in the present on the basis of the past. We can hear Loewald's preoccupations with time, and we can think also of Freud's idea of *Nachträglichkeit*, the activity whereby the work in the present reworks the past, which then dialectically reworks the present. Loewald is perhaps a most intriguing person to evoke in this context. He was attentive to the regressive element in primary process and thus in certain archaic aspects of speech. These ideas are at the heart of Spielrein's work on speech and embodiment.

In her work on language development, Spielrein consistently weds the disciplines of psychoanalysis and developmental psychology in a fascinating analysis of the potency and meaning of sound making, the music of language, intonation, mouth movement, babbling as it cascades into symbol use, and the development of semantic and syntactic aspects of speech. Using both case material and developmental observation, Spielrein (2015a/1922) works in a conjoined way of theorizing, seeing the onset of speech as carrying the regressive oral experience of feeding, nursing, and babbling. Speech arises in the embodied and intentional motive to link and find another, which then becomes routed through the forms of language (rules, meanings, etc.). We may see the evolution and appearance of these ideas in Loewald's work on primary and secondary process in language and symbolization (Loewald, 1980a).

In her 1922 paper on the origin of a child's words "Mama" and "Papa" (Spielrein, 2015a/1922), she anticipated by some years Klein's papers on weaning and orality. Some version of her ideas in this work were in the 1920 presentation at the IPA Congress at The Hague, a congress attended by both Klein and Anna Freud. Interestingly, in her paper on infant analysis, Klein (1926) cites Spielrein only in a somewhat enigmatic footnote (p. 56) as noted above, meanwhile drawing explicitly on her work on the words "Mama" and "Papa."

Spielrein begins always with the premise that all aspects of speech carry unconscious or, as she comes to term it, "subconscious" meaning. The melodic, rhythmic, and gestural forms of speech progress into more verbal and then symbolic features. Sound elements in early wordplay carry desire, anxiety, shame, aggression, and other affect states. In this paper, she begins her analysis of the stages of speech and thought development, seeing in the early wordplay and naming a magical formation, or an even earlier autistic stage, a term she adopts from Bleuler. Barbara Wharton (2015) has called the links to Winnicott in this paper "uncanny" (p. 249), noting the early forms of ideas about play and its interactional effects that Winnicott would develop in his ideas about transitional objects and transitional spaces. Words are actions, feeling states, carrying both links to the parent and processes of separation. The early magical properties of words allow the child to attempt to manage loss or absence in conjuring speaking as a form of action.

Speech and conscious and unconscious levels of thought interpenetrate. Spielrein gives a set of clinical examples in which "Mama" and "Papa," in different languages and different family constellations, mean different things: sadness, dismay, contentment. The words that she links to suckling and orality are endowed with magical properties. Speech is designed to make pleasure last. *Fort-da*? At one point in the essay, Spielrein notes some indebtedness to William James, to his ideas about the role of speech in the generation of affect.

In listening to a mother and child, Spielrein (1913) speculates on the nicknames and playful speech of mother to child and child to mother, noting that from each side there is a muddling of identifications, a slippage of gender from parent to child, projections and introjections, with speech signaling the deep somatic and affective ties. In a theoretical move she will use later in looking at mother–daughter envy, she notes how much love and threat live in the speech practices of child and parent. Her little patient develops a phobia of monkeys, and Spielrein speculates on the impact of the boy calling his mother "marmoset" (see also Harris, 2014).

Her conclusion, and it resonates with her thinking generally about psychic life, is that speaking partakes equally of the pleasure principle and the reality principle, toggling between these two spheres of psychic reality. What is Loewaldian here is the consideration of the primary process in words and language, his ideas of nonlinear, often ambiguous development between oedipal and pre-oedipal levels, and between levels of mental functioning. It is important not to declare these ideas her property, but rather to enter her claim to a place in an unfolding genealogy of ideas, her contribution to questions with which many of us in psychoanalysis continue to grapple.

The clinical implications of this are fascinating: the gratification and erotics of speech within the analytic process, the conflicts between reality and pleasure as it might appear in distortions of speaking, the hypnotic effects of speech. Spielrein is asking us to attend to something quite obvious and usually unremarked: the link between speech and the mouth. But Spielrein's work is always a particularly interesting corrective to the modern tendency to airbrush sexuality from early dyadic life.

In a paper based on her work with children in the clinic in Geneva (Spielrein, 1923a; see also Chapter 13, this volume), we can see Spielrein's capacities, both clinical and intellectual, in full flower. She begins with an interesting theoretical commitment to the instability of the lines between conscious and unconscious thought and to the importance of clinical judgment in regard to the subtle interplay of the unconscious and conscious aspects of words. She makes a point of the centrality of the role of "free association" in the language play of children and then turns her attention to a transcript of phrases and "babbling" or wordplay of a two-and-a-half-year-old. She draws on dream work, condensation, and displacement as ways of seeing the play of the unconscious in the child's language and the linked experiences of conscious and unconscious forms in this simple verbal output. This is of course good clinical listening, but it is also a deep encounter with the nature of thought and language. As her work matured and deepened, she continued to find strong parallels between the analysis of dreams and the analysis of speech. I think here of how the idea of reverie has entered our considerations of analytic listening (e.g., Ogden, Bion, Ferro). There are Loewaldian notes here as well, as preoccupations familiar to any psychoanalysts drawing on field theory (Baranger & Baranger, 2009).

In the 1960s, in an appreciation of Piaget's work, the American developmental psychologist John Flavell (1963) described Piaget's first five books in English, which appeared in the period 1923–1932, as galvanizing the field of child development with regard to content and methodology. It is in this period that Piaget crystalized a form of close observation, the naturalistic observation of children's activities alone and with others – original yes, in some sense, but derived also, in another. Given Spielrein's formation in child clinical work, we can see that what Piaget adapted rather than invented is the clinical method of listening to children talk and play that is at the heart of child psychoanalysis. In Piaget's early writing, his work often centered on observations of his own children. Every feature of his working method is first or simultaneously present in Spielrein's; she is the portal from child psychoanalysis to child development.

In other words, Piaget's early work, rightly considered to be both creative and revolutionary, is built on ideas Spielrein was teaching and researching. We will see a similar line of influence with Vygotsky a scant few years later. What is important to remember in thinking of the direction of influence is that Spielrein's method as imported into child study draws a great deal from psychoanalytic ideas, from the history of thinking about clinical listening, of finding the structure and meaning in the everyday processes of engagement, play, and narrative. Spielrein did not of course inaugurate this method; it was central to Freud's thinking and was already embedded in the clinical ideas regarding child analysis in the work of Hug-Hellmuth. Spielrein was a transmitter, a conduit of these traditions, and she must be considered in large part responsible for the rootedness of these perspectives in Geneva and later in Moscow.

Ironically, but perhaps characterologically, Spielrein, so unremarked or underrepresented in the work of others, was herself good at citations. It gives us a sense of the breadth of her reading: William James, the British neurologist John Hughlings Jackson, Théodore Flournoy, the Swiss linguist Charles Bally, initially Jung, and always Freud. If the style of the first paper on destruction and creativity was intense, charged, wildly evocative, and associative, the writing Spielrein was doing by 1913 was increasingly sober, carefully argued, and grounded in the science and philosophy emerging in the first two decades of the twentieth century.

Moscow and Rostov-on-Don

In reflecting on the evolution of psychoanalytic thinking and the coordinates of psychoanalysis and developmental psychology in the Soviet Union, and in trying to reestablish Spielrein's central place in this incandescent but brief period, we are hampered by much missing information due to the chaos of both the Soviet period, World War II, and the postwar Stalinist period. We do know that psychoanalysis takes hold in Russia in the early 1920s and was flowering most powerfully in the years 1920–1924. Spielrein was there at the high-water mark, but she had also given an influential talk in Russia much earlier, in 1912. Miller (1986), Etkind (1997), and Wharton and Ovcharenko (1999) have provided important documentation and analysis of this period. Political suppression was underway by the mid-1920s, and by 1928, psychoanalysis had been broken and forced underground. Institutional life and analytic publishing were curtailed, while the Children's School, in which Spielrein was involved, closed down, as psychoanalysis becomes the devilish marker of bourgeois mentality. Spielrein's departure from Moscow to Rostov, probably to continue her practice in very reduced circumstances and in secret, seems in retrospect both prudent and tragic.

Reading Wharton and Ovcharenko's (1999) brief history of the periodization in Russian psychoanalysis, one understands the place of ambition, along with nostalgia for home and family, in Spielrein's return to Moscow and Rostov-on- Don in 1923. Russian psychoanalysis was flourishing and in a transdisciplinary way in which Spielrein would have thrived and felt at home (see also Chapter 3 in this volume).

Reviewing what is known of Spielrein's arrival and work life in Russia in 1923 is to encounter again and immediately the enigma of her erasure. In moving back to Russia, she was reconciling with her estranged husband, with whom she had another child, a second daughter, born in 1926. She was returning to a difficult person and a difficult situation: her husband had started a new family with another woman. But as so frequently seems to have happened, from the early biographies and certainly the Cronenberg film (2011), a masochistic storyline trumps a narrative in which ambition, professional interests, and family alliances hold importance.

As one of two IPA-sanctioned training analysts in the Soviet Union, Spielrein would have been a person of great stature in the psychoanalytic community. Coming from the West, she would have been an exciting and sophisticated intellectual figure. In her role in several organizations, including the Russian Psychoanalytic Institute, she had administrative responsibilities, as she did at the State Psychoanalytic Institute and the State Children's House-Laboratory, a fascinating and apparently quite radical experiment in treatment and pedagogy operating along psychoanalytic lines (Spielrein, 1929). She would have been a teacher providing a highly sophisticated psychoanalytic education on such topics as child analysis, language, and symbolization, as well as the study of consciousness and unconscious phenomena. Her course on child development had the largest enrollment, with over thirty candidates. If you had been exposed to psychoanalysis in Russia in that time, you would have passed through her classroom, and that experience would surely have included Vygotsky and Luria, both significantly her juniors in age and experience. One could imagine that Spielrein was a complex figure there, perhaps intimidating, perhaps the object of some competitive envy, perhaps also fragile. What is harder to imagine is how she disappeared.

I am indebted to many scholars writing about the Soviet period and psychoanalysis, most particularly Alexander Etkind (1997).[15] John Launer's book (2015) finally has moved Spielrein's story in a more expansive direction. Many of the early Spielrein biographers minimize the periods in Geneva and Moscow in favor of the years with Freud and Jung, just as many Vygotsky scholars minimize psychoanalysis to the point of erasure. Spielrein's work and reputation in Geneva and Moscow, and the links between those worlds, have therefore been slighted in both literatures. Modern cognitive psychologists working on Vygotsky stress instead the importance of Kurt Lewin and field theory and of Gestalt psychology, while Spielrein's writing on dialectics and pattern becomes obscured. One of the more irritating tendencies in the assessment of Spielrein, Piaget, and Vygotsky is to see her pictured as empirical and clinical, interested only in early development, while the two men are lionized for having built formal models. To my ear, there are deprecating and misogynist tones to that judgment.

Vygotsky's first important lecture series, in 1924, was an attempt to move beyond Pavlovian reflexology to more complex ideas about consciousness. Oddly, he cites Jung, but not Spielrein or Freud. He goes on to talk about the "hidden somatic stimuli" in reflex systems and chains of associations with complex unconscious roots, an idea surely emerging from psychoanalysis. He sees self-consciousness as arising always from consciousness of others: "We are another to ourselves." These are ideas that appear to be lifted right from Spielrein's "Destruction" essay (1912). What makes this odd is that these lectures were delivered at the high-water mark of psychoanalysis in the Soviet Union, a time when institutes, training programs, journals, and Russian editions of Freud's work were flourishing. Spielrein and her link to Freud would have given the writings of Luria and Vygotsky considerable cachet.

Vygotsky might be said to have centered his intellectual and theoretical concerns on the ways that language and speech are "perched on the world–mind boundary" (Frawley, 1997, p. 1). In ways reminiscent of and yet different from the approaches of Spielrein and Piaget, he focuses on the problem – indeed, the necessity – of creating a developmental theory. Like Piaget and, before him, Spielrein, Vygotsky delineates a three-stage model of the unfolding of thought and speech. The terminologies differ, with Vygotsky's focus on the constitutive role of the social and with Piaget's on the evolution of structured thought. These differences increased over time and with subsequent interpreters. But at this epicenter of discovery in the early 1920s, all three are tracking language and thought through subtle, close observation of children, a method drawn, I believe, from Spielrein's use of psychoanalytic inquiry and attunement. The developmental models indebted to her mode of thinking put the emphasis on transformation and nonlinearity.

Vygotsky developed a number of other ideas that seem deeply tied to Spielrein's projects: the tie between intellect and affect; the intermingling of thinking and wanting; a link at the heart of Spielrein's attention to embodiedness as also constitutive of thought and word; the presence of otherness as an aspect of personal consciousness; and the encounter of speech as a splitting of the subject (see Spielrein, 1931, trans. this volume, Chapter 16).

In all of these figures (Piaget, Spielrein, Vygotsky, Luria), one tracks the struggle to sort out the external and internal forces feeding development. In subtle ways, all of these thinkers are interested in tracking how intentionality emerges as an individual process from a dialogic one. One hears Laplanchian and relational notes here, the process of recoding and transposing the move from inter- to intra-psychic experience, the "internalizing of the external," and the "in-growing of lived experience into personal meaning" (Frawley, 1997, pp. 21, 95), the asymmetric, uneven, and "revolutionary" aspects (Vygotsky's term but Spielrein's concept) of developmental change.

Vygotsky read and was influenced by Lewin's (1947) field theory – development as a spiral process. He knew Lewin personally, and subsequent commentators on Vygotsky's work have tended to give Lewin the credit for the Russian's interest in nonlinearity and transformation, the tie of thought and affect. Doubtless Lewin is a powerful vector in the intellectual climate in which Vygotsky was working, but I think too much is attributed to this influence, while Spielrein's contributions and projects are eclipsed – again.

One can find, for example, the psychoanalytic features of Vygotsky's (1962/1934) concept of the "zone of proximal development." This concept refers to a process where social interaction is transformative and where dialogue is the wellspring of transformation. Transference and countertransference phenomena, even ideas like the effect of container on contained, are ways of looking at what Vygotsky built as the site of emerging understanding and mastery. Knowledge was not a matter of what you can produce on a test, but what you could master with help; that is, in an intersubjective space with others. One needs two minds to understand one. We have no trouble hearing Bion in these ideas, but it is important to notice that this concept appears first in Spielrein as early as 1911.

In Vygotsky and Luria's (1925) introduction to a new Russian translation of *Beyond the Pleasure Principle* – the very work in which Freud names Spielrein's influence, as noted above – Spielrein is absent in their text, yet present in their ideas. Wherever psychoanalysis was headed in the Soviet Union (particularly after the death of Trotsky), the level of interest and involvement in psychoanalytic work was still quite high in the Soviet Union. Why, then, leave out the name and work of a senior Russian analyst who is mentioned in the Freudian text they are presenting? I have been a psychoanalyst long enough to know that she must have had a role in this omission, but I have been a feminist long enough to know that something is wrong here. Did she become for these brilliant men the "environmental mother" who does not have to be named or noticed because she is the water in which they swim? Where does gender factor in here?

I am left with a paradox. It does matter how ownership of all of these idea and concepts gets parsed out. What is irrefutable is that these historical moments in Geneva and Moscow are powerful sites of transdisciplinary creation. Child observation, philosophy of mind, gestalt psychology, field theory, ideas about development, revolutionary ideas, and ideas about consciousness all intermingle here, creating the bedrock of arguably the most powerful ideas we have regarding child development and the growth of thought and language. If you don't add psychoanalysis to that mix, you miss powerful elements in the picture (affect, embodiment, splits in subjectivity, otherness, unconscious projects of pleasure and destruction). And if you do add the force of psychoanalytic thoughts and methods, Spielrein is one of the key portals of transmission. I wish simultaneously to restore her individuality and brilliance and to engage her as a member of several extraordinary groups.

It is interesting to note that the intersection between psychoanalysis and cognitive psychology has waxed and waned, but mostly waned. The period in which Spielrein worked in interaction with Piaget, Vygotsky, and Luria is one in which these two bodies of thought interpenetrated. Many factors – personal and political – forced the separation. Perhaps the renewed interest in mentalization, in models of representation, and in Bion's (1984a, 1984b) focus on the conscious and unconscious function of thought constitute new beginnings. These beginnings would be aided by the refinding of Spielrein's history and work.

Conclusions

I became interested in the meaning for Spielrein of two myths: the myth of Laocoön and the mythic figure Siegfried. Laocoön is the priest who raises doubt and gives voice to suspicions about the Trojan horse after it was taken inside the city. He and his two sons are eaten by a sea serpent, and so are returned to the sea as a punishment from some god whose bet was on the Trojans. Punishment for insight: that is how the myth is often interpreted, and one encounters that idea very often in Spielrein's letters and diaries.

I think the rescue from various seas, swamps, fires, and internecine battles must be deep in my agenda in this chapter. I can see this trope in my professional life going back to work with Lew Aron on the revival of Ferenczi (Aron & Harris, 1993). In some ways, Spielrein's fate is all too familiar. It is against this tendency in our field to erase conflict and difference that I am speaking.

A persisting thought about the restoration of Spielrein's reputation that has surfaced for me is generational and cultural. For my generation, which Chodorow (2002) has described as a generation born into war and coming into consciousness in the chain of liberatory movements in America (civil rights, anti-war, feminism, through identity politics and gay liberation), the period between the wars (from grandparents to parents) still represents an extreme challenge. My/our generation imagined a fresh start, a break with the past, in the so-called New Left, the anti-war movements of the 1960s, and the unfolding identity politics involving race, ethnicity, gender, and sexuality. I think that what is required is to recover the unexpected continuities and so to be able to place into a genealogy lost figures and lost history from the first half of the twentieth century. In thinking intergenerationally and psychoanalytically, we are all infused with forms and forces outside our full conscious awareness. As a discipline, we are not yet consciously placed in the moving histories that formed us, though there are important moves in that direction (Makari, 1994; Cooper-White, 2014, 2017; Kuriloff, 2014). This essay is part of that project.

In the diaries, and in several biographical essays (see Lothane, 2015), Spielrein writes of her longing for a son, Siegfried, to be born of an incestuous bond. The struggle to be – and to be punished as – an oedipal winner, and to vanquish the disdained mother/wife, dominates most of Spielrein's preoccupation with Siegfried – as myth and dream. Recruited to a heteronormative scene, the woman is fulfilled by a son, born of oedipal victory and incest.

Why is the passion for Siegfried so fiercely recruited to these transgressions, but nonetheless to transgressions within a system of order and hierarchy and heterosexuality? Why cannot Siegfried, through the creative offspring born of various exciting and creative unions/couplings producing unique new forms of thought and creativity, be a strange attractor? Why isn't Siegfried standing for Spielrein's ambition, her hope for productivity and fecundity that would belong to her? Perhaps we might ask if Spielrein was the object of envy from many sides, as well as being an object of censure or disdain. It is this determination to recruit Spielrein's story to a cautionary tale about female sexuality that I want to object to. Our reading of Spielrein's preoccupation with Siegfried might also be our cultural trope to write a cautionary tale about female ambition. Perhaps both ambition and sexuality can seem too costly. There are certainly punishments for imagined oedipal victory and ambitious striving in many narratives about Spielrein.

I have been unable to resist the thought that Piaget and Vygotsky are Siegfrieds and that the maternal subject is, as so often, sacrificed to male offspring. Was Spielrein for these younger, ambitious men simply the environmental mother, her individuality and power seamlessly airbrushed out? There is one very telling shift in Piaget's acknowledgment of Spielrein's work on child thought and child speech. In the English edition of his first book, he differentiates their projects, consigning her to the study of very young children and empirical work, as noted above. Yet in the earlier French edition of his first paper on child thought (Piaget, 1923), he notes the closeness of their work and the intention to interweave and bring together their hypotheses ("*nous espérons reprendre ensemble ces hypothèses* [we hope to bring these hypotheses together]," p. 286]).

In the more biographical and fictional treatments of Spielrein, the stress is on her masochism, sacrifice, and destructiveness. My Siegfried associations take me there as well. A documentary film (Márton, 2006/2002) presents a diary entry that predicts death in burning fields. We shudder, knowing her actual fate in 1942.

Why does the biographical trump history and politics? Looking at the fate of the Russian psychoanalytic movement, one sees the terrible pattern. There is a scattering of survivors, summary executions, or more protracted deaths in the gulags, and along with that, a few migrations. One of Spielrein's chief colleagues – the other IPA-sanctioned psychoanalyst, Moishe Wulff – goes to Berlin in 1927 and Palestine in 1933. What kept Spielrein from that path? Again, the narratives of this period in her life vacillate between masochism and family duties. All three brothers and her husband had perished in the late 1930s, victims of Stalin's purges. Perhaps she stayed too long; perhaps it was unthinkable to leave again (cf., Chapter 2, this volume). Let us stay, although it is difficult and anxiety-producing, with enigma. But we might be less obsessed with self-destructiveness or idealizations of masochism. Rather, there is the heavy hand of history.

Spielrein and her daughters were murdered in 1942 in the company of over 10,000 Jewish citizens who had been rounded up in Rostov, taken to a ravine at the edge of the town, shot, and buried in unmarked graves. In a series of massacres over a three-month period, 27,000 Jews were murdered. Once you know of Spielrein's and her family's fate in Rostov, that image never leaves you. But I want to offer you another image to hold alongside it. Alexander Etkind interviewed Spielrein's stepdaughter about Spielrein's last years in Rostov. Etkind tried to describe to a sixty-something Soviet citizen of the 1990s what psychoanalysis was. Lying on couches. Talking. "'Oh yes,' Nina answers, 'In that old stable' – (she is referring to Spielrein's workroom in the ramshackle quarters to which she and her family had been assigned) – 'there was a room that was totally empty except for a huge, lonely sofa'" (Etkind, 1997, p. 176).

Etkind imagines that Spielrein must have seen patients there sometime in that long expanse from 1923 to 1942, a practice that would have been dangerous and yet also intentional. My association was to the work of scholars like Judit Mészáros (2014) and Martin Mahler (2014), who track the intense and courageous need to preserve psychoanalysis in Budapest and Prague, even as an underground practice across half a century of oppression from Hitler to Stalin. They were compelled. Maurice Apprey (2015) might call this an "errand." My thought is that Spielrein, too, carried that project, that errand. She was compelled. In an employee questionnaire during a period in the 1920s in which Spielrein held positions in three central psychoanalytic institutions, she wrote, "I think that I was born for this job, that it is my calling. My life would have no meaning without it" (Etkind, 1997, p. 172).

Psychoanalysis in the 1920s needed a thinker able to link it to other related disciplines and to advance ideas. The loss of Spielrein, someone who was actually performing this function at a quite crucial juncture in psychoanalytic history, is significant. It has taken decades for this kind of project to reappear and flourish (Schore, 2003; Mayes, Fonagy, & Target, 2007). We are in such a moment now in imagining the intersects of infancy research, neuroscience, clinical theory, and a renewed interest in the body and materiality. It is fascinating to me that these interests were clearly Spielrein's interests as well. We often think of what she lost, of how she was lost and eclipsed. But I ask us to think of the loss to psychoanalysis, and therefore of the loss to us.

Notes

1 An earlier version of this paper was given as a plenary address at the American Psychoanalytic Association in January 2015, and published in the *Journal of the American Psychoanalytic Association* (Harris, 2015) – adapted by permission. I am indebted to many helpful readers: Ken Corbett, Steven Cooper, Donald Moss, Wendy Olesker, Bonnie Litowitz, and John Launer. I am also deeply grateful for the assistance and translating efforts of Judith Gresh.
2 For many people, the Cronenberg film (2011) was a particularly destructive intervention in understanding Spielrein. A recent biography (Launer, 2015) restores a careful balance to accounting for a long and productive life, albeit a complex one.
3 "By 1910, there were 362 Russian students at Zürich University. The majority were women, and more than half were studying medicine" (Launer, 2015, p. 54).
4 Otto Rank is usually accorded this distinction for his dissertation on Lohengrin in Vienna in October 1911, but Spielrein in fact completed her doctorate in January 1911! – PC-W.
5 Later published as Spielrein (1912a); cf. Spielrein (1994/1912, 1995/1912; newly trans. in this volume, Chapter 6).
6 Minutes of that meeting record eighteen people present, including Freud, Spielrein, Dattner, Federn, Friedjung, Hitschmann, Nepallek, Rank, Reinhold, Reitler, Reik, Rosenstein, Sachs, Sadger, Steiner, Stekel, and Tausk, plus two guests (Nunberg & Federn, 1974, p. 329). We might wonder at the underground circuitry of these figures spreading different versions of Spielrein's ideas beyond the perimeter of that meeting. For more on the reception of Spielrein's paper, see Chapter 2, this volume.
7 Carotenuto (1982) made the first crucial discovery, and this work led to biographies by Kerr (1994) and Richebächer (2012). Most crucially, work by Covington and Wharton (2015) and their colleagues, particularly Zvi Lothane (2015) and Cifali (2001), widen our experience of Spielrein, her era, and her work. There is important scholarship within developmental psychology by Santiago-Delafosse and Delafosse (2002) and Vidal (2001). I am indebted to crucial archival excavation and contextualizing work by Etkind (1997) and Miller (1998). The continuing recovery and rehabilitation and widening scope of work on Vygotsky has also been crucial (Vygotsky, 1994; Frawley, 1997). This large community of scholars scattered internationally is a joy to know of and encounter. For everyone engaged in working on Spielrein, this is all still so much a work in progress. Mistakes and misleading judgments will inevitably occur. There will be revisions, of course. For me, the work of Alexander Etkind and John Launer have offered the deepest insights and guidance. The present volume continues the trajectory of research. A new International Association for Spielrein Studies founded by Klara Naszkowska in Warsaw, Poland

(www.spielreinassociation.org), promises to offer further opportunities for collaborative research.
8 These writers approach language with a deep appreciation for the power of somatic, preverbal, unmentalized experience and so lean on models of consciousness and unconscious life that appreciate the layering of consciousness.
9 Mawson (2011), in an introduction to his edited collection *Bion Today*, notes "The degree of collaboration between Hannah Segal, Wilfred Bion and Herbert Rosenfeld in their work with psychotic patients during the late 1950s, and their discussions with Melanie Klein at the time, means that it is not always possible to distinguish their exact individual contributions…" (p. 3).
10 Hug-Hellmuth herself cites several early sources of child observation, some going back to the 1880s, all of them producing powerful and subtle observations of infant life (Preyer, 1880; Shinn, 1900). One such researcher, Mildred Shinn (an American), was awarded a doctorate at Berkeley in 1900 for a thesis – later published as a book – that detailed a highly intricate and close observation of infant life, observations she made of her young nephew from birth to about two years. Both Hug-Hellmuth and Shinn are little known today.
11 As will be discussed further below, Piaget was in Geneva for roughly the same years as Spielrein, and even was analyzed by her around the year 1921 (Launer, 2015, p. 201). They both presented papers at the Berlin Congress in 1922 (ibid., p. 203).
12 There are conflicting views on the degree to which Freud diverged from Spielrein's views on a death instinct and destructiveness (see also Chapter 2, this volume).
13 Translated in this volume (Chapter 6) variously as "species-psyche" and "collective psyche."
14 Spielrein's work here sits in an anomalous and difficult spot. Psychoanalysis might be said to have a century-long concern, low grade but insistent nonetheless, with the danger posed by the mother. Managing maternal envy may require a masquerade (Riviere, 1929); the impact of maternal envy may require strict regulation (see Bernstein, 1990, on the archaic female superego). See also Elise (1997) on the female oedipal situation and Harris (1997) on envy's excitements and terrors, the fear of being the object of envy that constricts ambition and excitement.
15 Others include Miller, Ovcharenko, Launer, van der Veer, Valsiner, Frawley, and Wertsch.

References

Apprey, M. (2015). The pluperfect errand. *Free Associations: Psychoanalysis & Culture, Media, Groups, Politics*, 77, 15–28.

Aron, L. & Harris, A. (Eds.) (1993). *The legacy of Sándor Ferenczi*. Hillsdale, NJ: Analytic Press.

Baranger, M. & Baranger, W. (2009). *The work of confluence: Listening and interpreting in the psychoanalytic field*. London. Karnac.
Bernstein, D. (1990). Female genital anxieties, conflicts and typical mastery modes. *International Journal of Psychoanalyasis*, 71, 151–165.
Bersani, L. (2010). *Is the rectum a grave? and other essays*. Chicago, IL: University of Chicago Press.
Bion, W.R. (1984a). *Learning from experience*. London: Karnac. (Orig. publ. 1962.)
Bion, W.R. (1984b). *Elements of psychoanalysis*. London: Karnac. (Orig. publ. 1963.)
Bonomi, C. (2014). *The cut and the building of psychoanalysis, Vol. 1: Sigmund Freud and Emma Eckstein*. New York: Routledge.
Botella, C. & Botella, S. (2005). *The work of psychic figurability: Mental states without representation*. A. Weller & M. Zerbib (Trans.). London: Karnac.
Butler, J. (2004). *Undoing gender*. New York: Routledge.
Carotenuto, A. (1982). *A secret symmetry: Sabina Spielrein between Freud and Jung*. A. Pomerans (Trans.). New York: Pantheon.
Chodorow, N.J. (2002). Born into a world at war: Listening for affect and personal meaning. *American Imago*, 59, 297–315.
Cifali, M. (2001). Sabina Spielrein, a woman psychoanalyst: Another picture. *Journal of Analytical Psychology*, 46, 129–138.
Claparède, E. (1923). La conscience de la ressemblance et de la différence chez l'enfant. *Archives de Psychologie*, 23, 67–80.
Cooper-White, P. (2014). Beyond "A dangerous method": Sabina Spielrein and the "death instinct." Fulbright lecture presented at the Sigmund Freud Museum, Vienna, January 17.
Cooper-White, P. (2017). *Old and dirty gods: Religion, antisemitism, and the origins of psychoanalysis*. New York: Routledge.
Covington, C. & Wharton, B. (Eds.) (2015) *Sabina Spielrein: Forgotten pioneer of psychoanalysis*, 2nd edn. New York: Routledge.
Cronenberg, D. (Director) (2011). *A dangerous method* (film). Los Angeles: Sony Pictures Classics.
Dimen, M. (2003). *Sexuality, intimacy, power*. Hillsdale, NJ: Analytic Press.
Elise, D. (1997). Primary femininity, bisexuality, and the female ego ideal: A re-examination of female developmental theory. *Psychoanalytic Quarterly*, 66, 489–516.
Etkind, A. (1997). *Eros of the impossible: The history of psychoanalysis in Russia*. New York: Westview Press.
Ferenczi, S. (1989). *Thalassa: A theory of genitality*. London: Karnac. (Orig. publ. 1924.)
Ferro, A. (2005). *Seeds of illness, seeds of recovery: The genesis of suffering and the role of psychoanalysis*. P. Slotkin (Trans.). New York: Routledge.
Flavell, J. (1963). *The developmental psychology of Jean Piaget*. New York: Van Nostrand.

Fonagy, P. (1995). Playing with reality: The development of psychic reality and its malfunction in borderline personalities. *International Journal of Psychoanalysis*, 76, 39–44.

Frawley, W. (1997). *Vygotsky and cognitive science: Language and the unification of the social and computational mind*. Cambridge, MA: Harvard University Press.

Freeman, W. (1990). Chaos: The new science of the brain. *Concepts in Neuroscience*, 2, 275–285.

Freud, S. (1955). Beyond the pleasure principle. *SE*, 18, 1–64. (Orig. publ. 1920.)

Freud, S. (1958). Psycho-analytic notes on an autobiographical account of a case of paranoia (dementia paranoides) ("The Case of Schreber"). In J. Strachey (Ed.), *The standard edition of the complete psychological works of Sigmund Freud* (hereafter *SE*), 12, 1–82. (Orig. publ. 1911.)

Gross, O. (2012). On the symbolism of destruction. In O. Gross, *Selected works, 1901–1920*. L.L. Madison (Trans.) (pp. 261–270). Hamilton, NY: Mindpiece. (Orig. publ. 1913.)

Harris, A. (1976). The function of speech rhythms in the regulation of non-speech activity. In K. Riegel & J. Meacham (Eds.), *Development of the individual in a changing world, Vol. 1: Historical and cultural issues* (pp. 172–180). The Hague: Mouton.

Harris, A. (1997). Aggression, envy, and ambition: Circulating tensions in women's psychic life. *Gender and Psychoanalysis*, 2, 291–325.

Harris, A. (2005). *Gender as soft assembly*. Hillsdale, NJ: Analytic Press.

Harris, A. (2014). Curative speech: Symbol, body, dialogue. *Journal of the American Psychoanalytic Association*, 62(6), 1029–1045.

Harris, A. (2015). "Language is there to bewilder itself and others": Theoretical and clinical contributions of Sabina Spielrein. *Journal of the American Psychoanalytic Association*, 63(4), 727–767.

Hug-Hellmuth, H. (1919). *A study of the mental life of the child*. J.J. Putnam & M. Stevens (Trans.). Washington, DC: Nervous and Mental Disease Publishing Company. (Orig. publ. 1912.)

Kerr, J. (1994). *A most dangerous method: The story of Jung, Freud, and Sabina Spielrein*. New York: Vintage.

Klein, M. (1926). Infant analysis. *International Journal of Psycho-Analysis*, 7, 31–63.

Klein, M. (1932). *The psychoanalysis of children*. London: Hogarth.

Kress-Rosen, N. (2003). Kindred spirits. In C. Covington & B. Wharton (Eds.), *Sabina Spielrein: Forgotten pioneer of psychoanalysis* (pp. 251–261). New York: Routledge.

Kuriloff, E.A. (2014). *Psychoanalysis and the Third Reich: History, memory, tradition*. New York: Routledge.

Lampl-de Groot, J. (1933). Problems of femininity. *Psychoanalytic Quarterly*, 2, 489–518.

Laplanche, J. (1999). *Essays on otherness*. J. Fletcher (Trans.). New York: Routledge.
Laplanche, J. (2002). Sexuality and attachment in metapsychology. In D. Widlöcher (Ed.), *Infantile sexuality and attachment* (pp. 37–54). London: Karnac.
Laplanche, J. (2016). *New foundations for psychoanalysis*. J. House (Trans.). New York: Unconscious in Translation. (Orig. publ. 1990.)
Launer, J. (2015). *Sex versus survival: The life and ideas of Sabina Spielrein*. New York: Overlook Duckworth.
Levine, H.B., Reed, G.S., & Scarfone, D. (2013). *Unrepresented states and the construction of meaning: Clinical and theoretical contributions*. London: Karnac.
Lewin, K. (1947). Frontiers in group dynamics: Concept, method and reality in social science; social equilibria and social change. *Human Relations*, 1, 36.
Loewald, H.W. (1980a). Primary process, secondary process, and language. In H.W. Loewald (Ed.), *Papers on psychoanalysis* (pp. 178–208). New Haven, CT: Yale University Press. (Orig. publ. 1978.)
Loewald, H.W. (1980b). Instinct theory, object relations and psychic structure formation. In H.W. Loewald (Ed.), *Papers on psychoanalysis* (pp. 207–218). New Haven, CT: Yale University Press.
Loewald, H.W. (1988). Psychoanalysis in search of nature: Thoughts on metapsychology, "metaphysics," projection. *Annual of Psychoanalysis*, 16, 49–54.
Lothane, [H.]Z. (2015). Tender love and transference: Unpublished letters of C. G. Jung and Sabina Spielrein (with an addendum/discussion). In C. Covington & B. Wharton (Eds.), *Sabina Spielrein: Forgotten pioneer of psychoanalysis*, 2nd edn. (pp. 126–157). New York: Routledge.
Mahler, M. (2014). Underground Psychoanalysis in Prague. Paper presented at the Sándor Ferenczi Center. New School University, New York, April.
Makari, G.J. (1994). In the eye of the beholder: Helmholtzian perception and the origins of Freud's 1900 theory of transference. *Journal of the American Psychoanalytic Association*, 42, 549–580.
Márton, E. (Director) (2006). *My name was Sabina Spielrein* (DVD). Chicago, IL: Facets Video. (Orig. released as *Ich hieß Sabina Spielrein*, produced by Helgi Felix/Idé Film Felixson AB, 2002.)
Matte-Blanco, I. (1975). *The unconscious as infinite sets: An essay in bi-logic*. London: Duckworth.
Matte-Blanco, I. (2005). The four antinomies of the death instinct. R. Carvalho (Trans.). *International Journal of Psychoanalysis*, 86, 1463–1476. (Orig. publ. 1973.)
Mawson, C. (Ed.) (2011). *Bion today*. New York: Routledge.
Mayes, L.C., Fonagy, P., & Target, M. (2007). *Develomental science and psychoanalysis: Integration and innovation*. London: Karnac.

Mészáros, J. (2014). *Ferenczi and beyond: Exile of the Budapest School and solidarity in the psychoanalytic movement during the Nazi years*. London: Karnac.

Miller, M. (1986). The origins and development of Russian psychoanalysis, 1909–1930. *Journal of the American Academy of Psychoanalysis*, 14, 125–135.

Miller, M. (1998). *Freud and the Bolsheviks: Psychoanalysis in imperial Russia and in the Soviet Union*. New Haven, CT: Yale University Press.

Muller, J. (1932). A contribution to the problem of libidinal development of the genital phase in girls. *International Journal of Psychoanalysis*, 13, 361–368.

Nunberg, H. & Federn, E. (Eds.) (1974). *Minutes of the Vienna Psychoanalytic Society, Vol. 3: 1910–1911*. M. Nunberg (Trans.). New York: International Universities Press.

Nunberg, H. & Federn, E. (Eds.) (1979). *Minutes of the Vienna Psychoanalytic Society, Vol. 4: 1912–1918*. M. Nunberg (Trans.). New York: International Universities Press.

Ogden, T.H. (1997). *Reverie and interpretation: Sensing something human*. Northvale, NJ: Jason Aronson.

Ovcharenko, V. (1999). Love, psychoanalysis and destruction. C.J. Wharton (Trans.). *Journal of Analytical Psychology*, 44, 355–373.

Piaget, J. (1923). La pensée symbolique et la pensée de l'enfant. *Archives de Psychologie*, 18(72), 273–303.

Piaget, J. (1927). La causalité chez l'enfant. *British Journal of Psychology*, 18, 276–301.

Piaget, J. (2001). *The language and thought of the child*. M. Gabain (Trans.). New York: Routledge. (Orig. publ. 1923.)

Piaget, J. (2013). *The moral judgment of the child*. M. Gabain (Trans.). New York: Routledge. (Orig. publ. 1932.)

Preyer, W. (1880). *The mind of the child: The senses and the will*. New York: Appleton.

Reich, A. (1953). Narcissistic object choice in women. *Journal of the American Psychoanalytic Association*, 1, 22–44.

Richebächer, S. (2012). *De Freud à Jung* [From Freud to Jung]. D. Martineschen (Trans.). Sao Paolo: Editora Civilização Brasileira.

Riviere, J. (1929). Womanliness as a masquerade. *International Journal of Psychoanalysis*, 9, 303–313.

Saketopoulou, A. (2015). On sexual perversions' potential to act as portal to unformulated mental states. In A. Lemma & P. Lynch (Eds.), *Sexualities: Contemporary psychoanalytic perspectives* (pp. 205–218). New York: Routledge.

Santiago-Delafosse, M.J. & Delafosse, O.J.M. (2002). Spielrein, Piaget and Vygotsky: Three positions on child thought and child language. *Theory and Psychology*, 12(6), 723–747.

Schore, A. (2003). *Affect dysregulation and disorders of the self; affect regulation and repair of the self.* New York: W.W. Norton.

Segal, H. (1957). Notes on symbol formation. *International Journal of Psychoanalysis*, 38, 391–397.

Shinn, M.W. (1900). *The biography of a baby.* Boston, MA: Houghton Mifflin.

Spielrein, S. (1911). Über den psychologischen Inhalt eines Falles von Schizophrenie (Dementia Praecox) [On the psychological content of a case of schizophrenia (Dementia Praecox)]. *Jahrbuch für psychoanalytische und psychopathologische Forschungen*, 3, 329–400. (Excerpt trans. this volume, Chapter 5; for full English trans., see Spielrein, 2018, pp. 14–96).

Spielrein, S. (1912). Die Destruktion als Ursache des Werdens. [Destruction as the cause of becoming]. *Jahrbuch für psychoanalytische und psychopathologische Forschungen*, 4, 465–503. (Trans. this volume, Chapter 6 cf., Spielrein 2018, pp. 97–134.)

Spielrein, S. (1913a). Beiträge zur Kenntnis der Kindlichen Seele. [Contributions to an understanding of the child's mind.] *Zentralblatt für Psychoanalyse und Psychotherapie*, 3, 57–72. (Trans. in Spielrein, 2018, pp. 135–154.)

Spielrein, S. (1913b). Mutterliebe [Maternal love]. *Imago*, 2, 523–524. (Trans. this volume, Chapter 7.)

Spielrein, S. (1914). Der vergessene Name. [The forgotten name.] *Internationale Zeitschrift für Ärtzliche Psychoanalyse*, 2, 383–384. (Trans. this volume, Chapter 8.)

Spielrein, S. (1920a). On the question of the origin and development of speech. *International Journal of Psychoanalysis*, 1, 359–360.

Spielrein, S. (1920b). Renatschens Menschenstehungstheorie [Little Renate's theory of human origins.] *Internationale Zeitschrift für Psychoanalyse*, 6, 155–157. J. Gresh (Trans. – unpublished).

Spielrein, S. (1920c). Das Schamgefühl bei Kindern [The feeling of shame in children]. *Internationale Zeitschrift für Psychoanalyse*, 6, 157–158. J. Gresh (Trans. – unpublished).

Spielrein, S. (1920d). Verdrängte Munderotik [Displaced oral eroticism]. *Internationale Zeitschrift für Psychoanalyse*, 6, 172–174. J. Gresh (Trans. – unpublished).

Spielrein, S. (1921). Russische Literatur: Bericht über die Fortschritte der Psychoanalyse in den Jahren 1914–1919 [Russian Literature: Report on the progress of psychoanalysis in the years 1914–1919]. *Beiheft der Internationale Zeitschrift für Psychoanalyse*, 3, 356–365. (Trans. this volume, Chapter 10.)

Spielrein, S. (1922). Psychologische[r Beitrag] zum Zeitproblem: Bericht über den VII Internationalen Psychoanalytischen Kongress in Berlin (25.–27. Sept. 1922) [Psychological contributions to the problem of time: Report of the 7th International Psychoanalytical Congress in Berlin.] *Internationale Zeitschrift für Psychoanalyse*, 8(4), 496–497.

Spielrein, S. (1923a) Die drei Frage. [The three questions.] *Imago*, 9, 210–211. (Trans. this volume, Chapter 13.)

Spielrein, S. (1923b). Die Gedankengang bei einem zweieinhalbjahrigen Kind [The thinking processes in a child of two-and-a-half years.] *Internationale Zeitschrift für Psychoanalyse*, 9, 251–252. J. Gresh (Trans. – unpublished).

Spielrein, S. (1923c). Quelques analogies entre la pensée de l'enfant, celle de l'aphasique et la pensée subconsciente [Some analogies between a child's thought, aphasic thought, and subconscious thought]. *Archives de Psychologies*, 18, 305–322. (Trans. this volume, Chapter 14.)

Spielrein, S. (1929). K'dokladu Doktora Skal'kovskovo [Dr. Skalkovskiy's report]. Proceedings of the 1st Congress of Psychiatry and Neuropathology of the North Caucasus Region, Rostov-on-Don. (Trans. this volume, Chapter 15.)

Spielrein, S. (1931). Kinderzeichnungen bei offenen und geschlossenen Augen [Children's drawings with eyes open and closed], parts 1 and 2. *Imago*, 17, 159–391. (Trans. this volume, Chapter 16.)

Spielrein, S. (1994). Destruction as a cause of coming into being. K. McCormick (Trans.). *Journal of Analytical Psychology*, 39, 155–186. (Orig. publ. 1912.)

Spielrein, S. (1995). Destruction as cause of becoming. S.K. Witt (Trans.). *Psychoanalysis and Contemporary Thought*, 18, 85–118. (Orig. publ. 1912.)

Spielrein, S. (2001a). Animal symbolism and a boy's phobia. C.J. Warton (Trans.). *Journal of Analytical Psychology*, 46, 202–204. (Orig. publ. 1914.)

Spielrein, S. (2001b). A dream and a vision of shooting stars. P. Bennett & B. Wharton (Trans.). *Journal of Analytical Psychology*, 46, 211–214. (Orig. publ. 1923.)

Spielrein, S. (2001c). The mother-in-law. C.J. Wharton (Trans.). *Journal of Analytical Psychology*, 46, 205–208. (Orig. publ. 1913.)

Spielrein, S. (2001d). The unconscious phantasies in Kuprin's *Duel*. C.J. Wharton (Trans.). *Journal of Analytical Psychology*, 46(1), 201–202. (Orig. publ. 1913.)

Spielrein, S. (2015a). The origin of the child's words Papa and Mama: Some observations on the different stages in language development. B. Wharton (Trans.). In C. Covington & B. Wharton (Eds.), *Sabina Spielrein: Forgotten pioneer of psychoanalysis*, 2nd edn. (pp. 233–248). New York: Routledge. (Orig. publ. 1922.)

Spielrein, S. (2015b). Unedited extracts from a diary (with a prologue by Jeanne Moll.) J. Moll, P. Bennett, & B. Wharton (Trans.). In C. Covington & B. Wharton (Eds.), *Sabina Spielrein: Forgotten pioneer of psychoanalysis*, 2nd edn. (pp. 14–29). New York: Routledge. (Orig. unpubl. manuscript, c. 1906–1907.)

Spielrein, S. (2018). *The essential writings of Sabina Spielrein: Pioneer of psychoanalysis*. R. Cape & R. Burt (Eds. & Trans.). New York: Routledge.

Stein, R. (1998). The poignant, the excessive, and the enigmatic in sexuality. *International Journal of Psychoanalysis*, 79, 253–268.

Tausk, V. (1933). On the origin of the "influencing machine" in schizophrenia. *Psychoanalytic Quarterly*, 2, 519–556.

Vidal, F. (2001). Sabina Spielrein, Jean Piaget: Going their own way. *Journal of Analytical Psychology*, 46, 139–153.

Vygotsky, L.S. (1962). *Lev Vygotsky: Thought and language*, 2nd edn. A. Kozulin (Ed. & Trans.). Cambridge, MA: MIT Press. (Orig. publ. 1934.)

Vygotsky, L.S. (1978). *Mind in society: The development of higher psychological processes*. M. Cole & S. Scribner (Eds.) Cambridge, MA: Harvard University Press.

Vygotsky, L.S. (1987). *The collected works of L.S. Vygotsky, Vol. 1: Problems of general psychology*. R.W. Rieber & A. Carto (Eds.). New York: Plenum Press.

Vygotsky, L.S. (1994) *The Vygotsky reader*. R. Van der Veer & J. Valsiner (Eds. & Trans.). Oxford: Blackwell.

Vygotsky, L. & Luria, A.R. (1925). Foreword. In S. Freud, *Po to storonu principa udovol'stvija* (pp. 3–16). Moscow: Sovremennye Problemy.

Wharton, B. (2015). Comment on Spielrein's paper "The origin of the child's words Papa and Mama." In C. Covington & B. Wharton (Eds.), *Sabina Spielrein: Forgotten pioneer of psychoanalysis*, 2nd edn. (pp. 249–250). New York: Routledge.

Wharton, C.J. & Ovcharenko, V. (1999) The history of psychoanalysis and the problem of Periodization. *Journal of Analytical Psychology*, 44, 341–352.

Part II

Samples of Spielrein's writings – new translations in English

Chapter 5

On the Psychological Content of a Case of Schizophrenia (Dementia Praecox) (An Excerpt)

Sabina Spielrein

1911 Translated by Judith Gresh with Pamela Cooper-White

Introduction

Studies in recent years[1] have shown a certain understanding of schizophrenia (dementia praecox), which requires a broader empirical basis from a different point of view. I decided to investigate a case of paranoid dementia, although at first without taking into account established scientific opinion, with the unique intention to gain a deeper understanding of these patients' mental processes. I chose this case because the patient, an educated, well-read woman, is very productive, which at first glance seems to be a complete mess of entirely meaningless sentences. I think it is best to communicate this material as completely as possible, literally the way the patient told to me, so that the reader has the opportunity to check the validity of my conclusions. I would only ask the reader not to consider my conclusions arbitrary merely on the basis of a fragment: we cannot avoid the fact that, taking into account the whole analysis, I am getting ahead of myself with practically one explanation; the proof of the correctness of the "interpretation" [*Deutung*] will be presented later.

Evidence that made interpretation irrefutable for me, in many cases, was immediate, spontaneous information from the patient. In other cases, it turned out that the patient was unable to answer questions directly. Moreover, she preferred making very ambiguous comments leading to other areas, which then needed to be decrypted again, thus, in the end, there is the risk of getting lost in details.

The urge for a definite interpretation further deprives us of the advantage of clearly seeing the spontaneous chain of associations;

there is also a risk of forcing the patient to talk about embarrassing things, provoking feelings of discomfort about the study. Following these reflections, I had to make a good many conclusions from what was said earlier, and from the general context. At first, I had to be thorough, to ensure the correctness of my conclusions; then, in reverse, I devised a shorter route, as I tried to translate the patient's statements directly into our language without making her say a word – see, for example, the chapter "*Impressions of childhood*," etc., where I had already mastered the patient's language.

To avoid suggestion, I looked through the medical history, the anamnesis, only shortly before the end of the study, when I had finished everything. I was now controlling the extent to which what was discovered by me coincided with the anamnesis and could explain it. It is not easy to follow the tangle of thoughts. Therefore, repetition seemed to me necessary in many places. However, anyone who wants to check the correctness of my conclusions should act as a forensic investigator, and must get involved in the work to the point of taking into consideration every word.

Anamnesis (from the medical history)

The husband reports: he has known the patient since she was eleven. Any childhood diseases are unknown to him. She has always been healthy, and from a mental [*geistiger*] point of view, he also did not notice any abnormalities. At school she was an educated girl, curious about many things, especially literature. She always had religious tendencies. She married thirteen years ago. In sexual relations she was cold. Soon she became pregnant. The pregnancy went normally, the birth went well, and in the postpartum period everything was normal as well. Once her baby almost swallowed a small ball; because of this, she was so frightened that she was agitated for several days. Six years ago, she became pregnant for the second time. Then she was very worried: the doctor told her that her mother suffered from cancer of the esophagus. As a result, she started to have attacks, during which she thought she should die and her heart would stop. The attacks lasted for half an hour, an hour. Often she immediately calmed down as soon as the doctor came. She had no appetite, she had been suffering from stomach pain even before. The birth was difficult, with forceps. During the induction of anesthesia, ether spilled on her face and burned her eyes. This feeling bothered her a long time after the incident. After her mother's death, which occurred two years later, she calmed down. In the spring of 1903, she had an abortion (at around seven months pregnant). It was a curettage [*Auskratzung*[2]], after which she had a fever and severe weakness. She spent three months in the hospital. There she had her third anesthetic. During the anesthesia, she saw horrible dreams, about which she spoke again and again. (The informant [*Referent*][3] knows none of the details!) When she returned home, she showed, as before, a strong need for love, which, however, often seemed exaggerated to the informant, and very demonstrative. She always felt pressured to work, but was often very tired. In the summer before her illness, she enjoyed happy vacations. The patient was exuberantly happy. After that, she felt tired, completely exhausted, and thought she was pregnant again, but it was not so. Beginning in autumn 1905, she diligently cared for a poor family – she had always been immensely happy when she sent something to the poor. November 16, she visited a deaconess, was obviously very excited, prayed with the deaconess. At night, she woke her husband and told him that he was not religious enough. November 17 she was calm and behaved normally. The patient operates an embroidery business. She now kept a piece of fabric from a dress that she had already delivered. She wrote to the lady in question that she had kept the fabric (from whom she had been given too much) and now reproached herself for it. In the evening, she reproached her husband again because of religion, and said that she would give him no rest until he and his family also found salvation. The morning of November 18 – euphoric. At noon she cried, and suddenly made a big scene because her husband didn't have the right faith; she claimed that her sister was sick and should stay in bed, thought she herself was dirty, and therefore should not go to bed. From that moment she spoke in a wild jumble, argued that everybody was dirty and they should all wash their hands, her feet would have to be washed. Then she prayed again. So it was until hospitalization.

This is what we learned from her husband. It was impossible to obtain data of the history from the patient herself, as her speech was a confused muddle, as her husband also reports. Let us now consider the further course of the disease: I always bring from the case as much as necessary for an understanding of the relevant chapter. Here I should mention that the patient was Protestant, and her husband Catholic.

She said many times that her husband, a professor by occupation, was seduced by two students; one of them was especially guilty; she was a beautiful rich girl. She characterizes this girl with the name "Wench" ["*Frauenzimmer*"].[4]

Mental status exam [*Status praesens*]

The patient is pale and tired, no other obvious signs of physical disorders.

Orientation – in both time and space – good.

Perception and memory – not impaired.

Affectivity – inadequate. The patient gives the impression of a bad actor who cannot express his feelings in relation to the outside world, and to compensate for this deficiency, his expression is exaggeratedly emotional. Patient's pathos has features of something forced: her expression is variously tough, then serious, then not expressing anything, then smiling. The tone of voice shows little modulation. Pathos seems empty and basically "affectless."

Speech – highly tangled, sometimes accompanied by a meaningless play on words. Blockage and loss of thinking often occurs.

Hallucinations – primarily visual, auditory (voice), bodily sensations, such as electrostatic feelings.

Delusions – completely meaningless, for example: she is "catholicized" ["*katholisiert*"], is contaminated by urine, "makes her way through Basel," she was anesthetized and is waking up in the form of a horse, as a little trout [*Forel*[5]], she was dissected [*seziert*], is "phrenologized" ["*phrenologiert*"], has "mythological cures," etc.

Mannerisms – sometimes she is lying "on the body" ["*auf dem Leibe*"[6]], sometimes she falls to her knees before God and whispers something to herself in a solemn voice; in general, mannerisms are not very characteristic.

Psychomotor abnormalities – in the sense of catatonia – as good as absent: no continuous negativity ["*Negativismus*"], no catalepsy; no stereotypes or perseveration of action; echolalia, echopraxia – absent.

Is mostly housed in the ward for agitated [patients], sometimes is very violent.

Diagnosis: paranoid form of dementia praecox.

I. "Catholicizing"

From the medical history, we conclude that the patient did not love her husband in the sexual sense, and often quarreled with him; she believes that her husband chose one of his students. Her husband is Catholic and the patient is Protestant. The patient says a lot about the fact that, here in the hospital, she was "catholicized." Question: "What do you mean by "catholicizing?" Answer: "The history of art is in contact with Michelangelo, Sistine art, and the Madonna. That came into contact with Lao art; it is connected with Laocoön. Sistine art is sexual art. The derivation of Sistine art is Lao art, generation art. Sistine art gives rise to sexual art: through the beautiful image one can be transformed into poetry, [and] perhaps forget obligations. Sistine poetry – Catholics' poetry; it must be linked with the Madonna, Raphael, with all Catholic poetry."

This is the opinion of the patient. Everyone knows the Sistine Chapel in Rome, which serves the Catholic[7] religion, and at the same time houses Michelangelo's frescoes. The Madonna, whom the whole world worships as a symbol of beauty, also belongs to the Catholic religion. Raphael's Madonna is known as the Sistine. "Sistine art" (chapel), and the Catholic religion (art = "poetry"), respectively, are linked with beauty (Madonna, Raphael, Michelangelo). Sexual art is derived from Sistine art: [as] the patient expresses, "through a beautiful image one can be transformed into poetry, perhaps, forget obligations." With the phrase "forget obligations," delivered from the mouth of a married woman, "poetry" is viewed as an explicit erotic element, so that we can compare "poetry" ["*poesie*"] = "amorousness."[8] In fact, the patient confirms that her husband was delighted with beauty and forgot about his responsibilities in relation to his wife and children. Without waiting for further questioning, she continues:

> "The psychology of vanity is not related to the psychology of motherhood; clothes are chosen with the greatest care only when required by aesthetics. I have no respect for the soul [*Psyche*] who promotes beauty above internal purity."

However, she believes that her husband preferred the "beauty" ("the Wench") over "inner purity" (the patient). Since her husband is Catholic, then, accordingly, his sexual love in general is called "Catholic," "poetry," "art," "religion," and so on. In creating symbols, a similarity in sound between the words "Sistine" ["*sixtinisch*"] and "sexual" ["*sexuell*"] also played role. The patient even creates a verb corresponding to Catholic ("husband"): "to catholicize" that means "to treat like a Catholic" (who is enthused by sexual love = catholic poetry). From sexual art, it is clear there is "generation art" (the creation of new generations), which is called "Lao art," because it is a symbol of Laocoön. ("The derivation of Sistine art is Lao art, or generation art.") The choice of the Catholic religion, as well as "religion" in general, as a symbol of sexuality, is mainly determined by the patient in the way that religion as a spiritual element represents the opposite of sexuality and the physical element. The reason for this seemingly paradoxical statement is the following: naming the sexual component through the negative (spiritual) is due to the strong resistance [*Abwehr*] to this component, but whereas the most sublime element – namely religion – represents sexuality, sexuality comes to be valued as sublime. The expression of the idea through its negative, or through its reversal, is repeated again and again in the symbolic imagery of the patient. This is confirmed in the following examples: to my question, whether she knows Catholics outside the institution, she cites the example of a family in which the husband was Protestant and the wife Catholic; there was always conflict between them, etc., then she remarked that it could also be that the husband was Catholic and the wife Protestant.

The patient is furious that her husband beat the children; soon after, she refers to a "case of poverty" ["*Armenfall*"] in which the mother perhaps beat the children. These people had the plague. She knows this because the woman reeked of "an impure atmosphere, prostitution." In addition, the patient claims that she was infected with prostitution from her husband and was thus made contaminated, sick, and so on. Everything about her husband that so arouses indignation in the patient is performed by a woman in her illustrations.

II. "Psycho-Sistine experiments"

When the patient said that she could have been unfaithful to her husband spiritually [*geistig*] and physically because his "soul" ["*Psyche*"] was in no way similar, I asked her if she had met a better soul yet.

"In the hospital it was Professor Forel,"[9] the patient said. "I found many well-known literary souls who brought sexual love to my mind. I came to know sexual love in a Forel-nature [*Forelnatur*] as a navitic [*navitische*] (?)[10] duty. Somewhere there should be a more sublime religion, a more sublime soul [*Psyche*]: God-seeking airs that sought Sunday; but the wench (the husband's student) took religion, faith from me. This is an animal bisection [*Diszentrie*], bisectional [*Diszentric*][11] of sexuality, associated with Dr. Laocoön.[12] There are psychological, animal, and vegetarian [*vegetarische*] *Marmite* (French for cooking pan). The pan is vegetarian, associated with contempt for the flesh. If the vegetable is impurely sexualized, than the vegetarian pan is also insufficient. *Marmite* is the pan; it is associated with the gifts of God, who sends the food."

We see that the patient comes to speak about three types of pan (using the word "*Marmite*" instead of pan), to explain the sexual "Dizcentrics." We can provisionally give the psychological pan a special position above the animalistic and the vegetarian ones. The patient might also be treated as a psycho-Sistine experiment; which would correspond at the same time to a psychological and a Sistine pan – the latter, in turn, being divided into two: a "vegetarian" one, associated with "contempt for the flesh" (that would be denial of sexuality), and an animal one (affirmation of sexuality). The association of the pans with sexuality is confirmed by the following proposition: "*If the vegetable is impurely sexualized,*" etc., speaking our language, this means: if the denial of sexuality (vegetable) is defiled by affirmation, i.e., it becomes an affirmation, then what use is the vegetarian pan with respect to defense?

So she continues: "Vegetables can become dirty, because farmers fertilize the ground with human excrement and with urine."

"People can be dissolved in water and dust; it enters in the animal, as it goes through ground, for example. This is the genetics of mythology or mysticism."

I ask her: "How can a person can be dissolved in water?"

Answer: "This is linked to the female anatomy. To the stone, which is formed of sand, we can give colors associated with Professor Tino-Forel.[13] Forel possesses a sculpture of spirit [*hat eine Plastik des Geistes*]; he is a sculptor of the soul [*plastische Künstler der Psyche*], who would lend the soul of the dust to the recreation [*Neuschaffung*][14] of people. The development of dust that comes from the dust of persons is brought into plastic beauty through the purity of a color."

The patient sees contamination in that the ground takes in human excrement and especially urine next to the seeds. Here I must anticipate a point that we will see more clearly later: the patient understands the underground to be a woman. The woman (earth/ground) is defiled by the fact that along with sperm she also takes in urine. Consequently follow fantasies of human origins. The explanation of how a person is dissolved in water should be sought in the remark of the patient: "This is linked to the female anatomy." In this sentence, the patient expressly indicates that the "how" of this dissolution (my question goes: How could a person be dissolved in water?) needs to be found in the female genital organs. The idea is beautiful: from the dust a stone is formed, which can then be brought to life. A new person can emerge from human dust, whilst he (here: Forel) lends his soul. Sculptural beauty is due to the purity of the colors – blood, as we will understand later. Concerning that, we should be thinking of [the Book of] Genesis, in which God created the human from dust and breathed[15] life into him.

The patient continues: "The stone figures must be dissolved in a mythological-pious way, similar to the rigidity of the soul [*Seele*] on the cross. This is associated with Laocoön poetry and painting."

From the preceding representation, it becomes apparent that creation from a stone is equivalent to creation of a human being. "The stone figures are dissolved" is a parallel to the dissolution of the person in water, which, according to the sentences above, is understood as a new creation [*Neuschöpfung*]. "The mythological is associated with the new creation [*Neuschaffung*] of people." (Patient's expression.) "Pious" (the opposite of "sin") is, as we have already seen,[16] the flight from sexuality into religion ("compensation"), as well as affirmation through defense.

The expression "*the rigidity of the soul on the cross*" is an identification with Christ, who dies rigidly on the cross. But Christ will be resurrected [*auferstehen*]! So the people (stone figures) will also be resurrected. Both sentences could now be read as follows: the stones are brought to life (a new person is created), the excruciating rigor mortis (Christ-Laocoön soul[17]), is thus "*dissolved*" ["*erlösen*"],[18] and that happens through procreation, which itself comes from sexuality (cf., "Sistine art is sexual art." The origin of "sexual art is Lao art or generation art").

"Mythological – that means through magic or the power of fire: Does fire purify everything? – It cleans coal and slag."

This sentence is closely connected with the one above – "magic and the power of fire" is a poetic expression for both heavenly and earthly love. Jung drew my attention to the analogy, observable in the Persian myths. The sun (fire) purifies the seed of the first man; the seed of the primal animal also comes into the moon (female light) for purification.[19]

"The ashes can turn into a person." This sentence which immediately follows proves that, for the patient, fire is also a fertilizing force.

"Slag and stains that remain in the soul must be melted by the fire of education," the patient goes on to say.

She then claims that once she was treated with "enthusiasm" ["*enthusiasmus*"] but she did not feel clean enough, so she fell, for the sake of a brother, sister, or friend. She then goes on to talk about the "*complexes.*" She heard about "complexes" from "Professor Forel, or perhaps from his brother" (note the uncertainty!). His brother was Dr. J.[20] Dr. J. is the student of Professor Forel:

> "He began with the spiritual dissolution of the question of religion, or the Sistine question."

Here we arrive at a deeper level, where – entirely uncertainly – instead of Forel, a new person appears – Dr. J.[21] He treated her as a "psychological experiment."[22][23] "Sistine" – is discarded at first; the second sentence corrects the error and cloaks "Sistine" as a "spiritistic [*spiritistische*] (i.e., "spiritual" ["*geistige*"]) solution." Again the surface (negative) "question of religion" comes first, then the deeper – "Sistine" question, linked by an "or." The word "question" ["*Frage*"], which the patient uses very often, is fully borrowed from the "sexual question" of Dr. Forel, whom the patient knows, at least by name.

Further we hear: "Dr. J. must have worked on suggestion and hypnosis[24] in order to get to the bottom of insanity; this is associated with alcohol: the spirits [*Spirituelle*] of wine, which are transferred into the soul. Alcohol is used in medicine for purification."

Mental treatment is thus associated with alcohol, i.e., with "the spirits of wine, which are transferred into the soul." Both terms, emphasizing the asexual meaning of wine, suggest to us that behind wine something truly animal is hidden, that is transferred into something animal. Alcohol, as well as fire, purifies everything, and in accordance with its role, is identified with the latter.[25] After cleansing with fire, we saw new people emerge from the ashes. Is it the same thing after cleansing with alcohol? "It is a description of Italian lakes," explains the patient, "they come to light through a splitting of the land; the Italian mythological legends come from this, ... or how to say it?"

The word "Italian" is used by the patient as an expression of beauty, poetry, art, and the like (as we have seen – love); an Italian lake would, therefore, be a beautiful or love-filled lake. The designation of earth [*Erde*] refers to the woman, as the patient later proves without a doubt. The new water (lake) appears through the split in the woman's body (earth). This process leads to the emergence of "mythological" legends, i.e., legends that are "associated" with the emergence of human beings.[26] So the water that comes from the woman's body could already be associated with the emergence of the human being; let us think of amniotic fluid! Dr. J.'s psychological treatment would therefore be, according to this, "the description of the processes of human origin." For the moment, let us not take this interpretation as a certainty, but as a possibility…

Notes

1 Here, in general, I am referring to Freud's and the Zürich school's researches. Cf., bibliography. *Jahrbuch für Psychoanalytische und Psychopathologische Forschungen* in 1909 and 1910.
2 Translator note: As in the modern procedure of dilation and curettage; lit. "scraping." – PC-W
3 Translator note: We presume the "Referent" here refers to the husband as informant. – PC-W
4 Translator note: "*Frauenzimmer*" now has this negative connotation; in archaic German it meant "Lady." Perhaps the double entendre was in some way meant by Spielrein's patient. – PC-W
5 Translator note: Auguste Forel (1848–1931) was the Director of the Burghölzli Hospital before Eugen Bleuler (1857–1939), where Spielrein herself had been treated. As noted in the translation of the "Destruction" paper in the next chapter of this volume, "Forel" was both the doctor's name and a homonym for *Forelle* (trout).
6 Translator note: From other contexts (Spielrein, 1911, 1912), this may mean lying on the ground in a cruciform position, imitating Christ (see, e.g., Chapter 6). – PC-W

7 Translator note: Spielrein capitalizes "*katholish*" inconsistently throughout this work. Because "catholic" means "universal" in both English and German, and this is clearly not her meaning here, we have chosen to capitalize the word whenever it refers to the religion. – PC-W
8 Translator note: Here we have the origin of Spielrein's own use of the word "poetry" in her diaries as a code word for whatever transpired sexually between herself and Jung. – PC-W
9 Translator note: In addition to the association with the word for trout, the fish is of course also a symbol for Christ – as noted by Bettina Mathes in the next chapter.
10 Translator note: Spielrein marks this neologism of the patient with a "?" in the original text. There may be some association in the patient's mind between "*Forel*" (trout) and some kind of "*nautisch*" (nautical) navigation. The meaning was not clear to Spielrein herself. "*Forelnatur*" is also obscure, though referring to her doctor in some way – perhaps in his manner or personal character, but also with some association again perhaps to the symbol of the trout. The entire sentence, like the entire paragraph, is slippery, echoing the symbolism and also the loosening of associations of the patient. – PC-W
11 Translator note: Another neologism of the patient, suggesting the splitting of a whole or center. – PC-W
12 Translator note: Laocoön – a priest of Apollo in Greek mythology who was required to remain celibate. According to some sources, Laocoön violated the prohibition and, together with his sons, was killed by serpents as punishment; in other versions, he was killed by snakes sent by Poseidon for revealing the truth about the Trojan horse. – JG, PC-W
13 Tino Moralt is the hero of a novel (Walther, 1911); he is an artist committed to beauty, which he cannot achieve. Tino Moralt and Forel Tino-Forel result in the condensation Tino-Forel. – JG
14 Translator note: Here, the patient is quoted as using the word "*Neuschaffung*," literally "new creation" or "production," and not "*Neuschöpfung*," which might carry a more obvious theological or cosmic connotation of creation. Later, Spielrein herself in referring to this sentence uses "*Neuschöpfung*." – PC-W
15 Translator note: Here, in keeping with the biblical citation, Spielrein uses the archaic/poetic word *Odem* for breath. – PC-W
16 For example, Section I, "Catholicizing."
17 Jung points to the similarities with Laocoön (martyr's life): Christ with two thieves, Laocoön with two sons, besides Mithras Tauroktonos with two dadophores (cf.: Cumont: Myst.d.Mithra [Cumont, 1902]).
18 The word has a special meaning, to be discussed later.
19 Jung points to the importance of the cleansing function of heavenly urine among the Persians. The Indians cleanse themselves with cow urine. The heavenly sea of fertilization, Vorukasha, is purified with the urine of the three-legged donkey that lives in it.

20 Translator note: Almost certainly referring to C.G. Jung, who was hired by Eugen Bleuler (Forel's successor as Director of the Burghölzli). It is unclear whether the patient sensed the complex relationships of mentoring and rivalry among the three men. For more on Jung and the Burghölzli, see Bair (2003, pp. 55–69). – PC-W
21 By Dr. J., as shown below.
22 An association experiment was conducted with her one time.
23 Translator note: This refers to Jung's research using word associations to access the unconscious (see Bair, 2003, p. 64). Jung described this research in detail (Jung, 1973/1904–1910). – PC-W
24 What the patient knows from Professor Forel. "Alcohol" must also be associated with Forel's striving for abstinence from alcohol.
25 The Indian Soma is sometimes fertility, at other times an undying pool of fire. Soma is the ejaculation (Brihadâranyaka-Upanishad 1, 4, Deußen). At the same time, he is also a God, also known by the Persians as Haôma. Cf., Rig Veda VI, 47, 57, 59 (demonstrated to me by Jung).
26 Jung points out that mythologically, water has rich associations with "Mother"; one example of many: Mary is venerated as "Pege," as a source. (Cf. [Albrecht] Wirth: Ἐξήγησις περὶ τῶν ἐν Περσίδι πραχθέντων. [*Exegesis peri tōn en Persidi prachthentōn* – Account of the Things that Happened in Persia] – *From the Oriental Chronicles* [1894]).

References

Bair, D. (2003). *Jung: A biography*. Boston, MA: Back Bay Books/Little Brown.
Cumont, F.V.M. (1902). *Les mystères de Mithra*, 2nd edn. Paris: A. Fortemoing.
Jung, C.G. (1973). *Experimental researches*. In *Collected works of C.G. Jung*, Vol. 2. G. Adler (Ed.), R.F.C. Hull (Trans.). Princeton, NJ: Princeton University Press. (Orig. publ. 1904–1910.)
Spielrein, S. (1911). Über den psychologischen Inhalt eines Falles von Schizophrenie (Dementia praecox). *Jahrbuch für Psychoanalytische und Psychopathologische Forschungen*, 3(1), 329–400.
Spielrein, S. (1912). Die Destruktion als Ursache des Werdens [Destruction as the cause of Becoming]. *Jahrbuch für Psychoanalytische und Psychopathologische Forschungen*, 4, 465–503. (See Chapter 6, this volume.)
Walther, S. (1911). *Tino Moralt: Kampf und Ende eines Künstlers*. Berlin: Meyer & Jessen.

Chapter 6

Destruction as the Cause of Becoming

Sabina Spielrein

1912 Translated by Bettina Mathes with Pamela Cooper-White[1]

In my work on sexual problems, one question has especially interested me: why this most powerful drive, the reproductive drive, houses within itself, besides the a priori to-be-expected positive feelings, negative ones such as anxiety and disgust, the latter of which ought to be overcome in order to arrive at positive activity. The individual's negative attitude toward sexual activity is of course especially obvious in neurotics. To my knowledge some researchers have sought to explain this resistance with our mores – our upbringing – which aim at keeping the drive within limits and thus teach the child to regard the fulfillment of the sexual wish as something bad and prohibited. Some have remarked on the frequency with which sexual wishes are tied to mental images [*Vorstellungen*] of death which were however interpreted as a symbol of the moral Fall (Stekel[2]). Gross derives the disgust for the sexual products from their spatial proximity to dead excrement (feces). Freud traces the resistances – the anxiety – back to the repression of otherwise positive feeling-toned wishes. Bleuler sees the defense as the necessary negative, which must coexist with the positive feeling-toned representation. In Jung, I found the following passage[3]:

> The passionate longing, i.e., the libido, has two sides: it is the power that beautifies everything and, under certain circumstances, destroys everything. One often pretends to not quite understand what the destroying quality of the creative power could possibly be. A woman who abandons herself to her passions, especially under today's cultural circumstances, experiences the destructive quality only too soon. One must take one's thoughts a little outside the realm of bourgeois morality in order to understand the feeling

of boundless insecurity that overcomes the human being who surrenders to fate unconditionally. To be fruitful – that in itself is self-destruction, for with the birth of the next generation the previous one has passed its peak. And so our descendants become our most dangerous enemies, with whom we cannot come to terms, for they will outlive us and take the power from our enfeebled hands. This fear of erotic fate is entirely understandable, for there is something entirely unforeseeable in it. Fate generally holds unknown dangers, and the continual reluctance of neurotics to take a chance on life is explained by the wish to be permitted to stand aside, in order not to have to wrestle in the dangerous struggle of life. Those who forgo the venture of experiencing [life] must stifle the wish for it, i.e., commit a kind of suicide. This explains the death fantasies that so readily accompany the renunciation of the erotic wish.[4]

I purposely quote Jung's words in such detail because his remarks correspond best to my own conclusions, in that he points out an unknown danger of erotic activity. Moreover, it is very important to me that a male individual, too, is aware that this is not only a social fear.[5] To be sure, Jung does not bring the death representations into accord with the sexual representations – rather, he sees them as opposed to the sexual representations. From my experiences with girls I can say that anxiety is the feeling that normally moves to the forefront of feelings of repression precisely at the moment when, for the first time, the fulfillment of the wish seems possible. It is a special form of fear: one feels the enemy within oneself; it is one's own ardor which compels one with iron necessity to what one does not want. One feels the end, the passing away, from which one wants to escape into unknown distant lands. Is that all?, one might ask. Is this the climax, with nothing beyond? What happens to the individual engaged in sexual activity that warrants such a state of mind?

I. Biological facts

In procreation, a union between a female and a male cell occurs. Each cell is thereby destroyed as a unit and from the product of this destruction new life begins. Some lower forms of life, e.g., the mayfly, die after procreation because they have forfeited their lives in the production of the new generation. For these beings creation is also destruction, downfall [*Untergang*] which in itself is most terrifying to the living. If this particular destruction puts itself in the service of the new creation, then the individual yearns for it. With the more highly organized individual, which no longer consists of a single cell, the whole individual is, of course, not destroyed in the sexual act. However, the sexual cells, disappearing as a unit, are by no means indifferent elements to the organism but are most intimately connected with the entire life of the individual. They contain in concentrated form the entire progenitor by whom they are being influenced continuously during development, and whose development they, too, continuously influence. These most important extracts of the individual are destroyed in the process of impregnation. Due to the fusion of sexual cells, what happens during copulation is the most intimate union of two individuals: one pushing forth into the other. The difference is merely quantitative: it is not the whole individual that is being sucked in, but only a part of it – a part, however, which at that moment represents the value of the whole organism. The male part dissolves into the female; the female part, stirred into restlessness, receives a new form from the foreign intruder. This transformation affects the whole organism: destruction and restoration – which are always part of the organism's general functioning – now occur abruptly. The organism discharges the sexual products like any other excrement. It would be unlikely that the individual would not have at least a feeling (however vague) of these processes of destruction and reconstruction which are occurring in its organism. Just as wonderful feelings of Becoming[6] [*Werden*] are inherent in the reproductive drive, so are feelings of resistance, such as fear, anxiety, and disgust, which are part of the destructive component of the sexual instinct. Which is to say, they are not the consequence of a faulty association with the spatial proximity of excreta, i.e., they are not the negative, which leads to the renunciation of sexual activity.[7]

II. Individual psychological observations

The claim that psychically we experience nothing at all in the present sounds paradoxical, and yet it is accurate. We experience an event as feeling-toned [*gefühlsbetont*] only insofar as it may stimulate earlier feeling-toned contents (experiences) that lie hidden in the unconscious. An example will make this clear: a girl likes to read witch stories with great joy; as it turns out, as a child she liked to imitate a witch. Analysis reveals that in the girl's fantasy [*Phantasie*], the witch is a stand-in for mother with whom the girl identifies. Thus, for the girl the witch stories are tinged with pleasure only insofar as her mother's life, which the girl also wants to live through, is pleasurable for her too. The witch stories are mere similes, standing in for what she wishes for, i.e., the life story her mother already lived, with the feeling tone merely displaced onto similes. Without her mother's experience, the witch stories would not be pleasurable for the girl. In that sense, "all that is transitory"[8] is only a parable for an unknown primal event [*Urereignis*] seeking analogues in the present. In this sense, we do not experience anything at all in the present – even though we project the feeling tone onto current mental representations [*Vorstellungen*]. In my example, what was conscious was the presentation of the witch; what was unconscious was the assimilation of the past (experience of witch = experience of mother) out of which the present differentiated itself. Every conscious thought or mental representation content is accompanied by a corresponding unconscious one, which translates the results of conscious thinking into the language of the unconscious. This parallel train of thought is most evident in the states of fatigue described by Silberer. Two of his examples may make this parallel process clear.

Example no. 1: "I'm thinking of my plan to mend a rugged spot[9] [*eine holprige Stelle*]." Symbol: "I see myself planing a piece of wood."

Example no. 2: "I'm thinking of the human spirit descending into the mystifying obscure realm of the mother-problem" (Faust, part II).

Symbol: "I am standing on a lonely stone pier, extending far outwards into a dark sea. At the horizon, the waters of the sea meld with the equally dark-hued and mysterious black air."

Interpretation: Being extended into the dark sea corresponds with entering into the dark problem. The fusion of air and water, the blurring of above and below, may symbolize that in the realm of the mother (as Mephistopheles describes) all times and places melt into one another; that there are no boundaries between "above" and "below"; and that therefore Mephistopheles may say to Faust: "Plunge then. – I could even say, soar!"

These examples are very instructive: one sees how a train of thought adapted to the present is assimilated in the unconscious to "events" that have occurred over many generations. The term "rugged spot" [*holperige Stelle*] (ex. 1) is a simile taken from another presentation: the planing of wood [*Holz hobeln*].[10] The conscious mind metaphorically adapts the expression to the present, which means that it becomes differentiated from its source. The unconscious, however, returns the words to their original meaning, i.e., smoothing a rugged spot when planing wood. This way, the unconscious transforms the present activity of mending things into the previously and oft performed activity of planing wood.

The second example is interesting inasmuch as it, just like the ancient peoples, sees the sea as mother (the maternal generative water from which all life has sprung). The sea [*das Meer*] ("the mother"), into which one enters, is the obscure problem, the state in which there is neither time, nor place, nor opposites (above and below) because it is still undifferentiated, not creating the new, therefore an eternal Being [*ein ewig seiendes Etwas*]. At the same time, the mental representation of the sea (mother) is the representation of the depth of the unconscious, which simultaneously lives in the present, the past, and the future, i.e., outside of time[11]; where all places merge into one (the origin); and where all opposites mean the same thing.[12] In this Ur-mother (the unconscious) all the representations that once differentiated themselves from her seek to be dissolved, that is, they want to transform themselves into an undifferentiated state. When, for example, the patient I analyzed[13] says, "The earth was punctured," instead of saying "I was impregnated," this means that the earth represents the Ur-mother both in the conscious and unconscious idea of all peoples.[14] The mother = patient precisely metamorphoses into this Ur-mother from which she once differentiated herself. With good reason philosophers such as Anaxagoras sought the origin of world-weariness [*Weltschmerz*] in the process of Being differentiating itself from the primal parts. The pain stems from the fact that each particle of our being yearns to return to its original state from which, in turn, a new Becoming [*Werden*] will emerge.

Freud detects our adult love impulses [*Liebesregungen*], be they straightforward or sublimated, in the infantile age where we experienced the first pleasurable sensations, brought about by the persons who took care of us. Later we seek to reexperience these sensations of pleasure [*Lustempfindungen*]. And even when consciousness has long worked out a normal sexual aim, the unconscious is occupied with those representations that gave us pleasure in earliest infancy. Freud's opponents tend to indignantly reject the sexualization of innocent infantile sensations of pleasure. Those, however, who have been in analysis themselves have no doubt whatsoever that the innocent infant's erogenous zones become the adult's source of achievement of sexual pleasure, whether they are conscious of it or not. Why an individual prefers one erogenous zone over another may be based on their constitution. In any case, we see especially clearly in neurotics that the infantile pleasure zone becomes the source of sexual excitation toward the persons who took care of the child, with all the corresponding unconscious symbolism that goes with it. This gives us the right to maintain, in accordance with Freud, that the infantile sources of pleasure are the germs of sexual pleasure in the adult. As concerns the controversy regarding the role of sexuality, I was told that provided one has the will to do so, we might just as well derive everything from the drive for food [*Nahrungstrieb*]. I do not want to leave unmentioned the views of a French author who traces all psychic activity [*seelische Regungen*] back to the drive for self-preservation. He believes that a mother loves her child because when sucking the baby relieves the mammary glands; accordingly one loves a man or a woman because through coitus, irritating excretions are being discharged from the organism or rendered harmless. Pleasure is then transferred to the object that causes the relief. These objections have nothing to do with Freud's theories: for Freud does not inquire what constitutes a feeling of pleasure and how it comes into being. Rather, he begins at the stage in which the feeling of pleasure is already there, and here we do indeed find that infantile feelings of pleasure are earlier stages of feelings of sexual pleasure later in life. It is exactly the same as growing fond of the caring hand of the nurse who satisfies our need for food. There can be no doubt that the relation between the drives for food and for self-preservation respectively, and the drive to preserve the species (thus to the sexual drive as well), is an intimate one. Experience has taught us that in sexual arousal eating can sometimes substitute for coitus. Two factors are at work here: on the one hand, the pleasure in the process of eating, and on the other, the often increased appetite is due to general arousal. The opposite has also been noted: the need for food cannot be completely satisfied by coitus, and yet, we often find an overwhelming sexual drive in those who are physically weakened.

If we are looking to find the *causa movens* [motivating cause] of our conscious and unconscious ego, Freud, I believe, is right in assuming that the search for attaining pleasure and the suppression of unpleasure is the foundation of all psychic work. Pleasure stems from infantile sources. The question then is whether our entire psychic life consists of this life of the ego?[15] Isn't it true that there are within us driving forces that set in motion our psychic content regardless of the weal and woe of the ego? Do the well-known drives of preservation (self- and species-) have the same meaning for the entire psychic life as they do for the life of the ego, namely being the source of pleasure or unpleasure? I must emphatically contend that the ego-psyche [*Ichpsyche*], conscious and unconscious, is governed by impulses that lie still deeper, and that do not concern themselves at all with our emotional reactions to the demands made by said impulses. Pleasure is nothing but the ego's affirmative response when confronted with these demands that spring from deep down below. We can derive pleasure from unpleasure, and pleasure from pain – pain that in itself is deeply tinged with unpleasure. Why? Because pain is equal to harming the individual, which the self-preservation drive tries to avoid. There is thus something deep inside us which, as paradoxical as it may sound, wants, even desires, this self-damage, for the ego responds to it with pleasure. The wish to put oneself in harm's way, the pleasure in pain, is, however, completely incomprehensible if all we consider is the pleasure-seeking life of the ego. Mach supports the idea that the ego is something quite inessential, continually changing, a certain momentary grouping of eternally existing elemental sensations [*ewig seienden Elementeempfindungen*]. Being a philosopher, Mach is satisfied with this schematic concept. For me, the name Mach is intimately linked to Jung, for it is the latter who believes the psyche to consist of numerous individual beings [*Einzelwesen*]. It is Jung who speaks of the autonomy of complexes, which means – according to Jung – that we do not have an undivided "I" within us, but rather various complexes competing for predominance. Schizophrenic[16] patients confirm Jung's theory most beautifully. They feel controlled by their individual complexes – complexes that are separated from the "I" – to the extent that they view their own unconscious wishes (my patients call those wishes "assumptions") as though they were viable hostile beings. "The assumption could become reality in order to demonstrate its right to exist," said a female schizophrenic patient I analyzed.

I was led to believe that the main characteristic of the individual consists in being a "dividual" [*ein Dividuum*]. The closer we get to conscious thinking, the more differentiated our mental representations; the deeper we enter into the unconscious, the more general, more [arche]typal[17] they become. The depth of our psyche knows no "I," it only knows its summation, the "We"[18]; or the current "I," viewed as an object, becomes subordinate to other similar objects. A patient's skull was trepanned [*trepaniert*].[19] Under the influence of anesthesia his ego consciousness [*Ichbewußtsein*] faded away, and with it the feeling of pain. And yet he perceived impressions of the external world because as his skull was chiseled, he called out, "Come in." This shows that he indeed perceived his skull, but he did so as an object, a room apparently, separated from his ego. In this way, individual parts of the personality become objectified. In the following example we will see the objectification of the whole personality. My patient[20] reported that during anesthesia, in one of her states, she no longer felt the pain inflicted by the surgery. Instead of herself, she saw wounded soldiers for whom she felt compassion. This objectification is also at work in the soothing effects of little children's sayings: may the dog, the cat, etc., hurt, but not the child's own self. Instead of perceiving the injured little finger as part of him- or herself, the child sees it as somebody else's. "My finger" has been replaced with the more general idea of somebody's finger. In times of personal misfortune, how often do we console ourselves with the thought that others are suffering just as much, as though the pain we feel were to be alleviated by the thought that it occurs regularly, by the elimination of the personal and the accidental. What happened and happens by and large is no longer a misfortune but an objectively perceived fact. Pain consists in the differentiation of the separated ego-idea. By this I mean an idea that is linked to the "I"-consciousness. As is well-known, compassion means to put oneself in a state of pain. In people suffering from schizophrenia, however – people who transform ego-ideas into objectively perceived ideas of the species – we observe an inadequate affect: indifference. But this indifference quickly fades away when we succeed in establishing a relation to the ego [*Ichbeziehung*]. For example, the patient says, "The earth was polluted with urine,"[21] instead of "I was polluted during sexual intercourse." This, in my opinion, is the meaning of symbolic speech.

While the symbol means the same as the embarrassing representation, it is less differentiated in terms of the ego-idea. One can associate many more things to the word "woman" – they only need to resemble each other with regard to the essential – than one associates to the much more sharply defined ego-idea of a certain Martha N. One could object to this: if the dreamer puts another person in his place, this other person is no less differentiated than the person of the dreamer. This is correct only objectively: other people exist for us only insofar as they have access to our psyche – I perceive in the other only what agrees with me. If the dreamer substitutes another person for himself, he does not care to represent the other person as clearly as possible. On the contrary, what occurs is a condensation of different persons into one: the dreamer is only concerned with representing those traits of the substituted person that are in agreement with the realization of his wish. If for example the dreamer would like to be envied for his beautiful blue eyes, he condenses several people with beautiful eyes to one composite person, which means that here, too, the type rather than the individual prevails – a type which, as the analyses of dreams of people suffering from schizophrenia have shown, corresponds to archaic thinking.[22]

Hysterics, who display a hypertrophic ego, show an increased sensitivity as well. It would be wrong, however, to state that the psychic life of hysteria is richer than the psychic life of schizophrenia. We find the most meaningful thoughts in schizophrenic patients. The lack of ego-activity is responsible for the fact that in schizophrenia we encounter [arche]typal, archaic, analogous ways of thinking. Freud thinks that in schizophrenia we are dealing with (1) the withdrawal of the libido, (2) the return of the libido, and then (3) the battle between the withdrawal and the cathexis of the libido. In my opinion, it is a battle between the two antagonistic currents: the species-psyche versus the ego-psyche. The collective psyche strives to turn the ego-psyche into an impersonal, [arche]typal one; the ego-psyche defends itself against this dissolution, such that patients anxiously transfer the feeling-tone of the disappearing complex to a lateral association onto which they fasten the "I" (inadequate affect). Patients, however, realize that the feeling-tone does not correspond to the representation [*Vorstellung*] it has been transferred to – that, in fact, they themselves "produced" the previous affect. This explains why they often laugh at their own pathos and at the same time perceive everything as a comedy. At the onset of the illness, we often observe states of severe anxiety and depression. In the ill person the tendency to flatten the feeling-toned ego-parts is experienced as a stream that undermines the need for ego-relatedness and adaptation to the present. It is as though the feeling tone, awakened earlier, has not yet subsided, while the objects are no longer linked to the ego. The predominant sensation is this: the world has changed, has become uncannily foreign, like a theatre play. At the same time, this insight is forced upon me: "I am a stranger to myself." Thoughts become depersonalized, they are "made," not thought, because they emerge from depths outside of the ego, from depths that turn the "me" [*ich*] into "we" or rather "they." The feelings that are still available are articulated with pathos precisely because they no longer find objects [to attach to]. This is just like an overly melodramatic speaker, who instead of performing the corresponding idea performs the feeling itself. As long as the still present feeling, i.e., the need for an ego-relation, allows the patient to perceive the disintegration of his ego [*Ichzerfall*] (alien power), fear and anxiety will persist. As the illness progresses, the well-known indifference sets in: patients no longer take anything personally; even when they say "I" ["*ich*"], they are objects which neither signify "I," nor obey the will of the ego [*Ichwollen*]. This way a woman, who wishes to have many children, can with a smile on her face tell about her twenty-two thousand boys as if she wasn't really longing to have children. At times, though, the sick person is able to have genuinely adequate feelings, something I have observed in the production of non-symbolic, i.e., direct ego-relations. In those who come to our clinic, the disorder is fairly advanced so that the patient reverts back to his inadequate attitude right away. Only the future knows whether analysis can improve things for those patients.

Thus, as feelings of pleasure and unpleasure become diminished, psychic life does not expire in equal measure (even though the need for differentiation and the fulfillment of personal wishes does come to an end). To the contrary, what ensues is the assimilation (meaning dissolution) of ego-differentiated ideas into ideas that entire peoples have developed, which is to say that they become transformed into [arche]typal ancient collective ideas and representations. These affectless ideas and images, developed by entire peoples, teach us about the content associated with our drives. The ego-psyche [*Ichpsyche*] is only able to wish for feelings of pleasure, whereas the collective psyche [*Artpsyche*] teaches us what exactly we wish for when we wish for pleasure; what exactly we feel as positive or negative; and here we find that the collective wishes [*Artwünsche*] that are alive in us do not at all correspond with the ego-wishes [*Ichwünsche*]; that the collective psyche strives to assimilate the existing ego-psyche while the ego – every little part of it – possesses the determination to preserve the species in its current form (perseverance) [*Beharrungsvermögen*]. The collective psyche, which negates the current ego, creates it anew through this negation, for the drowned ego-particle surfaces richer than before, adorned with new representations. We see this most beautifully in artistic creation. Of course, the regression in the ego consists in wanting to reexperience pleasurable infantile experiences. But why, I ask, are infantile experiences so pleasurable for us? Why this "joy in recognizing what is known?"[23] Why does this strict censor, which seeks to modify experiences in us, persist long after we have ceased to feel the grip of parental power over us? Why don't we experience the same and keep reproducing it?[24] Obviously, the wish for perseverance goes along with a wish for transformation, the latter of which means that a singular-representational content might be dissolved into similar material stemming from the past, and so, at the expense of the individual wish, the representational content becomes an [arche] typal – that is, collective – wish, which the individual projects into the external world as a work of art. We seek what is similar to us (parents, ancestors), we seek to dissolve our own ego-particle, because the act of dissolving into what is similar is not brutal destruction but a process that goes almost unnoticed. And yet, what does this dissolution mean for the ego-particle, if not death? It returns, of course, in a new, perhaps more beautiful form, but it is not the same; it returns as an Other that came into being at the expense of that particle. Just like a tree growing tall from its seed is the same in relation to the species, but is not the same in relation to the individual; and it is really more a matter of taste where we want to put the emphasis in the new creation (which came into being at the expense of the old): on its existence, or on the disappearance of the old life. The same is true for the pleasure or unpleasure when the dissolution of the entire ego-complex is concerned. There are neurotics who are quite explicit about their fear of sexual contact: they believe that with the discharge of semen, a piece of the individual is lost.

Everything that moves us wants to be communicated, understood, and felt: every mental representation [*Vorstellung*] that we hand over to our fellow human beings either directly or as a work of art is a differentiated product of the primal experiences that make up our psyche. Let's take the example of an already differentiated experience, e.g., a sunny spring day that has brought joy to countless generations before us. When we reproduce this experience, we cannot help but differentiate by shaping the trees, the grass, the sky according to our current consciousness. We are no longer dealing with *a* spring day but with *this* special spring day, imbued with my personal experience. And vice versa, when this differentiated product finds its way into the psyche of another person, a retransformation occurs: the other individual consciously processes the spring day and thereby gives it a different, an individual imprint [*Gepräge*]. Besides being processed consciously, the mental representation also falls prey to unconscious processing, which seizes its current individual imprint, takes it down to the "Mothers," and dissolves it. In the unconscious we may find the spring day broken down into its components, sun, sky, plants, with the latter rearranged or, to put it more accurately, "formed back" ["*rückgestaltet*"] into mythological shapes known to us from folk psychology. With every thought we express, with every representation we describe, we also generalize; for words are symbols serving to shape the personal into the universally human and thereby making it intelligible, i.e., robbing it of its personal imprint. The purely personal can never be understood by others; and it doesn't surprise us when Nietzsche, a man with a mighty ego-consciousness, comes to this conclusion: language is there to bewilder itself and others. And yet we feel relieved when we express ourselves in language, when we, at the expense of our ego-ideas and ego images, form a collective mental representation. And the artist, too, takes joy in the "products of his sublimation" when he creates the [arche]typal instead of the individual. Every representation seeks similar but non-identical material to dissolve it and transform it. This similar material is the understanding – resting on the same content of the representation – with which the other person receives our representations. This understanding evokes in us a sympathetic feeling which means nothing less than that we want to give even more of ourselves, to the point that affection, especially when we deal with individuals of a different gender, increases so far that we want to surrender our whole being [*im Ganzen*] (the whole ego). For the ego this most dangerous phase of the reproductive (transformation) drive goes along with feelings of bliss, because the dissolution takes place within the beloved, who is similar (= in love).

Since in the beloved we love our parents (who are similar to us), it is understandable that we thereby also seek to experience, in reality, the destiny of our ancestors, especially of our parents[25] (cf., Jung, 1961b/1909). Chance plays a role in life only insofar as sexual experience, already predestined in our psyche, either becomes activated, or remains in our psyche as a possibility for future experience. In the first case, the complex is satisfied; in the second case, however, the tension-inducing element has not been eliminated and has to continually free itself by draining the ever-replenishing analogue content of representations. Thus, for psychic life, the activation of the experience has only a negative meaning as it removes the content of the representation along with the corresponding tension. Let us assume, for instance, that we had achieved the longed-for union with the love object. As soon as reality claims its rights, as soon as the word becomes deed, the group of mental representations that correspond to this reality dissolves and produces a blissful feeling of relaxation; at that moment we are completely unproductive psychically. Every representation reaches its maximum life when it most intensely awaits its transformation into reality: its realization is its destruction. This does not mean that with the fulfillment of a powerful complex all psychic life comes to a standstill, for the complex is just an extremely tiny particle that has differentiated itself out of primal experience. The primal event continues to create new products of differentiation that the psyche transforms, now into abreactions, now into works of art. Importantly, as far as their content is concerned, the products of sublimation do not stand in opposition to the wish for reproduction, which has adapted to reality. They [the products of sublimation] only seem to be in opposition because they are less adapted to reality, i.e., less differentiated. They are more [arche]typal in form, such as ideas of "higher" love for nature or for Christ. Jung shows that in worshipping the sun we worship our own libido, the father who lives within us.[26] Since activation does not destroy these representations, they remain in the psyche in the form of a most intense longing for a return to the original source, specifically, to dissolve oneself in the progenitors (which shall be proven below). This explains why religion, the most elevated, so readily becomes a symbol of the lowest, i.e., sexual activity. Take, for example, the Duke of Zinzendorf, analyzed by Pfister,[27] or my own analysand Frau M.[28] By negating the existence of love objects that are outside of the ego we only achieve one thing: to take ourselves as the object of our own libido including the self-destruction that ensues.

In his "Contributions [to Dream Interpretation]" Stekel states:

> Just as the dream does not know negation in general, so it also does not know negation of life. Death in a dream just as often symbolizes life, and even the most intense lust for life often expresses itself in a wish for death. Similar psychological factors apply to suicide as well. And even the choice of the manner of death is influenced by certain erotic fantasies. Poets have repeatedly discussed these ideas, and philosophers often have shed light on the relations between Eros and Thanatos. In dreams, as so frequently in life, murder is merely sexual murder and represents nothing but a sadistically charged sexual act.[29]

Thus far I can agree with Stekel. But now he goes further:

> A typical dream of a young girl is that she is standing naked on a street, and a large man throws himself on her and thrusts a knife into her belly. Here murder serves to illustrate a violent defloration; it is [her] honor which is irretrievably destroyed; it is the death of virginity, which signifies the life of Woman.

I see absolutely no evidence that permits us to interpret death in these dreams as a moral death. After all, Stekel himself interpreted even real death as nothing more than a sexual act with an intense sadistic charge. In accordance with the fact that during intercourse the woman is bored through [*durchbohrt*], in the dream the girl, but also woman in general, sees herself as a victim of this sadistically tinged sexual act. This is the reason why wartime events are so conducive to the outbreak of a neurosis which, as we know, has its origin in the disturbances of sexual life. There is no war without mental representations of destruction. And since one representation invokes other, related representations, in times of war representations of destruction stir up precisely those representations that are connected to the destructive element of the reproductive drive. These latter representations can spoil Being [*Dasein*] even for normal people, and they are all the more damaging for the neurotic, in whom the mental representation of Destruction outweighs that of Becoming [*Werden*], and who is waiting for suitable symbols that may represent this destruction fantasy. Young people, and particularly girls, in their dreams often have fantasies of lying in a coffin. Freud teaches that resting in a coffin is a symbol of lingering in the mother's womb (coffin = womb). Stekel adds, and accurately so, that [in dreams] *grave* [*Grab*] has the same symbolic meaning as coffin; whereby "'grave digging' [*graben*'] has an unmistakable meaning similar to 'bore and being born' ['*bohren und geboren sein*'; '*graben und begraben*']. And so the grave becomes heaven [*Himmel*], as people believe that we enter heaven through the grave (through death)." My analysand Frau M.[30] has developed a rich symbolism: she will, as Christian doctrine teaches, come to new life as she dies with Christ. If she thinks of death as a sexual union – which her numerous fantasies about Christ prove – she would, as I have argued earlier, have to identify with Christ (the beloved), to transform herself into him. And indeed, she does become Christ, lies stretched out on the ground, claiming she was crucified; she wants to redeem the sick; and she has become, just like Christ, the life-giving grave. Prof. Forel = Dr. J. to whom she developed a transference, comes to her like Christ in her death chamber (her room); he is "buried alive" and returns to the world as a grapevine. This vine, which signifies new life, symbolizes the child. Sometimes the patient says that she had changed herself into a little trout [*Forel*].[31] She becomes this little trout/Forel when she is being treated harshly, beaten – again, there is destruction. At other times her child-producing [*kinderproduzierend*] organism (organ) is a glass coffin or a broken porcelain bowl containing the bones of her stillborn child. The porcelain shards, the child's bones, and other fertilizing substances must be ground finely, then cooked, etc., in order to bring forth a child. What is essential is the fact that in order to bring forth life, death is necessary; and, in accordance with the Christian faith, what is dead is made alive through death. In mythology to bury = to fertilize. The accuracy of this assertion is virtually forced upon us when we study mythology.

"To produce a new generation," my patient says, "the entire body must be prepared. The new generation comes into being from the head (psyche) and from the spermatic development in the animal." "Novozoo (– sperm) is a dead substance."

The last sentence shows that sperm is thought of as a dead excrement. Binswanger's analysand Irma is disgusted by coitus and animals feeding on carrion [*Leichenfraß*].[32] If eating equals copulating, the corpse = sperm which is being received in the act. Moreover, Irma has developed an extensive symbolism of coffins. But in contrast to normal individuals she is permanently terrified of her ideas. For a normal young woman, the idea of being buried becomes bliss as soon as she thinks about passing away [*vergehen*] in her beloved. A young woman told Binswanger that "the greatest happiness for her would be to linger in the body of the beloved." Irma too sometimes thinks "death is a handsome man," but only for a short while; soon the idea of pure destruction and the understandable anxiety that goes along with it take over. Irma describes the feeling as "a feeling of wildness, of romping around, of surrendering, and of being overpowered in such a way that you don't know what you are doing or what will become of you."

As Frau M.'s and other patients' symbolism demonstrates (which is why the elongated shape of the snake is so fitting as a sexual animal), one is poisoned, becomes dangerously ill. Then later, during pregnancy, one is destroyed by the child who develops at the expense of the mother, like a malignant tumor [*Geschwulst*]. My female medical colleagues availed themselves of this rich material for the creation of their own symbol formation, and their unconscious knew how to make good use of it as well. One colleague dreamt her little brother (wish-personality [*Wunschpersönlichkeit*])[33] had a dove growing in his stomach (dove as symbol of innocence); then a dove comes out of his mouth. Another colleague develops abscesses on her neck, just like Frau M. Still another dreams of having cancerous tumors on her fingers, or she dreams that a university lecturer, to whom she has developed a "transference," asks her about her tumor (exhibition dream). Others contract scarlet fever, etc. In dreams as well as in mythology, every sexual symbol signifies the life- and death-bringing god.

One example might stand for all: the horse, a well-known sexual animal, is both the life-bringing animal of the sun god as well as the animal of death, indeed the symbol of death.[34]

Mental representations of Destruction are very instructive with regard to the various forms of masturbation. Nietzsche is an excellent example by which to study this psychic autoerotism. Nietzsche, who spent his entire life alone, had his libido turned toward his own person. How then did Nietzsche conceive of love, or more accurately, how did he feel about love? Tormented by loneliness, he created an imaginary friend, Zarathustra, with whom he identified. The longing for a love object made Nietzsche become his own man and woman, husband and wife, both in the form of Zarathustra.

> For she is coming already, the glowing one – her love for the earth is coming! Innocence and the creator's desire is all solar love! Look there, how she glides impatiently across the sea! Do you not feel her thirst and the hot breath of her love? She would suck at the sea and drink its depths into herself in the heights; now the sea's desire rises with a thousand breasts. It wants to be kissed and sucked by the thirst of the sun; it wants to become air and height and footpath of light and light itself! Indeed, like the sun I love life and all deep seas. And this I call perception: all that is deep shall rise – to my height! Thus spoke Zarathustra.[35]

For Nietzsche, both love and knowledge consist in sucking in the depth of the sea, like the sun. Thus, for Nietzsche knowledge is nothing other than a desire for love, for creation. The glowing sun suckles at the sea like a lover, and the wildly heaving sea rises with a thousand breasts toward the sun, hungry for kisses like an enraptured woman. The fantasy of suckling suggests that the sun relates to the sea like a child to a parent. Let's not forget that Silberer[36] too, in the second example of the hypnagogic phenomenon, describes the land of the Mothers as a sea. Just as the sun sucks up the sea, Zarathustra, in the act of knowing, sucks up the depth (the deep sea). For the poet, his yearning for love is nothing more than the longing for his mother living in this depth. If mother is his own depth, the union with mother has an autoerotic meaning, i.e., it is a union with himself. In another passage Nietzsche mocks the preachers of so-called "pure love," of immaculate conception [*Erkenntnis*] without any desire, who deceive themselves by disguising the snake in the mask of a god (see Jung: deity – one's own libido – snake).

Indeed, you do not love the earth as creators, begetters, and enjoyers of becoming!

> Where is innocence? Where there is will to beget. And whoever wants to create over and beyond himself, he has the purest will. Where is beauty? Where I must will with my entire will; where I want to love and perish so that an image does not remain merely an image. [Cf., the earlier discussion: activation destroys psychic content – "image" – or destruction activates it.] Loving and perishing: these have gone together since the beginning of time. Will to love: that is also being willing for death.
>
> (p. 96)

By uniting in love with mother, Nietzsche himself becomes a mother: begetting, creating, becoming. This mother-being expresses itself even more clearly in the following passage:

> You creators, you higher men! Whoever must give birth is sick; but whoever has given birth, is unclean. Ask women: one does not give birth because it is enjoyable. Pain makes hens and poets cackle. You creators, in you there is much that is unclean. That's because you had to be mothers.
>
> (p. 236)

We have learned a lot about Nietzsche, or so it seems; and I believe that this process can shed some light on the question as to why we so often, if not always, encounter the homosexual component[37] in people suffering from schizophrenia and the autoerotic isolation that comes with it. By identifying with mother – by sucking her up – Nietzsche becomes a woman. One contributing factor is the fact that Nietzsche, as a consequence of his autoerotic isolation, does not consciously live in the present but in his own depth, which belongs to the time when he was still a child – for a child, still insufficiently differentiated in his sex life, behaves in a passive feminine way when sucking at the mother's breast. If Nietzsche is in the female position, his mother acts like a man toward him. The same is true for the depth that later takes the mother's place, or his "abysmal thought" (which I will discuss in a moment), with which he fought as if fighting with himself. For Nietzsche, the mother is himself, and he himself – his mother.

In every kind of love, we must distinguish two orientations of a mental representation: how we love, and how we are being loved. In the first orientation we are ourselves subjects who love the object that we projected outward. In the second orientation we have changed ourselves into the beloved, and we love ourselves, as his object. In man, who has the active task to conquer woman, subject representations prevail; in woman on the other hand, whose task it is to seduce man, regressive presentations normally gain the upper hand. This relates to the familiar coquettishness we see in women: the woman contemplates how to please "him." Woman's stronger homosexuality and autoeroticism is connected to this as well[38]: changed into her beloved, she has to feel masculine to a certain extent; as the object of man she can love herself or another young woman who is her "wish personality," i.e., this is how as lover she wants to see herself, always beautiful, of course. Once I met a colleague in great indignation over a number of envelopes she herself had addressed; on none of them was she able to reproduce the beautiful handwriting she had achieved on the first one. Upon my questioning what the wished-for handwriting meant to her, she all of a sudden remembered, entirely correctly, that it was her beloved's handwriting. Her need for identification with the beloved was so great that she could only tolerate herself as him. We see the same in "Tristan and Isolde." Tristan says: "Tristan, thou – no more Tristan I-Isolde." Isolde says: "Isolde, thou – no more Isolde I-Tristan."[39] The child, too, is autoerotic because it relates to the parents in a passive way: it must struggle to arouse the parents' love, and never forget to please them; it must imagine how it is loved, thus putting itself in the parents' place. In later years, the girl will see her mother as her rival, but also as her wish personality whom she loves; likewise the boy does with his father. If children are angered by their parents, the normal reaction would be an act of revenge; but this is precisely what children must not risk. They therefore either unleash their rage onto an object, any object, or in the throes of the first wave of rage, they know nothing more sensible to do but, for instance, pull their hair, whereby they put themselves in the place of the parents who make them angry. In "The Government Inspector," for instance, Gogol [1972/1856] describes an immensely conceited governor who shamelessly exploits his subjects. At the end, however, he himself is duped by a young impostor whom he mistakes to be the long-awaited inspector. When, in a letter that everybody gets to read, the impostor makes fun of everyone, including the governor, the governor turns his scorn against himself. "Look at this old fool," etc., he shouts. In this case too, failed aggression gives rise to a regressive series of mental representations, i.e., the transformation into the subject who scornfully turns against himself as object. In line with the destructive element inherent in the sexual drive, man, who is more disposed to activity [than woman], has more sadistic wishes: he wants to destroy the beloved. Woman, on the other hand, who is more inclined to imagine herself as the object of love, wants to be destroyed. Of course the boundary is not that sharply drawn, firstly because all humans are bisexual, and secondly because, in women, subject representations are just as available as object representations in men; that's why woman is sadistic, and man – also masochistic. If in the effort to put oneself in the beloved's place, object representations gain in intensity, the love turned against the self will lead to the destruction of the self, e.g., self-castigation, martyrdom, and even to the total annihilation of one's own sexuality, as in castration. These are merely different forms and degrees of self-annihilation.

The procreative act itself is self-annihilation. Nietzsche's words refer to this:

> "Human being is something that must be overcome," teaches Zarathustra, "in order for the overman [*Übermensch*] to appear." "And if now all ladders should fail, then you must know how to climb on your own head – how else would you climb upward?"
>
> (pp. 5, 121)

The sense of this sentence is: you have to learn to overcome (destroy) yourself. How else would you create the higher, the child? In the chapter entitled "On Unwilling Bliss," Zarathustra complains:

> But I lay chained to the love of my children; desire set this snare for me, desire for love, that I might become the prey of my children and lose myself to them.
>
> (p. 129)

Zarathustra the child – the "abysmal thought" of the eternal return of things – threatens to die unborn in Zarathustra, but he summons it to life.

> You stir, you stretch, you gasp? Up! Up! No gasping – you will speak to me! Zarathustra summons you, the godless one! I, Zarathustra, the advocate of life, the advocate of suffering, the advocate of the circle... Hail to me! You are coming – I hear you! My abyss speaks, I have unfolded my ultimate depth to the light! Hail to me! Here now! Give me your hand – ha! Let go! Haha! – Nausea, nausea, nausea – oh no!
>
> (p. 174)

Just as Zarathustra, the sun (the Highest), sucked up the deep sea, he now pushes out his deepest self toward the light (analogue of the sun = love). We know that Nietzsche is that light (the height) which his mother = the deep sea sucks up. It is this union with mother which made Nietzsche himself a childbearing mother. Here, too, he turns his depth inside out into his light, thereby bringing it forth into the world as his child. This recalls the children's wells of mythology: the deceased are changed back into children and as such are reborn.[40] Wünsche,[41] who presents numerous examples, clearly states: "In Holda's kingdom, the souls of the deceased, ascending to heaven, cannot return unless they have been revitalized in her well." Wünsche argues that the idea that newborns are retrieved from wells and ponds stems from the belief that vegetative and animal life sprouts up from the underworld. This is certainly correct. However, if the unconscious in order to describe the birth of human beings takes its symbolism from the world of plants, something analogous must occur when a child is being born: children come from ponds, because in the womb they are indeed in a pond (= the waters, amniotic fluid) from which they ought to enter into the external world. In his paper "Psychic Conflicts in a Child" [1954/1910], Jung shows how little Anna, who is very busy trying to figure out where children come from, searches for answers in the realm of plants. She is interested in how her eyes, mouth, and hair grew, and, finally, how her little brother Fritzchen grew inside her mother (Mama = earth). She asks father: "But how did Fritzchen get into mama? Did someone set him out there (plant him), have seeds been set?" She also sees other analogous processes in the world of plants to which her unconscious draws her attention, because they lend themselves to the symbolization of the secret that occupies her imagination. At the age of three, Anna heard that children were little angels living in heaven and brought to the earth by the stork. One day she asked her grandmother:

ANNA: Grandmother why are your eyes so withered?
GRANDMOTHER: Because I'm old.
ANNA: But won't you become young again?
GRANDMOTHER: Actually no; I'm growing older and older, and one day I'll die.
ANNA: And then will you be a little child again?

It is extremely interesting that to little Anna the idea that her old grandma could be changed back into a little child seemed completely natural. Even before grandma mentions death and little angels (which, as Anna heard, came to earth), Anna asks grandmother whether she will be young again; therefore it doesn't strike her as odd that grandma will become a little angel, and she immediately completes the answer according to the principle of changing back into a previous state [*Rückverwandlung*]. There are numerous examples of sick persons who want to have children and who see themselves changed into children. The nun in the temple of Amida,[42] as Riklin reports, is a wonderful example. Another one is Frau M. who becomes a little Forel through the sexual act with Prof. Forel. Rank draws our attention to dreams that feature reverse birth symbolism: instead of pulling a child out of the water, the child is brought into the water, for instance. This symbol is born by way of identification. One evening a colleague (medical doctor) told me how much she would like to have a child. The following night she dreamt she had to creep into a narrow passage that didn't have an opening at the end but opened into a building (just as the birth canal ends in the mother's womb). I let her show me how she crawled into the passage and she recalls that she mimicked the birth movements of a child in the first or second cephalic presentation. She feared that she wasn't able to get in again, that the passage was too narrow, and getting ever narrower so that she was almost crushed. Frau M. (schizophrenia) sees herself and the children abandoned at sea; Christ will then save their souls, i.e., the children are being born again (since Destruction leads to Becoming). Nietzsche, too, employs similar symbols of destruction when he describes the birth of his thought as a stand-in for the child. Zarathustra defends himself against the act of creation with expressions of disgust, as though creation was something impure – which reminds us of his words: "Whoever must give birth is sick; but whoever has given birth is unclean" (p. 236). Naturally, the thought which replaces the child must be able to hold both the most desirable as well as the most dreaded, in order for it to do justice to Zarathustra's yearning for losing himself in his children. This is indeed the case: the thought expresses the Highest, i.e., the eternal return of the superhuman, and the Lowest, i.e., the eternal return of the smallest human. Since Nietzsche is constantly concerned with the highest affirmation of life, at the same time his wishful thought tells him that affirmation without negation [*Vernichtung*] does not exist; that the Lowest is part of the Highest. And this dreaded element is indeed capable of overwhelming Zarathustra: for seven long days he lies motionless, as if dead, wrestling with a terrible animal – his own depth, i.e., his own sexual personality. He bites the animal's head off, thus murdering his own sexuality, and by murdering himself, his abysmal thought attains its highest vitality [*Lebenskraft*], and with it arises a resurrected Nietzsche.

The saga of the Russian prince Oleg is interesting. It is prophesied that his most beloved horse will bring about his death. To escape this verdict he gives his horse to his servants, telling them to treat it with exceptional care. After some time he learns that his horse has died. Moaning, he stands at its grave, cursing the devious soothsayer. And while he laments, a snake emerges from the horse's skull and administers the deadly bite to the hero. The horse is Oleg's sexuality. It dies, and with it Oleg dies as well, because the snake = sexual desire turned against him.

In this case destruction does not become creation, as it does in Nietzsche. On the contrary, the saga shows that the life-bringing sexual animal can become the source of death. It is quite remarkable how readily passionate poets die in their works. Take for example Shakespeare's *Romeo and Juliet*. The motif of a love that develops between the descendants of two families who hate each other is indeed instructive. In a certain psychological sense, hate and love are the same: the same actions are taken out of hatred as out of passionate love. As regards the conscious present, as regards its activation, hatred is negative love. But because hate most opposes the annihilation of the content of the representation [*Vorstellungsinhalt*], which its activation will bring about, in the hater's unconscious, the representations of love are exceptionally vigorous.[43] If in normal cases, the tamed libido goes along with weak destruction fantasies, e.g. teasing, hurting – which has given rise to the proverb, "he teases the one he loves" – the wild passion of a sadist unloads itself in hideous scenes that can build up to the point of sexual murder. While a weak aversion changes into a weak sympathy once the factors that inhibit the positive accentuation of the libido disappear, the unleashing of representations whose activation thus far hatred did not permit become white-hot passion. This passion must destroy; it is too strong to observe the bounds of self-preservation. We can see this in Shakespeare: his protagonist-lovers are not satisfied with the activation of just a small part of the libido indispensable to an ordinary love union [*Liebesvereinigung*]. They require more and more obstacles upon which to unload their destructive impulses; but no obstacle, not even the greatest, will suffice to satisfy their passion, which finds peace only in total destruction, the death of the personality. While, on the one hand, an overly strong fixation on the parents' libido makes the transference of their own libido to the external world impossible, because no object will ever completely match the parents,[44] so too the unsatisfied libido becomes reattached to the parents, resulting in either incest fantasies directed at reality, or in more-or-less sublimated fantasy symptoms, such as the worship of nature, or religious symptoms. Concurrently, the unsatisfied reproductive drive, contained within the destructive drive, gains vitality [*Spannkraft*], generating either more concrete or more sublimated death fantasies. However, the death fantasy associated with the incest wish does not mean: "I will die because I want to commit this sin," but: "I am dead," meaning: "I have achieved the longed-for reinstatement [*Rückversetzung*] into the progenitor, I am passing away/I am losing myself in him." With the less differentiated incestuous love we find a stronger than usual wish to Become [*Werdewunsch*] which corresponds to the more strongly pronounced wish for Destruction in sadistic love. Dreams and myths in which one has children with one's parents and siblings provide ample evidence that the incestuous thoughts per se are not the source of the death fantasies; rather, they are fantasies of Becoming [*Werdephantasien*]. Freud showed that every dream image always, already, and at the same time, means its opposite. Freud also showed that linguistics recognizes the "antithetical meaning of primal words."[45] Bleuler's notion of ambivalence and Stekel's concept of bipolarity suggest that within us every positive drive coexists with a negative one. Jung believes that when we don't notice them, both drives are of equal strength. However, a small preponderance of just one drive, one wish, is enough and it seems to us as if this wish were the only one we had. This theory explains very well why we overlook the presence of the death drive within the sexual drive. Under normal conditions, the mental representations of Becoming [*Werdevorstellungen*] must predominate somewhat, particularly because Becoming is the result of Destruction, is conditioned by Destruction. Now, it is much easier to focus on the successful end result, instead of always searching for its cause. However, it does not take much, especially in children and emotive persons, to confer predominance to the mental representations of destruction. In neurosis, the destructive element is predominant and expresses itself in all symptoms of resistance to life and natural destiny.

Summary

Every content that appears in our consciousness is the result of a process of differentiation from older psychological contents. This new content is adapted to reality and assumes a specific and immediate coloring that endows it with the quality of the ego-relation. In other words, there is within us a tendency toward differentiating. If we want to make this very personal, very specific content, to which only we have access, accessible to others, we de-differentiate [*Rückdifferenzierung*]: we strip the content of its personal aspects and express it in general and [arche]typal or collective terms, i.e., in symbolic form. In this, we follow the second tendency in us (which stands in opposition to the first one): the tendency to assimilate and dissolve. Assimilation causes the unity which refers to the "i"[46] to be transformed into the unity which belongs to the "We" ["*Wir*"]. The dissolving and assimilating of a personal experience into a work of art, a dream, or a pathological symbolism transforms this personal experience into a collective experience, turning the "I" ["*Ich*"] into a "We."[47] The appearance of pleasure or unpleasure is tied to the production or disappearance of the ego-relation. If the personal experience has already been transformed into a collective experience, we relate to it like spectators who feel empathy only if they can see themselves in the performance and identify with the actors. People suffering from schizophrenia, and we as dreamers, are such spectators. The self-preservation drive in us matches the tendency to differentiate and the capacity for perseverance [*Beharrungsvermögen*] which we see in both a crystalized ego-particle [*Ichpartikel*] or in the entire ego-personality [*Ichpersönlichkeit*]. The drive for the preservation of the species is a reproductive drive; psychically it expresses itself in the tendency to dissolve and assimilate (transformation of the "I" into the "We"), followed by a new differentiation from the "primal material" ["*Urstoff*"]. "Where love reigns, the I, that sinister despot, dies." In love, dissolving the "I" in the beloved is the strongest form of self-affirmation; it is a new I-life [*Ichleben*] which takes place in the person of the beloved. Without love, the idea that an individual changes both psychically and physically under the influence of a foreign power, as in the sexual act, is experienced as destruction and death. The drive for self-preservation is a simple drive consisting only of a positive [tendency]; the drive for the preservation of the species, whose task it is to dissolve the old in order for the new to be created, has both a positive and a negative element, i.e., the drive for the preservation of the species is ambivalent in its nature. This is why arousing the positive element always also provokes the arousal of the negative element, and vice versa. Inasmuch as the self-preservation drive strives to protect the individual from alien influences, it is a "static" drive. The drive for the preservation of the species however is a "dynamic" drive, aiming at the transformation, the "resurrection" of the individual in a new form. Without the destruction of the old state, change cannot and will not happen.[48]

III. Life and death in mythology

Clinical experience with dreams and with those suffering from schizophrenia teaches us that in its depth, our psyche houses ideas that no longer conform to our current conscious way of thinking, and which we cannot immediately understand. We do however find these ideas in the consciousness of our forebears, a conclusion based upon studying their mythology and other cultural products. Thus, our unconscious way of thinking corresponds to our ancestors' conscious way of thinking. Instead of saying inherited "ways of thinking that lead to the formation of corresponding mental representations," I will for the sake of brevity speak of inherited "ideas and images" ["*Vorstellungen*"].[49]

The idea that new life emerges from the four elements (earth, water, fire, air) is already present in oriental[50] symbolism. For my purposes I shall discuss life and death as it manifests in earth and water symbolism. I mainly rely on the historical material compiled by Wünsche and Kohler.

We are familiar with the two trees (of Knowledge and of Life) which according to the Bible grow in paradise. In older cultures, however, there is just one tree, the Tree of Life,[51] which serves two functions: to the dead or the severely ill, the tree (or its fruit) gives life; to the healthy and strong however, the tree brings death. If we desire to eat from the forbidden fruit, i.e., if we want to succumb to the pleasures of the procreative act, death will ensue – from which we shall arise to new life. Adam and Eve, who fell victim to sin, shall be delivered from death when Christ, the son of God, dies for them. Christ takes the sins of the world upon him, he suffers as humankind should suffer, and he comes to new life as it has been decreed for the dead as well. Thus, Christ is a symbol of humankind. As for humans, so for Christ, the Tree of Life becomes a source of death. Wünsche richly cites material indicating that the wood used for Jesus' cross was taken from the Tree of Life. Among his examples is a riddle in Middle High German which reads as follows: "A noble tree grew in an elaborately designed garden. Its roots reached down to the bottom of hell (in the English-language version of this poem, the name for hell is "hall of worms" ["*Wurmsaal*"], filled with snakes and dragons); its apex touches God's throne; with its broad branches it holds the entire world in its embrace. The tree stands in full splendor and marvelous is its foliage." What we have here is a description of the Tree of Knowledge (= Tree of Life) described as having the shape of a cross.

When Adam falls seriously ill, he sends his son Seth to Paradise, asking him to fetch oil from the Tree of Mercy. The angel gives him three twigs (and no oil) – according to other legends, Seth receives three apple seeds – which he was to plant under Adam's tongue. Adam will die but from the twigs spring trees, one of which shall later redeem humankind, i.e., Adam as well. (In some versions of the story only one twig is planted in Adam's mouth; the number three points to the tree's relation to Creation.) When Adam learns that his death is near, he laughs for the first time in his life.[52] Now that he is dead, he no longer needs to die but, having been fertilized, comes into this world as a new being. The twig is planted in the mouth (Freudian displacement upward [*Verlegung nach oben*[53]]). As Riklin[54] has demonstrated, in fairy tales, the twig signifies the phallus and as such is a symbol of the highest power.[55] In the hands of Moses it works miracles. The twig is transplanted into the garden of the emperor, who is the father of Moses' future bride: for only those may court his daughter, who are capable of controlling the tree that grew out of the twig. It is, as it were, a test of sexual potency: Moses, who receives the tree from the young woman's father, from now on fills the place of the father as the man in the girl's life. According to Wünsche, the royal scepter stems from the Tree of Life as well; basically the king's power is a symbol of sexual power. In most legends, the life-giving tree (from which twigs have grown) serves as a bridge over water. Let us recall Nietzsche, for whom the human being serves as bridge for the superhuman: "Human being is something that must be overcome," he says. This way the tree, as a bridge which the new generation crosses, must be overcome too. Since the tree is a symbol of sexuality, of the life-giving phallus, we overcome ourselves as we cross over on the tree. After the tree has served for a while, God drowns it in the water. Water, too, is a procreative primal force [*Urkraft*], and so is Adam, in whose mouth the torn twig was implanted; this reimplantation [*Rückversetzung*] brings about rebirth. The sunken tree was then forgotten and only when the time for the crucifixion of Christ came, one of his enemies remembered the tree.

> Ah! this tree will serve, thought he,
> For Jesus' cross the weight to be.
> So soaked, already half like stone,
> So may its burden press him down.
> It grew from the first man's grave
> The tree that Life to mankind gave,
> And redemption, just as death will be
> Once again dispensed by this living tree.[56]

What role does Christ, God's son, play in this? How does he redeem humankind? Wünsche mentions several Germanic fairy tales in which a sick father or mother is saved from death by holy water or paradisiacal fruit respectively. The fruits are the offspring of the Tree of Life (more on water below). Wünsche interprets fairy tales as myths of spring: both the fruit of the Tree of Life and the Water of Life are symbols of the vital force that rejuvenates nature every year. The sick father and mother, argues Wünsche, represent nature in the throes of winter. In Nordic sagas we find numerous myths of spring in which the sun god saves earth by fertilizing her with his rays. In *The Nibelungenlied*, Siegfried and Brünhilde figure as sun and earth.[57] The hibernating Brünhilde (earth) is saved by Siegfried's victorious light (sun), who cuts through her suit of armor (ice-crust) with his sword, thereby impregnating her. As opposed to the sagas, in *The Nibelungenlied*, the process is not described as an act of fertilization or impregnation, as with sun and earth, but it is represented as a cutting-through; its erotic significance is emphasized by a kiss. What is important is that, through Brünhilde, Siegfried impregnates his mother. True, Siegfried's mother is Sieglinde but Brünhilde is her sister; she loves whomever Sieglinde loves, namely Siegmund. She feels herself into Sieglinde's role, and this way Sieglinde becomes her wish-personality, her sexual personality [*Sexualpersönlichkeit*], respectively. By saving Siegfried, she saves her own wish, her own child. Prof. Graf's work demonstrates the accuracy of this interpretation of Brünhilde as Siegfried's mother. Like Eve, Brünhilde violates the father's commandment and is banished from the kingdom of the gods, just as Eve is banished from Paradise. This violation (the defense of her wish-personality, whose sins she takes upon herself, as it were) brings a death-like sleep upon Brünhilde from which the spring sun Siegfried awakens her.[58] Very often, for example in Wagner's [*Götterdämmerung*], the yearning for death is a yearning for *Liebestod* [love-death], for dying while consummating love.

> Not goods nor gold[59]
> For godly state;
> Not house nor hearth
> For lordly pomp;
> Not empty treaties' treacherous bonds
> For false tradition's
> Pitiless law:
> Blessed in joy and sorrow,

Only love I bequeath![60]
Grane, my horse!
I greet my friend!
Can you tell, my friend,
To where I must lead you?
In fiery glory
Blazes your lord,
Siegfried, my hero and love.
To follow your master,
Oh! Are you neighing?
Lured by the fire,
The light and its laughter?
I too am yearning
To join him there;
Glorious radiance
Has seized on my heart.
I shall embrace him,
United with him,
In sacred yearning,
With him ever one!
Hiayoho! Grane!
[Greet] your [friend]![61]
Siegfried! Siegfried!
[Blessed is my greeting to you!][62]

Here, death is a victorious song [*Siegeslied*] of love! Brünhilde, as it were, passes away in Siegfried: Siegfried is the fire, the redemption that comes from the sun's blazing heat. In this primal progenitor [*Urerzeuger*], Brünhilde dissolves, becoming fire herself. In Wagner's oeuvre death is often nothing other than the destructive component of the instinct to become [*Werdeinstinkt*]. *The Flying Dutchman* is a good case in point. [The Dutchman's] redemption depends on finding a woman/wife [*Weib*] who will be faithful to him. Senta is the one. Agreeing to be destroyed completely in her love for the Dutchman, i.e., to die with him, is the highest expression of love. She loves according to what Freud called the "rescue motif" [*Rettertypus*]. Freud notes that there is an [arche]typal fantasy of rescuing someone from water. A man who dreams he rescues a woman makes her a mother, whereas "a woman rescuing someone else (a child) from the water acknowledges herself in this way as the mother who bore him, like Pharaoh's daughter in the legend of Moses." We have already seen in Nietzsche that sucking up the sea (Mother) makes him a mother. In dreams of births we have noted the same procedure. In the same way, Senta can become a mother as she dissolves herself in the Mother (sea), and the Dutchman becomes a progenitor through the retransformation [*Rückbau*] (death) in the progenitor. Like newborns, Senta and the Dutchman rise from the water, intimately entwined.[63] What Wagner's protagonists have in common is the fact that they love according to the rescue motif, like Siegfried and Brünhilde, for example, who sacrifice themselves for their love, and die. The similarity between the Nordic Siegfried and the oriental Christ are remarkable. Christ too is a Savior type [*Rettertypus*] who sacrifices himself for humankind. Siegfried is the sun god and his beloved is mother earth; Christ is also a sun god.[64] Christ dies at the Tree of Life; he is fastened to it as though he were its fruit. Like the fruit, Christ perishes and enters Mother Earth as seed. Fertilization leads to the formation of new life, to the resurrection of the dead. Through Christ's death and resurrection Adam's guilt is paid [*begleicht seine Schuld*]. Let us now address the question of Adam and Eve's punishment. In Paradise they wanted the forbidden fruit which was denied to them on the grounds that this fruit could only be tasted after one's death. Thus, as God condemns them to death, he also grants them the forbidden delight. Their other punishment – Adam being condemned to till the earth (Mother) by the sweat of his brow, Eve to bear children in pain – has the same meaning. What is the essence of this punishment? It inflicts harm on the individual; because the reproductive drive demands the destruction of the individual. It is therefore quite natural that ideas of punishment so readily assume a sexual coloration.

In order to deflect God's punishment, a sacrifice is offered, i.e., instead of oneself, one gives him another being to destroy, so that one can come into being oneself. What once was the most valuable [i.e., literal human sacrifice] was replaced by a series of symbols and tokens, each less valuable than the preceding one. Symbols fulfill a similar function in the unconscious, because in the unconscious, a symbol is substituted for reality. The most valuable sacrifice was Christ, who took upon him the sins of humankind, and whose death saved all human beings. But Christ does not die for humankind over and over again every time [a human being sins]; it suffices to remember his deeds and thus bring them back to life: when his body and blood are received in the form of bread and wine, [the receiver] identifies with Christ. And by doing so, one says: "I, who am now one with Christ, have performed the required sacrifice – I died – which will bring about my resurrection." To understand how exactly this identification with the sacrifice-victim [*Opfer*] (Christ whose flesh and blood we ingest) works, I want to mention Eysen's interesting account.[65] In the *Marienkirche zu Großgmain*,[66] many of the votive tablets that describe misfortunes also contain information about the motivation for the sacrifice, what it should accomplish [*Wunschtätigkeit*], as well as information about the desired activity and the beloved victim. One of them reads: "A child was drowned in a bath; when the mother learned of it, with a heavy heart, she pledged[67] the child with a living sacrifice, and the child came to life again." "A sow bit a child in the head and tore it apart; the child was pledged out with a living sacrifice and it recovered."

Thus, passing away [*Vergehen*] falls to the sacrificial animal, and Becoming falls to the one who suffered the misfortune. The same is true in this example: "A child born of a dead mother was brought to be baptized as soon as the father had pledged himself with a living sacrifice." Again, instead of the child, a living sacrifice is offered. Christ, the child, who dies for the father, is a part for the whole ["*pars pro toto*"], is what the father with total conviction [*all seiner Gesinnung nach*] becomes in the very moment of procreation: it is always the father who dies in the child; and it is also always the father who is restored in the child. At some point in history, living animals were replaced by inanimate symbols and tokens as sacrifices. Eysen also mentions vases that look like human heads. The vases are filled with grain and they serve as a remedy for headaches. These jars (called "little heads" ["*Köpfl*"]) were used to bless [those suffering from headaches], for healing, for they were taken from the altar and put on the head of the sufferer, just as one would give a blessing by laying on hands. The meaning of the "*Köpfl*" becomes even clearer when we learn of heads modeled on saints who, out of love, just like Christ, welcomed death, and, like Christ, died as a sacrifice. In the Museum of Reichenhall (Eysn) examples of these sacrificial heads, modeled after St. John, can be found. Symbolically they are seed-filled fruits, as surmised earlier, another symbol for Christ. They were supposed to heal through fecundation, which is indeed the case: J. Arnold reports the discovery of wooden heads, which, he explains, were used as sacrificial objects [to cure] headaches and to promote marrying. The juxtaposition of two evils – headaches and being unmarried – shows that the headaches are to be thought of in Freudian terms as a "displacement upward"; the same can be said about the choice of the head as a container for seeds. In other regions, heads made from clay were used to remedy childlessness. These heads contain three types of grain – with three being the symbol of procreation! Still other sacrificial objects mimic the entrails rather than the head. The figure of the entrails usually represents the sick organ greatly enlarged: the destruction demanded by the deity for the continuation of life is diverted to something else of lesser value. A children's saying puts it beautifully: holding the hurt finger of a little one who is crying, one whispers: "May the cat, the dog, the hare, etc. hurt; and in XX [name] may the pain go away." Then one spits 3 times to the side for fear of the evil eye. The number 3 is a symbol of procreation, and the spitting equals the sprinkling of holy water which scares away the demon. Reverential acts of contrition and salutations are akin to the sacrificial act. When we fall to our knees or prostrate ourselves before the ruler, we are saying: "Look, my life is in your hands, here I am lying before you, destroyed (imagined death), now grant me life (rebirth)." When Seth reaches Paradise in order to plead for mercy for his father, he sprinkles his head with earth: "Dust you are, and to dust you shall return," God says to humans. By sprinkling earth on his head, Seth shows that he has already become dust (that he has entered into the earth because the earth is now above his head). From this return to the origin [earth], new life begins.

As regards humankind's origin in the earth, K. Kohler's[68] work compiles interesting religious symbolism. In what follows, I am drawing from his paper. Rabbinic literature describes men of the field and men of the forest who are plugged into the earth up to their navel through which they draw in their sustenance from the earth. As Maimonides explains in his Mishna commentary, these man-like creatures also have man-like voices. In Arabic they are called "Little Man" or "Dwarf Man." According to Salomon Buber, this fabulous creature is a plant in human form whose human-like head only shows itself once it has been pulled from the earth. Simeon from Sims[69] claims that the animal was identical to Jadua: shaped like a pumpkin and tied to the earth by a long cord growing out of the root. Nobody may advance closer than the range of the cord permits, lest he be torn to pieces. The animal can be killed by cutting the cord: it will scream loudly and then die. It is quite obvious that this little plant-man is plugged into the earth as a child is plugged into the womb and tied to its place of origin by an umbilical cord. Just as in algebra, the essence of a formula does not change whether we use α or β as a symbol for the same value, so too for the unconscious it is irrelevant whether we depict what is essential – in our case the genesis of children – using the symbolism of plants or of humans. For example, we designate breath waves as "Traube–Hering waves," thereby highlighting the contribution of both researchers to its discovery. The unconscious does the same with its plant- and animal-men and other composite creatures (cf., Freud, *Interpretation of Dreams*).[70] The plant screams like a child upon its birth. This scream is a scream of death. As long as the child remains within the mother, it has no life of its own. Mythology describes this condition as "apparent death/suspended animation" or "shadow existence" [*Schattendasein*], as for instance in the kingdom of Proserpina, where all we have is a pale reflection of life or a presentiment of life, where everything is just hinted at, as in a shadow. In relation to "Mothers," there is no light or darkness, no above and below, no opposites, because one has not yet differentiated from the primal matter, from the Ur-Mother. Only with differentiation into an independent organism is one doomed to live and to die (return to an undifferentiated state [*Rückdifferenzierung*]). Life itself is the source of death, death the source of life. The development and genesis of a child occurs at the expense of the mother. At birth, it is the mother's life that is endangered the most. The mother is being harmed. In order for her not to be completely destroyed, the death element requires a substitute: a sacrifice is needed. Growth [*Gewächs*] is pulled out (gives birth to it), sprinkling it with the blood of sacrificial animals or urine, both of which are death products [*Todesprodukte*]. In Jewish antiquity there is a plant, *baarah*, with a fiery glow, whose root has the power to exorcise demons and ghosts of the deceased. Tearing the root out of the ground brings death immediately, which is why the uprooting is performed at night by a dog; the plant is also showered with urine or menstrual blood. Treating urine and menstrual blood equally shows that both products are sexual products[71] that possess healing and fertilizing powers. The analogous Persian *Haoma* herb (according to Kohler, a plant- or tree-man revered as a god who possesses divine magical powers; a kind of

Tree of Life in the figure of herbs and plants, a substitution we see quite often in folklore) is ground by night in a mortar while invoking Hades and darkness, pouring the blood of a slaughtered wolf over it. The *Haoma* herb was used to kill demons. A potion made from *Haoma* gives immortality and fertility. Jesus, the fruit of the Tree of Life, must die in order to be resurrected and to bestow life on those who identify with him. In a similar vein, the divine *Haoma* herb, like Jesus, a "tree-man," must be destroyed in order to become, just like Jesus, the fertile seed, the potent potion. Corresponding to the dangerous nature of this plant, Arabs regard agriculture as dangerous.[72] In Arabic belief, every year a worker must die during the harvest. The death-bearing nature of the soil is also attributed to the "earth-people." Therefore, they used to irrigate the land with the blood of an animal sacrificed as a peace offering. On the one hand, the earth plays the role of mother who feeds the little man via the umbilical cord; pulling the child from the earth is thus a birth. On the other hand, the earth carries fruits (children) such as the Tree, which is often thought of as male. With regard to the tree symbolism, I have shown how child and genitals coincide,[73] which is why the act of giving birth may also be a coitus.

To Prof. Freud I owe the communication that circumcision was a symbol of castration. Certain aboriginal Australians [*Australneger*[74]] hold castration rites, while neighboring tribes hold ceremonies in which two incisions are made. These are sacrificial ceremonies: one castrates oneself, i.e., symbolically kills one's sexuality, in order not to be destroyed in reality. As we know, without Destruction, Becoming is impossible! A woman who had undergone a tooth extraction told me that while she was anesthetized, she dreamt of delivering her child. It is not surprising that in dreams tooth extraction becomes a symbol of childbirth [*Entbindung*].[75] Now childbirth = tooth extraction = castration; which means procreation is thought of as castration. Tausk informed me of a case in which the patient understood coitus as castration: during coitus the penis is cut off by the vagina. Notably, masturbation is represented (in dreams) as tooth extraction = castration. We can thus draw the equation:

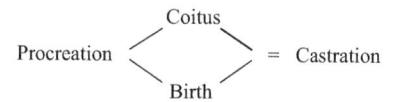

$$\text{Procreation} \genfrac{}{}{0pt}{}{\text{Coitus}}{\text{Birth}} = \text{Castration}$$

The destruction of a sacrificial animal or object can take the place of self-destruction. Seen from a Christian point of view, Christ suffers a sacrificial death, and dies in lieu of human beings, who figuratively suffer death with him. This figurative self-destruction achieves the same aim, as it were, as Christ's self-destruction – namely, resurrection. In the Christian view, self-destruction occurs in the act of placing Christ in his tomb, this burial is a reimplantation into Mother Earth. Resurrection is rebirth.

Pliny reports this Greek custom: "that the presumedly dead body remained unclean until it had undergone a symbolic rebirth" (Kohler). As Liebrecht has shown, rebirth occurred through a circular opening in the roof that resembled a womb. In India, the instrument of rebirth [*Wiedergeburtsinstrument*] is a golden cow: the person to be reborn is placed into the cow and then drawn out through her birth parts [*Geburtsteile*]. In Jerusalem or in Mecca, a person who is returning [home] may go inside [the house]; but instead of making him enter back into the Mother, a sheep or goat is sacrificed for him. This is proof that the sacrifice is seen as analogous to the implantation into the Mother's womb. Kohler describes the sacrificial rite as follows:

> Before he crosses the threshold into the house, he stands with his legs spread apart, making room for the sacrifice to be placed between them. Then the animal is placed on its left side and its head is adjusted – Muslims turn it toward the south or toward Mecca, Christians to the east or toward Jerusalem – then he slits its throat either just in front of or on the door's threshold. If he is a Christian, a cross is drawn on his forehead with blood. Then he enters the house, not stepping on the animal and the blood, and takes the clothes he will wear to the church where the priest will bless them.

Placing the sacrifice between the splayed legs of the returning person corresponds to the position of the child at birth. The bloody cross that is drawn on his forehead refers to Christ's death. Like Christ, he dies and is reborn.

In this chapter, I have once again demonstrated that Becoming comes from Destruction. The progenitor = the life-giving god changes into a child who is returned to the mother's womb. Death in itself is pure horror; death in the service of the sexual instinct, i.e., its destructive element which leads to Becoming, is salutary and health-giving. And yet, eternal life does not bring salvation to human beings, which we see clearly in the legend of the Fountain of Life. I will cite an example from the Alexander Saga (according to Friedländer). By mere coincidence, Alexander's cook found the fountain they were searching for. He wanted to wash a saltwater fish, when all of a sudden the fish came alive and slipped away. The cook, too, bathes in the same fountain and attains immortality. But immortality does not bring him any good: the king, whom he tells about the miracle, falls into a rage for not having been told about this earlier, and has the cook, whose life cannot be taken, thrown into the sea. The cook becomes a dangerous sea demon to whom people (according to other versions of the saga) bring sacrifices. The cook who wanted to attain [eternal life] is being punished, and his punishment consists precisely of being put back into the water, i.e., the primal element (Mother's womb),[76] and his vitality, which cannot be destroyed, becomes dangerously destructive. We have encountered an analogy to the cook in the mandrake plant and in the dangerous little earth-men who are not yet fully born. Killing the dangerous plant makes it wholesome (killing = birth). *The Flying Dutchman* is another analogy of the restlessly raging cook. Friedländer, too, noticed this analogy. According to Graf, the Dutchman's restless sailing about from place to place is an expression of his mental state: he longs for a suitable object that he cannot attain. The cook longs for his death. And the Flying Dutchman shows us that what we long for is erotic death, i.e., a death that leads to new Becoming – Senta and the Dutchman rise from the waves in an intimate embrace.

"According to an ancient saga, when Adam left Paradise he was not given a staff (= Tree of Life according to Wünsche) but a geomantic ring bearing a world cross (⊕, ☉) that he passed on to his descendants, who took it to Egypt where it was perceived as the secret of all knowledge."[77] According to Wünsche, the Tree of Life is replaced by the ring. Both ring and Tree are genesis symbols. Wünsche draws our attention to a passage in Goethe's "Reynard the Fox" (Canto 10, V, 7ff): the ring, engraved with three Hebraic words – which the fox pretends was meant for the king, is described as follows: Seth, the pious, brought the three names down from Paradise, where he had been searching for the Oil of Mercy. We know that Seth brought back three apple seeds or three twigs from which the Tree of Life develops. The three words engraved on the ring are thus symbols of its life-giving power. This sheds new meaning on the ring in *The Nibelungenlied*, where it is also a symbol of procreation and new creation, of the life force which brought about the Fall.

The world can only be saved when life returns to its primal source, symbolically portrayed as the ring being returned to the original place from which it was taken.

In this second section [of this Part III] I have confined myself to discussing a few quite heterogeneous examples, with the intention of illustrating the views on mythology developed in the first section. More comprehensive and in-depth research is needed to prove, respectively, the existence of the destructive element of sexuality, both in recent psychological phenomena, and, as well, in mythological formations. I do believe, however, that my examples sufficiently show that psychologically, and congruent with biological facts, the reproductive drive consists of two antagonistic components, therefore, both a drive for Becoming and a drive for Destruction.

Notes

1 Translator note: Two earlier translations of Spielrein's essay (1912) have been published: first in 1994 as "Destruction as the Cause of Coming into Being" (by K. McCormick) in the Jungian *Journal of Analytical Psychology* (Spielrein, 1994/1912), and then partially (parts I and II) in 1995 as "Destruction as Cause of Becoming" (by Stuart K. Witt) in the psychoanalytic journal *Psychoanalysis and Contemporary Thought* (Spielrein, 1995/1912). Both versions contain numerous errors; however, this new translation owes much to the previous efforts to translate this difficult text into English. – BM
2 When I wrote this essay, Dr. Stekel's *The language of dreams* [1911] had not yet been published. In his work he shows in numerous dreams that next to the wish to live we have the wish to die. The latter he regarded as contrary to the nature of the sexual instinct underlying the wish to live.
3 Translator note: Spielrein is quoting precisely from Jung's (1911) first version of *Wandlungen und Symbole der Libido*. This text was translated into English by Beatrice Hinkle (Jung, 1961a, pp. 116–117). Where necessary, Bettina Mathes has amended Hinkle's translation. The parallel text in Jung's *Collected Works* (Jung, 1967/1911,1950) is based on a later significant revision by Jung made in 1950 in which the sentences "A woman who abandons herself… to be fruitful… our enfeebled hands," so relevant to Spielrein's own argument, no longer appear. – PC-W

4 [C.G. Jung, 1911], *Transformations and Symbols of the Libido*.
5 Translator note: We variously translated "*Angst*" as "fear" or "anxiety," depending on the context, and whether or not there was an identified object of the affect ("fear") or not ("anxiety") – not dependent on the level of intensity. Readers may want to choose the alternative interpretation.
6 Translator note: Although normally German nouns are capitalized and not translated as such into English, we have chosen to capitalize the words "Becoming" and "Destruction," when appropriate in context, to highlight their importance as philosophical themes in Spielrein's thought.
7 Translator note: Spielrein writes very long paragraphs, which are tempting as a translator to divide up for ease of reading. However, we have preserved the original structure in order to enable easier reference to the German original (Spielrein, 1911).
8 Translator note: Witt notes (Spielrein, 1995) that this quote, "*Alles Vergängliche*," is a line from the end of Goethe's Faust, part II. "All that is transitory is only a likeness… the Eternal-Feminine [*das Ewig-Weibliche*] shows us the way" (trans. PC-W). Spielrein cites the passage directly a few sentences later.
9 Translator note: Literally presented here as an action; possibly also a "rough spot" in life. – PC-W
10 Translator note: The English language cannot reproduce the visual and auditory similarity between *holperig* (rough, rugged, bumpy) and *hobeln* (to plane). – BM
11 According to Freud the unconscious is timeless insofar as it only consists of wishes which it represents for the present as being fulfilled. Freud: *Interpretation of Dreams* [= Freud 1953/1900].
12 Freud: "The Antithetical Meaning of Primal Words" [Freud, 1957/1910].
13 "On the Psychological Content of a Case of Schizophrenia (Dementia Praecox)" This *Jahrbuch*, Vol. 3, p. 329ff [= Spielrein, 1911].
14 Translator note: This is the same patient discussed in Spielrein's dissertation "On the Psychological Content of a Case of Schizophrenia" (Spielrein, 1911) (excerpt trans. in this volume, Chapter 5). – PC-W
15 Translator note: We have chosen the convention from the James Strachey translations of Freud in the *Standard Edition*, translating "*das Ich*" as "the ego" whenever Spielrein appears to be referencing Freud's use of the term.
16 Translator note: Spielrein uses "Dementia praecox" throughout this paper – the term traditionally used to refer to schizophrenia in the psychiatry of the time. The term *schizophrenia*, coined by Eugen Bleuler at the Burghölzli hospital in Zürich (where Spielrein herself was treated), was also coming into regular use around the same time – cf., Freud's (1958) Schreber case, also published in the *Jahrbuch* one year before, and in Spielrein's dissertation "On the Psychological Content of a Case of Schizophrenia" in 1911 (excerpt trans. in this volume, Chapter 5). – PC-W
17 Translator note: Spielrein uses the term "*typisch*" throughout this paper in a way that suggests that she is referring to Jung's theory of archetypes. We

are therefore choosing to translate *"typisch"* as "[arche]typal" rather than the more literal "typical," which does not convey an archaic, collective meaning. – PC-W
18 Cf., Spielrein, "Schizophrenia," *Jahrbuch*, III, part I, Conclusion.
19 Translator note: An ancient procedure of drilling holes in the skull for medical and/or ritual reasons. – PC-W
20 Cf., [ibid.].
21 She may also display a strong negative affect when imagining the contaminated earth, if she feels that Earth = I [*Ich*].
22 Translator note: Here, too, Spielrein appears to be referring to Jung's theory of archetypes. – PC-W
23 Cf., Freud [1960/1905], *Jokes and Their Relation to the Unconscious*.
24 Why, for instance, does an artist not always paint the picture of his beloved mother but creates perhaps a Renaissance painting? The censor does not prohibit us from loving mother in "sublimated" form.
25 We experience, or rather we regard and designate experiencing, only as that which we have previously experienced in our ancestors.
26 Jung, Transformations and Symbols of the Libido, *Jahrbuch*, Vol. 3, part I. [Jung, 1911].
27 Translator note: Oskar Pfister (1873–1956), Swiss "analyst pastor" and longtime correspondent with Freud, wrote several psycho-historical works on Count Zinzendorf. The one Spielrein most likely had seen by 1911 was his monograph (Pfister, 1910). NB: In this translation we only are providing citations for sources where Spielrein did not (either in the text or as an original footnote). – PC-W
28 Translator note: The subject of Spielrein's (1911) dissertation. – PC-W
29 Translator note: Our translation of Stekel's *"Beiträge zur Traumdeutung"* (1909) – BM
30 Cf., my above-cited work.
31 Translator note: For German-speaking readers the professor's name *Forel* brings up *Forelle*, the word for trout. The fish is of course another symbol for Christ. Spielrein does not elaborate on this association, perhaps because the connection seemed obvious to her. – BM
32 Translator note: The German word *Leichenfraß* is another word for *Tierfraß* = the act of an animal feeding on carrion. – BM
33 Translator note: Spielrein's *"Wunschpersönlichkeit,"* literally "wish-personality," which seems to be a term she invented, may refer to a personality that only exists as a wish, or to a wished-for personality.
34 Cf., Negelein: "The Horse in Spiritual Belief and the Cult of Death" [*"Das Pferd im Seelenglauben und Totenkult"*], [*Jahrbuch*, Vol. 4].
35 Translator note: Nietzsche (2006/1883–1891, p. 97). Unless otherwise noted, all subsequent quotes are taken from this translation. – BM
36 Translator note: Presumably Silberer (1909). – PC-W
37 Cf., Otto Rank: "Beiträge zum Narzissmus" ["Contributions to Narcissism"], *Jahrbuch* 3(1).

38 One only need to think of the passionate kissing and hugging among young girls. This type of friendship, not remarkable among women, would seem very peculiar among men.

39 Translator note: Spielrein does not give a source for her quote, but it can be assumed that she refers to Wagner rather than Gottfried von Straßburg. As Witt notes (Spielrein, 1995, p. 108n19), Wagner's libretto in the Schirmer edition differs from Spielrein's quote:

> Isolde: *"Du Isolde, Tristan ich, nicht mehr Isolde!"*
> Tristan: *"Tristan du, ich Isolde, nicht mehr Tristan!"*
> Isolde: "Thou Isolde, Tristan I, no more Isolde!"
> Tristan: "Tristan thou, I Isolde, no more Tristan!"
>   (Wagner, 1906, pp. 191–192; BM trans.)

Spielrein puts it differently:

> Tristan: *"Tristan, du — nicht mehr Tristan Ich-Isolde."*
> Isolde: *"Isolde, du — nicht mehr Isolde Ich-Tristan."* – PC-W

40 Cf., Otto Rank: "The Saga of Lohengrin" [*"Lohengrinsage"*], in *Writings on Applied Psychology* [*Schriften zur angewandten Seelenkunde*], ed. S. Freud.

41 *The Sagas of the Tree of Life and the Water of Life, Old Oriental Myths* [*Ex oriente lux. Die Sagen vom Lebensbaum und Lebenswasser, altorient. Mythen*] by A. Wünsche, Leipzig, 1905.

42 Riklin: "Wish Fulfillment and Symbolism in Fairytales" ["Wunscherfüllung und Symbolik im Märchen"], *Schriften zur angewandten Seelenkunde, Writings on Applied Psychology*].

43 Translator note: This sentence is ambiguous in German. The language is convoluted; previous translations are not quite accurate. – BM

44 Cf., *Imago* by Spitteler.

45 Translator note: Freud (1957/1910).

46 Translator note: Sic: *ich* is original – not *Ich*. – BM

47 "On the Psychological Content of a Case of Schizophrenia" [*"Über den psychologischen Inhalt eines Falles von Schizophrenie"*] [Spielrein, 1911].

48 Translator note: Witt's translation (Spielrein, 1995) ends here.

49 Translator note: In this section, where Spielrein is concerned with literature and mythology (i.e., external representations), the intrapsychic term "representation" we have used in parts I and II does not seem to convey Spielrein's intention as well as "images." – BM

50 Translator note: While "oriental" is no longer considered appropriate to denote "eastern" or (better) "Asian," Spielrein's original "*orientalische*" is kept here because it conveys the racialized, romanticized "orientalism" of the period. – PC-W

51 Wünsche notes that indeed death does not stem from the Tree of Life but from the Tree of Knowledge, but numerous legends do not distinguish between the Tree of Life and the Tree of Knowledge. In the beginning there is only one tree, the Tree of Life.

52 According to one legend, Adam, after having heard God's message, shouts: "There, next to my grave, a tree is sprouting. This means, alas, that you have seen the Tree of Death. But Heaven's clemency willing, from my dust shall sprout the Tree of Life."

53 Translator note: Here, Spielrein uses the term *"verlegen,"* but seems to be referring to Freud's term *"Verschiebung,"* referring to the symbolic mental displacement of the genitals to an image of an upper part of the body as a defense against conscious awareness of the libidinal drive (cf., Chapter 9, this volume). – BM

54 Riklin, "Wish Fulfillment and Symbolism in Fairytales," in *Fairytale Writings on Applied Psychology* [*"Wunscherfüllung und Symbolik,"* in *Märchenschriften zur angewandten Seelenkunde*].

55 Here twig or tree figure as a male sexual symbol; Otto Rank compiled numerous examples in which the tree is thought of as female. This supports Stekel's hypothesis that symbols are bisexual.

56 Translator note: Spielrein does not provide a citation for this poem. The first stanza is newly translated here by PC-W. The second stanza is quoted from the 1994 translation (Spielrein, 1994/1912, p. 176).

57 Cf., *Das Nibelungenlied*, [trans. by] Max Burkhardt, edited by Brandis.

58 [Riklin], *Fairytale Writings on Applied Psychology* [*[Märchen]schriften zur angewandten Seelenkunde*.]

59 Translator note: Translation from Porter (1985, pp. 123–124).

60 Translator note: Porter notes that these verses were translated by Elizabeth Forbes, and "were not set to music: 'As these verses, because their meaning was already conveyed with the greatest clarity by the musical effects of the drama, became unnecessary in live performance, they were not set by the composer' – Richard Wagner." This shows that Spielrein (and no doubt Jung as well) were familiar with the libretto as a literary source, apart from its usual operatic performance practice (ibid., p. 123n). – PC-W

61 Translator note: Porter translates this as "ride (sic) to your master" based on a later German version of the text *"Grüss deinen Herren!"* (ibid., p. 124). Several other minor variations occur in the 1985 libretto. Spielrein correctly quotes the original Wagner text. – PC-W

62 Translator note: Here, Spielrein changes *"Selig grüsst dich dein Weib!"* ("Blessed, your wife/woman salutes you!") to *"Selig gilt dir mein Grüss!"* ("Blessed is my greeting to you!"). – PC-W

63 Cf., Otto Rank, "The Saga of Lohengrin," *Writings on Applied Psychology* [*Lohengrinsage, Schriften zur angewandten Seelenkunde*]. Edited by Freud.

64 Translator note: As in English, one perceives the homonym here: Jesus is both a sun god and a son god: *Sonne* and *Sohne*. – BM

65 *Journal of the Society for Folklore*. "On some votive offerings in the Salzburg Flachgau region" [*Zeitschr[ift] des Vereins für Volkskunde*, 1901. *Über einige Votivgaben im Salzburger Flachgau*].

66 Translator note: Presumably this refers to the church by this name in the spa village of Reichenhall, Bavaria. – PC-W
67 Translator note: This archaic use of the word "pledged" reflects Spielrein's quotation of the archaic German. – BM
68 "A lecture on the comparative study of folklore by K. Kohler in Cincinnati. Strange ideas and customs in the biblical and rabbinic literature." *Archive for Religious Research*, 13(1). [*Ein Vortrag zur vergleichenden Sagenkunde von K. Kohler in Cincinnati. Seltsame Vorstellungen und Gebräuche in der biblischen und rabbinischen Literatur*"], *Archiv f[ür] Religionswissenschaft*, 13/1].
69 Kohler [ibid.].
70 Translator note: Freud (1953/1900).
71 Apparently they stemmed from the same organ.
72 [Samuel Ives] Curtis: *Primitive Semitic Religion in the Folkways of the Orient Today* [*Ursemit. Religion im Volksleben des heutigen Orients*], German edition, 1903. [Orig. publ. Chicago, 1902.] Quoted in Kohler [ibid.].
73 In line with Stekel's claim. To be sure, some have tried to explain the process of child development [*Kindsbildung*] after coitus, with the man putting the child into the woman.
74 Translator note: Literally, "Australian Negros." Because "Negro" is neither an accurate term for indigenous Australians, nor is it an appropriate term due to its racist connotations, we have used the word "aboriginal." However, the original terminology conveys the cultural bias of the time. – PC-W
75 Translator note: One of several German words for childbirth, "*Entbindung*," literally = "untying," makes reference to the cutting of the umbilical cord by which the child is severed or untied from the mother. – BM
76 Cf., Rank, *The Myth and Birth of the Hero: A Psychological Exploration of Myth* [*Der Mythus von der Geburt des Helden. Schriften zur angewandten Seelenkunde*] [Rank, 2015/1909].
77 Wünsche, *From the Tree of Life to the Water of Life* [*Vom Lebensbaum zum Lebenswasser*]. According to Wünsche in some legends the Tree of Life = the Tree of Knowledge. Cf., Nietzsche for whom knowledge = love, and others. [Citing, J.W. Goethe, *Reineke Fuchs* [*Reynard the Fox*] (Stuttgart: Cotta, 1866.)]

References

Freud, S. (1953). The interpretation of dreams. In J. Strachey (Ed.) *The standard edition of the complete psychological works of Sigmund Freud* (hereafter *SE*), Vols. 4–5 (entire). London: Hogarth. (Orig. publ. 1900.)
Freud, S. (1957). The antithetical meaning of primal words. *SE* 11, 153–162. (Orig. publ. 1910.)

Freud, S. (1958). Psycho-analytic notes on an autobiographical account of a case of paranoia (Dementia paranoides) [The "Schreber" case]. *SE*, 12, 1–82. (Orig. publ. 1911.)

Freud, S. (1960). Jokes and their relation to the unconscious. *SE* 8 (entire). (Orig. publ. 1905.)

Gogol, N. (1972). Ревизор [*Revizor – The government inspector*]. P. Raby (Trans.). Minneapolis, MN: University of Minnesota Press. (Orig. publ. 1856.)

Jung, C.G. (1911). Wandlungen und Symbole der Libido: Beiträge zur Entwicklungsgeschichte des Denkens, Erster Teil. [Transformations and symbols of the libido: Contributions to the history of the development of thought, Part 2.] *Jahrbuch für Psychoanalyse und Psychopathologische Forschungen*, 3(1), 120–227.

Jung, C.G. (1954). Psychic conflicts in a child. R.F.C. Hull (Trans.). In *The collected works of C. G. Jung*, Vol. 17. G.A. Adler & R.F.C. Hull (Eds.) (hereafter CW). (pp. 1–36). Bollingen Series XX. Princeton, NJ: Princeton University Press. (Orig. publ. 1910.)

Jung, C.G. (1961a) *The psychology of the unconscious*. B. Hinkle (Ed. & Trans.). New York: Dover.

Jung, C.G. (1961b). The significance of the father in the destiny of the individual. *CW* 4, 301–323. (Orig. publ. 1909, rev. ed. 1949.)

Jung, C.G. (1967). Symbols of transformation. *CW* 5 (entire). (Orig. publ. 1911–12, rev. ed. 1952.)

Nietzsche, F. (2006). *Thus spoke Zarathrustra: A book for all and none [Also sprach Zarathustra]*. A. del Caro & R.B. Pippin (Eds.). A. del Caro (Trans.) Cambridge, UK: Cambridge University Press. (Orig. publ. 1883–1891.)

Pfister, O. (1910). *Die Frömmigkeit des Grafen Ludwig von Zinzendorf* [*The Piety of Count Ludwig von Zinzendorf*]. Leipzig: Deuticke.

Porter, A. (1985). *Richard Wagner: Twilight of the gods/Götterdämmerung*. English National Opera and Royal Opera Guide No. 31. A. Porter (trans. – also using a portion of trans. by E. Forbes). London: John Calder.

Rank, O. (2015). *The myth and birth of the hero: A psychological exploration of myth*. G. Richter & E.J. Lieberman (Trans.). Baltimore, MA: Johns Hopkins Press. (Orig. publ. 1909.)

Silberer, H. (1909). Bericht über eine Methode, gewisse symbolische Halluzinations-Erscheinungen hervorzurufen und zu beobachten. [Report on a method for evoking and observing certain symbolic hallucinatory phenomena.] *Jahrbuch für Psychoanalytische und Psychopathologische Forschung*, 1(2), 513–525.

Spielrein, S. (1911). Über den psychologischen Inhalt eines Falles von Schizophrenie (Dementia praecox). [On the psychological content of a case of schizophrenia (Dementia praecox).] *Jahrbuch für Psychoanalytische und*

Psychopathologische Forschungen, 3, 11–93. (Excerpt trans. in this volume, Chapter 5; full trans. in Spielrein, 2018.)

Spielrein. S. (1912). Die Destruktion als Ursache des Werdens. [Destruction as the cause of Becoming.] *Jahrbuch für Psychoanalytische und Psychopathologische Forschungen*, 4, 465–503.

Spielrein, S. (1994). Destruction as the cause of coming into being. K. McCormick (Trans.). *Journal of Analytical Psychology*, 39, 155–186. (Orig. publ. Spielrein, 1912.)

Spielrein, S. (1995). Destruction as Cause of Becoming. S.K. Witt (Trans.). *Psychoanalysis and Contemporary Thought*, 18, 85–118. (Orig. publ. Spielrein, 1912.)

Spielrein, S. (2018). *The essential writings of Sabina Spielrein: Pioneer of psychoanalysis*. R. Cape & R. Burt (Ed. & Trans.). New York: Routledge.

Stekel, W. (1911). *Die Sprache des Traumes* [*The language of dreams*]. Wiesbaden: Bergmann.

Wagner, R. (1906). *Tristan and Isolde*. New York: Schirmer.

Chapter 7

Maternal Love

Sabina Spielrein

1913 Translated by Judith Gresh and Pamela Cooper-White[1]

A six-year-old girl wanted to sleep in the same bed as her little brother. "Mama" ["*Muttchen*"[2]], she asked, "allow me to enjoy his wonderful little body."[3] The girl, raised under strict supervision, has "no idea" ["*keine Ahnung*"] about sexual things. Here, it's a question of "maternal" feelings, which the older sister has for the "little body." Presumably for the brother, the sister's proximity also gives satisfaction. Why are we surprised, therefore, when this experience leaves such a strong impression in our mind? Why does the assertion seem so improbable, that the adult's first "physical love" goes back to childhood experiences, when the blissful touch of the beloved woman could be compared with the once-beatific touch of the sister, of the mother? If we have recognized this recourse to childhood experiences, then neurotic manifestations do not seem strange: if there is a strong fixation [*Fixierung*] on the maternal role model, any sexual love object would meet with great resistance [*Widerstand*], because the mother's figure would be superimposed on any female figure, consciously or in the subconscious [*Unterbewusstsein*].[4] Also, if the mother's image itself does not reach consciousness without analysis, emotional reactions will occur, because they correspond to "normal" ideas about incestuous love. These are feelings of disgust, shame, fear.

The following communication from philosopher I[saak] Spielrein[5] (Rostov) is, among other things, evidence of the fact how repressed psychic content can generate feelings of unpleasure.[6]

Notes

1 Translator note: Translated from the original German (PC-W) with reference to the Russian translation (JG).

2 Translator note: Diminutive for "Mother."
3 In Russian: *"Doj ninie nasladitjsia ewo trehudnym tielzein."*
4 Translator note: Spielrein frequently uses the term "subconscious" [*"das Unterbewußtsein"*] rather than Freud's preferred term "unconscious" [*"das Unbewußte"*] in her writings. – PC-W
5 Translator note: Isaak Spielrein was Sabina's middle brother. At the time she wrote this brief essay, he was in his early twenties, married, with a doctorate from the Sorbonne. He had "a formidable German education in philosophy and psychology," with a strong "interest in Jewish history and culture as well as the Yiddish language" (Launer, 2015, p. 158). A loyal socialist and communist, he would go on to be a rising star in Soviet Moscow under Trotsky in the field of industrial psychology (ibid., p. 228), but under Stalin was arrested along with their father, Nikolai, and sentenced to five years of hard labor. One day after Christmas in 1937, Isaak was murdered by a firing squad and thrown into a mass grave (ibid., p. 232) – PC-W
6 What follows is a brief commentary by Isaak Spielrein entitled "Das unbewußte Träumen in Kuprins 'Zwiekampf' [sic]" ["Unconscious dreaming in Kuprin's [novel] 'The Duel.'"]

References

Launer, J. (2015). *Sex versus survival: The life and ideas of Sabina Spielrein.* London: Overlook Duckworth.
Spielrein, S. (1913). Mutterliebe [Mother love]. *Imago*, 2(5), 523–524.
Spielrein, S. (2008). Материнская любовь [*Materinskaya liubov* – Maternal love]. In S.F. Sirotkin & E. C. Morozova (Eds.), *Psychoanalytischeskie trudi* [*Psychoanalytic works*] (pp. 180–181). Izhevsk, Russia: ERGO.

Chapter 8

The Forgotten Name

Sabina Spielrein

1914 Translated by Judith Gresh with Pamela Cooper-White

A lady of my acquaintance could not remember the name of the hero of the novel she had just read. "Leon? – No. George? – No. Martin? – No. What was he called? His last name is Mendlin. Ah! I remember now! Kurt Mendlin."

I must add that the lady wanted to draw my attention to the similarity between the hero's fate and hers. In this regard, she forgot the main similarity: her boyfriend had the same name as the hero of the novel – "Kurt!" She wanted to forget her lover's name; this is why she forgot the name of the hero of the novel.

Reference

Spielrein, S. (1914). Der vergessene Name. [The forgotten name]. *Internationale Zeitschrift für Ärztliche Psychoanalyse, 2,* 383–384.

Chapter 9

Two Menstrual Dreams

Sabina Spielrein

1914 Translated by Pamela Cooper-White with Jan Rehmann

Communicated from Dr. S. Spielrein:

In Freud's *Interpretation of Dreams*,[1] he highlights the similarity between dreams and popular art: how the dreamer, just like the popular poet, receives drive energy from the unconscious, which is occupied by infantile wishes. So we also understand, conversely, how it is that we readily employ once-heard folk legends and myths in our dreams. In a well-known children's and folk tale, a son or daughter is born of noble parents, whom s/he later meets only by chance; whereas, up until then, people took the simple foster parents for the rightful ones. Thirteen-year-old Erna dreamed during her menstrual period that she was dancing in a torn little red dress. Undoubtedly, the idea of menstrual blood contributed to the image of the red dress in her dream. But that by itself does not explain everything. Where did the dreamer derive the model of the girl who danced so? If we know that, then we also know what fantasies occupied her in the formation of her dream image. "Have you ever seen anyone dance like that?" I ask her. Puzzling [*irindliehou*][2] dreams are easy to decipher. Immediately Erna remembers having seen "Mignon" in the theater. Mignon is a noble child kidnapped by gypsies. One day, she refuses to obey the beggar's command to dance her usual dance. This could go very badly for her; she is only saved by chance: she finds rescuers, one of whom later turns out to be her long-missed father, and the other of whom is a young nobleman who then marries the rescued girl. Erna lives in quite modest circumstances with her mother and a little brother. Often, with longing, she hears stories about her long-absent father. The father is supposed to love his children above all else. Erna has a strong need for love, all the more so as the mother pampers the younger brother much more.

Now we understand why it is that the girl identifies with Mignon in her dream. She also would rather not be the child of a poor mother, but would prefer to belong to rich people. She would like to find her father, who would belong to her alone, and to find a "hero" to whom she could surrender in love.

Dream II[3]

A patient (Miss U.) sees images of the saints in her dream. Among others, there is the Mother of God with the Child. Her head is split, and smoke rises out of it. The patient awakes in a masturbatory [o[n]anistisch] position with an urgent need to urinate, and sees that her menses have begun. For the expert, the dream is immediately clear. Already the images of saints reveal enough: we lay emphasis on the "holy" as a defense against internal "unholy" wishes. I once analyzed the fantasies of a schizophrenic patient,[4] who claimed that her head was split in two and the "spirit" ["*Geist*"][5] of the animal that plagued her came out. It became apparent that the patient was symbolically describing here the process of giving birth. In the same way, when she spoke about splitting of the earth and emerging from the waters, she meant the birthing process.

This patient also produced an analogical sequence of associations. One day she recounted, under some resistance, that a woman was torn giving birth. Someone said that the uterus looked like a cook-oven. Thereupon, I ask the patient, hasn't she already dreamed of ovens or smoke?[6] I wanted to bring her a memory of her dream of the Mother of God, but the patient only remembered very generally: "Oh, yes, I have often dreamed of smoke." That means joy was not pure. Fire is pure joy. "Once I dreamed that a building was burning and smoke was coming out of it." I must remark here that the previously mentioned schizophrenic patient also spoke of pure fire, and she also had a dream of a building (the house of her parents), which went up in fire and puffs of smoke. Patient H. went on to tell how, after such a dream, she fell out of bed; once she dreamed that someone was lifting her up. That reminded her of an earthquake that caused the lamp to totter [*wackelte*] (again a fire association). Constellated from the image of tearing at birth, the patient produced a series of pictures that symbolically represent the rip, the convulsion, the yawning gap: the oven, which looked like a split-open "birth canal wound," the building from which smoke was coming, the vibration during the lifting up, the vibration during the earthquake. Jung, in his work "Psychic Conflicts in a Child" [Jung, 1954/1910][7] has described a case of earthquake anxiety. Here also the earthquake was a symbol of giving birth.

Patient H. provides us with even further evidence. She recounts how as a child she was afraid of the devil, the chimney sweep, and Krampus[8] (all of whom come out of the chimney). I have her come up with some further associations, and then ask if she couldn't think of a similar dream in which an oven or smoke occurred. Now she immediately recalled the portrait of the Mother of God from whose head smoke rose up. In addition, the myth we were long expecting came to her. "Hera came out of Zeus' head," she said. Until now I had not interpreted to her the meaning of her dream. But it is strange that the patient had not already got to the true contents of the dream through objective signs, such as the masturbatory position, the urinary urgency, the bleeding. The idea of birth, which emerges easily from menstrual bleeding, was too horrific for the patient to tolerate consciously. She only dared to express it symbolically, by representing the blood as smoke, moving the process upward to the head (displaced upward [*verlegte nach oben*[9]]), and attributed everything to the Holy Mary.

The child whom Mary holds in the dream also shows that the patient had likewise thought of motherhood (the product of birth) in the dream. The same is shown to us by the interassociations of the devil, the chimney sweep, and Krampus, which (like the child) come out of the "oven."

Notes

1 Translator note: Freud (1953/1900).
2 Translator note: There are a number of misspellings or typographical errors in the original German publication, which required some contextual interpretation. Such words are noted in brackets throughout this translation, as well as other words that could be open to alternative interpretations. – PC-W
3 Translator note: There is no "Dream I" subheading in the original text. – PC-W

4 Translator note: This refers to one of the case studies in Spielrein's doctoral dissertation (Spielrein, 1911; excerpt trans. this volume, Chapter 5; full translation in Spielrein, 2018). – PC-W
5 [Spielrein], "Emphasis on the spiritual in contrast to the animalistic: On psychology." "On the Content of a Case of Schizophrenia" ["*Betonung des Geistigen im Gegensatz zum Animalischen. Über den psycholog*"] [Spielrein, 1911].
6 Translator note: Tense changes in the original.
7 So Jung elaborates: "On the Meaning of the Earthquake in Mythology" ["*Über die Bedeutung der Erdspaltung in der Mythologie*"], in "Transformations and Symbols of the Libido, [Part 2]" ["*Wandlungen und Svmbole der Libido*"], *Jahrb[uch] für Psychoanalyt[ische und Psychopathologische] Forschungen*, 4 [Jung, 1967/1912, 1952].
8 Translator note: In Austria, Krampus is a familiar fantastic monster figure who accompanies St. Nicholas (Santa Claus) on his rounds. He is usually depicted as entirely covered in red fur, with staring eyes and sharp fangs. – PC-W
9 Translator note: Here, Spielrein uses the term "*verlegen*," but seems to be referring to Freud's term "*Verschiebung*," referring to the symbolic mental displacement of the genitals to an image of an upper part of the body as a defense against conscious awareness of the libidinal drive. – JR. See also Chapter 6, this volume.

References

Freud, S. (1953). The interpretation of dreams. In J. Strachey (Trans.), *The standard edition of the complete psychological works of Sigmund Freud*, Vols. 4–5 (entire). London: Hogarth. (Orig. publ. 1900.)

Jung, C.G. (1954). Psychic conflicts in a child. R.F.C. Hull (Trans.). In *The collected works of C. G. Jung*, Vol. 17. G.A. Adler & R.F.C. Hull (Eds.) (hereafter CW) (pp. 1–36). Bollingen Series XX. Princeton, NJ: Princeton University Press. (Orig. publ. 1910.)

Jung, C.G. (1967). Symbols of transformation. *CW* 5. (Orig. publ. 1912, rev. ed. 1952.)

Spielrein, S. (1911). Über den psychologischen Inhalt eines Falles von Schizophrenie (Dementia praecox). [On the psychological content of a case of schizophrenia (Dementia praecox).] *Jahrbuch für Psychoanalytische und Psychopathologische Forschungen*, 3, 11–93. (Excerpt trans. this volume, Chapter 5; for full translation, see Spielrein, 2018, pp. 14–96.)

Spielrein, S. (1914). Zwei Mensesträume. [Two menstrual dreams]. *Internationale Zeitschrift für Psychoanalyse*, 2(1), 32–34.

Spielrein, S. (2018). *The essential writings of Sabina Spielrein: Pioneer of psychoanalysis*. R. Cape & R. Burt (Ed. & Trans.). New York: Routledge.

Chapter 10

Russian Literature on Psychoanalysis

Sabina Spielrein

1921 Geneva

Translated by Judith Gresh, Anatoli Samochornov, and Felicity Kelcourse, with Ekaterina Golynkina and Sergey Trostyanskiy

Preliminary comments of the editors[1]
German editions

1921: Russische Literatur // Bericht über die Fortschritte der Psychoanalyse 1914–1919. – Leipzig, Wien, Zürich: Internationaler Psychoanalysticher Verlag, 1921. – *Beiheft der Internationalen Zeitschrift für Psychoanalyse.* [*Supplement to the International Journal for Psychoanalysis*] – No. 3.-S. 202–212.

Russian editions

1999: Russian Literature. Report on Success of Psychoanalysis (1914–1919)/Translation from German M.I. Spielrein // Ovcharenko, V.I., Leibin, V.M. Anthology of Russian Psychoanalysis in 2 volumes – Volume 1. – Moscow, Moscow Psychological Sociological Institute: Flinta, 1999. – Pages 207–211.

A short article – a review of Russian Language Psychoanalytical Literature form the period of 1909 to 1920.

Translation from German by M.I. Spielrein.

Citations

1. Asatiani, M.M. The concept of "conditioned reflexes" as applied to the symptoms of psychoneurosis. *Psychotherapy* [*Psychotherapiya*] – 1913. – IV / 4.

2. Asatiani, M.M. Mental mechanisms of symptoms in a case of hysterical psychosis. *Psychotherapy*. – 1912. – No. 3. – [pp. 141–155].
3. Benny, [V.I.] On the method of psychoanalysis // *Review of Psychiatry and Neurology* (St. Petersburg). – [1911. – Year] XVI. – [pp. 257–384].
4. Beloborodov, L.Y. Psychoanalysis of a case of hysteria // *Psychotherapy*. – 1912. – No. 2. – [S. 84–103]; No. 6. – [S. 277–298].
5. Birstein, I.[A.] On the psychology of neuroses // *Psychotherapy*. – 1913. – No. 5. – pp 290–297.
6. Birstein, I.A. On the psychology of smoking // *Psychotherapy*. – 1913. – No. 6. – pp 366–377.
7. Droznes, L.M. The bio-psychological basis of the mental patient's delusions. *Therapeutic Review*. – Odessa, 1914. – No. 4. – [pp. 108–117].
8. Droznes, L.M. About masturbation. [A popular presentation concerning the views of Prof. Freud's psychoanalytic school on the nature of masturbation and its treatment]. – *SPB.*, [1911. – 16 p.].
9. Feltsman, O.B. On the issue of suicide // *Psychotherapy*. – 1910. – No. 6. – [pp. 227–243].
10. Goloushev, S.S. About a case study of psychoanalysis // *Psychotherapy*. – 1913. – No. 5. – [pp. 287–290. Reprint. M., 1913. – 4 p.].
11. International Congress on care for the mentally ill [26–29 Moscow. XII. 1913.] Russia. // Ref. Münchener med. Wochenschrift 1914. – Nr. 11.
12. Joffe, A.L. About the unconscious in the life of the individual // *Psychotherapy*. – 1913. – No. 4. – [pp. 234–238].
13. Kannabikh, Y.V. Evolution of psychotherapeutic ideas in the XIX century // *Psychotherapy*. – 1910. – No. 1. – [pp. 1–10; No. 3. – pp. 106–116].
14. Aihnitskiy, V.N. About the current state of psychotherapy in America // *Psychotherapy*. – 1913. – No. 1. – [pp. 35–42].
15. Orshansky, I.G. Artistic creativity and psychoanalysis // *Bulletin of education*. – [1914. – Year XXV. – May.] – No. 5. – [pp. 1–33].
16. Osipov, N.E. About psychoanalysis // *Psychotherapy*. – 1910. – No. 1. – [pp. 11–28].
17. Osipov, N.E. Idealistic moods and psychotherapy: [About the book of Professor Yarotskiy] // *Psychotherapy*. – 1910. – No. 6. – [pp. 244–255].
18. Osipov, N.E. Thoughts and doubts about a case of "degenerate psychopathy" // *Psychotherapy*. – 1912. – [No. 4. – pp 189–215;] No. 6. – [pp. 299–306. Separate printing. M., 1912. – 34 p.].
19. Osipov, N.E. "Diary of a madman," the unfinished work of L.N. Tolstoy (regarding the question about the emotion of fear) // *Psychotherapy*. – 1913. – No. I.1 – [pp. 141–158].
19a. Osipov, N.E. Psychotherapy in the literary works of L.N. Tolstoy. [(Excerpt from the work "Tolstoy and Medicine")] // *Psychotherapy*. – 1911 – [No. 1. – pp 1–21].

19b. Osipov, N.E. About Freud's "pansexualism" // *Journal of Neuropathology and Psychiatry* [In honor of S.S. Korsakov]. – 1911 – [Bk. 5–6. – pp. 749–760].
19c. Osipov, N.E. About the sick soul // *Journal of Neuropathology and Psychiatry* [In honor of S.S. Korsakov]. – 1913. – No. 5–6. – pp. 657–673.
20. Dr. Tatiana Rosenthal. About Dostoevsky (Part 1) [Rosenthal, T.K. Suffering and creativity of Dostoevsky: Psychogenetical study // *Challenges in Studying and Educating an Individual.* – 1919. – No. 1. – Pg., 1920. – pp. 88–107].
21. Zaharchenko, [M.L.]. On the semiotics of alcoholism [(On the aversion to wine in alcoholics during abstinence)] // *Problems in Psychiatry and Neurology.* – 1914. – [Year 3 – May.] – No. 5. – [pp. 193–204].
22. Zalkind, A.B. Questions concerning factors, nature and psychotherapy of neuroses // – 1913. – No. 1. – [pp. 8–25].
23. Zalkind, A.B. On the issue of the origins of psychoneuroses // *Psychotherapy.* – 1913. – No. 3. – [pp. 172–187]. – No. 4. – [pp. 214–221].
24. Schrader, N.N. Psychotherapeutic observations // *Psychotherapy.* – 1912. – No. 6. – [p. 269-T].
25. Tutyshkin, P.P. Psychoanalysis as a method of psychological diagnosis and therapy (Prof. Freud's method) // *Review of Psychiatry, Neurology and Experimental Psychology.* – 1912. – No. 3. – pp 173–181.
26. Vyrubov, N.A. On the question of the genesis and treatment of anxiety neurosis by the combined hypnoanalytic method // *Psychotherapy.* – 1910. – No. 1. – [S. 29–41].
27. Vyrubov, N.A. Concerning the psychopathology of everyday life: Psychoanalysis of the recent struggle for parliamentary seats // *Psychotherapy.* – 1913. – No. 1. – [pp. 25–35].

Translations of Freud's works

1. Three essays on the theory of sexuality / Trans. Under ed. [N.E.] Osipov. – First ed. 1909; Second ed. 1911 [= Freud, 1953c/1905].
2. The psychopathology of everyday life (new ed.). Trans. Medem. M., 1910. [– 162 p.] [= Freud, 1960/1901].
3. About psychoanalysis. Five lectures at Clark University. / Trans. [N.E.] Osipov. – (Psychotherapy Library). – M., 1911. [– 67 p.]. 2nd ed. 1912. [– 67 p.]. 3rd ed. 1913. [– 67 p.] [= Freud, 1957a/1910].
4. Delusions and Dreams in Gradiva [// Jensen, W. *Gradiva. Fantastic adventure in Pompeii.*] – Odessa, 1912. – [pp. 87–190] [= Freud, 1959/1906].
5. A childhood memory of Leonardo da Vinci. – M., 1912. – [119 p.] [= Freud, 1957b/1910].
6. Formulations on the two principles of mental functioning // *Psychotherapy.* – 1912. – No. 3. – [pp. 155–162] [= Freud, 1958c/1911].

7. The interpretation of Dreams. – M.,² 1913. – [2, 448, VII p.] [= Freud, 1953a/1900].
8. Practical application of dream interpretation in psychoanalysis // *Psychotherapy*. – 1913. – No. 2. – [pp. 79–84] [= Freud, 1958a/1911].
9. Recommendations to physicians conducting psychoanalytic treatment // *Psychotherapy*. – 1913. – No. 5. – [pp. 297–306] [= Freud, 1958b/1912].
10. About types of neurotic illness // Ibid., *Psychotherapy*. – 1913. – No. 5. – pp. 306–313] [= Freud, 1958d/1913].
11. Some comments on the concept of the unconscious in psychoanalysis // Ibid. – 1913. – No. 5. – pp. 313–320] [= Freud, 1958e/1912].
12. Phobias of a five year old boy // Trans. O.B. Felzman. – M., 1912. – (Psychotherapeutic library no. 9) [= Freud, 1955].
13. About dreams. – St. Petersburg 1909. [= Freud, 1953b/1901].

I hope my Russian colleagues will not be offended if this statement on Russian literature is quite incomplete. Wartime conditions and their aftermath led to our being completely cut off from Russia for years.

I have only a few issues of the Moscow magazine *Psychotherapy* [*Psychotherapiya*]³ (from years 1909–1914) at my disposal, in which a number of psychoanalytic works appeared. This magazine was founded in 1909,⁴ and is edited by Dr. N. Vyrubov.

Already, the contributors' names show that, at least until 1913, the magazine brought together psychoanalysts from very different fields. Different nationalities are represented as well, namely, representatives from Vienna, Russians from Moscow (M. Asatiani, A. Bernstein, Y.V. Kannabih, N.E. Osipov, O.B. Felzman) and from Odessa (I.A, Birstein,⁵ V. Likhnitskiy). In Moscow, psychoanalysis apparently fell into fertile soil. When, in the winter of 1911–1912, I read a report about psychoanalysis in Rostov-on-Don, my attention was also drawn to the psychoanalytic movement in Moscow, the chief representatives of which were Osipov, Felzman, and Vyrubov.

Osipov, First Assistant at the Moscow Psychiatric Hospital, according to works available to me (references 16–19 above), is a faithful follower of Freud's views, which he courageously defends against attacks; he also cites interesting clinical cases from his medical practice. There is no mention of children's sexuality, perhaps because Osipov, like many practitioners, does not have the opportunity to carry out pure psychoanalysis but uses a combination of treatment methods instead.⁶

In No. 19 Osipov points to the fact that, in the work mentioned,[7] Tolstoy describes his own psychological state. An analysis of drawings based on Freud's principles follows. The author shows how precisely the development of the patient's pathological symptoms of fear is observed, and corroborating examples in psychiatric or (correspondingly) psychoanalytic experiments are presented. He speaks about fear hysteria [*hysteriya strax*]. In the theoretical part, Osipov contests the views of Dubois and Oppenheim, who challenge each other on the basis of Janet's theory of feelings. Osipov also finds Janet's theory insufficient; with Stumpf, Lossky, and others, he emphasizes that the bodily sensations described do not represent the essence of the state of fear, since we can observe the accompanying sensations of body parts belonging to a fear state, without developing fear. From this Osipov concludes that we can have an effect on the pathological condition of fear in a psychotherapeutic way, namely by means of psychoanalysis. If we accept that the basis of the emotion of fear (anxiety) is the organic (bodily) sensations, it will be possible to conclude that anxiety appears (develops) with the breakdown (damage) of sexual feeling. Osipov has not seen a single case of anxiety hysteria without problems in sexual life.

In fairness to the author, I follow his terminology, with which, despite great appreciation for his theoretical interpretations, we do not always agree.

Vyrubov (citations 26, 27) serves us well too, although he is not a pure psychoanalyst. His concise analysis of (Freudian) slips [*opechatka*] made by conflicting political factions is very good. Y.V. Kannabikh (13) mentions increasing interest in psychoanalysis. O.B. Felzmann (9) emphasizes the importance of psychoanalytic experience in order to understand and avoid suicidal tendencies. True, he does not want to call himself a perfect follower of Freud, but he cites some cases of suicidal tendencies that he had observed, and finds in all cases a sexual etiology. M.M. Asatiani (2) describes a case of hysteria with a twilight state, treated with psychoanalysis. L.Y. Beloborodov (4) talks about a case being cured by psychoanalysis. Unfortunately, I have only the end of this interesting analysis. A.B. Zalkind (22) raises the question of whether there are innate neuroses, and whether there is a specific constitution that predisposes one to disease by some form of psychoneurosis. He believes that we cannot establish a predisposition to certain psychoneuroses, but that one must assume a common congenital psychoneurotic basis acting as a predisposition. He incorrectly criticizes Freudians for allegedly denying every kind of organic predisposition. After this criticism, he still shows respect for the "individual-psychological" law of development discovered by Freud's followers. The author acknowledges that neurosis is based on conflict but denies that this conflict should always be of a sexual nature. One of his peculiar views deserves attention: "I even believe," he says, "that in recent years the number of neuroses attributed to sexual reasons could rise because of the fact that Freud's school focuses all our attention to this area; it increases the role of sexuality in the eyes of ignorant society, i.e., increases the pathogenic significance of sexuality."

Conclusions are absent in the essay, but I do not think this work is of special interest for us analysts, since the author, like most of the ignorant, does not offer his own arguments but argues a priori.

Zalkind's views (23) can be summarized in the following statements: "Neurosis appears due to [an] excess of unspent affects within an immature psyche which has not yet been able to adapt." "Neurosis is inharmonious, unplanned, irrational sublimation of affect, the result of unstable, incomplete and immature positions of vital systems in the individual."

Judging from this article, Zalkind subscribes to a Jungian orientation. He also describes two psychological types, analytical and synthetic, which think deductively and inductively; the latter is not through intuition, but through slowly forming a whole system of logical constructions. The first type in pathological cases results in the hysterical state; the second, in the psychoanalytic state.[8] Neither Freud nor Jung was mentioned.

N.N. Schreider (24) investigates three methods of psychotherapy – hypnosis, psychoanalysis, and rational psychotherapy (according to Dubois) – and their application in various cases of diseases. He recommends hypnosis where it is possible to clearly see the development of the illness without psychoanalysis, that is, where nothing "repressed" is found, for patients of lower classes, not the intelligentsia, and in cases where heavy, painful conditions make a quick intervention necessary. For hysteria, psychoanalysis is always recommended. Here the author finds every possible reason for disease, yet sees the main basis of disease in sexual injury. However, the author does not believe in a complete cure by psychoanalysis since for neurotics it is necessary to deal with the predisposed pathological constitution. In spite of this, psychoanalysis is recommended as a much more effective solution compared to hypnosis. In some cases, the combined method of psychoanalysis and hypnosis is recommended. Rational psychotherapy is a method that aims to confront the patient, as opposed to hypnosis and psychoanalysis, whose methods seek to eliminate contention.

Rational psychotherapy should be applied to psychasthenia, especially for psychasthenic states of elderly persons who are much less suitable for psychoanalysis.[9]

A. Yoffe (12) discusses a case of homosexuality in a medical assistant who constantly threatened suicide to attract attention from those close to him. When they finally stopped believing him, he really made good on his threat: this also led to the impression that he decided to do it from vanity, so that he would not be mocked. Yoffe concluded that homosexuality in this person resulted from his childhood relationship to the father, where the boy always identified himself with the mother. What follows, however, is not clear:

> He loved his mother and "hated" his father; he was always thinking that the mother knows everything. She makes everything better than his father, [she is] more important than his father. Since he "played the role of his mother," he knows everything, does everything better than the others, etc. ... "Father was a tyrant"; Mother had always been insulted by him [the father].

This supposedly explains the son's sensitivity to insults. Hatred can be interpreted as a reaction against homosexual fixation on the father, which Yoffe talks about. It is striking that Yoffe refers to Jung and Teller, but not to Freud, even though he analyzes the case according to Freud.

Goloushev (10) treated an interesting case of disgust toward women's genital parts on the part of a married man, which for years made normal coitus impossible for him. The author discovered, under hypnosis, a childhood trauma: at the age of six years the boy was attacked by shameless laundresses who looked at his penis and showed him their genitals; he began to cry, and the nanny took him away. The author learned of additional examples without hypnosis. When the patient was nine years old, he and his friend saw a little girl's genital area when she raised her dress. This body part seemed disgusting to him, and he felt an impulse to torture it. This feeling was then transferred to the whole female [body], causing the children to force the girl to run barefoot, with her dress lifted, across some small scattered nails. After this limited analysis, Goloushev applied the following method: he tried under hypnosis to separate his patient's representation of women's genitals from representations of these parts of the laundresses. When that was achieved, he suggested to the patient that women's parts are something very attractive and [that] coitus is very pleasant. In two weeks, the patient was so recovered that he wanted to have normal coitus with his wife, but the wife refused. Then he tried it with another woman, and he managed it. Since then he is cured.

Two brochures of Dr. L.M. Droznes (Odessa) are written in clear language and very worthy to be recommended. The author shows (7) that neither new theories of metabolism nor descriptive clinical psychiatry can explain the nature and causes of the psychic content of mental illness. What is the reason that not all syphilitics have progressive paralysis, but only 4.7%? We cannot explain this by materialist–monist concepts. The theory of heredity seems inadequate as well because, firstly, it is not possible in all cases – with all good intentions – to prove a hereditary predisposition. And secondly, we have quite a lot of hereditarily burdened individuals, but in spite of this they do not develop psychosis. Thus, the author arrives at the extraordinary value of education and experience regarding early childhood sexual experiences, following Freud, although the author's term "homosexual dependency" is not entirely clear and may lead to error; good examples from psychoanalytic practice sufficiently compensate for the error.

The second small work (8) is a popular, easy-to-digest summary of Freud's views about the nature of masturbation. The author especially emphasizes the great harm that may arise from excessive fear and reproach of oneself about masturbation, which is practiced by over 95% of normal people over a long period of time.

In addition to original works of Russian authors, the journal *Psychotherapy* offers foreign authors' works, translated into Russian, including Freud's work (see No. 6 and 11 of translated literature). Further abstracted [are] works in the *International Journal of Psychoanalysis* and other psychiatric literature, and reports on congresses.

Among works of Russian researchers, abstracted in *Psychotherapy*, I am interested in Dr. Netkachev's work "Symptoms and Therapy of Stuttering: New Psychological Treatment," 1913, VI, and p. 126 (abstracted by Vyrubov). The author considers stuttering as psychoneurosis, which he treats based on the methods of Dubois, Freud, Dejerine, and others, as well as with hypnosis.

Next: "Proceedings of the Psychiatric Clinic of the Imperial University of Moscow," edited by Professor F.E. Rybakov, No. 1, 1913, p. 384 (abstracted by Vyrubov).

The first volume contains F.E. Rybakov's papers, "Influence of Sex and Age on Mental Illness," "Influence of scientific trends in psychiatry for diagnosis of mental illness." Dr. Ermakov, "Hysterical epilepsy, pathology of emotive breathing." Articles of E. Petrov, Tarasevich, M.P. Kutanina, Dr. I.A. Azbukin raise a rather general psychiatric interest. Among the abstracts one should note Bleuler's essay "On Schizophrenia" ([1950/1911] p. 60, annotated by Kutanin).

The Fifth International Congress on Care of Mental Illness in Russia, Moscow, 8–13 January 1914 (26–29 December 1913) is reviewed by Drs. I.D. Mackewitch and A.I. Prusenko in the monthly *Questions of Psychiatry and Neurology*, edited by M. Lakhtin.

Dr. Maria and H.H. Bazhenov talk about dementia praecox and degeneration. They refer to various views on dementia praecox and criticize the French school's concept of "degeneracy," the exaggerated etiological significance attributed to inheritance, and the differential diagnosis of Kraepelin, which is based on clinical and pathological–anatomical symptoms. Only taking all the symptoms into account (in their opinion) allows a correct diagnosis.

In discussions, Rosenbach (St. Petersburg) argues against Magnan. Weygandt (Hamburg) believes that even in somatic diseases it is difficult to make the diagnosis on the basis of physical symptoms, and in psychiatry it is especially risky. We cannot yet diagnose forms of psychosis based on physical signs of degeneracy.

S. Orshanskiy: "Secondary Mental Degeneracy as Symptom of Some Chronic Psychoses." P.P. Tutyshkin: "The Legal Responsibility of Mentally Ill People."

Hess: "Raising the Legal Age for Psychopaths." For psychopathy with moral defects one should have longer supervision time and education, which should be psychiatric and pedagogic.

Karpov: "About the Drawings of Mentally Ill People."

1. Drawings of normal people are created under the law of symmetry, that is, if part of the drawing deviates from the original, the other parts are subject to the same deviations.
2. Among drawings of mentally ill people, according to the attached original, we find drawings that are little different from drawings of healthy people.
3. In drawings of mentally ill people, symptoms of disease sometimes are visible that may not be detected by other research methods.
4. When a doctor and the patient work on drawings together, the relationship between doctor and patient becomes more cordial, and there is growing confidence in the doctor.

G. Rossolimo: "A Simplified Research Method for Defects in Intelligence."

S. Rabinovitch, "Results of Children's Examinations according to Rossolimo's Method."

Other reports (according to the report in "Münch. Mediz. Wochenschrift," 1914, No. 14).

Bazhenov: based on the theory that a genius is a hyper-typical form of the human spirit under [in the case of] certain pathological symptoms, as well as on other theories that artistic creativity is subject to the influence of the subconscious, Bazhenov discussed first Goethe (cyclothymia), then Rousseau, then the cyclothymic Gogol, the depressive state of Schiller, J.S. Mill, Newton, etc. Dostoevsky was epileptic; Maupassant was suffering from headaches and arterial disease. The author defends himself against the reproach that doctors try to maliciously diminish great people with such studies.[10]

Mrs. Dr. Strasser-Eppelbaum (Zürich) discussed autistic thinking in dementia praecox. To understand schizophrenia, the study should not be simplified by being broken in parts, but it would be necessary to trace what is possible to grasp in its relations to its development and try to understand it genetically. To understand, one should intuitively feel the specific kind of thinking. Dementia praecox, psychologically, is a result of an overwhelming reaction to the perception of the world that has not yet led to the recovery of the real self but [rather] a turning away from what is real.

Notes

1 Translator note: This is in the original Russian text.
2 Translator note: Full name not given in original.
3 Later, I found some short works by different authors that could have been partially considered here.
4 Translator note: Spielrein gives 1909; other sources state 1910 (e.g., Ovcharenko, 1999: 343; also see Chapter 3, this volume). – PC-W
5 Birstein's work is written from the perspective of Alfred Adler.
6 Translator note: "Combination treatment" is mentioned in Spielrein (2008a/1929) as well. Presumably, this refers to alternative methods of treatment that are not exclusively psychoanalytic (see Chapter 15). – EG, FBK
7 L.N. Tolstoy, *The Memoirs of a Madman* (1912) [= Tolstoy, 1982/1912].
8 Translator note: Re: Jung, the context does not support a reference to "psychological types" as in introversion and extroversion; it seems more likely the reference is to directed and non-directed thinking. This is more akin to Freud's (1958/1911) "two principles of mental functioning." – FBK, PC-W
9 Translator note: "Psychasthenia" referred to a psychological disorder characterized by phobias, obsessions, compulsions, or excessive anxiety. The term is no longer in psychiatric diagnostic use. – EG, FBK
10 Translator note: For example, the author Guy de Maupassant (1850–1893) suffered from fear and paranoia caused by syphilis. He attempted suicide in 1892 and died in a private asylum in 1893. – FBK

References

Bleuler, E. (1950). *Dementia praecox or the group of schizophrenias*. J. Zinkin (Ed. & Trans.). New York: International Universities Press. (Orig. publ. 1911.)

Freud, S. (1953a). The interpretation of dreams. In J. Strachey (Ed.), *The standard edition of the complete psychological works of Sigmund Freud* (hereafter *SE*), Vols. 4–5 (entire). (Orig. publ. 1900.)

Freud, S. (1953b). On dreams. *SE* 5, 629–686. (Orig. publ. 1901.)

Freud, S. (1953c). Three essays on the theory of sexuality. *SE* 7, 125–148. (Orig. publ. 1905.)

Freud, S. (1955). Analysis of a phobia in a five-year-old boy. *SE* 10, 1–150. (Orig. publ. 1909.)

Freud, S. (1957a). Five lectures on psycho-analysis. *SE* 11, 1–56. (Orig. publ. 1910.)

Freud, S. (1957b). Leonardo da Vinci and a memory of his childhood. *SE* 11, 57–138.

Freud, S. (1958a). The handling of dream-interpretation in psycho-analysis. *SE* 12, 89–96. (Orig. publ. 1911.)

Freud, S. (1958b). Recommendations to physicians practicing psychoanalysis. *SE* 12, 109–120. (Orig. publ. 1912.)

Freud, S. (1958c). Formulations on the two principles of mental functioning. *SE* 12, 213–226. (Orig. publ. 1911.)

Freud, S. (1958d). Types of onset of neurosis. *SE* 12, 227–238. (Orig. publ. 1912.)

Freud, S. (1958e). A note on the unconscious in psycho-analysis. *SE* 12, 255–266. (Orig. publ. 1912.)

Freud, S. (1959). Delusions and dreams in Jensen's *Gradiva*. *SE* 9, 1–96. (Orig. publ. 1906.)

Freud, S. (1960). The psychopathology of everyday life. *SE* 6 (entire). (Orig. publ. 1901.)

Ovcharenko, V. (1999). The history of Russian psychoanalysis and the problem of its periodisation. C.J. Wharton (Trans.). *Journal of Analytical Psychology*, 44, 341–353.

Spielrein, S. (2008a). Doklad doktora Skalkovskogo [Dr. Skalkovskiy's report]. In S.F. Sirotkin & E.C. Morozova (Eds.), *Psychoanalytischeskie trudi* [*Psychoanalytic works*] (pp. 352–358). Izhevsk, Russia: ERGO. (Orig. publ. 1929.)

Spielrein, S. (2008b). Russkaya literatura po psychoanalyzu. [Russian literature on psychoanalysis]. In S.F. Sirotkin & E.C. Morozova (Eds.), *Psychoanalytischeskie trudi* [*Psychoanalytic works*] (pp. [235]–247). Izhevsk, Russia: ERGO. (Orig. publ. 1921.)

Tolstoy, L. N. (1982). The memoirs of a madman. In M. Katz (Ed.), *Tolstoy's short fiction: Revised translations, backgrounds and sources, criticism*, 2nd edn. (pp. 303–312). New York: W.W. Norton.

Vasilyeva, N. (2000). Psychoanalysis in Russia: The past, the present, and the future. *American Imago*, 57(1), 5–24.

Chapter 11

Who Is the Guilty One?[1]

Sabina Spielrein

1922 Translated by Judith Gresh and Felicity Kelcourse with Anatoli Samochornov

Mr. Lenormand's play,[2] recently performed at the Pitoëff Theatre, deserves to be studied from the standpoint of the psychological problems it raises.

> *The Lord said to his child:*
> *Go through the clear innocent garden of*
> *Angels where apples and*
> *Roses shine. It is yours. This is your kingdom.*
> *But pick among these only the flower,*
> *Leave the fruit on the branches,*
> *Do not deepen happiness. Do not seek to know*
> *The secret of the earth,*
> *And the mystery of human beings.*
> *Do not listen to the voice that draws you from*
> *The depths of the shadows, the voice that tempts,*
> *The voice of the serpent, or the voices of sirens,*
> *Or that of the ardent doves in*
> *The dark groves of Love.*
> *Stay ignorant.*
> *Do not think; sing.*
> *All knowledge is vain,*
> *Love only beauty*
> *And may this be for you the whole truth.*
> (Charles van Lerberghe, *The Song of Eve*)[3]

Live! Enjoy life! But no! Still the forbidden fruit attracts us and, despite all the good advice, we forget the Creator God's words; we forget the sad experiences of our ancestors Adam and Eve. Again and again, we want to taste the fruits of the tree of evil. Oh, that human soul, that rebellious spirit, full of longing, never satisfied and always seeking! Where does it lead us? It is not enough for us to know the laws that govern planets' motions; not content to study the development of plants and animals around us, we tackle the supreme creation, man in the image of the Almighty. In addition, research concerning his physical nature is not enough for us, we want to see into ourselves, to know our soul in all its profundity, to the depths of the subconscious. Is it surprising that the Almighty loses his patience, that he cries "Stop!" to these upstarts and causes them to perish, devoured by their passions risen from the abyss of the unconscious?

This is what was revealed, in an artistic form, in Mr. Lenormand's play. Fearon, the mistress of Luc, is the image of his own unconscious and instincts, unleashed in all their nakedness, which he has revived, and can no longer control. Jeannine, the person he has come to love, collapses, unable to endure the discovery of his intimate tendencies.[4] Similarly, Luc, after fruitless struggles, is brought low by his own deeds, his own instincts having turned against him. We are certainly right to be wary of all kinds of healers [who are] quite wrongly called psychoanalysts. Moreover, on the program for this play, we read this: "It would be a mistake to interpret this work as a representation or as a refutation of the famous doctrine (Psychoanalysis). If Luc professes Freudian ideas, it is that he is a psychologist of today, reflecting the beliefs of his time. The outcome illustrates the failure of an individual, not of a proven approach."

Here is the fascinating question: Who is the guilty one? Who caused Jeannine's death? Via Fearon's mouth, the author tells us that it is Luc, the psychologist. Fearon is only an aspect of the latter.[5] Yet, wasn't Jeannine already dead before her actual suicide? We see her wandering, staring, always dressed in green, drawn to water, where she already once made a suicide attempt. Jeannine, pursued by remorse that she cannot explain, incapable of any joy, feels compelled to give up all that is life. She no longer finds satisfaction in any work; for whole days she is devoured by her inner anxiety, unable to do anything. Is she not seriously ill? A skilled doctor would approach this frail and suffering soul gently. If the patient, guided by him, had come to a recollection of her childhood tendencies of being hostile to her mother, he would tell her: "Do not condemn yourself so severely. The unconscious does not make the value of the man!

"In our unconscious we are all children and primitives, we all live the powerful Oedipus tragedy, but we have learned to resist these basic tendencies. The value of man consists in his power to control his instincts, which allows us to have our energy available for actions of a higher social order."[6] The value of a man is proportional to his capacity for "sublimation." Luc, in contrast, reveals to Jeannine the secret of her unconscious suddenly, without waiting for her memories to emerge by themselves, as a psychoanalyst would have done.

But this is most contrary to psychoanalytic treatment: Luc, who is himself a man unable to control his instincts, claims the right of a supreme judge: "I absolve you," he says to Jeannine; he allows her to unleash the beast, and he lets himself go so far that he becomes Jeannine's lover. What a sharp difference between this sudden invasion and the delicate method taught by the Viennese psychologist!

Despite everything, Jeannine begins to revive, only because she begins to see a bit more clearly what's going on in her. But this change is incomplete: Jeannine, without being fully aware, is pursued by the haunting conviction of having killed her mother. She flees before this idea and seeks the light. In the most brutish and cynical way, Fearon then tells her that, as a child, she unintentionally caused the death of her mother. At the same time, Fearon slips a revolver into the hand of her victim, suggesting suicide. Jeannine's delicate soul is not able to handle this sudden revelation. She succumbs. A psychoanalyst at the height of his powers might be able to save her by reducing the emotional shock; he wouldn't reveal anything himself to the patient; if the latter arrived spontaneously to see clearly for herself, he would have supported and encouraged her in her liberating insights. It's not the crime of an irresponsible child that kills Jeannine. How many people should then commit suicide, having caused the death of their mother during their birth!

If Jeannine falls victim to her remorse, it is because her act was perhaps more intentional than she dares to admit; this is also why she cannot dress in other than green, the color of the scarf by which she caused the death of her mother. It is quite likely that Jeannine might have committed suicide without ever having met Luc. It is also possible that Luc helped to destroy her, not Luc the seeker, but Luc in his second personality, that of Fearon. While interested in psychology, Luc is not a real psychoanalyst, his delicate task is beyond his ability: to be a psychoanalyst one must first of all be sufficiently unburdened to be able to control one's instincts. Luc had not reached this initial stage, and that is why his selfish, unleashed instincts in the person of Fearon result in the death of Jeannine.

"He would have done better to focus on healing his patients than eating their dreams," says Professor Claparède in his introduction to the play. If Luc had been analyzed himself and been able to fight his instincts, who knows? Jeannine perhaps would have been able to live a happy life, as do many of our patients who are treated with psychoanalysis. Have we solved the problem? – No! Why not? – Luc would never have been able to kill Jeannine if there was not something else, if it was not remorse, sick in its exaggeration, that made her a zombie, a shadow, well before Luc's intervention.

Evil is much more deeply rooted than one would think at first sight: there is a common cause to Jeannine's sick conscience and Luc's incompetence. It is due to this same cause we now have such an increase in suicides, madmen, and criminals. It's the lack of love in our society, the lack of education. Religion has become a dead letter. We are too advanced to believe anything else, we want to know everything. Children of previous generations had at least the advantage of educating themselves close to nature – our generation, however, since tender childhood suffocates under the weight of lies and social conventions. There is no heart, there is no understanding, no natural frankness between parents and their children.

We doctors and teachers are quite isolated in our efforts to win parents' support, or at least their interest. Patients are referred to us when it is already late, frequently too late.

I do not mean that reasonable education always knows how to protect children from mental and nervous diseases, there are still many things that are beyond our power – but this is not a reason to dull our conscience and attempt nothing. Jeannine's example proves very clearly that we can't fight evil by ignoring it, otherwise Jeannine, who is ignorant, would be the happiest of creatures. On the contrary, only a deep knowledge by parents of psychological laws, an entire frankness between parents and their children – obviously not to an extent that exceeds the understanding of the child – only a natural and healthy education, can contribute to the man of the future, able to resist the instincts of which he is well aware, and that he knows to condemn, yet without developing, in reaction, a sense of failure and a remorse so deep that he succumbs to it. This is what we must learn from Lenormand's play, and that is why we thank him.

Dr. S. Spielrein

Notes

1 Spielrein's original title *"Qui est l'auteur du crime?"* may be a reference to a Russian philosophical discourse: two eternal questions – who is to blame and what is to be done? The translation "Who is the guilty one?" was chosen with this in mind. – AS
2 A review entitled *"Qui Est l'Auteur du Crime?"* appeared in *Variété* in 1922 while Spielrein was living in Geneva. The play in question, *Le Mangeur de Rêves* [*The Dream Eater*], written in 1922 by Henri-René Lenormand (1882–1951), is sometimes classified as surrealist (Amiot, 1992). Spielrein and Claparède attended this play together (Launer, 2015, p. 194), and it reminded Spielrein of her own relationship with Jung (Roudinesco, 1990, p. 79). The play was a thinly veiled autobiography, as Lenormand's own mistress separated from him after seeking analysis with "a psychologist from Küsnacht" (ibid., p. 78). It caused a sensation in the psychoanalytic communities in both Geneva and Paris, and Freud himself welcomed a visit from Lenormand in 1927, calling the play's title "witty" (ibid., p. 79). – FBK, PC-W
3 Charles van Lerverghe (1861–1907) was a Belgian symbolist poet and playwright known for his collection of free verse poetry *La Chanson D'Ève* (1904). Gabriel Fauré (1845–1924) used these poems as the text for his song cycle Op. 95 of the same name, composed 1906–1910 (Fauré, 1910). – JG, FBK
4 In the original, *"tendances intimes,"* presumably of a psychological and sexual nature. – FBK
5 *"Fearon n'est qu'une oeuvre de ce dernier."* As noted above, Fearon represents Luc's unconscious, in the form of his anima. – FBK
6 This quotation is presumably taken from the program notes for the play, authored by Spielrein's Geneva colleague, Édouard Claparède (1873–1940), whom she references below. Claparède was a Swiss neurologist and psychoanalyst, cofounder (with his cousin Théodore Flournoy – 1854–1920) of the journal *Archives de Psychanalyse* in which Spielrein (1923) also published, and founder of the Rousseau Institute in Geneva, where Spielrein and Piaget were both affiliated. – FBK, PC-W

References

Amiot, A.-M., Ed. (1992). *Mélusine: Le surréaliste et son psy: Études et documents réunis par Anne-Marie Amiot* ["*Mélusine: The surrealist and his psy[che]: Collected studies and papers by Anne-Marie Amiot*"]. Cahiers du Centre de Recherches sur le Surréalisme [Notebooks from the Center for Research on Surrealism], Vol. 13 (entire). Paris: L'Age d'Homme.

Fauré, G. (1910). *La chanson d'Ève*, Op. 95. Paris: Heugel.

Launer, J. (2015). *Sex versus survival: The life and ideas of Sabina Spielrein*. London: Overlook Duckworth.

Lenormand, H.-R. (1922). *Le mangeur de rêves* [The dream eater]. Paris: Éditions G. Cres.

Roudinesco, E. (1990). *Jacques Lacan & Co.: A history of psychoanalysis in France, 1925–1985*. J. Mehlman (Trans.). Chicago, IL: University of Chicago. (Orig. publ. 1986.)

Spielrein, S. (1922). Qui est l'auteur du crime? *Journal de Genève*, 93, 15 January.

Spielrein, S. (1923). Quelques analogies entre la pensée de l'enfant, celle de l'aphasique et la pensée subconsciente. *Archives de Psychologie*, 18, 305–322. (Trans. in this volume, Chapter 14.)

van Lerverghe, C. (1904). *La chanson d'Ève*. Paris: Société du Mercure.

Chapter 12

Time in Subliminal Psychic Life

Sabina Spielrein

1923 Translated by Judith Gresh, Pamela Cooper-White, Felicity Kelcourse, and Robby Kongolo[1]

Ladies and gentlemen! Psychoanalysis lacks a concept that encompasses the preconscious and the subconscious. I would like to put forward the concept of "subliminal psychic life" ["*das unterschwellige Seelenleben*"]. Do not expect me to explain the complex problem of time as a problem already resolved. It is rather a case of sequential research methodically carried out. Here, too, it was Freud who placed the cornerstone. More than in any of his subsequent works, he considered in *The Interpretation of Dreams* the structure of thought in dreams – in other words, preconscious thought. Aside from general laws regarding the formation of dream images (displacement, condensation, *pars pro toto*, etc.), we find here specific observations devoted to preconscious language; thus Freud gives us examples of the way in which the concepts of "if" and "why" are represented in dreams, and other examples of the same kind. This preconscious language, as an expression of mechanisms of thought, has always especially interested me. According to Freud, one can observe the same laws in primitive and infantile thought. This is why I have systematically devoted myself to the study of preconscious and infantile mentation. In so doing, I met the respected researcher and also psychoanalyst at the Rousseau Institute in Geneva, Docent Piaget,[2] who has the aim of studying the child's thought – or "autistic" thought, as he calls it – following Bleuler. Since then, though working independently, we are essentially working on the same subject.

Our consciously directed thought relates to three conditions: time, space, and causality. We have known for some time that these are not mental categories or concepts a priori, as Kant believed, but a posteriori concepts we acquire slowly in the course of our development. The concept of space appears to become familiar first, followed by that of causality,[3] and only lastly the concept of time. For the concept of time itself, we must distinguish between duration and orientation. An action, an event, can be short or long; in addition, we can place it in the direction of the future or in the inverse direction of the past, or have it in the middle, which corresponds to the present. When speaking of time, we think generally of the direction of time, but here we will have to take into consideration both aspects [e.g., orientation and duration].

I noted the following observations about my daughter Renatchen[4] when she was two years and one-and-a-half months old. Concerning the three basic concepts of space, time, and causality, the concept of time causes the most difficulties for Renate. She clearly understands the question "Where?" and expressions like "under the bed," "under the pillow," and "under the rug," etc., are completely familiar to her. She also has a sense of near distance. She knows that something can come or go, [and] that something can be far away, very far away.

She understands "inside," "outside," "enter," "leave," and also distinguishes round forms from other shapes. So, for her, apples or objects with a similar form are balls. She also distinguishes between "big" and "small."

Likewise, she understands the question "Why?" For example, yesterday she said, "Poor, poor sseeep [*Ssaaf*]." I asked her, "Why poor sheep?" "Legs broken," answered the little one.

Renate does not understand the question "When?" at all. For her, everything takes place in the present. I have just helped her understand "after," "soon," "later," and "next," which exist for her only in the moment, and which must not last too long. I often tell her during her bath, "First the little face, then the little hands." I do not remember that she has ever repeated that, because, although she still has a sense of the near future, for her there is nothing in the past. She always uses verbs in the present tense. I often say to her, "My good Renate has eaten so well" – this becomes "Eat well," and sometimes "Eat! Have!" even when she is not hungry at all.

As we can see, these observations concern time as direction.

It is understandable that she prefers the present and the future to the past: the child behaves first in a will-directed manner, and is primarily interested in what she already possesses or wishes to obtain; the fact that everything in the world is perishable and subject to transformation means nothing to her at first and escapes her awareness. It is another matter to know how the child conceives of the future, and to what extent she distinguishes the future from the present. The study of dreams and linguistics offers some hints.

Does the dream recognize the present, past, or future? Yes and no! We know that the dream mixes past, present, and future in a completely arbitrary manner, as if this distinction into three parts did not exist at all! Yet this is not completely true. The vision of a person we no longer love, not yet dead but dying, represents a transformation in a future sense. Each action is, in fact, a becoming,[5] and in this sense announces the future – but it is at the same time an enduring present, a present which then transforms itself constantly. One also recognizes the idea of the future in the sense that very often in dreams we await or fear something. But we never find the future represented in an independent manner; this idea is better suggested by the duration of an action, in such a way that one can also speak of the present. Is a freestanding representation of the future possible in dreams?

Regarding the future understood in this sense, representations of the past are much rarer in dreams, but at the same time more independent. For example, a woman sees in a dream the pallid image of her analyst; this pallor, an image of what was and is no more, immediately makes a big impression on her. A man who has decided on a definitive separation from his beloved, which causes him great suffering, sees the woman in a dream as an object overgrown with moss. The image expresses his desire that the distressing moment of farewell might already be over and done with, becoming an old moss-covered thing. This patient often refers to the past in his dreams to be rid of distressing experiences.

The past in dreams is not understood in the same way that we comprehend it now: the emphasis is not on what was, but on what is not here, what no longer exists.[6]

Little children also represent the past in this way, since the idea of the past must be suggested to them by the realization that something has disappeared. The child initially thinks of disappearance as a special distance: an object or person is "far away, very far away, absent." Dreams of departure as a representation of death, mentioned by Freud, are now understandable; it is the representation of time through the medium of space. Freud notes here that the dream proceeds like a child who does not understand extinction [*Vernichtung*], and thinks of death as leaving on a journey. Another dream of the man cited above is even more clearly spatial; he sees a situation he finds distressing as a receding landscape, moving away into the distance. Regarding this, as in his earlier dream, he said, "This belongs to the distant past" – more precisely, "This will soon belong to the distant past." This is once again a becoming, an enduring present that is like a future.

And here is another interesting example where the evaluation of temporal duration in preconscious thought is represented; I received this from a young teacher. One morning, he awakes at 5:00 a.m.; he tells himself it is too early; he could still sleep for two more hours. In fact, he goes back to sleep and reawakens at 7:00 a.m., as he had wished. During these two hours, the following occurred: "I dream," he writes, "that I find myself in a large white asphalt plaza. There are roads going off in different directions. The road to the east goes toward a lake. I go toward the west and I tell myself that I must wake up in two hours. The road to the west slopes gently toward the mountain and is intersected twice by perpendicular roads. I think: here is the first hour and here is the second." Beyond that, the memory fades.

Are we really dealing with a dream here? – a dream, and also something else. We can directly observe how a conscious intention, namely, waking oneself in two hours, dressed in the image language of the preconscious, lives on, and how it continues to work. The two temporal distances (two hours) become two spatial distances; this image is used in this way as dream material.

Once this temporal distance has become a spatial distance in the preconscious, it also acquires the significance of a life path [*Lebensweg*], by which the effective content of the dream is introduced. There are two paths between which the dreamer must choose: the road to the east is that of free love, as the patient has indicated in his analysis; the one to the west signifies the renunciation of this love and a return to his father, who is a pastor. The white asphalt plaza is overdetermined by numerous erotic desires. It is exactly here that the problem of two life paths begins.

The rest of the analysis, which, out of regard for this person I will not cite, reveals that the road to the west only signifies an *apparent* renunciation.[7] Desire [*Der Wunsch*] knows how to claim its rights, using the familiar mechanism of representation by negation.

Most of our dreams proceed in the same way when they use the representation of the dreamer's present situation immediately in his favor, and reinterpret it accordingly. There are cases, however, where the thought process of the dream is content simply to process our actual situation, without being able to prove the slightest wish-activity. In a state of great fatigue, a gentleman "dreamed" of a boat that was pulling a heavy weight. Upon waking he felt that he himself was the boat. Should we still discuss dreams in these cases? Freud is of the opinion that one can only discuss a dream when wish-forming activity is present. This should be an essential definition [*definitio sine qua non*]. It is very difficult to decide this question. Some elements could speak in favor of this definition. I have observed, for example, that these dreams, provisionally said to be imperfect, in which the transformative activity of desire is missing, occur in cases of heavy fatigue. A lady, for example, sees herself in a dream hanging from a hook, and does not dare to jump to the ground. In despair, she looks around for help. She tells herself: "I don't really need someone to help me; if I were just certain that someone could help me in an emergency, I would risk jumping." The lady fears life. She feels alone and in need of help.[8] After the conscious thought had lost its force she allowed the image from her preconscious thought to come more and more to the fore. In principle, I do not find any difference between this and hypnagogic phenomena. After these imperfect dreams, one feels completely depleted. We could say that we miss the well-being that the dream otherwise procures by its action of fulfilling our desire, just as in anxiety dreams, for example, in which resistance thwarts the enforcement of desire [*Wunschdurchsetzung*]. The activity we desire has realistically already begun in the hypnagogic state, which gradually passes over into the state of sleep, just as hypnagogic hallucinations pass over into dream images. This wish-generating activity can, then, as experience shows, be manifested with more or less force. If the activity has enough force to assert its rights, then the dream is perfect. If, as in the case of exhaustion, anguish, or deep depression, it is too weak, too uncertain, then the dreams are imperfect, approaching states that are pure or almost pure representations of hypnagogic situations.

The results of linguistic research are in many respects amazingly similar to those of dream research. What is interesting is that the results of the study of languages and of children have brought me to the hypothesis that languages do not distinguish temporal directions – thus no present, past, or future. Upon questioning, Professor Bally,[9] the well-known linguist in Geneva, confirmed my hypothesis.

Bally has informed me that there are languages that do not know time as direction, but simply as duration, in the sense in which, for example, the imperfect tense is distinguished from the perfect tense by duration (cf., in French, *"je parlais"* and *"je parlai"*). Duration itself is often replaced by the distinction between a single action and one that is repeated. This certainly does not mean that the peoples in question have no understanding of temporal direction; it is simply a question of a corresponding expression in the language. Language is always more archaic than thought; it drags along modes of thought that we have long since surpassed. It takes centuries for us to get rid of linguistic nonsense [*Dummheit*] that we consciously recognize [as such]. For analysts this should be clear: language is not formed consciously, but mainly in the preconscious. Moreover, it must not only meet the requirements of conscious thought, but also of preconscious thought (which, in turn, is influenced by the unconscious).

Language, like the thought process of dreams, adjoins the past to the present much more than it does the future; Bally states[10]: "In Indo-European languages, ancient as well as modern, the past is much more clearly marked than the present or the future. Expressions about the future are of much more recent origin. One might even doubt that there is a true future tense in Indo-European languages; each Indo-European language has formed a future in its own way; it is a tense that takes root with difficulty and therefore oscillates continually; in each group of languages, it is formed differently; the form *"amo, amabo"* in Latin is completely independent; it is not found in any other Indo-European language. The Romance languages (French, Italian, etc.) form their future by circumlocutions, for example, the Latin *amare habeo*, I love you (translated in German *"ich habe zu lieben"* = *soll lieben* ["I have to love" = should love]), if translated into French one would say *J'ai (à) aimer* [I have to love]. Instead of this, we have the inverse construction: *(je) aimer ai* [I to love have], which was later contracted to *"j'aimerai"* ["I will love"]. We also encounter "soll" ["should"] as an expression of the future in English; so, for example, "I shall like"[11]; so the English also use *I will* (*I will like*). By using the auxiliary word will, they primitively emphasize intention, which gives the idea of a developing action, and therefore the future. The German language, like the dream, uses an ongoing present for the future, a becoming.[12] Now we are no longer aware of this becoming, but this is the origin. Language puts it before the idea of action, for example, the idea of writing. Duration activated in this way gives us the idea of the future: I will write [*"Ich werde schreiben"*]. Germans also say "I want to write" [*"Ich will schreiben"*].

The Russian language is quite idiosyncratic and instructive. It has so-called imperfect forms that indicate duration (forms for actions that repeat), and perfect or completed forms (for actions that only happen once). There are also two forms for the infinitive: preterate and future. For the present, there is just the imperfect form, which indicates duration. Within the imperfect form, however, the language distinguishes a fairly short, more continuous duration, from a rather long, more discontinuous duration – for example *"ja pischu"* ("я пишу") = "I am writing" [*ich schreibe*] and *"ja popischu"* ("я пописываю") = "I sometimes write." These nuances of duration and frequency are so finely differentiated in the Russian language that it would be impossible to name them all here. Within one and the same tense, a modification of duration is achieved by means of both suffixes [*Suffixen*] and preverbs [*Präverbien*].[13] For example, from an imperfect or continuous form *"ja pissal"* ("я писал") (I was writing – ongoing), adding the preverb *"na"* ("на") gives the perfect form: *"ja napissal"* ("я написал") = "I wrote – once." The future imperfect that expresses duration is formed in the same way in German, with the auxiliary verb "to be" [*"werden"*] (in Russian *"budu"*). For the perfect future, one could say that there is no special form: it is a present perfect, i.e., completed or one-time present; because, as we have seen, the Russian language knows no perfect present. The future perfect is formed from the present imperfect with the addition of preverbs. Thus, *"ja pischu"* ("я пишу") = "I am writing" [*"ich schreibe"*], and *"ja napischu"* ("я напишу") = "I will write") [*"ich schreibe"*] in the future, are formed in the same way as the perfect from the imperfect in the past – by adding the preverb that indicates duration (compare *"ja pissal"* – *"я писал"* = "I was writing" [*"Ich schrieb"*] (continuous) and *"ja napissal"* – *"я написал"* = "I wrote" [*"Ich schrieb"*] (one time).[14] Consequently, the future perfect is not an independent grammatical form; it can be considered as a present perfect, and can be distinguished from the actual present just by the suppression of duration.

It is worth noting one more analogy with the language of dreams: Bally showed me that all prefixes, like temporal adverbs, are taken from spatial representations. For example, the French *"après"* (after) is formed from *"près"* (near, in the sense of space); *"tard"* (late) from the Latin *"tardus"* = slow (as movement in space), and so on.

Now I would like, at my own risk, to attempt an explanation. Bally warns me against temptations of this kind. For this reason I do not want to present my opinion with certainty, but as a possibility that personally strikes me as very likely.

Let us recall that language forms in the preconscious. If verbal language is formed consciously, why is it so poorly adapted to our conscious thought, and showing so many points in common with the image language of dreams? Why is the concept of temporal direction so imperfectly expressed in so many languages, or almost nonexistent? Why, as in the thought process of dreams, does duration take the place of direction? Why is the past more independent in relation to the present and the future, as is so clearly evident especially in the Russian language? Because verbal language draws its representations from preconscious material in these cases, as in the language of dreams. If this is the case, as Bally freely admits, why should language not also have the mechanism, respectively, of representing time by spatial means? Bally himself says that all the prefixes as well as the spatial adverbs for time are taken from spatial representations! Among the prefixes indicating the future in Russian, we most frequently find *"na"* [*"на"*], *"po"* [*"по"*], and *"s"* [*"с"*]. Literally *"na"* means over; *"po"* means spreading over something. In Russian *"napischu"* [*"напишу"*] (I will write) literally means "I write on [something]"; *"ja popischu"* [*"я попишу"*] (I will write a bit) means "I write about." I therefore claim that a concept of time in language is also based on a subliminal representation of spatial distance: if, in our example, we imagine the action of writing as a movement that extends linearly upwards – this movement is repressed or stifled by something that is placed above or on top. The preconscious, as we have seen above (the example of the representation of two hours by means of two paths), conceives this trajectory as a distance in space. It is as a spatial distance of this type that we represent duration or the imperfect tense, by which, by limitation of this duration, we form a perfect tense. I am moreover supported in my hypothesis by the fact that the preverb *"na"* does not act in all cases as a limitation of duration; if the *"na"* is understood as an overcrowding we associate the action with the idea of multiplicity; *"ja goworiu gluposti"* ["я говорю глупости"] means "I say nonsense," *"ja nagoworiu gluposti"* ["я наговорю глупости"] means "I will say a lot of nonsense." This is not a unique case in which the *"na"* has this connotation: there are in fact numerous cases in which *"na"* acts simultaneously as a limitation of duration and as a multiplier. The German term *"Zukunft"* [future] also strikes me as being characteristic of a spatial representation in the formation of a temporal direction – something that is added to what already exists. While Russians associate the idea of the future with a representation of a limitation of duration, the Germans would prefer to represent an elongation of duration. These representations are barely conscious. They have their foundation in the original representations, issuing from the preconscious, of duration as a spatial distance.

Linguists adopt a law of inertia, or of conservation of older language forms. But what is this inertia? Nature knows no standstill. Inertia that opposes all new development is therefore a force working in us in the opposite direction, a tendency to assimilate [*assimilieren*][15] all that is new into the past, an urge to experience the past again and again. If we understand the force of inertia in a dynamic manner, as I have just mentioned, then we can link the findings of linguists to our own without difficulty.

The following example offers us an excellent proof: Bally highlights the fact that in many languages, a word, as it passes from one grammatical category to another, is not only indicated under a new category, but is also indicated in a way that reveals its connection to an older category. Take for example the verb *"achten"* [to respect, pay attention to]. When this verb becomes a noun, it receives the suffix *"ung."* *"Achten"* becomes *"Achtung"* [danger/attention to danger]. The suffix *"ung"* indicates a new category, the category of nouns. But at the same time, this suffix indicates the former category of verbs, since only nouns that originate as verbs receive the suffix "*ung.*"

It is not enough to say that the dream, which is thought in images, cannot represent the abstract concept of temporal direction. If the dream needed this concept it would also know how to represent it. It is precisely the criterion of our consciousness that exists in time – that is to say, that we peel off [*ausschälen*] a certain constantly changing duration from the continuous stretch of time [*Zeitstrecke*] that we call the present, and in one direction, we differentiate the past from this present, and in the other direction, [we differentiate] what is to come [*das Kommende*]. Language once again offers us a fine example. During one of his presentations, Bally noted the paradox that time in *consecutio temporum* [Latin: sequence of time] (*concordance des temps*)[16] is not time at all. Thus the French say: "*Paul m'annonce qu'il viendra demain*" ["Paul tells me that he will come tomorrow"] and "*Paul m'a annoncé qu'il viendrait demain*" ["Paul told me that he would come tomorrow"].

But in both cases, Paul arrives on the very same day! Other languages, such as Russian, for example, are more faithful to the objective facts here. These [languages] say in both cases "that he will come."

While we consciously search for a fixed point in the passage of time, to which we relate everything, in the preconscious, we do almost the reverse – all that we experience now, we assimilate to what we have experienced before. What was previously experienced, we experience, however, in the present and, inasmuch as the present is a duration that is constantly changing, we live it as the future, as becoming. The preconscious is aware of a general duration, which for it, as we have already seen, is both present and future. It is Being-there [*Da sein*].[17] The child learns only with time that something he wishes for can also be "Not-there." Thus is formed on the one hand the idea of the present and the future = "Being-there" ["*Da sein*"], and on the other hand the idea of the past = "not-being-there" ["*nicht da sein*"]. Hence, the idea of present and future on the one hand = "Being-there," and the idea of the past on the other hand = "not-being-there." The dream also does not need to know anything more about the past.

We are still far from what we understand as the concept of time, that is to say, the abstract concept of a temporal direction. To be able to establish an idea of direction, we must be able to distinguish opposites.

According to Freud, we know that in dream thought, as with children, opposites are not mutually exclusive. We do not need to understand this in an absolute manner. If there were a complete inability to exclude opposites, no mental representations could be formed at all. I believe that we learn anew to master opposites in the course of each new psychic operation. Alongside each impulse, a contrary impulse rises up; alongside each representation, a contrary representation that we must suppress. We can master opposites in the course of one psychic operation, and then be once again incapable of this in the course of another. The child, just as in preconscious thought, masters contrary representations quite imperfectly. Direction is often represented by its opposite in a dream, and [again] in a contradictory manner in the very same dream. I have collected several examples of the way in which a thought that appears in one portion of a dream as water symbolism, occurs as fire symbolism in another.

To give an example, we can observe this in Flournoy's article,[18] in which he mentioned water and fire symbolism. I have recently studied these cases of reversals to the opposite in a case of motor aphasia with alexia, agraphia, and so on.[19] I would simply like to mention one very remarkable case. The patient in question, whom Professor Claparède kindly sent to me for observation, was afflicted with a stroke [*Schlaganfall*]. The patient is paralyzed on one side.[20] Speech mechanisms are intact. He understands all that is said to him and can also read, but can neither speak nor write himself. I ask my patient to draw a circle and then a triangle. He always finds the two forms correctly in what is called a game of surfaces.[21] The table below shows how he draws these two forms. The attempt is repeated a short time later during the same day (see table). After having drawn an angle the patient probably had the idea that one should somehow reconnect the two ends, *a* and *b*. It would seem to us self-evident that one could simply draw a line between *a* and *b*. Clearly, this did not seem so obvious to the patient – he reverses the direction instead and linked the two ends by a semi-circle. He was reinforced in his erroneous approach by the preceding task, in which he had to draw a circle. He began to draw quite correctly; it was only when the task became more difficult, when he had to link the idea of three sides and that of a triangle, that he lost all certainty as to direction and fell into doing the opposite, because he did not know how to switch off the preceding mental representation of movement in the direction of a circle. It is remarkable that this man, whose most basic mental functions were so profoundly disrupted, knew very well how to count. He was even able to do bookkeeping himself, because he retained the ability to write numbers, the four arithmetic functions, and the date.

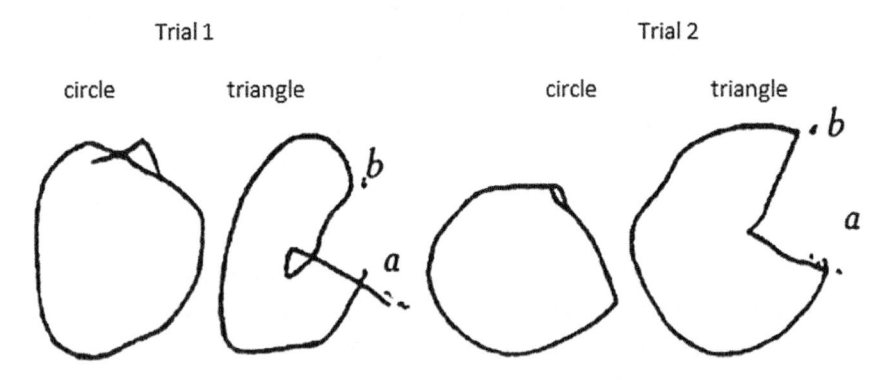

Trial 1 — circle, triangle

Trial 2 — circle, triangle

He can distinguish today, tomorrow, yesterday, etc. But he lost his way each time when it came to forming words, or the separation of sounds or letters.

For the child, who for a long time can replace reality with fantasy [*Phantasie*], the mental representation of temporal direction remains unnecessary for a fairly long time, and therefore is late to develop.

If I suppose, on the basis of observation, that in our ontogenetic development we discover time first as duration, and only later as direction, I am thinking only of [time as] the perception of duration, and not as the estimation of a length of time. The estimation of a length of time is a much more complicated operation that I will not address here for lack of time. I would just like to mention briefly that the estimate of a length of time presents mechanisms in common with rhythm, and with calculation skills, respectively. Werkoem speaks of this in his work on aphasia. Piaget has done interesting research on the procedures children of various ages use to do multiplication. To explore the thought mechanisms involved in arithmetic operations, Isaak Spielrein has performed calculation tests in the enneadic system[22] with various people. I would therefore like to compare this with the operations of thought in dreams, and would be very grateful to colleagues who could provide with me with dreams that include operations of calculation.

To sum up: I set myself the task of studying different functions of preconscious thought in their origin and development, on the basis of actual observations regarding subliminal image-language [*Bildsprache*], the language of children, linguistic evidence, and pathological disturbances of language. The focus of this lecture concerns the formation of the concept of time. The research revealed the following:

1. Of the three so-called categories of thought that are not a priori concepts but a posteriori concepts, it is the concept of space that develops first, then the concept of causality, and only lastly, the concept of time.
2. At first, the child knows only the present and the immediate future, which he probably separates one from the other just by means of duration! It is a Being-there [*Dasein*]. The idea of Not-being-there [*Nichtdasein*] develops over time. This "Not-being-there" is first conceived spatially, as "far, far away, gone" ["*weit, weit weg, fort*"]. Within the representation of "Not-being-there" is the core concept of the past, which will come later. The idea of duration develops first; the idea of direction comes later. The estimation of length of time comes much later.
3. a) Dreams cannot represent time as direction.[23]
    b) In dreams, direction is transformed into duration.
    c) The past is more independent in its means of expression, and is contrasted with the present and future, which form more of a block.
    d) In dreams, the past is not a proper past, but a "Not-being-there," with respect to a "No-longer-there."
    e) The temporal is represented by means of the spatial.
4. The preconscious is capable of a very precise estimation of length of time. But this estimation of duration does not take place in dreams, but rather occurs in the imagistic thought that unfolds in parallel with conscious thought: it is an image-thought [*Bilddenken*] that is not yet a dream, which we usually do not notice except in hypnagogic states, even though it accompanies all our conscious thoughts, and is transposed into its own particular language,[24] which it eventually processes.

    Preconscious thought is superior to conscious thought in its capacity to estimate length of time. This is a capacity that our ancestors mastered better than we did, that we apparently have lost. Is this due to the fact that we think more consciously, more narrowly? In a case where the estimation of length of time was symbolized, this was done by means of spatial evaluation of space (measuring the distance of a path).
5. Evidence from linguistic studies shows surprisingly similar results to dream research.
6. The lack of a concept of temporal direction corresponds to the inability to distinguish opposites. For each new psychic function, the retention of one direction and the exclusion of its opposite must be learned anew.

In the case of aphasia mentioned earlier, we have seen how the patient, who was able to orient himself so well in relation to time and problems involving calculation, failed in certain types of problems regarding spatial orientation, and fell back onto the opposite direction.

Why is it that the dream and the child do not distinguish opposites in temporal direction? Because both have at first simply the need for an ending, or a future direction [*Zukunftsrichtung*]; one could say they are one with this direction – they "live" it – so they do not notice it. What one wishes is simply there, in reality or in fantasy. [But] reality obliges the child to live more and more in the opposite direction, to also become acquainted with renunciation and annihilation. From this, the idea of an antagonist [*Antagonist*] is formed, and by the suppression [*Unterdrückung*] of this antagonist, the concept of a direction [is formed as well].

To conclude, I would like to express to my sincere thanks to Professor Bally for the valuable interest he has shown in this little work.

Notes

1 Translator note: First given as an address at the International Psychoanalytic Congress in Berlin in September 1922, published one year later in German (Spielrein, 1923a), and soon thereafter translated into French in Flournoy's and Claparède's journal in Geneva (Spielrein, 1923b). Our translation is based on the German original (PC-W) alongside the 1923 French translation by F. Paru (JG, FBK, and RK).
2 Translator note: Piaget (1896–1980) moved to Geneva in 1921 to work for Édouard Claparède as director of research at the Rousseau Institute, where he became a *Privat-Docent* (lecturer) (Launer, 2015, p. 201). – FBK
3 It is not impossible that what we merge together under the concept of causality is not a unified concept, but that one part of it develops earlier, and the other part later. That I do not know. But the reader will see from the examples here what I mean.
4 Translator note: Diminutive for "Renate." – FBK
5 Translator note: This theme of becoming and transformation echoes Spielrein's (1912) earlier preoccupation with destruction, transformation, and becoming elaborated in her first major paper (trans. in this volume, Chapter 6; see also Chapters 2 and 4). – PC-W
6 One could compare this to the "perfect" tense in some older languages. This grammatical form corresponds to the German "*er ist tot*" ["he is dead"], e.g., "*er ist gestorben*" ["he died"] would not be the perfect tense. The perfect tense puts us in the past; it is an ongoing state. When one says

"*er ist tot*" ["he is dead"], then one still thinks of death, while the phrase "*ist gestorben*" ["died"] emphasizes the moment of the past, a moment in which we no longer participate.

7 Translator note: Emphasis added for clarity. – PC-W
8 I no longer know whether someone in the dream had offered this help or not. In the first case, this would be a wish fulfillment [*Wunscherfüllung*]; in the second case, a simple representation of the situation. Even in the second case we cannot rule out with certainty a fulfillment of a wish – but neither can we can speak of this wish fulfillment if we cannot prove it.
9 Translator note: Charles Bally (1865–1947), a linguist from the Geneva School – FBK
10 Translator note: Quotation marks and italics are inconsistent in the original German text. – PC-W
11 Translator note: In English in the original German text, followed by "*ich werde lieben (soll lieben).*"
12 Translator note: Cf., Spielrein (1912). – PC-W, FBK
13 Translator note: This term is used for separable verb prefixes in Russian. – JG (Cf., "*Präfix*" in German = "prefix"). – PC-W
14 Translator note: In English, this distinction is actually clearer than in the German where "*Ich schrieb*" can be either continuous or one-time. – PC-W
15 Translator note: This understanding of assimilation echoes and likely mutually informed (see Chapter 4, this volume) Piaget's (1923, 1936) concept of "assimilation" (incorporating new knowledge into what is already known) vs. "accommodation" (adjusting to new information). – PC-W
16 Translator note: Both the Latin and the French are included in the original German text. – PC-W
17 Translator note: Although Heidegger's (2010/1927) *Being and Time* with the concept of "*Dasein*" was not published until 1927, he was lecturing on these concepts by as early as 1922, and Spielrein may have been alluding to him here. Spielrein does not collapse the term into one word here, but does use "*das*" before "*Da sein*," and always capitalizes "*Da*" or "*Nicht da*" before "*sein*," suggesting that it is a special term; later in this same essay she does use the unified form, "*Dasein*." – PC-W
18 H. Flournoy, "Some reflections on the subject of the symbolic significance of water and fire." ["Quelques rêves au sujet de la signification symbolique de l'eau et du feu."] *Internat[ionale] Zeitschr[ift] f[ür] Psychoanalyse*, 6 (1920).
19 This work was complete in the winter semester of 1922. Since then, I have continued to elaborate the ideas mentioned here and I have presented them, with more detailed proofs, in a work which recently appeared. "*Quelques analogies entre la pensée de l'enfant, celle de l'aphasique et la pensée subconsciente*" ["Some similarities between a child's thought, aphasic thought, and subconscious thought"], *Archives de Psychologie, XVIII*, May 1923. [Ed. note: Trans. in this volume, Chapter 14.]

20 Translator note: Spielrein often mixes past and present tense in the same paragraph, especially when discussing case material. We have retained the original tense shifts as representative of her writing style. – PC-W
21 Translator note: This possibly refers to a board game or a game involving various geometric shapes. – RK. The same patient is described again in Spielrein (1923c; see Chapter 14, this volume). – PC-W
22 Translator note: The word "*ennead*" comes from the number nine in Greek, a system of nine lines that may be joined to form shapes. Spielrein's brother, Isaak N. Spielrein, publishing between 1916 and 1933, was the founding father of Soviet psychological science and leader of psychotechnics in the USSR. – JG
23 Only in exceptional cases, where the wish [*Wunsch*] would depend in one way or another on the succession of time. I admit this possibility – but I have no examples at my disposal.
24 Translator note: Cf., Spielrein (1912, p. 486). – PC-W

References

Heidegger, M. (2010). *Being and time* [*Sein und Zeit*]. J. Stambaugh & J.D. Schmidt (Trans.). Albany, NY: SUNY Press. (Orig. publ. 1927.)

Launer, J. (2015). *Sex versus survival: The life and times of Sabina Spielrein*. London: Overlook Duckworth.

Piaget, J. (1923). La pensée symbolique et la pensée de l'enfant. *Archives de Psychologie*, 18, 273–303.

Piaget, J. (1936). *La naissance de l'intelligence chez l'enfant* [*The birth of intelligence in the child*]. Neuchâtel: Delachaux & Niestlé.

Spielrein, S. (1912). Die Destruktion als Ursache des Werdens [Destruction as the Cause of Becoming]. *Jahrbuch für Psychoanalyse und Psychopathologische Forschungen*, 4, 465–503. (Trans. this volume, Chapter 6.)

Spielrein, S. (1923a). Die Zeit im unterschwelligen Seelenleben. *Imago*, 9(3), 300–317.

Spielrein, S. (1923b). Le temps dans la vie psychique subliminale. F. Paru (Trans.). *Archives de Psychologie*, 18, 305–322.

Spielrein, S. (1923c). Quelques analogies entre la pensée de l'enfant, celle de l'aphasique et la pensée subconsciente. [Some analogies between thinking in children, aphasia, and the subconscious mind]. *Archives de Psychologie*, 18, 305–322. (Trans. this volume, Chapter 14.)

Chapter 13

The Three Questions

Sabina Spielrein

1923 Translated by Pamela Cooper-White with Jan Rehmann

It is sometimes interesting to see psychoanalytic experiences confirmed by other psychological methods. In the winter semester 1922–1923 with fourteen of my students at the Rousseau Institute, I conducted the following experiment: "Imagine," I said, "that you could ask God, Fate, or whatever you would like to call it, three questions that will certainly be answered. You may ask all possible questions, concerning this world and the world beyond; all questions are permitted; choose three questions that interest you most." The questions were to be written within the same hour.

In one week, I again wanted to have three questions, likewise unrestricted. But this time, I let the students spend about 1–2 minutes with their eyes closed; then they had to write down the first three questions just as they came to mind.

Only after responding to this second question assignment did I explain the purpose and the results of these experiments to the students.

First series: The consciously considered questions[1]
Purpose of life

1. What is the sense [*Sinn*] of life? (1)
2. What is the purpose of human life? (1)
5. What is the meaning [*Bedeutung*] of life? (2)
6. What is the real purpose of human beings on this earth? (1)
14. What is the real purpose [*Bestimmung*] of the human being? (3)

This world or the world beyond?

10. To see into the future! (2)

The future after this life

2. What is death? (2)
4. Where is the universe going? (2)
9. Is there life after life, and how should we imagine this life? (2)
14. What do we become after death? (1)

Personal future on this earth

3. Will I achieve my goal? (3)
5. What will my future be? (3)
10. To know the secret of life (in order to be able to create life)! (1)
13. Will I become a mother sometime? (1)

War

3. Is war among the European powers still possible, and when? (2)
7. Will it be possible for us to avoid wars in the murderous form they are now being conducted? (2)
11. Will we come to abolish war? (3)
13. Will people always kill one another, or will world peace come sometime? (2)

Other struggles (imperative questions)

8. Abolish money!
8. Abolish gravity! [the attractional force of the earth – *Anziehungskraft der Erde*]
8. To reach happiness without struggle or pain!

Religion and morality

(a) Future

3. From the religious standpoint: is there a future life? (1)
7. An absolute and genuine harmony among people – can that ever be realized? (3)

11. What difference does it make if there is a Judgment after death between those who effortlessly do good, and those who act scrupulously, tiring themselves out, but through their actions are harmful to humanity? (1)
12. Every being that is born – will it sometime live in the realm of perfect love? (1)
14. Will evil finally be defeated in humanity through the good? (2)

(b) Causes and means

6. Don't the laws of nature contain something special from which we would be able to create a universal religion? (2)
7. What are the influences that cause sublimation, which make these possible and safe? (6)
12. Will beings on this earth ever create perfection by themselves? (2)

(c) Considerations about religion and morality

4. Does religion have an absolute or a relative value? (3)
5. Does God exist? (1)
6. Is love the essence of the *élan vital* of life? (3)
7. Why does evil exist? (1)
11. Why do living beings who suffer or cause suffering sometimes... so long,[2] while others in full possession of their moral and spiritual powers often die so young? (2)
13. Is there a human being without any emotion? (3)

Duration in space and time

1. Is the human spirit [*Geist*] immortal? (3)
7. Is the universe finite or infinite? (5)
12. Perfect being, will it last forever?[3] (3)

Absolute and relative truth

1. What is the true reality? (2)
9. Is it science or moral conscience that comprises the correct truth? (1)

The I and the other

2. What am I? (3)
7. Are there human beings on other planets? (4)
9. What exists outside of our cosmos? (3)
10. To know how to read others' thoughts. (3)

Historical question

4. Formation of the universe? (1)

The question results are interesting in several respects. Forty-five questions in all were posed by 14 persons, because one person posed not 3 but six questions. Within these 45 questions, 29 covered the future (including 3 questions of duration and 4 of goals), 15 were on the present (e.g., what is the true reality?), and only one single question was on the past (the origin of the universe). This shows us how much our mind [*Geist*[4]] is oriented toward finality, at least in youth. The questions about religion and morality, 14 in number, form a third of all the questions, a result which perhaps is motivated by the especially Calvinist environment in Geneva. Now what is surprising, in spite of my many times emphasizing that the questions could also have to do with the hereafter – we have barely 9 questions on the duration of our lives after we have passed from the earth, i.e., barely 1/5 of all the questions. Two questions go into the space beyond the boundaries of our earth. With the previous 9 questions, these came to 11 overall, thus barely ¼ of all the questions go into time or space beyond the boundaries of our earthly being.

The spontaneous questions after closing the eyes differ significantly from the consciously considered questions. Regarding questions after closing the eyes, barely 6 people participated, with 17 questions in all (one person did not want to disclose one of the three questions, so she merely produced 2 questions). From these 17 questions, we can perceive that all, without exception, concerned the future, and [focused], moreover, on the immediate personal future on this earth. No questions inquired more than a year into the future. Religious, moral, philosophical, [or] scientific interests are not represented in any of the spontaneous questions – proof of how personal problems of our inner life get narrower and more personal when we move away from consciously directed thought, and how the more "social" intellectual curiosity becomes more and more clearly an egocentric thirst for knowledge adapted to the moment.

Some examples of the second series (spontaneous questions after closing the eyes)

What can the others be writing?
What might Madam Dr. S[pielrein's] opinion of us be?
What can happen this summer?
What's going on at home?
Where is my sister Marie?
Are Marie and Henry going after I [go]?
Where will I be next year?
Will I have a piano?
I would like to already be in the next year.
To already know ....[5]
To have time to paint.

The last three questions are at the same time statements of wishes or imperative questions. Such wish- or imperative questions are provided by No. 8 in the consciously considered questions. According to all the similarity of both types of questions, the spontaneous questions here are also very narrowly personal, and cover a much smaller span of time.

Notes

1 The number preceding each question indicates the research subject [numbered 1–14]; the number after the question refers to whether the question was put in 1st, 2nd, or 3rd place by the research subject. The objective classification of questions was subsequently made by me.
2 Translator note: Ellipsis in the original.
3 Translator note: While this is the literal translation, based on the context of previous questions, especially in the categories of "War" and "Other struggles," the intended meaning might also be: "Perfect being, will it take forever? (i.e., "Will it take forever before we see perfect being?") – PC-W, JR

4 Translator note: Alt. "spirit."
5 This was written too indecipherably; but we [may] observe that this second question is also personal [in nature], and stays on this earth.

Reference

Spielrein, S. (1923). Die drei Fragen. *Imago*, 9(2), 260–263.

Chapter 14

Some Analogies between Thinking in Children, Aphasia, and the Subconscious Mind

Sabina Spielrein

1923[1] Translated by Judith Gresh, Felicity Kelcourse, and Robby Kongolo, with Pamela Cooper-White

I

We distinguish a directed thought, where the aim [*le but*] is conscious to us, from a non-directed, spontaneous thought, where the aim is not conscious to us. This classification, like all classifications, is arbitrary; there is no definite boundary between directed thought and spontaneous thought, just as there is no boundary between the conscious and the subconscious. Nevertheless, this distinction has practical usefulness, and in the obvious cases that present themselves daily, we can easily say whether thought is directed, conscious, or not.

During psychoanalysis we ask the subject to abandon any conscious effort to direct his thought; he should say "everything that goes through his mind" without the slightest conscious criticism. I say "conscious direction" or "conscious criticism" because any thought must still be directed by some sort of principle [*un principe quelconque*]: if there were no choice, no direction, and all ideas were presented to us at once, we would not have any clear idea of ourselves – we would have typical "emptiness" or "blankness," as we can see in the experience of associations [*l'expérience des associations*] when we come to a group of affective ideas.[2] There must be some principle that brings out one idea and makes another disappear. This principle is different in conscious thought, or rather in the conscious part of our thought, and in its subconscious part. Among psychologists, logicians in particular have been occupied with the laws of conscious thought; we psychoanalysts deal with the laws of spontaneous subconscious thought. This thought appears to us most clearly in the free association of our subjects, during psychoanalysis, in dreams, in different cases of mental alienation [*alienation mentale*], and in very young children. All these cases of more or less spontaneous thought are not identical; the degree of adaptation to reality, the experience acquired in idea and verbal expression, the affective life – everything is more or less different; but not being identical, these different forms of spontaneous thought nevertheless reveal to us common laws of each spontaneous thought. The study of each of these forms has its difficulties and its advantages.

The thoughts of a child of two-and-a-half years old have not yet matured to become directed, logical thinking. The child, therefore, has no difficulty in saying everything that goes through his head, as we ask our subjects during psychoanalysis. Absolute spontaneity is the natural state of the baby. He babbles all day to himself, regardless of our presence or absence. With all this, the study of thought in the child is inconvenient: to study the sequence of the ideas in a subject we would like, as much as possible, to eliminate outside excitation [*excitation*]. We ask our subject during psychoanalysis to look within; outside excitations hardly influence his associations. In the same way, in the dream, outside excitations rarely play a role. In the spontaneous thought of the child, on the other hand, these excitations are heightened. It seems that the child will constantly abandon one group of ideas to follow another, which is suggested to him by an external impression. And yet this is not the case, or it does not happen as frequently as we would believe a priori. I would say that the thought of the child is "sticky" [*collante*]; left to itself, the child does not easily give up one group of ideas to move to another. Of course, there is nothing easier than changing a baby's ideas. He cries because he cannot have a toy; we draw his attention to another toy and he is happy; he has forgotten his sorrow. But let's not forget that in these cases, it is we who intervene abruptly with our authority and impose our will on the child in place of his choice. Also, for lack of observation, nothing proves to us that the child, while abandoning the object of his desire, abandons the group of ideas that surround it, and that this group of ideas does not continue to exist in him while assimilating the new object. The baby is quickly comforted, it is true, but have you not noticed that a child who has cried for a while does not stop sobbing? Sometimes the sobs continue all night. This proves that an innervation [*innervation*] as a result of an idea does not disappear so easily in the child, as we would be tempted to admit according to the current opinion of distraction, *Ablenkbarkeit*[3] [distractibility] in children. Abandoned to his occupations, without our intervention, the child is quite different. The elements of reality are there at his disposal. What does he do with them?

There are two attitudes with regard to reality: either we adapt to reality, or we adapt reality to ourselves.[4] The baby will choose, among the impressions that reality offers him, those that go in the direction of his groups of preconceived ideas; he will act in the same way as we do in our dreams, taking from reality what suits us and distorting reality in accordance with our dreams. The hypothesis is equivalent to reality for the baby. Even a question does not have the function of a question for him, which is the starting point of a search, of adaptation to the unknown. If the baby asks, "Where is the sheep?" it is not because he realizes that the sheep is not there; the baby answers to himself, "Here he is," or else "He is gone," without worrying in any way if this corresponds to reality. We say the child "plays," and he is still "playing."

There is an interesting dualism in the child's psyche: on the one hand, he realizes he is very small, helpless in relation to something that is reality; he relies on the authority of parents who know everything and can do anything. (Mr. Oberholzer, for example, cited the case of a little girl who thought her aunt could do anything, and asked her to make it rain.) On the other hand, at the same time doubt does not exist for him; he knows everything and can do everything. How many times have I heard the music teacher ask the little ones, "Did you understand?" "Yes, Miss." "Are you sure?" "Yes, Miss." "Are you really sure?" "Yes, Miss." "You will know how to do it?" "Yes, yes, Miss." The answer was always firm and unanimous, although in many cases the little ones did not know anything at all. The child does not realize the difficulties of reality because he is too used to realizing in his fantasy what reality denies him. All this proves that the danger of excitations coming from the outside world, which could influence the spontaneous thought of the baby, is not so great.

The little baby's thought is slow; it's "sticky," we said. This means that groups of ideas remain the same for a long time; objects, which a baby borrows from the outside world, change little and always remain the same. I observed a little baby in different periods of his life, recording word by word everything he said; I also noted, as much as possible, all his actions, all his habits. I repeated these observations several times. Here is one of these observations taken from a child at the age of two years and four-and-a-half months. To make it easier to read, I divided the words and gestures of the child, expressing her thought into four groups of ideas, each marked by a special sign.[5] Each line represents a phrase. The phrases are placed in the same order the child said them. The child spoke a mixture of German and Swiss German, which I translated into French, while adding the original. You see from the signs on the list below that the child does not state an idea once; the same idea always comes back and, characteristically, is repeated in virtually the same verbal form. These forms "stick," or "perseverate" [*persévère*], as we say in psychiatry.

Another of the most interesting phenomena is the one I call "crossing." According to [Gregor] Mendel's [genetic] research it is known that the crossing of certain plants with red flowers and those with white flowers can produce a new type, in which their descendants will have pink flowers as well as red or white flowers. The pink flowers only appear to be different, resulting from the cross pollination, and containing the paternal and maternal elements, the red elements and the white elements. An advanced microscope or a chemical reaction could perhaps show us these red and white elements in the flower, which appear to us to be completely pink.

The babbling of the baby is overflowing with phrases, parts of which belong to one group of ideas and other parts that belong to another group; this is not a simple condensation, because the crossed sentence is followed, or preceded, by simple sentences sometimes borrowed from one of these two groups of ideas, and sometimes from another. It is this condensation of two groups of ideas in one sentence, followed or preceded by their disassociation in the following sentences, which I would like to call "crossing." The baby's thought is overflowing with these crossed sentences. The rigidity of verbal expression makes it easy for us to say which group of ideas this expression represents. Let's look at the child's associations. I divided the combinations into four groups of more or less distinct ideas that always recur; obviously this does not exclude the possibility that there could still be a group of ideas that are expressed at the same time in the baby's phrase, or determining the appearance of that sentence at the same time. I identified each group of ideas with a special sign. Where I cannot say exactly which groups of ideas contain a phrase, I have not put any sign.

We will never be able to know all the groups of ideas that have contributed to the choice of the elements of a phrase, just as we can only follow the ideas that are expressed by gestures or words. I therefore limited myself to picking up the groups of ideas that seemed to me the main ones because they always reappeared and were easily pursued. It is obvious that such classification into groups of ideas must be more or less arbitrary; it is just a way to make it easier for us to follow the ideas. These four groups of ideas are: first group focused on the central idea of eating (+ sign); second group focused on the idea "Anna" (o); third group centered on the idea of sleeping (–); and the fourth group focused on the baby-mama idea (*) (see the list of associations).

List of associations

eating +; Anna o; sleeping –; baby-mama *

	1.	Mach guten Tag	fais bonjour	say hello[6]
	2.	Cravatte hat er an	il a col	he has a collar (on)
	3.	Den Bär	ours	bear
+	4.	Hat Hunger die Katz	a faim le chat	the cat is hungry
	5.	Will essen	veut manger	wants to eat
	6.	Soll ich nehmen die Mietsi Katz?	dois-je prendre le chat Minet?	should I take the kitty cat?
	7.	Soll den Hund…	dois (t) (le) chien	should (the) dog…
	8.	Der hat Freunde	il est content	He has friends/is happy[?][7]
*+	9.	Essen dem Bebi	manger à bébé	eat [food] to baby
*+	10.	Die Mama hat Hunger	la maman a faim	the mommy is hungry
*+	11.	Sie will essen (Will meine Uhr haben – ich lasse nicht; sie quieckst sagt dann noch einer Weile zu sich selbst:)	elle veut manger (la petite veut avoir ma montre – je ne permets pas; elle fait semblant de pleurer et se dit à elle même dans un instant:)	she wants to eat (the baby wants to have my watch – I don't allow it; she pretends to cry and says to herself after a moment:)
*	12.	Genug zu weinen	assez de pleurer	enough crying
–*	13.	Soll nichts passiert dem Bebi (Gähnt, ahmt das Gähnen nach)	doit rien arrive à bébé (Bâille, imite le bâillement)	nothing should happen to baby (yawn, imitates yawn)

(continued)

(Cont.)

o–	14.	Noch eine Tante	encore une tante	another aunt
o–	15.	Hat Taze an	a sac (mis)	has (put) on a pouch
o	16.	Hat Bändeli	a petits rubans	has little ribbons
o	17.	Hat Hosen an der Onkel	a (mis) pantalons oncle	uncle has (put) on pants
o	18.	Hat Hosen an der Onkel	a (mis) pantalons oncle	uncle has (put) on pants
	19.	Das Buch is zö	le livre est beau	the book is pretty [schön]
*o	20.	Nicht wahr?	n'est-ce pas?	isn't it?
–	21.	Puppe… (schläfft?)	poupée… (dort?)	doll… (is sleeping?)
–	22.	Läft im Betti	dort dans son dodo	sleeps in her crib [fait dodo]
–	23.	Das Buch läft auch?	le livre dort aussi?	the book sleeps too?
o	24.	Wo ist die Tante?	où est la tante?	where is the aunt?
o	25.	Sie macht Versteckis	elle fait cache-cache	she plays hide-and-seek
o	26.	Wo ist die zaf?	où est le mouton?	where is the sheep?
o	27.	Wo ist die Mietsi-Katz?	où est le chat Minet?	where is the kitty cat?
o	28.	Da ist die Mietsi-Katz	voilà le chat Minet	here is the kitty cat
*o	29.	Wo ist das Bebi?	où est le bébé?	where is the baby?
o	30.	Hat eine Taze an	a un sac (mis)	has (put) on a pouch
o	31.	Da ist die Balle	voilà la balle	here is the ball
o	32.	Da ist die Hosebueb	voilà la garçon en pantalons	here is the boy in pants
o	33.	Da ist die Hosebueb	voila la garçon en pantalons	here is the boy in pants
*o	34.	Zeig die Mama die Zuh	montre la maman la bottine	shows mama the (ankle) boot
o	35.	Anna hat die Hosebueb gemacht	Anna a fait le garçon en pantalon	Anna made [drew] the boy in pants
o	36.	Liese hat die Hosebueb gemacht	Liese a fait le garçon en pantalon	Liese made [drew] the boy in pants
*	37.	Hat Bauchweh der Siuck	mal au ventre a le Siuck	Siuck[8] has stomach ache
–	38.	Legen	coucher	lie down
*–	39.	Passiert dem Bebi	arrive à bébé	happens to baby
	40.	Das sind Mazinen	ce sont mazines	these are machines[?][9]
–	41.	Ferd Ferd laft	Zeval, zeval dort	horse, horse sleeps
*–	42.	Oh, Bebi laft im Buch	oh, bébé dort dans le livre	oh, baby sleeps in the book
–	43.	Oh Buch lafen	oh, livre dormir	oh, book to sleep
–	44.	Buch laf	livre dort	book sleeps
–	45.	Aa Buch	aaa livre	aaa book
*–	46.	Um komm zu Mama	oum, viens chez maman	um, come to mama
	47.	Lesen	lire	read
	48.	Lesen s'Buch	lire le livre	read the book

	49.	Buch	livre	book
	50.	Lesen s'Buch	lire le livre ("livre" s'associe à l'idée de "dormir"; ceci explique l'association qui suit, c.-a-d. l'association "maman" et puis les associations chants par lesquels la berçait la maman)	read the book ("book" is associated with the idea of "sleep"; this explains the association that follows: "mama" association and then singing associations by which the mama rocked her)
–	51.	Hu lu Hu lu Hu lu (singt)	Houlu, houlu, houlu, houlu (chante)	Hulu, hulu, hulu, hulu (sings)
–	52.	Siuk[10] hat keine Hasen mehr	Siouk n'a plus de lièvres	Siouk doesn't have any more rabbits [hares]
–	53.	Da sind Hasen im Buch	ce sont des lièvres dans le livre	These are rabbits in the book
–	54.	Da sind Hasen im Buch	ce sont des lièvres dans le livre	These are rabbits in the book
–	55.	Da sind farze Hasen	ce sont des lièvres noirs	these are black rabbits
–	56.	Aeuglein macht die Hasen zu	le lièvre ferme les petits yeux	the rabbit closes its little eyes
–	57.	Aeuglein macht die Hasen zu	le lièvre ferme les petits yeux	the rabbit closes its little eyes
–	58.	Lange Ohr hat die Ssaf	de longuès oreilles a le mouton	the sheep has long ears
–	59.	Hasen macht die Aeuglein zu	le lièvre ferme les petits yeux	the rabbit closes its little eyes
–	60.	Zlafen	dormir	sleep
	61.	Iii Iii (singt)	iii, iii (chante)	Iii, iii (sings)
	62.	Ssau! Das Midd pilt mit der Ball	regarde la fillette joue avec la balle	Look! the girl is playing with the ball
	63.	Armer Bär	pauvre ours	poor bear
	64.	Jack (quieckst)	Jack (gémit)	Jack (groaning)
	65.	Sei lieb (quieckst)	sois gentil (le) (gémit)	be nice (the) (groaning)
	66.	Sei lieb (quieckst wieder)	sois gentil (le) (gémit)	be nice (the) (groaning again)
	67.	Aa uu! unh um um!	aaa, ou, ou, oum, oum	aaa, uu! uu, oum, oum, oum!
	68.	Bär	ours	bear
	69.	Auf dem Bär	sur l'ours	on the bear
	70.	Auf dem Bär	sur l'ours	on the bear
	71.	Bär ist müde	l'ours est fatigué	bear is tired
–	72.	Will am Boden legen (singt)	veut coucher sur le plancher (chante)	wants to sleep on the floor (sings)
	73.	Sieh, nur, sieh (singt)	regarde seulement, regarde (sings)	just look, look (sings)

The child is busy looking at her picture book. "Say hello," said the little girl in the first phrase (in her picture book there is a cat paying visits). In the second sentence, "He has put on a collar" (*Kravatte hat er an*), the attention is focused on the cat character who put on a collar; the word "cat" has not yet appeared either in the first or in the second sentence: "Cat" is a "latent" association, which will appear later, linked to another group of ideas, which will be the strongest. This group of ideas is built around the idea of "eating." In phrase 3: "bear" appears as an awkward grammatical form (*den*) that could be translated into French by the preposition "*à*" (to); in German there are two cases, the dative and the accusative, in which the article is almost identical (*dem* and *den*). The child easily mixes up these two cases. The new grammatical form announces a new group of ideas. Unfortunately, I could not follow the whole sentence, which was pronounced too indistinctly. The child has the habit of feeding all her animals when she eats; her bear comes first, which is why I suppose the sentence also contains the latent idea of eating, or is perhaps expressed in the rest of the sentence that I missed.

The idea "to eat" appears clearly in the sentence 4, where the idea "cat" reappears, this time named as "Hungry cat"; the idea of "eating" is developed in sentence 5 "wants to eat." It disappears in sentences 6, 7, 8, to reappear in sentences 9, 10, 11, in a sequence of identical grammatical forms "eat to baby," "the mother is hungry," "she wants to eat."

Sentences 6 and 7 are interesting. The new form "should I" is not an interrogation, as one would believe. According to my many experiments, it is an optional imperative. The child often says, for example, "Do you want zwieback?" She also uses "or you do not want?" to say "I want zwieback" or "I do not want." We can consider sentence 6, and especially sentence 7, as cross-sentences; especially sentence 7, "should (the) dog (*Soll den Hund*)," must still contain the idea "to eat," which reappears in almost all the following sentences: 9, 10, and 11. At the same time the new optional imperative form "should" brings a new group of ideas, "baby-mama." I have sometimes explained to the child: "The dog keeps watch [*veille*] so that nothing happens to the baby" (*der Hund wacht, dass dem Bebi nichts passiert*).

The idea of the dog is therefore related to the idea of the baby. The expression "should" from sentence 6 perseveres in sentence 7, where it is associated with the "dog"; therefore, sentence 7 contains the latent idea of the baby (associated with the dog). This "baby" already appears in sentence 9 (eat to baby) and reappears through Mama (sentences 10, 11, and 12) in sentence 13, this time closely linked to "should" and "nothing should happen to baby." This grammatical form, as clumsy in German as it is in French, is in any case a combination of the idea of the baby with the more vague and wide-ranging idea of an optional imperative that we have seen appearing independently in sentence 6.

Sentence 13 is clearly crossed because its two component ideas, the "should" ["*doit*"] and the (that) "nothing happen(s) to baby," ["*rien n'arrive a bébé*"] are in the same independent monologue or well connected to other groups of ideas; for example, the "should" in sentence 6, i.e., before the clearly crossed sentence 13, and the "happens to baby" in sentence 39, i.e., after sentence 13. Sentence 13 was introduced, as we said, by intermediary associations with dog, baby, and mother, still linked to the idea of eating (sentences 9, 10, 11, "to eat to baby," "the mother is hungry," "she wants to eat"); the idea of "mama" begins to prevail: the attention of the child is on her mother's watch; the child pretends to cry and repeats the words of the mother, heard often on this occasion: "enough crying" (sentence 12). Since the little one desires the watch, there is one more reason to admit that the "should" in the following sentence is influenced by that desire, which persists and expresses itself in the form of an optional imperative. The child wanted to say "nothing happens to the baby," but the optional imperative "should" persists, is grafted, and contributes to forming the crossed phrase in its awkward grammatical form.

The idea of "sleeping," once pronounced in sentence 13 (since baby sleeps), becomes dominant, although expressed by gestures: the child starts yawning, then mimics the yawn. This prevalence at first glance is of short duration. The combination of "aunt" prevails (sentences 14 and 15, "another aunt," "has (put) on a pouch"). The idea of "sleeping" reappears, this time expressed in two sentences: "sleeps in her crib" (22) and "the book sleeps too" (23), but again the combination of "aunt" makes the group "sleeping" disappear. The idea of sleeping comes back again in sentences 38, 39, 41, 42, and so on, this time to reach its full development. The aunt exists in the picture book. What excites the curiosity of the child is her pouch: "has (put) on pouch" (15) and "has (put) on pouch" (30).[11]

The idea of "aunt" brings together two groups of different associations that alternate with each other. One group focuses on the clothes brought by the central idea "boy in pants" (*Hosenbueb*) with "has (put) on [is wearing a] pouch" (15); the other lifts up the idea of the game of hide-and-seek (sentence 24): "Where? Here." These two groups of associations are united by the idea or person, if you like, of "Anna." Anna often sang to the little girl, "Have (put) on the pretty pants with the pretty lace. Oh, you, yes, you, my dear little one!" (In Swiss German: *Hat schöne Höselili an, schöne Spit zelilz dran, Oh, du mein, ja mein, lieber kleiner.*)[12]

At the same time Anna was calling the little girls "boy in pants" (*Hosenbueb*). Sentences 15 and 16 have German grammatical forms where the idea of the boy in pants already appears (I translate it into French by the "*mis, mettre* [put, put on]." The aunt has (put) on a pouch (*Hat Taze an* "has [put] on small ribbons") and the boy has [put] on little pants (*mis*). It may be that in the song itself we speak of ribbons; it is also possible that while dressing the little girl, Anna also spoke of ribbons. In sentences 17 and 18, "uncle has (put) on pants," the idea of pants is expressed. The "pretty" in sentence 19 still belongs to the group of pants ideas (pretty little pants).

The idea of "Anna" is closely linked to the idea of "mama," just as the idea of "dressing" easily evokes the contrasting idea of "undressing," then sleeping. Sentence 20 contains the idea of Anna and Mama at the same time; "Isn't it?" Anna would often ask, as did Mama. The idea of "mother–baby" evokes, as in the following sentence 14, the idea of "sleeping" (21, 22, 23); on the other hand, the interrogative form is also in the game of hide-and-seek. After "sleeping" comes, as in the following sentences, 13–14, the idea of "aunt" (23–24), but the interrogative form, suppressed for the moment, reappears and is related to this idea: "where is the aunt?" She plays hide-and-seek (25, 26). The idea of "hide-and-seek" is obvious up to sentence 34. It gradually fades, giving way to the idea "boy in pants." This time, the central idea of Anna also appears (Anna made [drew] the boy in trousers, sentence 35).

In 36 "Anna" is traded with "Liese," who looked after the child some time before. Then the association comes back to the group of ideas "mama–baby," where, this time, the idea of sleeping is fully developed. All the rest is linked to the idea of sleeping and being at home, gently rocked by her songs, so, for example, the black rabbit and the long-eared sheep, two sentences with crossed elements drawn from the lullabies that the mother sang, etc.

The short monologue just analyzed appears to demonstrate that:

(1) Ideas do not appear to be isolated in the mind of the baby; they are interrelated and follow the laws of association;
(2) A baby's thought process is slow and lacks associations; in other words, ideas and associations do not vary much;
(3) The child does not express one idea after another, for example, the idea "the dog guards the baby." The idea first appears piece by piece, linked to other ideas; we find the isolated pieces with a number of other phrases, linked to other ideas, sometimes quite awkwardly, before the idea is expressed as a complete phrase. This can be explained by a fact that we will soon see more clearly as we study the way aphasics and children draw; the fact is that:
(4) The child's thought is not necessarily tied to a direction. We find two opposite directions at the same time. When the child has already arrived at a new idea, his thoughts return to a preceding idea that is then grafted onto the new idea. Consequently:
(5) The previous idea always reappears; it remains or perseveres;
(6) In grafting itself to the new idea, it produces the crossing effect.
(7) If we take a quick look at the list of associations, we notice that certain symbols take up little space, while others are fully extended. The sign + disappears relatively quickly. This is the sign that corresponds to the group of ideas "eating." There are four actions that preoccupy the child during this observation; the four actions are: eating, getting dressed, hiding, sleeping. Why does the idea of eating disappear so quickly, while other ideas so stubbornly persist? Is this by chance?

In the sign "o" we have distinguished two central ideas, united in the person of Anna: the idea "the boy in pants" and the idea of "hide-and-seek." Each time the little girl talks about pants she repeats the idea twice. Phrases 17 and 18, "uncle has (put) on pants" are also identical. Also, in phrases 32 and 33 ("Here is the boy in pants!") and phrases 35 and 36 ("Anna has made [drawn] a boy in pants" and "Liese has made [drawn] a boy in pants"), only the subject has changed. "Pants" appears three times, and each time the phrase is repeated. Now, Stern has already established that when a child repeats a word (or a phrase), he must be emphasizing something that is important to him. We often do the same, as when we say "That's very, very pretty." There is therefore an interesting relationship in a psychic, not biological, sense – an affective relationship. Sentence 18 is followed by an affective phrase: "the book is pretty." The associations are becoming ever more emotive. In the group of ideas "sleep" that persists for such a long time, joy is abundant. Sentence 41: "horse, horse sleeps." 42: "oh, the baby is sleeping in the book!" Pleasure increases and culminates when the book comes to sleep with Mama. Here we find several memories always grouped around the same idea: the desire to sleep with the mother, rocked by her lullabies.

Thus, we see that what causes a group of ideas to persist in spontaneous thought is the movement of affect.

II

There are two objections to be made regarding our analysis of the baby's thought. The first would be of a general nature: we study the expression of thought and we then draw conclusions about thought itself. Do we have the right to do this? – This is in sum the same question we might pose about the relationship between things as they are and as we perceive them. We must not confuse thought with what is within us as acquired experience, organized, stabilized, "organic" I would say, as in the case of an instinct. Thoughts do not exist for us other than through their expression. This expression or language is not necessarily a language in words. Thought can be translated into a melody, into movements (gestures, for example), into images, etc. The language that expresses our thoughts could be directed to ourselves, as in dreams, what we call *autistic* language, or could be directed to others, as in *socialized* language.[13] But in one way or another, it is always language that represents thoughts for us; it is after it has been expressed in a language of any sort that we draw conclusions regarding the mechanism of thought.

The second objection belongs to the special case that we have just considered: Isn't it possible that what we designate as the mechanism of thought for the baby can only be explained by the baby's limited capacity to express itself in words? Isn't it possible that the mechanism of thought would appear differently to us if the baby expressed itself in a language other than words, if we knew, for example, how the baby thinks within itself? Here we find the same problem posed in the case of aphasia.

We will now see that what we call the mechanism of thought for the child resembles, in many respects, the mechanism of thought in our dreams, and in the case of the aphasic patient.

"Aphasia" is an inability to speak that originates in the brain. Hearing is intact. The motor pathway is unaffected; in other words, the nerves, the muscles, all that constitutes the speech organs, is intact; in most cases the patient is [nevertheless] unable to repeat all that we say to him. Whether rightly or wrongly, we still identify three forms of aphasia: sensory, amnesic, and motor aphasia. In sensory aphasia the patient himself can speak but does not understand what we say to him. In amnesic aphasia, he no longer remembers the names for things; if he is able to remember, he understands everything and can say everything. In the third case, the patient knows the names for things, understands everything, but does not know how to say anything.

Scientists are far from agreeing on explanations for the phenomenon of aphasia. Some still note centers in the brain that each have a special function. They would say that a lesion in these centers would produce functional difficulties, localized in the corresponding center. Thus there would be a center – or more likely centers – for speech, in which lesions cause different forms of aphasia.

We have only recently accepted the current theory that the loss of speech in aphasia is independent of intelligence; as M.M. Weber, Claparède, Naville, and others note, intelligence may be intact without the power of expression; in motor aphasia it could possibly be a case of a problem in the pathway between the mental idea of a word and its physical expression: we may have the idea of the word in mind, as we have said, even be able to hear it within ourselves as a sound, and not have the image of its motor expression.

Jackson[14] was perhaps the first to give a completely different explanation for the phenomenon of aphasia. His idea was that lesions in certain regions of the brain produce a dissolution in the domain of superior functions that are [then] replaced by inferior functions. Here is a passage taken from Jackson's conference presentation on the subject of aphasia[15]:

"There is loss of intellectual language (the most voluntary) with persistence of emotional language (the most automatic). The patient cannot speak and his pantomime is very simple, yet he smiles, frowns, varies the tone of his voice (he may be able to sing), gestures, as well as ever. Gesticulation, which is an expression of emotion, must be distinguished from pantomime, which belongs to intellectual language," etc.

Monakow, who was not familiar with Jackson's work, arrived independently at his theory of the chronological localization of functions. English researchers Head, P. Marie, and others, also do not recognize a speech center.[16] For them the speech difficulty with aphasia is a special difficulty related to intelligence. According to them, aphasia is essentially the loss of the ability to adapt ideas to the symbolic signs they represent.

The observations of Dr. Saloz, as communicated by Dr. Naville, are very interesting from this point of view.[17] The patient, suffering from a motor aphasia, had sufficient intelligence to point to the place on his head where the site of his brain lesion was located; when his status had improved and he had regained the ability to express himself in writing and orally, he said that his will, his thoughts, his exact memories had remained intact, even the possibility of the motor mechanism of language, but he lacked the connection from an idea to a word, the use of a word as a symbol for an object. Words as symbols, or as signs for an object, are acquired by children, as for primitive peoples, in the course of their development. The first words are reflex phenomena or onomatopoeias. The inability to use verbal signs is therefore due to a lack of intellectual faculties. This lack of understanding is even more evident in the cases of aphasia we usually see; these are not the pure aphasias that some authors believe do not exist, but are mixed with alexia (an inability to read, of cerebral origin), agraphia (an inability to write, of cerebral origin), etc. In these cases we find the same problems as are found in the domain of spoken language. This in fact supports Jackson, Monakow, Head, and their adherents. My own personal observations also appear to support these authors. Here are some of these observations, made about a 55-year-old man afflicted with motor aphasia.

We work with the patient to pronounce: *"table, chaise, chambre"* [table, chair, room]. He repeats these three words several times, repeating after me in the same order; at the same time he points to the corresponding objects; then I touch the table and ask the patient to tell me the name. He replies, "*timbre*" [stamp]. Where does this word come from? The patient wishes to say "*table*" but the preceding word "*chambre*" is still present in his mind; we might say that he "perseverates"; as with the baby, the preceding idea is grafted for him to the idea that was beginning to develop, and we then find a crossed word, composed of *table* and *chambre*; since the word "*tambre*" does not exist, the patient replaces it with a known word, which he evokes from memory; this word is "*timbre.*"

If I ask the patient to give me the letter *r* from alphabet blocks [*alphabet mobile*], he frequently gives me *s*; the same thing happens when he is asked to pick another letter of the alphabet.

The phenomena of perseveration and crossing can be explained by the patient's incapacity to maintain a fixed direction in his thought. This conclusion is derived from the following observations: the patient, who was still quite good at drawing, must draw a circle from memory, then a triangle. He is quite able to pick out these two forms from a set of geometric shapes [*jeu des surfaces*].[18] He drew the circle well → ○ but instead of a triangle, he drew this form → ⋖. What is happening? Initially, the thought of the patient goes in the direction of the circle to the triangle ○ → ◁ (indicated by the upper arrow); for a moment he continues in that direction, by drawing a part of the triangle $_b{<}_{a'}^c$; here he changes direction and returns to the idea of the circle that he had already abandoned (the direction indicated by the lower arrow). The preceding idea revived again is grafted to the idea of the triangle, producing the strange crossing.

The following example is perhaps even more instructive: the patient must draw a square.

Instead of this he draws a standing rectangle ⎕ (fig. 1); then a recumbent rectangle ⎕ (fig. 2), and in the end a mixture of the two shapes ⎕ (fig. 3); the third is evidently a cross between the first and the second; his thought has been directed from idea 2 ⎕ to idea 1 ⎕. The patient begins to draw the rectangle 1 ⎕; here the patient changes direction, returning again to the previous drawing 2 ⎕ that, "perserverating" in this way and grafted onto idea 1, has become the obvious moment of fusion.

One must not confuse crossing with the juxtaposition Mr. Piaget speaks about.[19] The child juxtaposes details without worrying about their relationship to the whole; this is irrefutable, we see proof of this in the drawings of children where we find houses with windows outside of walls or faces of people with one eye in place and the other in a completely different place. Mr. Piaget had one of the children copy a diamond shape [*losange*]; Mr. Piaget said that the child no doubt thought of this shape as a square with a point. Hence he was able to produce a unique mixture of these two forms ⌂. No doubt, but how did it happen that the child considered a diamond shape to be a rectangle with a point? Here we have two distinct ideas, that of a quadrilateral form, and that of a pointed angle. These two ideas would be united in the form of the diamond if the child's thought were simply focused on the actual task of drawing a diamond shape. But the quadrilateral [diamond] form evokes in him the memory of the more familiar quadrilateral form, that of the rectangle. His thoughts turn back to this more familiar idea and attach to it; the idea of the rectangle "perseverates" and crosses with a new idea, that of a pointed angle characteristic of a diamond. This is therefore, in the domain of drawing, the same phenomenon as the one we have just studied in the case of aphasia.

We find more similarities between the baby and the aphasic with regard to the great importance of affective moments. My personal observations confirm those of other authors; the patient can easily recover lost words where there is an emotional [*emotive*] relationship.[20]

In conclusion, I must say this: with children, as with aphasics, the insufficiencies or difficulties with speech do not form an isolated deficit independent of intelligence; we find in each case, with children and with aphasics, the same features (in the domain of drawing, for example). We cannot consider speech as something isolated, independent of intelligence. Spoken language is, above all, a social language; thanks to speech, our thoughts can become logical, adapted to the requirements of reality. The child begins to acquire language from the moment he begins to leave the autistic stage, as he abandons, little by little, the mechanisms of his primitive thought, which becomes ever less conscious. Spoken language evolves before all the other languages, such as logical or social language, but these other languages also evolve in the same way; the child's spoken language and drawing traverse the same stages in their development – spoken language evolves first, and the language of drawing comes later.

We find these primitive stages in the unconscious where, as Freud has demonstrated, the pleasure principle triumphs over the reality principle [*le principe de joissance l'emporte sur la fonction du réel*]. If directed thought is altered for any reason, it experiences a regression [*dédéveloppement*] by once again becoming in a certain sense the primitive thought of the child. This is what we observe in aphasia, as much in the domain of speech as in the other domains.

While agreeing with Jackson, Monakow, and other scientists who reason that aphasia presents us with a phenomenon of regression in the domain of intelligence, I must on the other hand lift up the role that motor–verbal [*verbo-motrices*] images play in this regression.

Motor–verbal images are none other than a group of kinesthetic images that are, as I have shown in my (forthcoming) work on the origin of symbols, at the origin and basis of our thought.[21] Our conscious thought is primarily verbal thought; our subconscious thought has retained its primitive character, in that it consists primarily of kinesthetic–visual thought. Our conscious thought is always accompanied by parallel thought that is organic, hallucinatory,[22] translating conscious thought in images; this parallel thought is unconscious thought. We note the presence of this thought in the phenomenon of synesthesia, studied by Théodore Flournoy, but we can certainly observe it in hypnagogic states (A. Maury, H. Silberer),[23] that is to say, in states of great fatigue where thought is not sufficiently directed to suppress all the subconscious images, which allows us to see at the same time verbal thought and its expression in images simultaneously.[24]

Here are two examples: a young man finds himself faced with the problem of knowing if he should give in to the idea of free love or instead follow the austere ideas of his father, who is a pastor. In thinking about these problems he enters into a hypnagogic state, which we must not confuse with an actual dream. In this state he sees a plaza where two roads part ways.[25] The next day he tells me what he saw. I ask him what the plaza in his dream looks like – it is the place where he spoke to a young girl who suggested to him the possibility of free love. One of the roads leads to the place where his father lives; the other resembles a road where he had all sorts of erotic memories. Thus, subconscious thought expresses in images what conscious thought would have expressed in words. Another subject, a woman, thinks: "It is not worth the struggle to fight in this life; as soon as we get to the top, something intervenes that causes us to tumble down and we have to start again." In this depressed state she went to bed; as she was falling asleep she saw a beetle climbing along a grate. At the moment it got to the top a little girl touched its leg and it tumbled down to start the climb again. The woman did not realize immediately that this hypnagogic image was expressing in images her conscious thought of the day before. Concentrating on considering the first thing that came to her mind when she thought of this image, she said: "You want to go forward and the devil pulls your leg." At this point the memory of her thoughts returned.

Subconscious visual–kinetic images nourish [*donne la sève*][26] our conscious thoughts. Without them our thought would be uprooted, "stripped down" [*déracinée, "décortiquée"*], as Dr. Saloz felt, when he had recovered from his aphasia. In motor aphasia, it is probably not the loss of motor–verbal images but rather, as Saloz experienced it, the "loss of the connection of the idea to the word," that is the loss of the connection, or rather the weakening of the connection of the idea to its kinesthetic image. Deprived of its nourishment in this way, verbal thought falls apart in the sense that it suffers a regression [*dédéveloppement*] (Jackson) and returns to primitive thought; in other words, it becomes, in part, the thought of a child. What we see in the domain of [verbal] languages also occurs in the domain of other languages,[27] as in the domain of drawing, for example.

Also, in these domains we can agree on the influence of dissociation between the conscious idea and its expression, generally unconscious kinesthetic, particularly in the domain of motor aphasia (this would be a weakening of the connection between the word and the verbal–kinetic image).

I by no means pretend to have the last word on a subject as complicated as aphasia. I have simply wanted to draw attention to the possibility of reuniting two theories that might appear antagonistic, by seeing kinesthetic images as existing at the origin of our thought, constantly accompanying our conscious, verbal thought. The loss or weakening of their connections to our conscious thought would consequently result in difficulties consistent with the regression Jackson speaks of: thought once again becomes, in a certain sense, more primitive and resembles, as I have shown, the thought of a child. This does not exclude the fact that the thought of the aphasic is from many points of view superior to the thought of the child. The adult possesses a rich experience that the child has not yet acquired; it is only the mechanism of thought for the aphasic that becomes more primitive, like our unconscious thought, which is at the same time the thought process of the child.

Subconscious thought is, in fact, our primary thought; it is only the beginning and the end of our thought that we are conscious of; all the rest takes place in the subconscious. In many cases, we can persuade ourselves that subconscious thought may be superior to conscious thought, as in its collaboration with conscious thought, just as when we benefit from what we have acquired to resolve problems in conscious reality. Left to itself, subconscious thought suffices for a certain adaptation in this world, but it would lose its character of creative thought, because the momentum of creating something, of making something in this world, the absolute direction and concentration toward the functions of reality, is lacking in subconscious thought. [The latter] is not, as we have seen, necessarily a directed thought. [Subconscious thought] is destined to work for ourselves rather than for others. This explains how an aphasic, like Dr. Saloz, retained the high level of acquired understanding that allowed him to point at the place on his head corresponding to the cerebral lesion, while those around him noticed the rigidity of his [verbal] ideas and his inability to create an original thought.

It is only the collaboration of subconscious thought with conscious thought that can engender a creative work in this world; conscious thought must grasp what the unconscious offers it, and use it.

Notes

1 Translator note: First presented as an address in German to the Psychoanalytic Society of Zürich in January 1923 and in March 1923 to the Psychoanalytic group in Geneva (Spielrein, 1923b). Both German and French texts were consulted to prepare this English translation. – FBK, PC-W
2 Translator note: Spielrein is likely referring to the association experiments that she participated in as both subject and researcher with Jung at the Bürgholzli. Cf., Jung's publications in German between 1904 and 1906 (Ress & McGuire, 1979). – FBK

3 Translator note: German term in original French text. – FBK
4 Translator note: Parallel to Piaget's "accommodation" and "assimilation" (cf., Spielrein (1923a); Chapters 4 and 12). – PC-W
5 Translator note: We know from context (below) that the child was a girl. – FBK
6 Translator note: The German and French columns are original; the English column is our translation. – FBK, PC-W
7 Translator note: Spielrein's German and French in the original text do not correspond here. "*Freunde*" = friends; "*Freude*" = happiness. "*Freunde*" may be a typographical error in the publication or a translation error by Spielrein. – PC-W
8 Siuck is the name the child calls herself.
9 Translator note: *Maschinen* (German)/*machines* (French)/*machines* (English). The meaning of childish speech reproduced here is unclear. – PC-W
10 Translator note: Variations in spelling of this name are in original. – PC-W
11 Translator note: Spielrein misquotes her data here – above, the word "*Sac*" is repeated rather than "*poche*." – PC-W
12 Translator note: In the original text. – PC-W
13 Translator note: Italics in original. – FBK
14 Translator note: John Hughlings Jackson (1835–1911), English neurologist known for his work on epilepsy. – FBK
15 Hughlings Jackson, Croonian's lectures on the evolution and dissolution of the nervous system. *Lancet*, March 1884: French translation in the *Arch[ives] Suisses de Neurologie et Psychiatrie*, VIII and IX, 1921.
16 Translator note: Henry Head (1861–1940), English neurologist known for his work on the somatosensory system and sensory nerves. – FBK
17 F. Naville, Mémoires d'un médecin aphasique [Memories of an Aphasic Doctor]. *Ar[chives] de Psychologie* XVII, 1916.
18 Translator note: Or "board game" (cf., Spielrein (1923a; Chapter 12) – almost certainly the same patient. – PC-W
19 Jean Piaget, course at the psychology laboratory in Geneva, winter 1921–1922.
20 Doctors Brun and Minkowsky have also lifted up the importance of emotional moments that they have been able to notice during their observations of aphasics.
21 Translator note: This envisioned work was apparently never published as such, but the same concepts were incorporated in detail in Spielrein, 1928 and 1931 (trans. this volume, Chapter 16). – FBK, PC-W
22 Freud, *Totem and Taboo*, p. 112 [Freud, 1955/1913].
23 Translator note: Théodore Flournoy (1854–1920), Louis Ferdinand Alfred Maury (1817–1892), and Herbert Silberer (1882–1923) were all psychologists interested in altered, paranormal, and/or mystical mental states. – FBK, PC-W

24 S. Spielrein, Destruction as the Cause of Becoming, *Jahrb[uch] f[ür] psychoanalyt[ische] u[nd] patholog[isce] Forschungen*, Vol. 4, 486 [Spielrein, 1912, trans. this volume, Chapter 6]... Die Zeit im unterschweiligen Seelenleben [Time in Subliminal Life] (communication to the International Congress of Psychoanalysis, Berlin, Sept., 1922). [Spielrein, 1923a, trans. this volume, Chapter 12.]
25 Translator note: Cf., Spielrein (1923a, Chapter 12) – the same patient with new details. – PC-W
26 Translator note: Literally, to give sap, juice, to our thoughts. – FBK
27 The language of words is not our only language. Dreams, for example, principally use a visual language (of images) to express an idea. There is a language of gestures, a language of melody. See Spielrein, The Origin of the Child's Words Papa and Mama, *Imago* VIII, 1922 [Spielrein, 2015a].

References

Freud, S. (1955). Totem and taboo. In J. Strachey (Ed.), *Standard edition of the complete works of Sigmund Freud*, Vol. 13, 1–162. London: Hogarth. (Orig. publ.1913.)

Ress, L. & McGuire, W. (Eds.) (1979). *The collected works of C. G. Jung, Vol. 19: General bibliography of C. G. Jung's writings* (rev. ed.). Bollingen Series XX. Princeton, NJ: Princeton University Press.

Spielrein, S. (1912). Die Destruktion als Ursache des Werdens. [Destruction as the cause of becoming]. *Jahrbuch für Psychoanalytische und Psychopathologische Forschungen*, 4, 465–503. (Trans. this volume, Chapter 6.)

Spielrein, S. (1923a). Die Zeit im unterschwelligen Seelenleben. [Time in subliminal life.] *Imago*, 9(3), 300–317. (Trans. this volume, Chapter 12.)

Spielrein, S. (1923b). Quelques analogies entre la pensée de l'enfant, celle de l'aphasique et la pensée subconsciente. *Archives de Psychologie*, 18, 305–322.

Spielrein, S. (1928). Детские рисунки при открытых и закрытых глазах. [*Detskie risunki pri otkrytyx i zakrytyx glazax* – Children's drawings with eyes open and closed.] Lecture to the Pedagogical Society at North Caucasus University, Rostov-on-Don, Russia, winter, 1928. (Trans. this volume, Chapter 16.)

Spielrein, S. (1931). Kinderzeichnungen bei offenen und geschlossenen Augen. [Children's drawings with eyes open and closed]. N.A. Spielrein (Trans. from Russian). *Imago*, 17, 359–391. (Trans. this volume, Chapter 16.)

Spielrein, S. (2015a). The origin of the child's words Papa and Mama: Some observations on the different stages in language development. B. Wharton (Trans.). In C. Covington & B. Wharton (Eds.), *Sabina Spielrein: Forgotten pioneer of psychoanalysis*, 2nd edn. (pp. 233–248). New York: Routledge. (Orig. publ. 1922.)

Chapter 15

Dr. Skalkovskiy's Report

Sabina Spielrein

1929[1] Translated by Judith Gresh, Felicity Kelcourse, and Anatoli Samochornov, with Ekaterina Golynkina and Sergey Trostyanskiy

Preliminary comments of the editors[2]
Editions in Russian

1929 – On the report of Dr. G.A. Skalkovskiy[3] // Proceedings of the First Conference of Psychiatrists and Neuropathologists of the North Caucasus Krai. – Issue No. 1. / Published by N.C. (North Caucasus) Regional Health Department and N.C. Association of Scientific and Research Institutes). – Rostov-on-Don, 1929. pp. 95–97.

This article is in fact the only publication prepared by Spielrein in Russian. The text below follows the usage of names, psychoanalytical terminology, and spelling of the original.[4]

In practice, the author of the report[5] uses the same method for treating patients as Freud. Like all Freudians, the author of the report recommends to first explore [consider, uncover] repressed infantile sexual experiences. This is essential, because, according to Freud's teaching, therapeutic success with transference neuroses[6] (e.g., hysteria) depends exclusively on uncovering repressed experiences as completely as possible. Freudians also direct the patient to his unconscious protest, or his positive dependence, on the father or the mother. This is done based on what the patient himself says. If the patient remembers his hostile feelings towards the father, or critically hostile relations with the father, but does not remember any infantile sexual experiences, the experienced analyst will not suggest such experiences to the patient. Usually, talking about their fantasies with respect to one of their parents (dependence or protest), patients themselves make clear or symbolic associations with infantile sexual experiences. We became particularly convinced by many highly productive scientific psychoanalytic sessions during which the analyst said nothing except: "And now, what do you see?" What was said by the person being analyzed was set down verbatim and could be redacted [reconstructed, examined] for a long time afterwards. Freudians, such as the author of the report, show the patient how education and environment contribute to the development of pathological dependence or resistance. The author then explains his theory of dependence to the patient, stopping at development's various stages. Despite the theoretical interest, these explanations provide practically nothing, because effective treatment consists in the elimination of the repressed. Therefore, similar results are often achieved with analyses, especially children's, in which the analyst does not say a word, and gives the patient the possibility to play out, for example, hostile impulses against father or mother. This playing out forms the basis of the analytic method for children of preschool age. This method was reported and first described by Hug-Hellmuth.[7] All of us who have to deal with patients of preschool age employ it. Personally, having a different view from Hug-Hellmuth and Melanie Klein, I do not find it necessary to let a child consciously work through the repressed, as we do with adults. In preschool age analyses this is only necessary in exceptional cases. Often, as I described in one of my cases, the therapeutic effect occurs exclusively due to the influence of the expression of the repressed content, and without the analyst giving a word of explanation.[8]

Theoretical section

Freud's teaching surpasses that of [both] his enemies and his followers. A decade ago Freud defined neurosis as a social maladjustment and unsuccessful attempt at contact with the environment. On several occasions Freud noted that many people could have been spared from neurosis if the social situation stimulating the primal repression could have been changed. According to Freud, our behavior's primary instincts are not only of a sexual nature (contrary to the assertions of the enemies of Freudianism). Freud himself is not studying bio- and physio-genetic factors. He puts all the emphasis on socio-genetic factors, highlighting the study of social conditions' influence on the family environment of the child and thus on the child itself.[9] The meaning given by Freudian school analysts to the manifestation of dependency or protest can be seen for example in the book of Jung (at that time purely Freudian): *The Significance of the Father in the Destiny of the Individual* [*Über die Bedeutung des Vaters für das Schicksal des Kindes* – Jung, 1961/1909, 1949]. If Jung speaks in this case about the importance of individual experience, in other cases, he and other analysts explain maladjustment at work, asocial or antisocial behavior, etc. through the influence of father or mother (dependence or protest). Freudians explain neurotic dependency on parents (with either positive or negative [*plus ili minus*]) instilled through faulty education, exacerbating the child's original feeling of helplessness (a "protective reflex"[10]), an education that also perverts the normal feeling of attachment to parents. And in pathological protest, Freudians perceive the result of an incorrect education that does not allow the child to identify his personality in the form of a fight or protest concerning father's or mother's initial authority, as is natural for each child. In this and in the other cases, Freudians speak of pathological "fixations."

What is interesting in Dr. Skalkovskiy's report is the attempt to link the child's dependency and protest phenomena to certain forms of his/her development. Indeed, theorists know well the initial phase of dependence in the very young child, who relies on the powerful "instinct of imitation." Imitation, at first automatic, advances the ideal we would like to emulate.[11] On the other hand, as the personality of a child develops, a protest well known to all of us also develops. At the beginning, it appears as a general negativity, then the child's assertiveness requires a critical reversal of the initially unlimited parental authority. It needs to be noted that the way Skalkovskiy develops these phases is not always correct: dependency and protest do not proceed in a straightforward manner, but intermittently – furthermore, in adolescence, which also represents the period of sexual maturation where it appears again as a strong fight for self-assertion, by challenging[12] the initial parental authority. Teachers know well how difficult the child of this age can be. Peer influence emerges, to replace parental authority. It is only in the post-adolescence years that a normal person appears to attain an approximate balance between attention to the parents' critical judgment on the one hand, and the development of thoughtful social and philosophical/scientific judgment on the other. For a Freudian analyst it is quite acceptable to make an argument that education and the environment can either stimulate the correct development of what Dr. Skalkovskiy calls homofunction [healthy psychic balance[13]], or curb this development by creating "stagnation" or "regression" at a more primitive stage of development (according to Freudian terminology). Asking whether homofunction determines drives, or drives determine homofunction, is the wrong question, because one influences the other, and it all depends on the point of view from which we would observe this phenomenon: in mathematical language this means that formula "b" can be expressed by means of "a" and formula "a" can be expressed by means of "b."

Of course, homofunction is not the only manifestation of personality. For example, the psychoanalyst Piaget, Professor of Pedology[14] of Neuchâtel, followed the development of a "reality plan" based on age. The reality plan in adults and children is obviously not the same: here we see again the influence of bio-, physio-, and sociogenic factors on stagnation or regression to more primitive stages of development. Similarly we could explain all the phenomena in question from the "reality plan" point of view. This would be as restrictive as trying to explain everything by Adler's "masculine protest" or Skalkovskiy's "homofunction." In particular, it is the compromise (Freud), or interaction between our personality's different sides and our basic drives, that results in directing our actions. Most of our instincts, as well as other expressions of our personality ("homofunction," "reality plan," etc.) are governed directly or indirectly by bio-, physio-, and sociogenic factors. The main subjects of study for a psychoanalyst are the sociogenic ones.

Outpatient therapeutic practice (on the basis of Freud's teaching and my personal experience)

Freud's demand to treat patients, if possible, without modifying the conditions that caused the disease until the end of analysis, is fully achievable in outpatient practice.

1. During the treatment of the so-called "transference neurosis" of adults, as indicated, we reach a therapeutic outcome only by uncovering the repressed. A combination therapy[15] in this case is only indicated if the

analyst is inexperienced or there is a lack of time. The fuller the analysis, the stronger the treatment outcome.

2. In case of psychasthenia,[16] we combine psychoanalysis with Ferenczi's "active therapy."[17]
3. We cannot yet talk about concrete results with narcissistic neuroses[18] (exceptions include only mild neurotics of the narcissistic type). Classical psychoanalysis may even be dangerous, especially if we are dealing with symptoms of obsessionality or psychasthenia as defense mechanisms.
4. In psychoanalysis with children, special techniques must be used that we cannot discuss here for lack of time.
5. It would be desirable to devote to each adult patient a daily academic hour[19] for a few months. For us this is possible only in exceptional cases. For this reason we must restrict ourselves to psychoanalysis that I call "abortive." This releases some groups of repressed representations appearing to be the "material most pressing" for the patient at that time. The rest should be completed by developing one's will. Such an analysis lasts an average of six weeks, a half-hour session three times a week for two months.[20] During "abortive" psychoanalyses, the definition of what material is important must be done by the doctor due to lack of time; then, of course, the analyst's subjectivity is not excluded, which will be an even greater [impediment] if the doctor is inexperienced. That is why during abortive psychoanalysis it is imperative not only that the doctor knows the new psychoanalytic techniques, but also has enough psychoanalytic experience.[21]
6. In my opinion, for a working day of 5 hours, 3 hours should be devoted to therapeutic treatment and 2 hours to consultation. For 3 therapeutic hours, the doctor-analyst can receive an average of 7 people, counting ¾ hour for one patient and ½ hour for the others, with a few minutes' break between patients. The amount of patients the analyst can receive this way is approximately 15 people in 6 weeks. If we add to this 4 daily assessments/consultations, then our clinic can receive about 100 people per month. One must add that psychoanalysis exhausts the doctor like no other kind of psychotherapy. Experienced physician-analysts say it is not unusual for them to fall asleep during sessions. Thus, the physician-psychoanalyst needs prolonged rest, perhaps more than teachers, who enjoy two-and-a-half months of summer vacation.

Taking all this into account, we come to the conclusion that psychoanalysis, even if it is an expensive therapy, nevertheless saves more of a patient's subsequent costs for treatment, because during this therapy, even in abortive psychoanalysis, recurrences are rarer than in other types of therapies. In addition, we save the costs of keeping patients in sanatoriums, hospitals, hydrotherapy, electrification, etc.[22] It pays to think about all this.

Notes

1 Translator note: In Spielrein's collected works in Russian, this article is listed as 1929a, even though no 1929b appears in the table of contents (Spielrein, 2008/1929, p. 352). – FBK
2 Translator note: This heading appears in the Russian edition of Spielrein's collected works.
3 Translator note: G.A. Skalkovskiy was a psychoanalytically oriented psychiatrist and a convinced Marxist. He co-authored Drosneß & Skalikowskij, 1925 – reviewed by Lowtzky in the *Zeitschrift* – Lowtzky, 1928. Cf., Richebächer, 2008, pp. 274–275. – PC-W
4 Translator note: The editors' preface that appears in the Russian edition of Spielrein's collected works ends here. – FBK
5 Skalkovskiy, G.A., Theory of homofunction and the methodology of homofunctional re-education of a person // Works of the 1st conference of psychiatrists and neuropathologists of the North Caucasus Region. – Questions of social psychoneurology. – Edition 1/Published by North Caucasus Department of Health and North Caucasus Association of the Research Institutes). – Rostov-on-Don. – pp. 88–92.
6 According to the modern terminology: transference neurosis.
7 Translator note: Hermine Hug-Hellmuth (1871–1924), a teacher in Vienna, is often cited as the first to treat children with talk and play. Like Spielrein, she did not believe that conscious insight was necessary for healing (see Chapters 3 and 4 above). – FBK
8 Translator note: Here, Spielrein is aligning herself with Anna Freud's more psycho-educational approach to working with children (e.g., A. Freud, 1945), contra Klein. – PC-W
9 Translator note: This would appear to be overstating Freud's view of social, environmental influences on development (to be found more readily in Alfred Adler and later works of Otto Rank), but likely reflects the appropriation of Freudian theory within her Russian Marxist context. – PC-W
10 Translator note: Spielrein is likely alluding here to Pavlov's theory of reflexes, well-known in Russia (see Timeline in this volume). – ST
11 Translator note: Lit. "to which we would like to be matched." – AS
12 Translator note: Lit. "breaking." – AS
13 Translator note: The term "homofunction" appears to have been a term used by Dr. Skalkovskiy (Drosneß & Skalikowskij, 1925), with no clear correlates in Russian or English. In this context, "homofunction" may be comparable to the term "homeostasis," which was introduced by American physiologist Walter Cannon in the late 1920s to denote the necessary state of internal equilibrium in a healthy body. A similar idea, with respect to psychological balance, is apparently intended here. – EG, FBK
14 Translator note: "Pedology" – the study of children's behavior and development – was prominent in the Soviet Union during this period. – EG

15 Translator note: What exactly Spielrein means here is unclear – it could be medication plus talk therapy, or advice plus analysis; basically, when one combines analysis with anything else. – EG
16 Translator note: "Psychasthenia" referred to a psychological disorder characterized by phobias, obsessions, compulsions, or excessive anxiety. The term is no longer in psychiatric diagnostic use, although it still forms one of the ten clinical subscales of the popular self-report personality inventories (Minnesota Multiphasic Personality Inventory [MMPI] and MMPI-2). – EG
17 Translator note: Active therapy as practiced by Hungarian analyst Sándor Ferenczi (1873–1933) included role-play, psychodrama, and a more active role for the therapist, as later developed by "interpersonal" and now some relational psychoanalysts. – FBK, PC-W
18 In modern usage: narcissistic neurosis.
19 Translator note: In Russia, this meant 45 minutes. – AS
20 Translator note: This method anticipates much later methods of brief psychodynamic therapy. The term "abortive," however, suggests that Spielrein did not consider this optimal. It should be noted that analysis in this period, even with Freud, did not always last for many months or years. – PC-W
21 Translator note: Spielrein would have been familiar with the "Eitingon model" for the training of analysts inaugurated in Berlin in 1920 that required analysts in training to be analyzed, still considered best practice in psychoanalytic training institutes today. – FBK
22 Translator note: Spielrein is not referring to what we now know as ECT – electroconvulsive therapy – since this treatment was not in use in 1929, but an earlier form of electrical stimulation, already eliminated at the Burghölzli hospital in Zürich (Launer, 2015, p. 26), and which Freud (1955/1919) also opposed as inhumane. Spielrein herself was subjected to these treatments and depicted them in drawings as "electrocute" and "hell/the devil" during her own treatment at the Burghölzli (Wharton, 2015, pp. 59, 65). – FBK, PC-W

References

Drosneß, L.M. & Skalikowskij, G.A. (1925). *Grundlagen des durch das Milieu bedingten individuellen und kollektiven Entwicklungsprozesses. (Lehre von der Homofunktion)* [*Fundamentals of the individual and collective developmental process caused by the environment. (Doctrine of the homofunction)*]. Odessa: [n.p.].

Freud, A. (1945). Indications for child analysis. *The Psychoanalytic Study of the Child*, 1, 127–149.

Freud, S. (1955). Memorandum on the electrical treatment of war neuroses. In J. Strachey, (Ed.), *The standard edition of the complete psychological works of Sigmund Freud*, Vol. 17, 211–215. London: Hogarth. (Orig. publ. 1919.)

Jung, C.G. (1961). The significance of the father in the destiny of the individual. R.F.C. Hull (Trans.). G.A. Adler & R.F.C. Hull (Eds.), In *The collected works of C. G. Jung*, Vol. 4 (pp. 301–323). Bollingen Series XX. Princeton, NJ: Princeton University Press. (Orig. publ. 1909, rev. ed. 1949.)

Launer, J. (2015). *Sex versus survival: The life and ideas of Sabina Spielrein*. New York: Overlook Duckworth.

Lowtzky, [?]. (1928). Review of Drosneß, L.M. & Skalikowskij, G.A. (1925), *Grundlagen des durch das Milieu bedingten individuellen und kollektiven Entwicklungsprozesses. (Lehre von der Homofunktion)* [*Fundamentals of environmentally caused individual and collective developmental processes. (Doctrine of the homofunction)*]. Odessa. Internationale Zeitschrift für Psychoanalyse, 14(1), 114–115.

Richebächer, S. (2008). *Sabina Spielrein: Eine fast grausame Liebe zur Wissenschaft. Biographie*. [*Sabina Spielrein: An almost cruel love for science. Biography*.] Munich: Btb.

Spielrein, S. (2008). Doklad doktora Skalkovskogo [Dr. Skalkovskiy's report]. In S.F. Sirotkin & E.C. Morozova (Eds.), *Psychoanalytischeskie trudi* [*Psychoanalytic works*] (pp. 352–358). Izhevsk, Russia: ERGO. (Orig. publ. 1929.)

Wharton, B. (Trans.) (2015). Burghölzli hospital records of Sabina Spielrein. In C. Covington & B. Wharton (Eds.). *Sabina Spielrein: Forgotten pioneer of psychoanalysis* (pp. 57–82). New York: Routledge.

Chapter 16

Children's Drawings with Eyes Open and Closed

Sabina Spielrein

1928/1931 Translated by Judith Gresh and Pamela Cooper-White[1] Lecture to the Pedagogical Society at North Caucasus University, Rostov-on-Don, Russia, Winter 1928

Dedicated to my father

Research on subliminal kinesthetic representations

Before we begin to study the influence of kinesthetic experiences [*Erfahrungen*] on the structure of our thinking, I would like to give a short overview of prior observations on the forms of thinking up to this moment. At the same time, I want to use terminology used in psychology, although it is not exhaustive. But, in my opinion, in any case it is more justified than the "reflexology" terminology of the reflexology schools founded by Pavlov and Bekhterev.

How do we think? If this question were posed to a large number of people, the majority of answers, based on their own introspection, would be, "I think in words, in the form of language." But some of them would say that most thinking occurs in visually imaged representations. Some researchers, such as Professor Visilchikov, argue that children think in images, and adults in the form of language (compare also to the "eidetic" school's Marburg studies[2]; also Freud's reasoning about the probable organically hallucinatory nature of thinking in early childhood). Differences of opinion are due to the fact that adults think at the same time in a linguistic and an imaginative way – mainly with visual–kinesthetic images.

Upon introspection, we see according to our constitution, and the conditions of the moment or language or imaged part of the thinking process.

Evidence for the simultaneous cooperation of linguistic and imagistic activities of thought is presented both in theoretical and experimental ways.[3]

(I) If we want to give a name to any object or concept, whether it is in sound-imitating or symbolic form, we associate the name with a mental representation [*Vorstellung*], which consists of sensations of motion, color, odor, and other sensations/impressions. From this, it appears that the given name is based on our sensation of movement, color, and other sensations, and prompts us toward these imagistic representations, whether they are conscious or preconscious, or even "ready for representation" ["*Vorstellungsbereitschaften*"].

(II) If we want to make our language more understandable, we present "concrete examples" as an aid, we use "imagistic comparisons," i.e., we transform the abstract verbal form of our language into imagistic language, which originated from primitive sensations and sensations of bodies and is closely associated with them, and therefore is also called "organ language."[4]

(III) We clearly find imagistic language or organ language [*Bild- oder Organsprache*][5] in our dreams. Here linguistic thinking functions completely in the background. Operating in its place, respectively, are figurative thinking, visual thinking (visual-imagistic thinking), or, more correctly, visual-imagistic kinesthetic or symbolic thought. The problem of symbolization is not fully resolved at the moment, although many researchers have tried to do it. Psychoanalysis considers visual images, prevalent in dreams, as a reappearance of the pre-linguistic stage, according to Freud – the figurative-hallucinatory, organic thinking of a small child. If this definition is understood correctly, it appears irrefutable. Yet neither Freud nor his followers define our dream-thinking as little children's way of thinking. On the contrary, our dream-thinking progresses beyond the period of early childhood, as we bring into use all the complex experiences of all the domains of our mature consciousness. This is irrefutable. Freud simply believes that in adults' dreams, elements of preconscious thought from early childhood are ordered with elements of thinking from their present age. In an anatomical–physiological way, we can explain this fact on the basis of objective observation – that the function of the cerebral cortex during sleep, though not completely preserved, is, in any case, reduced. Accordingly, in a dream, earlier elements of young children's thinking ontogenetically break through into our present-age thinking. Elements of subcortical thinking correspond exactly to the thinking components of the visual-hallucinatory mode of infantile pre-linguistic thinking.

We find the same characteristic hallucinatory way of thinking in narcosis, in various psychoses, and in the so-called hypnagogic state, which was first described by the psychoanalyst Silberer.[6] In all these states, the function of the cerebral cortex partially gives up its dominance to intensified subcortical functions. However, I don't know the extent to which psychoanalysis joins with this indisputable premise that in a dream, we are dealing with a weak activity of the cerebral cortex. As we know, Freud explains the symbolization process in dreams in terms of regression and the action of the censor.[7] Unfortunately, here we cannot go into the details of this theory. Yet one thing is certain: Freud recognized the fact that in dreams we perceive emotions, desires, and the thinking mechanisms of our early childhood. Next, we would like to suggest that, in dreams, those parts of the brain are stimulated that at one time played an important role during ontogenetic development. In the end, if Freud speaks of the "organic," imagistic–hallucinatory, pre-linguistic thinking of early childhood, perhaps one cannot deny that, in this case, we are dealing with activities in terms of ontogenetics in older areas of the brain, in accordance with the activity of the subcortical region.

(IV) Hypnagogic thinking is very interesting for us, because here we can represent language in symbolic form, its transition to images – mainly to imagistic and kinesthetic language. I want to explain this with an example: a student[8] falls asleep with the following thoughts: "It makes no sense to strive for something. As soon as I draw near to my destination, there is something that makes me start all over again." Gradually drifting off to sleep, the student sees a beetle, which climbs up a grate, but as soon as it goes forward a little, a little girl touches its foot, and it falls down again. The sleeper wakes up with the words: "You climb the mountain; the devil pulls you down by the feet." The student remembers his dream and thoughts before sleeping, which focused on the hectic struggles of life.[9]

(V) We often find a simultaneous use of language and imagery-hallucinatory thinking in paranoid forms of schizophrenia, when the patient has loud hallucinations and then explains them. Such cases suggest that an initially unobservable series of images occurring synchronously with conventional thinking appear rather abruptly – I would say, autonomously – after strong disturbances.

(VI) The law of irradiation[10] moves in the direction of a synchronous, coexisting series of images as well. As we know, this law states that in the case of stimulation of a certain area of the brain, the stimulation is not localized, but extends to regions that are associated with the initially excited area of the brain. This means that if a certain area of the brain is stimulated when creating a linguistic symbol, it irradiates and causes stimulation of the activities of relevant brain areas that are in any relationship with imagistic thought. Bleuler and Freud represent creative thinking as "organic," because, finally, any imagistic representation comes from a certain feeling, but the feeling [is] associated with the stimulation of not only the centrifugal but also the centripetal part of our central and autonomic nervous system. Therefore, the action of the feeling moves to our body. Feelings affect our body, as do visual images, so they justify the name "organic thinking."

I mentioned earlier that from studying imagistic thinking [*bildlichen Denkens*] Freud himself called it "visual hallucinatory thinking" ["*gesichtshalluzinatorisches Denken*"].[11] So he and his students understand this thinking mainly as visual-imagistic thinking. This is not entirely correct. In our imagistic thinking, without a doubt we understand visual images best, because the visual sensations that are the basis of these images are most clearly objectified. For example, we always locate the sensations of heat and cold inseparably in our bodies and in our muscle sensations as well. It is no different with the sense of smell and taste. In contrast, visual sensations without a doubt appear to be located outside the body. Visual sensations intrinsically are not feelings, but impressions that we associate to the real object that generates them. We can feel movement, but the color blue or red does not call up conscious bodily sensations in us.

Kinesthetic imagery is absorbed more like all the others, by means of visual images, because visual images are most closely associated with kinesthetic ones. In the act of seeing, we distinguish between representations of light and of form. In the development of the representation of forms, along with the sense of light, kinesthetic sensations do not play the slightest role. (I deliberately do not take into account here the blind.) In relation to sighted people, I would like to explain the almost inseparable fusion of visual representations with primitive kinesthetic representations, partly using the kinesthetic nature of what we call the act of seeing. As a result of this fusion, we don't perceive the kinesthetic moment. The best way to describe the fusion of visual elements with the kinesthetic ones is by using a simple schematic line drawing. A line can be considered to be the simplest visual kinesthetic image. It is a visual image if we represent it in a steady state as a stroke; on the other hand it becomes kinesthetic for us if we represent it as a line arising from the movement of a certain duration and direction. The following hypnagogic hallucination appears as an example of a kinesthetic linear image: while falling asleep, a student in the physics and mathematics department is thinking about different things that she should do. In the hypnagogic hallucination that follows, *she believes that she is moving on the periphery of a polygon. In one of the corners of the polygon, she feels an uncomfortable stabbing feeling*[12] and wakes up. She closes her eyes again and tries to resume the previous interrupted movement on the line, but in the opposite direction. Reaching the starting point on the line, she recalls her thoughts before sleeping, what she did, and where she had to go, and every time, she mentally represented a line that, going out from her room, always led to the task with which she was occupied. Thus arose the interrupted line (unfinished polygon). The point of the polygon in which she felt the uncomfortable stabbing feeling corresponded precisely to the unpleasant task that she had to accomplish.[13] This case clearly shows that the image of the interrupted line in the student's hypnagogic hallucination was due to a representation of motion, a representation of her own motion. Thus, a purely kinesthetic representation produces a clear image, the image of an interrupted line.

Maybe in the process of formation, our dreams are kinesthetic in nature, but on waking we transform these dreams into visual–figurative form. The previous hypnagogic hallucination is, in fact, a schematic representation of actions that the student intended to commit. A schematic way of thinking is inherent to mathematicians. So we shouldn't be surprised that an image of a purely kinesthetic, schematic nature was produced by a student in the physics and mathematics department.

Also, it is easily explained that I could always perceive purely kinesthetic images in schizoid types, i.e., in those types who are known to have a tendency toward abstract thinking. In some cases, a visual-figurative form may not even be fully materialized. For example, one student at the Rousseau Institute in Geneva told me that he had a dream that awakened him with a strong sense of fear: the dream didn't consist of visual images, only of a sense of movement advancing on him. Another doctor says that he had experienced in a dream the feeling of growing in size, without perceiving an accompanying visual image. He had this dream a few times. I remember only a few cases of purely kinesthetic images of dreams. In all cases, we are talking about schizoid types.

Many psychologists who have studied the concepts of form and space, of course, have had to face the problem of kinesthetic sensations. Stanley Hall, Beaunis,[14] and others, believe kinesthetic sensations, namely, the feeling of muscles, tendons, articular surfaces [*Gelenkflächen*], to be the basis of our understanding of form and space. There is extensive literature on this. Up till now, the question of the priority of visual or kinesthetic sensations in representing form and space is still not resolved. Personally, I prefer the kinesthetic sensations, because, from the point of view of ontogenesis, they had to appear earlier. We already receive kinesthetic experience in the womb – a precursor of subsequent kinesthetic sensations. There is reason to believe that kinesthetic sensations in sighted people are due to superseding notions of form and space, because we are only using our vision based upon the distinction of light and shadow, [and] we can define the mutual relation between form and space. Despite the sensations (I have in mind here also the "readiness of sensations") that continuously accompany the movement of our eyeballs, we have some more evidence that the position and shape of the various organs and parts of the body are recognized by us even in the absence of vision. Here I am recalling Schreber's[15] notes.[16] Katz' interesting observations of a patient with a phantom body part after amputation inform us brilliantly about this.[17] It was found that the patient after surgery could absolutely, unmistakably indicate the shape and position of his phantom hand, at rest and in motion. Phantom limbs were merely indicated as elongated or shortened in size. If the patient was near to some object, he felt his phantom hand inside this object. The phantom limb was always felt in a position in which the un-amputated body part had been. This provides a new proof of the fact that we sighted people also represent shape and position in a state of rest or motion in a kinesthetic way. Kinesthetic representation of forms is distinguished by diminished accuracy in the specification of individual dimensions (lengthening or shortening in all directions), with a resulting disproportion. In addition, we acknowledge considerable independence of individual body parts in their relations of reciprocity and localization in space. This independence is distributed so that the form represented (the phantom hand) may occur in complete contradiction to the law of impenetrability inside of any object.

In my work on the problem of kinesthetic visual images in connection with the problem of symbolic thinking, I tried to determine the basic quality of these images in an experimental way. Since we, supposedly, borrowed the concept of form and motion from forms and movements of our own body, in accordance with this purpose, the shape of the human body seemed to me the most suitable. First, I conducted a survey of human figures. As a guide, I borrowed Leonardo da Vinci's words,[18] according to which the human hand while drawing always instinctively tries to represent the form and movement of one's own body. All knowledge about shape and movement, if we create them in a kinesthetic way, is produced from the shape and movement of our own body. According to this hypothesis, the reproductions from our own drawings made from memory, to some extent, should be more believable if they are executed on the basis of kinesthetic experiences without visual control.

Studies of drawings made with open and closed eyes confirm this in an amazing way.[19]

I studied about 20 adult drawings, and several hundred drawings of children aged 5 to 14 years. Most of them were children of school age from 8 to 13 years, of proletarian origin with a few exceptions. The subjects were divided by me into four groups. Each participant was separated from the other, was observed alone, and could participate in only one group. In all four groups, the subjects first drew a person in their own way. In the first group, they first drew under visual control, with open eyes. Then they were told: "Now close your eyes and try to draw the same person from memory." In the second group, they first drew with closed eyes. Then, the subject's drawing was shown to him, and he was told that he should now, without a template, with open eyes, put the man on paper as he had wanted to draw it with his eyes closed. In the third group, they drew both times with closed eyes. And finally, in the fourth group they drew once with open eyes; after that the subjects had to redraw from memory the same pattern again, with open eyes, on a new sheet of paper.

The results are very instructive, as is evident from a number of children's drawings presented here. Each experiment was followed by a short description of the child given by the teacher, by the school doctor's testimony, and finally by my personal diagnosis, on the basis of general pediatric verification.

Case 1. Twelve-year old student, son of a bookbinder. Behaves nervously, restlessly. Diagnosis: hysteria. Smart, capable boy. Exercise of the second group: draws first with closed and then with open eyes. At first the boy wanted to draw in accordance with the requirements, but could not resist and opened his eyes. Then again followed instruction to close his eyes and draw a person in his own way. So we got three pictures: one started with closed eyes, but unfinished, and then a completed reproduction of the previous figure, made from memory, and a reproduction made with open eyes (see 16.1). For the latter version, his first two works were given to the boy, and then they were hidden. Quite unexpectedly, these three figures convince us that, in any case, using predominantly kinesthetic memories, one can draw a man with closed eyes. As evidenced by Katz,[20] by observing representations of a patient with an amputated hand, this first – let's call it "blind" – reproduction from memory shows the following: in general, reproductions produced from memory preserved the outlines and some characteristic touches, even the direction of movement. Some parts of our blind drawings were lengthened, shortened, or dislocated in relation to the others. It's amazing how exactly the outline of the face of the second blind drawing matches with the shape of the first. They are not identical in length, but the angle between the forehead and the nose, the nose height, the angle of the upper lip, the entire line of the lower jaw – all this is almost completely alike in both blind drawings.

Fig. 16.1

So, we see that the blind drawing differs from an ordinary drawing, made under visual control. The difference appears only in those properties that coincide with the representations of the patient with amputated body parts. These differences on one side, and similarities on the other, prove that the characteristic elements of the blind drawings are attributable to the common elements between the blind drawings and the hallucinations of the amputated patient. Now it is clear that with blind drawings, as in hallucinations of amputated patients, we seem to be dealing with images that we obtain on the basis of kinesthetic experiences.

The third drawing of this boy, made with open eyes from memory, is hardly convincing. First, the task sounded different than at the beginning: draw a man as you thought to draw him with closed eyes. Second, it is difficult to determine which part of the picture really comes down to visual memory, and which to mechanical reconstruction based on the previous kinesthetic experience. One thing is for certain: when subjects in the fourth group first draw with open eyes, and once again they draw "exactly the same" man while seeing, we get an image that is inferior concerning the accuracy of individual forms and movements of the blind drawings made from memory. This is also confirmed by the third picture of our [first] case.

Children's Drawings   339

Fig. 16.2

Case 2. A girl, eleven years old, complains of nervous anorexia and constipation. Hysteria – constipation of hysterical origin. The child is self-centered, capricious. Mental abilities are average. Visual results based on Binet-Simon are average. The first drawing is made with open eyes, the second – with closed (see Fig. 16.2). The girl drew Line a–b independently, because initially she wanted to draw a foot there. Line d–e should mean the hand in blind reproduction. We can also see here features of the blind reproduction: traces of the individual parts of the body are very approximate, even if lengthened or shortened in different directions. Some parts are deployed in relation to each other; the skirt line is apart, the feet are included in the body (compare with phantom hands in Katz' table[21]), and so on. The leg direction relative to the lower line, the position of the head, the angle formed by the line of the head, and the line of hands d–e, all this is shown relatively correctly.

Case 3. Restless behavior during lessons. Inappropriate questions, such as: "How can you turn a ship into a living being?" Or "Man – is this a living being?" Big fighter, enjoys beating girls. Father died in war, was an accountant. Has no mother, lives with her very old grandparents. Pediatric study reveals hysterical type in puberty. Socially launched. Strongly aggressive, agile. Good mental abilities. It is noticeable that the boy's drawings are aggressive and motoric (see Fig. 16.3). This case is distinguished owing to good blind reproduction of direction, namely of the span of movement. Angles d–a–c and d'–a'–c' are identical in the blind and seeing drawings. (Later, I drew the dotted lines a–c and a'–c' myself parallel to the edge of the sheet). The position of the feet is unusually well reproduced, even the slight bend of the knee. Individual parts of the body are preserved, even some characteristic shapes, although disparities of static forms are expressed more eloquently than in previous blind reproductions. Here is movement that is retained and transmitted in the best way.

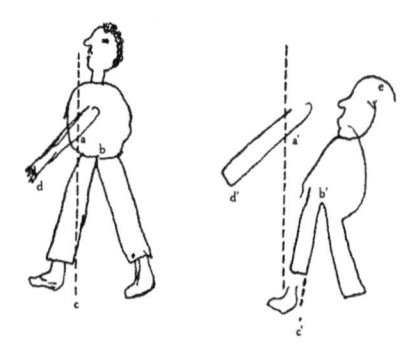

Fig. 16.3

Case 4. A girl, ten-and-a-half years. Capable. No complaints from school. Considered to be a "normal" child. But a more detailed examination reveals a lively play of affect and sensitivity, which is typical for young neurotics of the hysterical type. The father is a doctor. Unfortunately, I kept only one blind drawing from this girl (see Fig. 16.4). It offers proof here that one should not notice any significant difference between the blind drawings of so-called "normal" and markedly hysterical children. In this case, meanwhile, separate forms and general features are well transmitted. Concerning this, the ratio of individual fragments of the body is also deformed: the eyes are located outside of the head, the feet are in the upper part of the body, and so on.

Fig. 16.4

Fig. 16.5

Case 5 (Fig. 16.5). Drawn by an eight-year-old girl. Slightly neurotic, presumably hysterical, seems modest, advanced from a pedagogical perspective. A particularly interesting case: in the midst of doing the blind reproduction, the child had a moment of shyness, and suddenly sank her head deeply on her chest. As the figure shows, the child reproduced exactly this head position. Blind reproduction in this case is not particularly successful. At first glance, we have a brand new drawing, independent from the one made with eyes open, a drawing with all the characteristic qualities of a blind drawing. On closer examination, however, it seems strange that the direction of the hand movements, which are directed both toward each other as well as the bottom skirt line, coincides with the drawing made with open eyes. Even the distance between the legs is the same. Here we also have a research subject who transmits the movement and position of individual body parts better than their form. A good ability to reproduce movements perhaps gives the explanation of the fixed position of the head when making the blind drawing, or, on the contrary: a good reproduction of movement indicates a strong susceptibility of the child to the position of her own head. Through this case, my attention was especially directed toward similar events, and I have collected many such reproductions depicting the bodily position of subjects while drawing.

Case 6 shows us such an eyes-open picture from a child with a paralyzed right arm and right leg, and his blind reproduction (see Fig. 16.6). The slight tilt to the right throughout the seeing drawing is particularly pronounced in the blind reproduction.

Fig. 16.6

Case 7. The drawing of a child (see Fig. 16.7), who while drawing propped his head on his left hand.

Fig. 16.7

Case 8. An adult athlete's work. In the drawing (see Fig. 16.8), I noticed a pronounced incongruity between the right and the left sides, with an inclination to the left. Further investigation revealed: specialization – predominantly jumping. The right leg is strong. The left fibula is weaker, thinner than the right one. Same with the tibia muscle. The jump is always begun from the right side with the right leg, [whereas] 95 percent of all professional jumpers, and generally all people according to the subject, always start from the left side with the left foot. The man is skilled in shooting targets, but always starts on the right. To avoid this start from the right, when shooting, he always deliberately turns his torso to the left.[22] All the dimensions of the left hand are slightly smaller than the size of the right.

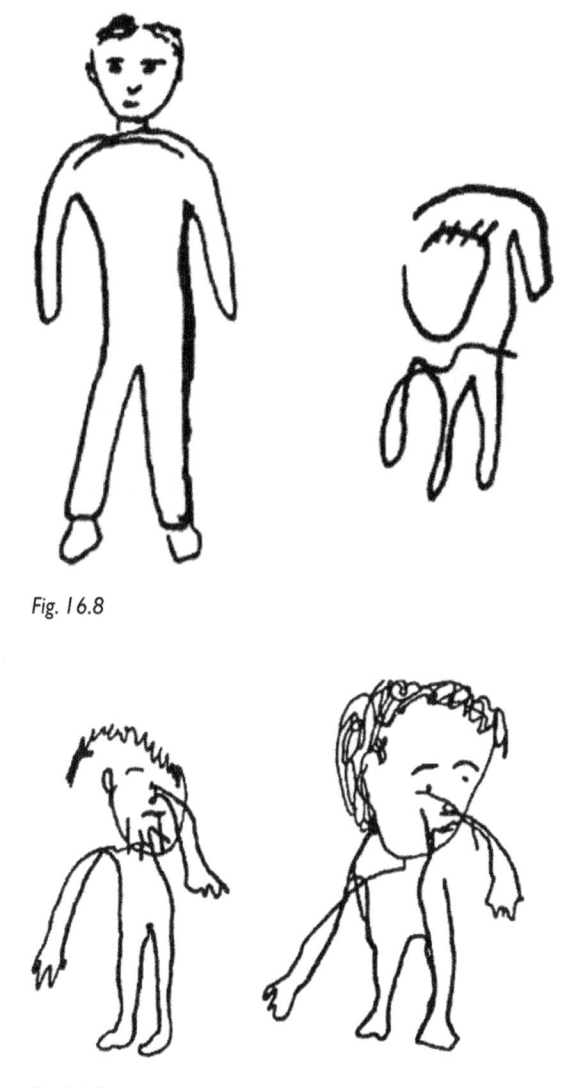

Fig. 16.8

Fig. 16.8a

I also tried – so far only with adult subjects – to intentionally give them an artificial body position while drawing, for example, strongly turning the head to the left, leaning on the left arm. Most subjects reproduce their artificially held body position in the blind condition, but in different ways: some drawings turn globally to left or to right according to the tilt of their own body, especially the head, or vice versa, some turned only one part of the drawn body in one way or another, [and] finally, some drew only the head tilted to the side of the artificially imposed position or toward the opposite side. In the latter case, the fixing of an experimentally produced body position seems to give the best result. But it is possible that the differences between reproductions are due to the different experimental conditions: one turns only his head to the left, as instructed, while the other, after positioning the head according to instructions, also moves his upper torso. Experimentally conceived movements may be followed by unforeseen counter-movements, which may explain the opposite direction of the turned head, torso, and other body parts in blind reproductions. This requires even more careful experimental treatment. In spite of those mistakes, which are inevitable in these imperfect experiments, we have therewith further evidence for the kinesthetic character of drawings, namely the blind works, in connection with the research on blind drawings in non-experimentally produced changes in posture.

As we have gained experience in the kinesthetic sensations of the body, in the absence of visual control we will unconsciously try to represent this position in kinesthetic drawings. Kinesthetic drawings must be in close relationship with the structure of our body with our constitution, and reflect its characteristic quality somehow. This allows us to wonder about the value of kinesthetic drawings for studying body structure. Unfortunately, I lost one of the most interesting drawings of a child with a dysplastic constitution, but with the help of the following two figures, I can sufficiently demonstrate related types of children.

Case 9 (Fig. 16.9). The drawing belongs to a boy of the athletic type. The constitutional diagnosis was made by Mrs. Dr. Voronova, the assistant in the psychiatric clinic of Professor Yushchenko.[23] The child's father is in the police. Noteworthy is a nearly square-shaped head in the seeing drawing, the pronounced lower jaw, the large mouth, the razor teeth drawn in bold lines, the piercing eyes, the raised arms, and the hands, fingers, and palms, as if clenched in a fist. The ears look plump too. The blind reproduction retained everything essential: thick, vigorously traced lines, a heavy form of separate parts, each of which here look even plumper, thicker, stronger than in the seeing drawing. The movement is broad and strong, [and] the direction of movement as a whole is well represented, for example, with the arms a. With the arms b the movement came out less well. Straight parts in the seeing drawing were kept straight in the blind drawing as well, i.e., head, torso, and legs. Angle H is noteworthy in both the seeing and the blind drawing. The boy wanted to represent the figure sideways, but then he changed his mind, and proceeded to draw a front view. Despite the decisions already made in the seeing drawing, in the blind drawing he returns to the original idea and makes a mixture of the front view and the side view. Next, I refer to the phenomenon of perseveration,[24] as we have discussed it earlier concerning the experiment with artificial changes in body position when drawing. The following characteristic representations serve as a contrast to the previously analyzed constitutional types.

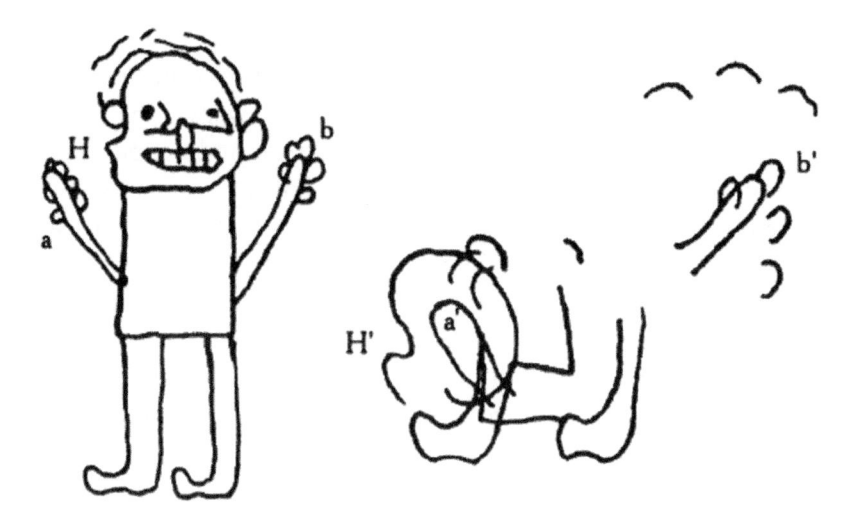

Fig. 16.9

Case 10. A drawing with stretched forms (see Fig. 16.10), soft, uncertain lines, drawn by a boy of the respiratory type. Here, too, in the blind reproduction we find sharply pronounced features, for example, a sharp right turn. At first I did not pay attention to the position of the body of the drawer, so I can only express assumptions. I cannot say for sure whether we are dealing with a slight inconsistency in the development of the right and left halves of the body, because of a curved spine, or if there a question of a simple habit of the child to sit in school, leaning in a certain direction, or finally, if the child has adopted a bent position "accidentally" in the study.

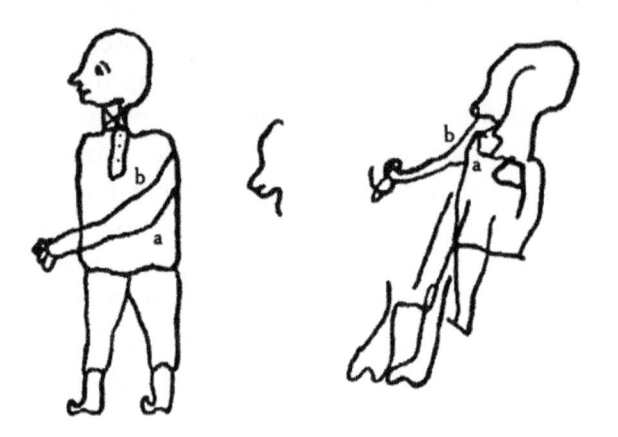

Fig. 16.10

Opposing the desire to express one's own constitution in drawing, one could mention, for example, Michelangelo's works, the weak Angelo, who created such powerful images of God and people. This should not confuse us: in considering Michelangelo's case, his own weakness is compensated by images of the Father-imago. In contrast, in our blind drawings we are dealing with "instinctive" ["*instinktiven*"] copying. It is also not impossible that one of our child subjects may produce in the seeing condition a type opposite to his own constitution. It would be interesting to observe whether in the blind condition the seeing type is maintained, or whether this type changes also according to the drawer's constitution.

The constitutional principle is not bad. What we emphasize in classification may possibly not be so important, and only later will it become clear on what principles the classification should be done. But in any case, we should use such extremely important points as representations of movement, and forms in kinesthetic images, to study the constitution.

Research on kinesthetic drawings may, under certain circumstances, be of unexpectedly great value concerning the definition of "illnesses of the personality" (following Yushchenko),[25] as well as in neuropathology. We have seen that paralysis and disproportionate development of drawers' body parts appear in their drawings. Also, body position and direction of movement, as well as the drawer's characteristics, are reflected in the blind drawing condition. In comparison with the seeing drawing condition, in the blind condition according to the force of movement, lines increase or decrease, become [more] vigorous, or vice versa, more modest, more trembling, chopped. Such differences could be used for diagnostic purposes, which I also partly tried to do. In my opinion, it would be advisable to start such a study of serious injuries in psychiatric clinics for the treatment of nervous diseases. My material from the Rostov-on-Don children's preventive outpatient clinic shows only cases with mostly minor injuries of the nervous system. I already showed that hysterical children make drawings that I still don't find significantly different from the drawings of so-called "normal" children. Schizophrenic children are less common, and therefore, for now, I did not study them in relation to kinesthetic drawings. Kinesthetic drawings of schizoids offer no possibility of making statements with certainty. Sometimes they look like drawings of a dysplastic constitution, self-control is often lacking, we observe forgetfulness, carelessness, omission, repetition, and anxiety, which we unite under the diagnosis of "emotional instability of the will" ["*Emotionale Willensunbeständigkeit*"].

This diagnosis is derived from Professor Belskiy's classification,[26] Leningrad, and is used in pediatric studies in our school outpatient clinic. Although the diagnosis leaves something to be desired, and is insufficiently differentiated, we use it for practical reasons only, among other things, to avoid possible differences in classification as much as possible. Under the name EWU ["emotional instability of the will"] we include active, easily excitable, noisy, restless children, whose will and attention tire easily. Their affects are superficial, [they] do not seem to go very deep. In these children, one enthusiasm is quickly followed by another, they are easily influenced by friends, and are led into various mischief. As a result of their will-weakness and irritability, it is easy for them to get off on the wrong path and take on all sorts of vices, such as smoking, gambling, alcoholism, lying, stealing. In addition to general hereditary influences, we also note that such children suffer the consequences of unbearable social and pedagogical neglect. Naturally, this EWU involves slow development at school. Often we see a relationship with mental retardation [*geistiger Zurückgebliebenheit*], but more often, on the contrary: EWU is attached to mental insufficiency. The children with EWU whose drawings we will now discuss are still passably tolerable in social life.

Case 11 (Fig. 16.11) shows us the work of a boy of eleven-and-a-half years, who is considered "incapable" at school. His blind drawing reproduces the individual shape and direction of motion (size of body parts) quite well, but differs from my earlier examples due to the disorder of body parts and multiple repetitions, so that the trunk follows after the head and ears, but then again the ears alone, then again the body, and lastly, arms and legs. The slight inclination of the head is sharply accentuated in the reproduction.

Fig. 16.11

Case 12. We will compare this drawing (Fig. 16.12) of a mentally retarded [*geistig zurückgebliebenen*] child, who, however, is quite normal in terms of EWU, with the previous case. Here [in Fig. 16.11] we clearly see that confusion and repetition of various body parts in the blind drawing is not a sign of mental retardation, but rather indicates excitability, confusion, anxiety, and both affective and volitional disorder of the child, loud symptoms of EWU.

Children's Drawings 349

Fig. 16.12

Case 13. We illustrate here (Fig. 16.13) the work of a mentally retarded boy suffering from EWU. He is the son of a Jewish tailor, ten-and-a-half years, with an infantile affective life, [who] lies, all the time trying to wriggle out of the noose, unreliable, noisy, likes to "argue" ["*zerworfen*"], in constant motion. The seeing drawing allows us to speak only about immaturity. But the blind drawing attests to mental retardation – a clumsy mixture of lines, resembling a bunch of twigs, generally lacking any form. Besides this, we already know that a child's character with EWU is characterized by disorder, repeated omission of individual body parts, which also points to forgetfulness: eyes outside of the head, the nose, and a little bit of the outline of the head, then eyes again, the nose and an indefinite hook form, then the torso with a not badly reproduced leg for a blind drawing; the second leg is forgotten. Finally come the arms (hands). It is striking that in both the seeing drawing and in the blind reproduction, one hand has three fingers while the other has all five. The direction of movement of the arms is depicted quite well.

Fig. 16.13

Case 14. An eleven-year-old boy from the fourth group. Previously complaints concerning his messy work were common, but now these have become rarer. Previously, he was unsatisfactory in all subjects, but now this only happens from time to time in arithmetic. The pediatric exam shows that reflection is difficult for the boy, but he is not mentally retarded. In character, he has shown some reliability, practical intelligence, cunning, and pedantry, but also suspicion, anxiety, awkward movements. This superficial diagnosis of EWU, which we had to make on the basis of our convention, is not very accurate. But for our present purpose, much depends not only on an accurate diagnosis, but also on the correct characteristics of the child. I was unable to identify what the strange zigzag on the head means (Fig. 16.14), or respectively, close to the head. Maybe at first he intended to draw the nose and eyebrows?

The exemplary reliability of the child's character is shown by the well-preserved forms in blind reproduction, even by the approximate determination of parameters. No particular disorder, no repetitions. Some parts of the body are well interconnected. The direction of movement is also satisfactorily reproduced. Yet, already in the seeing drawing, there is some anxiety in the movements, which is amplified in the blind drawing. Also absentmindedness is present – the eyes are forgotten. The center line is adequate, but some additional lines randomly diverge from each other. Motion in the blind drawing partly goes in the opposite direction. One leg, which was lower, is raised up high; the second, separated from the trunk, is at the bottom. The right arm was lowered; here it is raised up. The restlessness on the fingers has increased substantially in the blind drawing. It gives the impression that the child has completely lost himself in the abundance of random movements.

Fig. 16.14

Case 15. An eight-and-a-half-year-old boy, son of a railway doctor who was run over by train. After his father's death, a mental illness broke out in his mother. The teacher sent me the child with a diagnosis of "suspicion of mental instability and neurosis." The study found: EMU plus hysteria. Fear at night, restlessness, confusion, inattention, easy irritability, poor endurance, no patience. Slight fatigue. Intellectual processes are mediocre. Visual results following Binet-Simon are above average. History-taking [*anamnesis*] shows that the boy likes craft, reading, drawing, expresses a desire to sew.

Fig. 16.15

The kinesthetic drawing (Fig. 16.15) shows mobility, but the movements are unclear. The head shape is soft, not massive, surrounded by trembling, uncertain lines. Despite Binet-Simon's good visual results, the boy draws transparent clothing, as little children do, and the blind version does not have any clothes at all, lines are even weaker, trembling, and uncertain forms are even more blurry. Direction of movement is not retained anywhere. The whole picture is stretched in length, one foot goes down hard, head and hand are lifted upwards. Numbers of fingers are not specified. Above the arm there is a line that can equally well represent the line of the arm or the edge of the hat.

During these preliminary reports, I decided, as I have said, not to create clear diagnostic criteria. I simply wanted to show in general how important blind drawing is for the analysis of the little personality. Through forms and movements in blind drawings, the child shows us his "rhythm of life" ["*Lebensrhythmus*"]. There is no doubt that with further studies of such drawings among various diseases of the personality ("mental illness" ["*psychische Erkrankung*"]), we will find much that will contribute to characterize this pathology. Particularly important would be the study of blind drawings where there are central disturbances of the sensory or motor areas.

Case 16 (Fig. 16.16). This drawing was made in my presence by a normal boy of two-and-a-half years with eyes open. Both parents are doctors. The uncle is a painter. For a child of two-and-a-half years, the drawing is at a higher than normal level, but still corresponds to early childhood, which, as we believe, lasts up to four years. This drawing leads us directly to the issue of blind drawings. And although we are seeing some distraction and uncertainty of lines that can be easily explained by the child's age and lack of adequate motor habituation, otherwise the general outlines are properly transferred for both the whole figure and the individual fragments of body parts as well. One can also notice a relatively small dislocation of body parts relative to each other: the trunk is pushed into the head, the lower part into the middle, the arm pointing down, eyebrows outside the head, legs separated from the body.

Fig. 16.16

This case entitles us to the following conclusion: in early childhood we would rather draw on the basis of our kinesthetic experience than on the basis of what we see. While drawing with eyes closed, the adult in most cases comes close to that stage. I say in most cases, because before school age (between four and eight years), the child puts peculiarities in visual drawings that are otherwise typical of blind drawings. Most [researchers] who have already dealt with such drawings have noticed that children often draw a human face with only one eye, the other is outside of the head, [and] body parts are separated from the body; if there is a cap, it is removed far from the head. If there is a house, we find the window not on the wall, but to the side, in the air. These facts are well known from the literature (Kerschensteiner, Levinstein, Ricci, Sölli et al.).[27] Spatial deviations among individual parts are found not only in free drawing, but also in drawing from figures or models. Bülow[28] confirms it in his research and cites Kerschensteiner: "Throughout the entire public school track, drawing from memory is not qualitatively different from drawing from a model. Only in the upper grades do boys draw correctly from models, but the girls [still] do not."

This confirms, according to Bülow, that models bring no substantial benefit to children, and the same applies to younger children to a greater extent than to students. Drawing from an original is a hardly noticeable change from drawing from memory. This does not contradict the fact that some secondary features of the model are reproduced clearly in the drawing; but of course, experience shows that children's drawings represent elements that do not appear at all in the original. Some researchers explain these phenomena by the influence of "knowledge" ["*Wissen*"]. The child knows that a person has two eyes, two ears, two arms, two legs. Now he draws what he knows, without checking if the model has all these parts. Concerning this point, I remember my three-year-old daughter holding a picture of a woman presented from the side asked: "Here the lady has one eye, and where is the other?" It also confirms that a child relies not on the model she sees, but judges according to her knowledge. Now, by "knowledge," we mean experience that has reached consciousness. If the child draws, deviating from the model, two eyes, two ears, two arms, two legs, properly represents five fingers, and so on, we rightfully speak of "knowledge" ["*Wissen*"]. It is a different matter if the child draws the eyes on the stomach, puts the hat on the ceiling instead of the head, pushes the neck into the head, and so on. Then, of course, we cannot talk about conscious experience of knowledge and have to find another explanation. On the basis of what has been said up to this point, we first go back to the influence of kinesthetic experiences. Schematization, which is inherent in these drawings, namely blind drawing and drawing in early childhood, characterizes kinesthetic drawing to a greater or lesser degree. Sölli expresses it in the following way:

> We do not have to believe, however, that a three-to-four year old does not mentally represent a person's face better than she draws it. That seems senseless. The fact is that children's drawings of people with no hair, no ears, no torso and no hands lag behind their knowledge for a long time. In my opinion, this is based on the fact that the little artist actually just symbolizes. He is not a naturalist and does not care about a complete and exact correspondence; he only makes superficial indications.[29]

Bühler[30] sees a relationship between schematization in drawings and abstract–logical thinking, which functions not by concrete representations but by conceptual schemes. He proposes: "If the development of concrete thinking in otherwise mentally healthy people stops in some way, or for any reason, this must be reflected in the drawings of persons who are disabled in this respect."

In idiots [*Idioten*], whom we think of here first, we cannot anticipate nor deny any confirmation of the above, because they are recognized as incapable of drawing, and in general, everything that relates to the imagination. What is the case with deaf–mutes before they get any ability to speak or any substitute? We can also ask, conversely: "Do children with a marked talent for abstract, mathematical or philosophical thinking at an early age show any special penchant for schematic or symbolic thinking?" Following appropriate questioning, I think I have some basis for an affirmative answer to this question.[31]

At the time, I was engaged in similar issues, namely:

First: Doesn't a particularly strongly expressed schematization in drawing indicate a tendency to abstract logical thinking, and vice versa, especially if the child has already passed the age of schematization?

Second: Won't an inclination toward clear schematic drawings become noticeable in a child with abstract–logical thinking?

To answer the second question, I hope to be able to collect a sufficient amount of material in a short time. So far, I recall my statement about the student in the physics and mathematics department, who expressed clear hallucinations of a schematic–kinesthetic nature. Further, I have reported purely kinesthetic hallucinations that I observed in schizoid people, i.e., in people who are particularly prone to abstract logical thinking.

As for my first question, I refer to my research results, namely, that both mentally retarded children, and also children with abstract logical thinking, offer us drawings that, in terms of schematization, no longer correspond to the ages of these children. This seemingly paradoxical similarity has its validity. What do we mean by schematization? This is a process in which we represent the general situation of a phenomenon in its main outlines, i.e., we notice only the essentials in it, while all the rest we put aside. In accordance with this, schematization must go hand in hand with abstract–logical thinking. But the small child also thinks, even if not logically, still comprehensively; he first grasps a thing as a whole, and only gradually gets used to breaking down the whole into its component parts. We know, for example, that a child's first words are of a general nature. Different teaching methods, such as the Decroly reading lessons,[32] are based on this, in which we begin with whole sentences, and gradually move on to details. No wonder, then, that children's drawings during their early development also tend toward schematization.

But how can we reconcile the general schematic nature of a child's thinking with children's well-known concreteness of representation? One does not exclude the other. The most concrete representations that are most intimately associated with organic, subjective feelings are also the ones that lie at the foundation of our abstract–logical thinking. These are kinesthetic ideas. Since we are dealing with drawings, we will talk about the relationship of kinesthetic experiences to visual experiences. However, it is difficult to say how much we should attribute to the kinesthetic representations, and how much to the visual. Yet, one thing is certain: the visible elements of a drawing take away its abstract qualities. That means that all of what is drawn, to a certain extent, reflects concrete reality. Even a drawn line has its width, thickness, color, has attributes of an objectively existing real object. Likewise, a drawn picture at any level of schematization will evoke objects that remind us of something specific that actually exists. Only this line or that picture that we imagine in a kinesthetic way, i.e., in a form of movement, duration, direction, in other words, in the form of a line, as we draw it from a mathematical perspective without any subjective factors, remains purely abstract. Thus, abstraction separated from the subjective will exists precisely in the area of the most subjective kinesthetic elements. Abstraction may be more or less complete in our thinking – the most complete abstraction is the mathematical one. Not all areas of our thinking are suitable for abstraction. Therefore abstraction is subjectivized somewhere in the depth of consciousness, such as in the formation of a hypnagogic hallucination, or in infantile thought. Now it is clear to us that global or schematic thinking, despite similarities, still need not be the same as abstract thinking. A small child who thinks globally or schematically is still quite subjective and concrete in his consciousness [*Bewusstsein*].

As already mentioned, any abstract series in our thinking corresponds simultaneously to a free-flowing imagistic–kinesthetic series. This means that the abstractly conceived line is no longer abstract, nor does it remain a purely kinesthetic line, but becomes imagistic–kinesthetic. Imagistic representations, as it has already been emphasized more than once, will dominate when combined with kinesthetic representations. Thus, in the case of adults who think in an abstract–logical way, we get concrete visual representations along with abstract, "mathematical" representations. So we also get here, for example, instead of a mathematical–geometric representation of a line, a stroke; instead of a schematically conceived grouping of lines, we will have before us a visible, schematic picture of this relationship. It follows then, that the most abstract mathematical thinking should also yield visible schematic pictures. Now, it is very likely that individuals who feature a large number of such schematic pictures will express a disposition to schematization in drawing as well. The seemingly paradoxical coincidence between the penchant toward schematic drawings both in the mentally retarded and in people who are very good at abstract–logical thinking, now seems quite natural to us. As mentioned many times, the schematic drawings of mentally retarded children differ first in the feebleness of reference lines. Then we also find in visual drawings of older mentally retarded children phenomena that we recognize as characteristic of blind drawings and drawings of young children in general, e.g., placement of individual body parts, spatial independence, and so on. And, finally, along with schematization, subjectivity, and concretization, retarded children show a simultaneous accumulation of minor unnecessary details in [their] drawings. In contrast, the schematic drawings of talented children are striking because of their clarity, certainty of lines, and absence of all unnecessary details. Talented children's drawings usually do not differ from the drawings of their peers. Blind drawings have other attributes, along with schematization, that characterize kinesthetic images.

However, I also observed a tendency to schematization in several other children, whose imaginative reproduction wasn't below normal. These children also showed good abstract–logical thinking. But by no means did all children with well-developed abstract–logical thinking show a tendency to schematization in drawing. How can this be explained? Is it just a certain kind of abstract–logical thinking that, for example, tends toward geometric constructions, mainly producing schematic drawings? Or are there other circumstances that, up to this point, have not been adequately taken into account? This should be demonstrated by further research.

Fig. 16.17

Case 17 (Fig. 16.17) illustrates for us what was said about seeing and blind drawings of a twelve-year-old boy with particularly clear logical–abstract thinking. Typical hysteria of puberty. Sexual difficulties. Self-conscious. Adequate responsiveness [*Genaue Empfänglichkeit*]. Facial reproduction, following Binet-Simon, below average. Musically talented. Tuberculosis infection.

In his time, Piaget[33] was also struck by the "global" nature of children's drawings with disparate individual parts without any bilateral correlation. Piaget called this discrepancy "juxtaposition," and explained it by the distinctiveness of children's thinking. The child, according to Piaget, sees phenomena in their entirety. Only later does he notice different details, each of which he again considers as a special whole, yet he still does not understand how they are subordinate to the whole. Earlier Freud pointed out in his "Interpretation of Dreams"[34] the phenomenon of "juxtaposition" in the hallucinatory language of dreams, without giving the phenomenon a special name. As is well known, Freud perceives these mental mechanisms of the dreamer as mechanisms of early childhood.

Without a doubt, a child's thinking has its own mechanisms, which we find both in his drawings, and in verbal language, but also in the fantasies [*Schöpfungen*] and states [*Zuständen*] of adults, which in some way have to do with early childhood thought mechanisms. It remains unresolved whether we should explain the peculiar nature of children's works, especially children's drawings, by children's special mechanisms of thought and nothing else, or on the contrary, namely: that our thinking in early childhood drew at first exclusively, and later mainly, from kinesthetic experiences – then perhaps we should explain the peculiarity of children's cognitive mechanisms by the uniqueness of kinesthetic experience. Personally, I subscribe to the second point of view. "Being determines consciousness" (Marx): in terms of ontogenetics, we owe the characteristic uniqueness of early childhood thinking to the earliest kinesthetic experiences. One could reply: but a child, who must demonstrate early childhood mechanisms of kinesthetic thinking, has long used his visual, auditory, and other experiences. Of course, the impact of mental mechanisms through visual, auditory, and other experiences in very early childhood is undeniable, but it requires much too much time to change basic ideas, concepts, and the whole mechanism of thought, which was built up on the basis of deep-rooted experiences originating long before birth. Don't we know how hard it is for adults to get rid of certain strongly entrenched conceptual categories, even if we understand logically and with all our consciousness that we must renounce the legacy of earlier experience, because it prevents us from understanding something new? The influence of prior experience is even greater for a child. In addition, we may overestimate in the child, and possibly also in the adult, the amount of visual experience to the detriment of the kinesthetic one. Perhaps in the case of a child, it is not so exclusively a question of "vision" ["*sehen*"] as we believe (it is well known that adults owe three-quarters of their knowledge to visual experiences), because even in the process of seeing, we simultaneously get kinesthetic impressions. And children's drawings, with respect to infantile drawing or tracing, finally should teach us, as well, that there is still a big difference between what we call "seeing" and the actual use of impressions. From this we derive two didactic conclusions:

(1) The child must be taught not only to see, but also to use what he sees, i.e., we must give the child real, specific imagistic experiences that he can retain and, as needed, he can reproduce correctly. This requirement has already been stated by many educators who emphasize the advantage of drawing from memory before sketching [*abzeichnen*];

(2) It remains to be desired that kinesthetic experiences should take a more prominent place in instructional methods than they did previously. The education of kinesthetic sensations has the greatest importance, not only for general physical education, gymnastics, rhythmic gymnastics, and, in part, for musical instruction, but also for training special qualities of the intellect. Wherever we first think about exercises in visual acuity, as in visual determination of distance and magnitude, in spatial orientation, or as in determining time, the cultivation of kinesthetic sensations could make some contribution. Further, I think it is very necessary, especially for the development of abstract–logical thinking, especially perhaps during geometry lessons, to try to sketch with closed eyes. For we know how difficult it is at first for a student who is accustomed to concrete, visual perception of mathematical concepts, to master abstract representations. With algebra it is initially passable. But rarely can a student represent a planimetric sketch in his head, and certainly not at all to think about solving some geometric problems. When drawing planimetric sketches with closed eyes, we fix our attention more on the kinesthetic image, and this enables us to come closer to the aforementioned full mathematical abstraction, which for its part, as we know, leads us to the corresponding visual schemata.

This establishes the missing bridge between the planimetric sketch drawn by the child, which means nothing to him, and the abstract mathematical content that should be represented by this sketch.

Drawing with closed eyes could finally be used in systematic drawing lessons.

All of what has been stated above leads to the following conclusions:

1. Our abstract–logical, mostly linguistically expressed thinking corresponds to the "imagistic–hallucinatory" or "organic" way of thinking that runs synchronously with it… We can observe fragments of this thinking in those cases where, for whatever reason, the sharpness of our conscious mental activity is diminished, as in dreams, conditions of extreme fatigue, mental illness, intoxication, and the like.
2. The characteristic imagistic–hallucinatory thinking of very early childhood, which [in early childhood] is the only kind, originates primarily in kinesthetic experience. In the process of ontogenetic development, kinesthetic experiences merge with later experiences that come from other areas of the senses, especially imagistic experiences. This close association of kinesthetic impressions with imagistic ones explains the dominant visual–kinesthetic characteristic of imagistic hallucinatory thinking.
3. Kinesthetic images have not yet received enough attention in the literature. We have only heard about imagistic–hallucinatory thinking. This is because kinesthetic figures are absorbed by the more strongly objectified facial images.
4. Upon accurate observation, however, it appears that this absorption is only an apparent one: our unconscious mind has retained many of the unique properties that originate from kinesthetic experience.
5. The characteristic features of kinesthetic images can be found by observing children's drawings; they are the same as in Katz's experiments in the case of a patient with amputated phantom limbs.[35] Similar to the patient's phantom limbs after amputation, in children's blind reproductions we see: (a) approximately conceived forms of individual body parts; (b) individual body parts lengthening or shortening in different directions; (c) partial retention of the direction of movement, or respectively, the position of individual parts, is often reproduced with surprising accuracy; (d) the general preservation of the mutual relationship among different parts. The great independence of individual parts (Piaget's "juxtaposition") can go so far that they no longer take into account the law of impenetrability.

6. The characteristic properties of older children's blind drawings are typical of younger children's seeing drawings. It turns out that (a) younger children's drawings with open eyes are more kinesthetic than visual-imagistic, and that (b) with blind drawings, we come close to the drawings of the period of early childhood.
7. Many of the characteristic properties of early childhood thinking described by different researchers, such as schematization and juxtaposition, are explained by the nature of our kinesthetic primitive experiences, namely: children's drawings are not schematic because the child's thinking is schematic, but the other way around; children's thinking is schematic because it relies more than adults' conscious thinking on kinesthetic experience, from which, as we have seen, there is a tendency to schematization, juxtaposition, and so on.
8. Kinesthetic drawing sometimes reproduces the drawer's body position extremely precisely. The right or wrong development of the size of body parts, the whole "movement rhythm" ["*Bewegungsrhythmus*"] of the individual, comes much more clearly to light in the blind than in the seeing drawing. And since the body's shape and the body's movement form a direct expression of our "constitution," the significance of kinesthetic drawings for the study of the constitution is obvious. The great advantage of the study of drawings, in this case, consists in the fixation of the individual to be studied always in one and the same form, which we are free to examine again at our leisure.
9. The kinesthetic drawings also show us defects of body structure and movement, which are caused by diseases of the central nervous system, such as cerebral palsy of childhood, encephalitis, and so on. This allows us to make assumptions concerning the possible diagnostic significance of kinesthetic drawings in relation to central nervous system diseases.
10. In kinesthetic drawings, the particularities of a child's character are reflected, including acute pathological changes in personality [*Persönlichkeit*]. Thus, we see the importance of kinesthetic drawings for studying the normal and the abnormal personality.
11. Psychotechnics [*die Psychotechnik*] is a special part of personality studies concerning professional qualifications. Along with the somatic and general psychological depictions of personality,

kinesthetic drawing could offer us the possibility of commenting on special talents.
12. Kinesthetic drawings should also be used for didactic purposes, for the development of abstract–logical thinking, such as mathematics, and especially for studying geometry. Also, during drawing lessons, the evaluation of all that was said previously should be accompanied by results that should not be underestimated. Finally, in all cases where we want to develop students' accuracy, dexterity, exact sense of proportion, and eventually also estimation of time, we would recommend special kinesthetic sensation exercises, in particular, schematic drawing with closed eyes.

Notes

1 Translator note: This translation was made from the original Russian (Spielrein, 1928) (JG), with cross-reference to the German translation by Spielrein's father, Nikolai Spielrein (Spielrein, 1931). – PC-W
2 Jaensch, E.R. On the Structure of the World of Perception (and the Foundations of Human Knowledge [*Über den Aufbau der Wahrnehmungswelt (und die Grundlangen der menschlichen Erkenntnis)*] – 2nd ed. – Leipzig, 1927; [Ders.] On Eidetics [the study of visual memory] and the Typological Method of Research [*Über Eidetick und die typologische Forschungsmethode*] // *Zeitschr[ift für Psychol[ogie]. –* 1927. – 102. – Henning: The Archetype [*Das Urbild*] // *Ztschr[ift für] Psychologie.* – 1924. – 94; [Ders] New Types of Mental Images and the Development of Mental Representations [*Neue Typen der Vorstellungsbilder und die Entwicklung des Vorstellens*] // *Ztschr. f. angew. Psych.* – 1923. – 22. – Krager: The Eidetic System of Young People in its Significance for the Clinic and School Services [*Der eidetische Anlage der Jugendlichen in ihrer Bedeutung für die Klinik und die Schulleistungen*] // *Klin. Wochenschr.* – 1925. – Nr. 47.
3 Spielrein, S. Some similarities between child's thought, aphasic thought and subconscious thought [*Quelques analogies entre la pensée de l'enfant, celle de l'aphasique et la pensée subconsciente*] // *Archives de Psychologie.* – Vol. 18, May 1923; Time in Subliminal Psychic Life [*Die Zeit im unterschwelligen Seelenleben*] // *Imago.* – 1923. – Vol. 9. [Trans. this volume, Chapter 12]; Destruction as the Cause of Becoming [*Die Destruktion als Ursache des Werdens*] // *Imago* – 1912. [Trans. this volume, Chapter 6.] Also Varendonck: On Preconscious Fantasizing Thought [*Über das vorbewußte phantasierende Denken*]. – [Leipzig:] Int. PsA. Verlag. [1922. – 171 s.]
4 Freud, S. The Interpretation of Dreams [*Traumdeutung*] (1900).
5 Freud, Interpretation of Dreams [*Traumdeutung*], Ges. Schriften, vols. 1–2.

6 Silberer, H. Report on a Method to Evoke and Observe Certain Symbolic Hallucinatory Phenomena [*Bericht über eine Methode, gewisse symbolische Halluzinationserscheinungen hervorzurufen und zu beobachten*] // J. – 1909. – Bd. I.
7 Freud, S. [1953/1900], Interpretation of Dreams.
8 Translator note: Spielrein cites this case in her next footnote (Spielrein, 1923, trans. this volume, Chapter 14), but note that the gender and identifying information have been changed in this version. – PC-W
9 E.g., Spielrein, S. Some similarities between child's thought, aphasic thought and subconscious thought. [Spielrein, 1923, trans. this volume, Chapter 14.]
10 Translator note: By "irradiation" Spielrein is not referring to nuclear radioactivity. The "law of irradiation," first expressed by Sherrington (1906), refers to the ways in which neurons (and also muscles) when activated trigger similar responses in associated neurons (or muscles). – PC-W
11 Freud [1953/1900], Interpretation of Dreams.
12 Translator note: Italics in original German text.
13 Spielrein, S. Some similarities between child's thought, aphasic thought and subconscious thought.
14 Translator note: Presumably Henri Beaunis (1830–1925), a physiologist and director of a laboratory of physiological psychology at the Sorbonne, Paris. – PC-W
15 Translator note: Also the subject of Freud's (1958/1911) famous "Schreber" case, published around the same time Spielrein joined Freud's circle in Vienna. – PC-W.
16 Schreber, D.P. Memoirs of a Nervous Illness [*Denkwürdigkeiten eines Nervenkranken*]. – Leipzig, 1903.
17 Katz, [D.]: Ztschr. f. Psychol, und Physiol, der Sinnesorgane. – Leipzing, 1920. – Bd. 85. – Heft 1–4.
18 According to Merezhkovsky, "Leonardo da Vinci." u. [Perhaps we are talking about the following situation]: "A master whose hands are gnarled and bony, readily reproduces [in drawing] people with the same gnarled, bony hands, and this is repeated for each body part – every person likes faces and bodies similar to his own face and body. That is why if the artist is ugly he also chooses ugly faces for his pictures, and vice versa. Beware, that the women and men you portrayed would not seem to be sisters and twin brothers, either by beauty or by ugliness – a drawback of many Italian artists. In painting there is no more dangerous and treacherous mistake as an imitation of one's own body. I think it is because the soul is the artist of our own body: once he created it and fashioned it in his image and likeness; and now, when again he needs to create a new body with a brush and paints, he is more likely to repeat an image in which he has already once been embodied." Merezhkovsky, D.S. Resurrected Gods (Leonardo da Vinci) (1902) // Merezhkovsky, D.S. Works in Four Volumes. – M.: Pravda, 1990 – T. 1 – p. 454. Translator note: This note does not appear in the German translation. – PC-W

19 Translator note: As Launer (2015) notes, the idea for this experimental method no doubt stems from Spielrein's earlier experiment in "The Three Questions" (trans. this volume, Chapter 13) in which she asked students to pose questions about life with eyes open and then closed (p. 229). – PC-W
20 [Katz: Ztschr. f. Psychol, und Physiol, der Sinnesorgane. – Leipzing, 1920. – Bd. 85. – Heft 1–4.]
21 [Katz: Ztschr. f. Psychol, und Physiol, der Sinnesorgane. – Leipzing, 1920. – Bd. 85. – Heft 1–4.]
22 These days I have received quite similar blind drawings from one surgeon. The colleague is also adept at shooting at targets, and also shows a tendency to the right side, which he compensates by deliberately lean to the left (see Fig. 16.8a).
23 Translator note: Alexander Ivanovich Yuschenko (1869–1936) was a Soviet psychiatrist who, in the 1920s, directed a department of psychiatry with an emphasis on biochemical research in Spielrein's hometown, Rostov (http://bigmed.info/index.php/YUSHCHENKO_Alexander_Ivanovich). – JG
24 Translator note: Cf., Spielrein (1923; trans. this volume, Chapter 14).
25 Perhaps we have in mind the work: Yushchenko, A.I., "On studies of constitutions from evolutionary-genetic point of view," *Sovremennaia Psihonevrologiya*, 1927. This note not in German trans. – PC-W
26 [Belskiy, P.G. Typology of ethically-defective minors // Education Questions of the Normal and Handicapped Child / Ed. A.C. Griboyedov. – M.; L., 1925 – pp. 82–175.]
27 Kerschensteiner, [G.] The Development of Talent in Drawing [*Die Entwicklung der zeichnerischen Begabung*] (Munich: Verlag Carl Weber, 1905). – Levinstein: Children's Drawings Before Age Fourteen [*Kinderzeichnungen bis zum vierzehnten Lebensjahr.*] 1905. – Sölli: (Angef.: The Psychology of Childhood [*Die Psychologie der Kindheit.*]) – Ricci, [C] The Art of Children [*L'arte dei bambini.*] [– Bologna: N. ZanichelliJ 1887].
28 Bülow: The Mental Development of Children [*Die geistige Entwicklung des Kindes*] (Russian translation).
29 [Perhaps it's a question of the book: Sölli, D. Essays on childhood psychology. – M., 1901.] This note not in German trans. – PC-W
30 Translator note: Karl Bühler (1879–1963) was a German psychiatrist who taught at the University of Vienna from 1922 until forced to flee after the Anschluss (annexation of Austria by the Nazis) in 1938. He specialized in the nature of human thought; his paper "*Über Gedanke*" in 1907 "was a major contribution to the Würzburg school of imageless thought; it demonstrated that the mind is capable of purely abstract thinking and does not need to use images or past observations to conceive of an idea. Bühler made his subjects think by having them read a passage from Nietzsche or by asking them questions and timing their answers, then asking them to describe the experience. He called this experimental technique the *Ausfragemethode* – 'inquiry method'" (Sampaolo et al., 2016).

This work was no doubt influential on Spielrein's formulations in the present paper. – PC-W

31 [Perhaps it's a question of the book: Bühler, K. Spiritual development of the child. – M., 1924.] This note not in German trans. – PC-W

32 Translator note: Jean-Ovide Decroly (1871–1932) was a Belgian physician who developed a child-centered method of education based on his work with developmentally disabled children, with a focus on children's "biosocial needs." His methods somewhat resemble those of his Italian contemporary, the better-known educational pioneer, Maria Montessori (1870–1952). For more detail, see Dubreucq (2001). – PC-W

33 Jean Piaget: I. Language and Thought of the Child [*Le langage et la pensée chez l'enfant*] 1924; II. Judgment and Reasoning of the Child [*Le jugement et le raisonnement chez l'enfant*]; III. The Child's Conception of the World [*La représentation du monde chez l'enfant*]; IV. The Child's Conception of Physical Causality [*La causalité physique chez l'enfant*]; A Verbal Form of Comparison in Children [*Une forme verbale de la comparaison chez l'enfant*]. // Arch[ives] de Psychologie. Vol. 18, Nr. 69–70. May–October, 1921.

34 Freud [1953/1900], The Interpretation of Dreams.

35 [Katz: Ztschr. f. Psychol, und Physiol, der Sinnesorgane. – Leipzing, 1920. – Bd. 85. – Heft 1–4.]

References

Dubreucq, F. (2001). Jean-Olvide Decroly (1871–1932). *Prospects: Quarterly Review of Comparative Education*, 23, 249–275 (Paris: UNESCO: International Bureau of Education). Online at www.ibe.unesco.org/sites/default/files/decrolye.pdf. Accessed November 6, 2018.

Freud, S. (1953). *The interpretation of dreams*. In J. Strachey (Ed.) *The standard edition of the complete psychological works of Sigmund Freud* (hereafter *SE*), Vols. 4–5 (entire). London: Hogarth. (Orig. publ. 1900.)

Freud, S. (1958). Psycho-analytic notes on an autobiographical account of a case of paranoia (Dementia paranoides) [The "Schreber" case]. *SE* 12, 1–82. (Orig. publ. 1911.)

Launer, J. (2015). *Sex versus survival: The life and ideas of Sabina Spielrein*. London: Overlook Duckworth.

Sampaolo, M., Young, G., et al. (2016). Karl Bühler: German psychiatrist. Online at www.britannica.com/biography/Karl-Buhler. Accessed November 11, 2018.

Sherrington, C.S. (1906). *The integrative action of the nervous system*. New Haven, CT: Yale University Press.

Spielrein, S. (1923). Quelques analogies entre la pensée de l'enfant, celle de l'aphasique et la pensée subconsciente. *Archives de Psychologie*, 18, 305–322. (Trans. this volume, Chapter 14.)

Spielrein, S. (1928). Детские рисунки при открытых и закрытых глазах. [*Detskie risunki pri otkrytyx i zakrytyx glazax* – Children's drawings with open and closed eyes]. Lecture to the Pedagogical Society at North Caucasus University, Rostov-on-Don, Russia, winter, 1928.

Spielrein, S. (1931). Kinderzeichnungen bei offenen und geschlossenen Augen. [Children's drawings with open and closed eyes]. N.A. Spielrein (Trans. from Russian). *Imago*, 17(3), 359–391.

Index

Note: SS in parentheses refers to Sabina Spielrein; CJ to Carl Jung.

A Dangerous Method (film) 1
Abraham, K. 95, 118
active therapy 326n2, 328n17
Adam (Genesis) 84, 86, 235–236, 239, 245
affect: and anima 67n15; inadequate 217; in schizophrenia 216; and speech 162, 173, 175, 312; and the unconscious 78
aggressive drive 75, 79, 83, 97, 100, 165–166, 228
Aksyuk, O. 125, 137
Alexander III, Tsar of Russia 140n8
alienation 168, 173, 302
amnesic aphasia 313
Andreas-Salomé, L. 113, 115
anima 41, 45, 64
animus 64
antisemitism 99, 136, 140n8
aphasia 290, 292, 313–314, 316–319
Arkadyevich, Nikolai (father SS) 113, 115, 135
Aryanism 64, 87, 101
attachment theory 41, 50, 61, 64
Ausfragemethode ('inquiry method') 364n30
Australia, aboriginal people 243
autistic stage of development 131–134, 157, 175, 270, 312, 316
autoeroticism 82, 225, 226, 227

Bair, D. 47
Bally, C. 177, 284–288
Bauer, I. ("Dora") 65
Beaunis, H. 335
Bekhterev, V. 122, 128, 140n11
Belskiy, P.G. 347

Berlin 112, 115, 118
Bettelheim, B. 98
Binswanger, L. 224
Bion, W. 159, 165, 182
bisexuality 83, 101, 228, 250n55
Bleuler, E.: advice of 114–115; on ambivalence 167; and Burghölzli hospital 40; on creative thinking 333; Jung and 50, 52; as mentor 36, 56–58; and term "schizophrenia" 43; on treatment of Spielrein 1, 45
Bolshevik Party 114, 116, 117
Breuer, J. 65
Brünhilde, myth of 60, 74, 84–86, 104n8, 237–239
Buber, S. 241
Bühler, K. 354, 364n30
Bülow, H. v. 353
Burghölzli hospital, Zürich 45; admission of Spielrein 1, 36, 38, 40; Gross and 52; Jung and 42, 47, 53; training posts 115
Bykhovsky, B. 118

Calvinism 298
Cannon, W. 327n13
Carotenuto, A., *A Secret Symmetry: Sabina Spielrein between Jung and Freud* 2–3, 54–60, 74, 85, 87, 92, 96, 98, 110–111, 136
castration 243
Catherine II, Empress of Russia 140n8
"Catholicizing" 62, 200, 201–202
censor 332
chaos theory 159, 166
Chelpanov, G.I. 141n14

children: language 302–319; research on drawing 330–362; *see also* development, childhood
Chodorow, N.J. 183
Christ, crucifixion of 84, 236
Christian imagery 82
circumcision 243
Cixous, H. 133
Claparède, E. 110, 120, 129, 161, 277n6
collective psyche 80–81, 168, 217, 219; *see also* we-psyche
collective unconscious 78–79, 82, 100
conscious thought: Bion on 182; Jung on 60; Spielrein on 60, 78, 80, 134, 167, 175, 176, 212–216, 234, 291, 301, 317–319
Conquest, R. 123
countertransference 46, 49–50, 51, 64, 66, 68n19, 68n21, 157
Covington, C. 141n22, 60, 67n10, 94, 102, 104n8, 119, 126, 286
crossing 61, 158, 174, 304, 311, 315

Darwin, C. 63, 104n7, 120
Day, M. 98
death during love *see Liebestod*
death instinct 64, 75, 79, 83–84, 89, 98–101
"death tendency" (Jung) 93–94
Decroly, J.-O. 355, 365n32
dementia praecox *see* schizophrenia
development, childhood: destruction and 100, 211; and geometry 359, 362; and homofunction 325; and imitation 324; ontogenetic 332, 360; of professionals 38, 41, 102; proximal 161, 181; and schematization 354–355; sexual 171; Spielrein and 161, 162; and temporality 290; transdisciplinary 129, 156, 159; trauma 60; *see also* language (development); pedology
developmental psychology 123, 129, 159–162, 186n7
differentiation 167, 173, 213, 216–218, 220–221, 233–234, 242
distraction 303, 352
Downing, D. 60
dream images 78, 167, 174, 232, 257, 279, 283
dreams: Rank and 230; Spielrein and 56, 131, 133, 176, 217, 222–224, 232, 238–239, 243, 257–259, 281–284, 286, 291, 331–332, 334–335; Stekel and 222; *see also* Freud, Sigmund
Drosnes, L. 116

écriture féminine 133
ego-psyche 79–81, 167–168, 173, 215, 217, 218–219
Eitingon, M. 115, 152
"Eitingon model" of training 328n21
electric stimulation 328n22
Él'vova, V. 136
embodiment 167, 172–174
"emotional instability of the will" ("EWU") 347–351
envy 170, 175, 179
Erikson, E. 39
Ermakov, I.D. 116, 123, 125
Etkind, A.: on closure of Orphanage-Laboratory 128; on Jewish students 152; on political situation 117, 124; on Russian symbolism 163–164; on Spielrein's work 122, 129, 185
Eve (Genesis) 85, 235, 237, 239, 274

Fauré, G. 277n3
fear hysteria (*hysteriya strax*) 265
Federn, E. 89, 95, 99
Federn, P. 96–97
feminism 131–134
Ferenczi, S. 154, 155, 160, 164–165, 166, 170, 171, 183, 326n2, 328n17
field theory 176, 179, 181
Flavell, J. 177
Fliess, W. 158
Flournoy, T. 177, 277n6, 289, 317, 320n23
Fonagy, P. 173
food, drive for (*Nahrungstrieb*) 79
Forel, A. 40, 45, 206n5
formalism 173
Frawley, W. 180, 181
Freud, Anna 65, 68n24, 79, 98, 124, 125, 175, 327n8
Freud, Sigmund 14–31; *Beyond the Pleasure Principle* 75, 79, 89, 97, 123, 164; on creative thinking 333; on death instinct 84, 166, 100; on dreams 167, 232–233, 289; *The Ego and the Id* 75; on Germany 136; on hallucinations 330–333; internationalization of psychoanalysis 158; *Interpretation of Dreams* 43, 75, 257, 279, 358; and Jung

1–2, 51, 74, 89, 96; "Little Hans" case 103n4; on love 66; and metapsychology 158–159; *Nachträglichkeit* 174; on neurosis 323–325; Oedipus complex 74, 75, 103n4, 132; opposition to electric stimulation 328n22; outpatient system 44; on pre-oedipal stage 41, 64, 80, 104n8, 131–133; Psychoanalytic Congresses 47; on Russia 116; on sex and death 99; *Special Type of Choice of Object Made by Men* 103n4; and Spielrein 63, 74, 87, 92–93, 95, 102, 115, 167; *Three Essays on the Theory of Sexuality* 75; *Totem and Taboo* 103n4; translations into Russian 116; "Two Principles of Mental Functioning" 75; on Vienna Society 88–89
Freudism, USSR 117–119, 127–128, 135
Fröbel, F. 67n11

Geneva 65, 112–113, 153, 156, 158, 169–177, 182
German Psychiatric Association 43
Goethe, J.W. v. 245
Gogol, N. 227–228
Graf, M. 237, 245
Great Terror, USSR *see* purges, Stalinist
Gross, O. 51–52, 54, 164
guilt 86, 170, 273–277

The Hague, International Psychoanalytical Congress 65, 130, 160
Hall, S. 335
hallucinations 134, 283, 317, 330–334, 338, 358, 360
Hampstead Child Therapy Course and Clinic (later The Anna Freud Centre) 124
Hartmann, E. v. 47
Hasidic Judaism 39
Heidegger, M. 293n17
Heller Sanatorium, Interlaken 36, 40
Holocaust (Shoah) 7, 37, 111, 112, 123
homofunction 325
Hug, R. O. 119
Hug-Hellmuth, H. 119, 130, 160, 187n10, 323
hypnagogic state 225, 283–284, 317–318, 332, 334
hypersexuality 52

hysteria: cases of 217, 265, 266, 337, 339–341, 351, 357; Spielrein diagnosis of 36, 38–39, 41, 44, 45, 61, 80, 98
hysteriya strax see fear hysteria

Ich hieß Sabina Spielrein (My Name Was Sabina Spielrein) (film) 3
image-thought *see* preconscious thought
Imago (journal) 134, 174
imitation instinct 324
incest 132, 183, 232, 254
individuation 65, 78–79, 102
International Psychoanalytical Association (IPA) 120, 157
intersubjectivity 66, 80, 170
introjection 161, 171
Irigaray, L. 133–134
irradiation, law of 333

Jackson, J.H. 177, 313–314, 318
Jahrbuch für Psychoanalytische und Psychopathologische Forschungen (journal) 37, 57, 73, 90, 93
James, W. 175, 177
Janet, P. 42
Jean-Jacques Rousseau Institute of Psychology, Geneva 65, 171
Jews 86–87, 114, 115, 136–138, 185
Jones, E. 98, 117
Journal of Analytical Psychology 3
Jung, Carl 15–33; "anima/animus" 64; and Bleuler 57–58; and Burghölzli hospital 42, 53; childhood trauma 50; and collective unconscious 78; "complexes" 42, 80; on death instinct 84, 89–90, 100; family background 40–41; and Freud 47, 52, 74, 92–93, 96; "The Freudian Theory of Hysteria" 44; graduation 42; "individuation" 65, 78; influence of 166; on libido 163, 209–210; on love 66; *Memories, Dreams, Reflections* 41; on mother imagery 82–83; popularity of lectures 47; projection 54; "Psychic Conflicts in a Child" 229–230; psychological problems 38; *Psychological Types* 67n15; "On the Psychology and Pathology of So-Called Occult Phenomena" 42; *The Red Book* 2, 66, 2, 84, 85; sexual assault as child 41, 51; *The Significance of the Father in the Destiny of the*

Individual 324; and Spielrein 1–2, 36, 40, 43–50, 52–54, 74, 90–92, 94, 102; *Symbols of Transformation* 37, 51, 74, 97; *Transformations and Symbols of the Libido* 60, 75, 76, 93; "Two Kinds of Thinking" 75
Jung, Emilie Preiswerk (mother CJ) 41
Jung, Emma (wife CJ) 1, 52–53; *see also* Rauschenbach, Emma
Jurinets, V. 128
juxtaposition 316–317, 358

Katz, D. 335, 360
Kazan psychoanalytic circle 117
Kerr, J. 1, 3, 74, 95, 97–98, 99, 105n11
Kerschensteiner, G. 353
Khatyaturyan, M. 101
Kinderheim-Laboratorium, Moscow *see* Orphanage-Laboratory
kinesthetic imagery 133–134 *see also* Spielrein, Sabina, 'Chidren's Drawings with Eyes Open and Closed'
Klein, M. 65, 80, 98, 119–120, 125, 170, 174–175
Kohler, K. 241, 244
Kornilov, K. 122
Kraepelin, E. 269
Kraus, K. 99
Kress-Rosen, N. 138, 155–156

Lacan, J. 131–132
Lampl-de Groot, J. 164
language development: drawing and 330–333; and dreams 321n27, 358; linkages and 61; Nietzsche and 220; preconscious 279, 282, 291–292; Spielrein model of 132–134, 157, 160–162, 169, 172–176; and temporality 284–286, 288; Vygotsky and 122, 157, 180; *see also* aphasia
Laocoön, myth of 182, 201–202, 204
Laplanche, J. 166
Launer, J. 2, 64, 97, 104n7, 114, 120–121, 125, 127, 134, 137, 160, 179, 186n3, 255n5, 364n17
Lenin, V. 117
Leningrad 141n12, 141n13, 347; All-Russian Congress on Psychoneurology 122
Lenormand, H.-R. 273, 274
Lerberghe, C. van 273
Leung, A. 61

Lewin, K. 179, 181
libido 74–77, 83, 93, 163, 217, 221–222, 225, 232
Liebestod (love-death) 86, 99, 237
Liebrecht, F. 244
"Little Fridays" circle, Moscow 115
"Little Hans" case (Freud) 103n4
Ljunggren, M. 125, 126, 135, 136
Loewald, H.W. 154, 165–166, 173, 174
Lothane, Z. 43, 46, 47, 48, 135
Lubinskaya, Eva (mother SS) 38–39, 48–49, 55–56, 113, 114, 127
Luria, A. 117–118, 121–124

Maar, L. 138
Maeder, A. 63
magical stage of development 131–132
Maimonides 241
Makari, G.J. 158
Márton, E. 101–102, 126
Marx, K. 358
Marxism 117–119, 120, 123
masochism 79, 100, 169, 170, 228
masturbation 61, 170, 225, 243, 258, 268
maternal erotic 170
Matte-Blanco, I. 154, 173
Maury, L.F.A. 320n23
McGuire, W. 52, 89–90, 94–96, 103n1
Mendel, G. 304
merger 167, 173
Metchnikoff, E. 99
Mills, J. 60
Mirror stage (Lacan) 132
Monakow, C. v. 314
Montessori, M. 365n32
Moscow 65, 116–119, 120, 122, 178–179, 182; First All-Union Congress on Human Behavior 134; *see also* Orphanage-Laboratory (*Kinderheim-Laboratorium*)
Moses 236, 239
mother imagery 82–83
motor aphasia 289, 313, 314, 318
motor–verbal images 317
Muller, J. 164
multiplicity 80, 173, 287
Munich 74, 90, 91, 129
mythology: Brünhilde 60, 74, 84–86, 104n8, 237–239; and incest 232; Laocoön 182, 201–202, 204; life and death in 84–89, 224, 229, 234–246; menstrual dreams 259; in

schizophrenia 204–206; Siegfried 60, 64, 74, 84–87, 101–102, 126, 183–184, 237–238; symbols 81

narcissism 119, 326
Naville, F. 314, 320n17
Nazis 4, 7, 37, 65, 101, 103, 138, 364n30
neurosis 74, 75, 82, 222, 233, 265–266, 323–325
The Nibelungenlied 84, 237, 246
Nietzsche, F. 82, 225–226, 230–231
NKVD (secret police, USSR) 123, 135
North Caucasus University, Rostov 130–131
Noth, I. 65
Nunberg, H. 89, 95, 99

Oberholzer, E. 113
object relations theory 79–80
objective psychology *see* reflexology
observation, method of 160
October Revolution, Russia 113, 116
oedipal transference 74
Oedipus complex 74, 75, 103n4, 132
Operation Barbarossa 137
orality 122, 132, 173, 174, 175
organ language 331
Orphanage-Laboratory (*Kinderheim-Laboratorium*), Moscow 116, 118, 120, 124–125, 127–128
Osipov, N. 113, 115, 116, 264–265
'otherness' 45, 167, 173, 180
outpatient therapeutic practice 325–326
Ovcharenko, V. 130, 138, 178

Pappenheim, B. ("Anna O") 65
paranoia 197, 200, 333
Pavlov, I. 128
pedology (experimental pedagogy) 121, 128
Perepel, E. 128
perseveration 315, 345
Pfister, O. 99, 222, 248n47
phallic symbolism 84
Phanes 83
phantom limbs 335, 336, 338, 360
Piaget, J.: developmental psychology 161; and influence of Spielrein 65, 122, 130, 156–158, 160, 162, 165, 177, 184; *The Language and Thought of the Child* 171; "reality plan" 325;

Spielrein on 279, 290, 316; three-stage model 180
play therapy 130
pleasure principle 75, 79, 176, 317
Pliny 244
Poland, German invasion of 137
Polish–Lithuanian Commonwealth 140n8
poststructuralism 131
post-traumatic stress 38, 43, 79
preconscious thought 171, 173, 179, 282–284, 286–289, 291, 331
projection 44, 54, 159, 161, 170, 171
pre-oedipal stage 41, 64, 80, 104n8, 131–133
psychasthenia 267, 326
"Psycho-Sistine experiments" 202–206
psychoanalysis, banning of 101, 113
Psychoanalysis and Contemporary Thought (journal) 3
Psychoanalytic Institute, Moscow 116
Psychoanalytical Society, Vienna 112
psychosis 41, 63, 98, 168–169, 269; *see also* schizophrenia
Psychotherapy (*Psychoterapiya*) (journal) 115, 268, 269
purges, Stalinist 112, 123, 135, 184

Rabbinic literature 241
Rank, O. 88–89, 153, 230
"rational eating" 79
rational psychotherapy 266–267
rational thinking 75, 100
Rauschenbach, E. 42; *see also* Jung, Emma
reactology 122, 140n11
reality principle 65, 75, 176, 317
Red Army 113, 137
reflexology (objective psychology) 119, 122, 128, 140n11, 330
regression: Ferenczi on 164; Jung on 93; Loewald on 174; Spielrein on 169, 171, 173–174, 219, 227, 228, 317, 318, 325
Reich, A. 170
Reik, T. 99
Reisner, M.A. 118
religion 81, 84, 204, 205, 222, 241; *see also* Catholicizing
"repetition compulsion" 79
representation, mental: Bally on 286; Bleuler and 209–210; Freud and 282,

289; Jung and 209–210; Nietzsche and 225; Spielrein and 80–82, 165, 171, 212, 214, 216–223, 227–228, 232–233, 235, 249n49, 281, 283–284, 286–287, 290; subliminal kinesthetic 330–359
repression: Freudian 74, 75, 209, 322–323, 325, 326; Jung 42, 77; Lacanian 132; Spielrein on 210, 254, 266, 287, 322, 323, 325, 326; traumatic 7, 61
reproduction 78, 221
"rescue motif" (*Rettertypus*) 86, 238–239
reverie 105n11, 154, 172, 176
Richebächer, S. 98–99, 114, 127, 135, 138, 142n24
Riklin, F. 63, 230, 236
Robson, L. 61
Romanticism 99
Rosenthal, T. 118
Rostov-on-Don 36, 125–131, 137; First Congress of Psychiatry and Neuropathology of North Caucasus Region 134
Russia: Civil War 117; Cultural Revolution 117; female education 136; Nazi invasion 37; political situation and science 113; psychoanalysis 115–116
Russian Psychoanalytic Society 116, 121, 128

sacrifice 74, 86–87, 88, 184, 239–245
sadomasochism 97
Saint Petersburg 118
Saloz, J. 314, 318–319
Salpêtrière hospital, Paris 42
Salzburg, First International Congress for Psychoanalysis 51–52, 57
Sapir, I. 128
schematization 354–357
schizophrenia (dementia praecox) 38, 43, 58, 60–64, 80, 197–206
Schmideberg, M. 120
Schmidt, V. 118, 124, 128
Schore, A. 172
Schreber, D.P. 167, 247n16
Schreider, N.N. 266
Seetzen, H. 137, 138
Segal, H. 173
sensory aphasia 313
sexual etiology 43, 44, 60
sexuality: and destruction 63, 78, 82, 84, 87, 97, 99, 100, 163–169; female

83, 162, 170, 184; infantile 79, 171; Spielrein and 40, 54; *see also* libido; repression, Freudian
Shakespeare, W. 231–232
shame 172
Sheftel, Pavel (husband SS) 65, 96, 112–114, 116, 125–127, 129, 135
Shekhtel, F. 116
Sherrington, C. 363n10
Siegfried, myth of 60, 64, 74, 84–87, 101–102, 126, 183–184, 237–238
Silberer, H. 212, 225, 320n23, 332, 363n6
Simeon from Sims 241
Sistine Chapel, Rome 62, 201–205
Snetkova, O. 135–136
Snetkova, Nina (stepdaughter SS) 125, 135, 137, 138, 185
socialized language 133, 312
Society for Neurology and Psychiatry 130
species-psyche 168, 217
Spielrein, Emil (brother SS) 65, 113, 114, 135
Spielrein, Eva (daughter SS) 101, 119, 127, 129, 135, 137
Spielrein, Isaak (brother SS) 65, 114, 121, 128, 135, 255n5, 290
Spielrein, Jan (Yasha) (brother SS) 39, 65, 114, 140n9
Spielrein, Nikolai (father SS) 38, 65, 135
Spielrein, Rakhil (wife of Isaak) 119
Spielrein, Renate (daughter SS): birth of 73, 85; danger to 137; ill health 112; musical career 129; observation of 160, 280; psychological difficulties of 119, 127
Spielrein, Sabina 15–31; "Aphasic and Infantile Thought" 121; Burghölzli hospital 43–45; childhood 39; "Children's Drawings with Eyes Open and Closed" 330–362; "Contributions to an Understanding of the Child's Mind" 130; depression 40, 102, 127; "Destruction as the Cause of Becoming" 60, 64, 73–88, 98–101, 162, 163–169, 180, 209–246; discovery of diary 2–3; "Dr. Skalkovskiy's Report" 322–326; dreams 56–57; family history 38–40; financial difficulties 112–113, 129; "The Forgotten Name" 256; and Freud 49, 64, 76; on her work

110; "hysteria" diagnosis 1; idealism 101–102; influence as patient 65; on Jung 55, 58–59, 76–77, 126; on love 66; marriage 96, 125–126; on Marxism 135; "Maternal Love" 254; medical studies 45–51; "The Mother-in-Law" 170; murder by Nazis 7, 65, 103; murder of brothers 135; "On the Psychological Content of a Case of Schizophrenia (Dementia Praecox)" 197–206; "The Origin and Development of Spoken Speech" 65; passion 119; personal crises 101; psychological problems 38; "Russian Literature on Psychoanalysis" 261–270; self-awareness 54–55; self-sacrifice 102; "Some Analogies between Thinking in Children, Aphasia, and the Subconscious Mind" 301–319; "Some Brief Comments on Childhood" 130; "The Problem of the Unconscious in Contemporary Psychology and Marxism" 141n20; "The Three Questions" 295–299; "Time in Subliminal Psychic Life" 279–292; "Two Menstrual Dreams" 257–259; *Über den Psychologischen Inhalt eines Falls von Schizophrenie (Dementia Praecox)* (*On the Psychological Content of a Case of Schizophrenia*) 36, 58, 60–64; in USSR 110–139; "Who Is the Guilty One?" 273–277
Spielrein, Yasha (brother SS) *see* Spielrein, Jan
Stalin, J. 65, 117, 123, 128
State Psychoanalytic Institute, Moscow 125, 127
Stekel, W. 99, 167, 222, 246n2
subconscious thought 134, 158, 175, 254, 270, 301, 317–319
subjectivity 166, 168
subliminal kinesthetic representation 330–332, 333–338, 344, 346–347
Swiss Psychoanalytic Society 112
symbolic expression 80
symbolic language 133–134, 158, 217
symbolic thought 64, 75, 336
symbolism: of birth 229–230, 235, 242; Christian 86–87; contradictory 289; of destruction 223–224; Russian 163–164; sexual 214

Tausk, V. 89, 164, 243
"temenos" 66
three-stage model of development 131–132
transference 49, 64, 66, 74, 104n8, 151, 160, 181, 223, 224
transference neurosis 322, 325
trauma: Jung and 41; sexual 60, 267; Sheftel and 127; Spielrein and 7, 38, 40, 114, 142n23; traumatic object relations 170; triggers 174; *see also* post-traumatic stress
Tree of Life 84, 86, 235–237, 239, 243, 245–246
Trotsky, L. 114, 118, 128

Übermensch 101, 228
unconscious thought: Bion and 182; collective 78, 100; Freud and 247n11, 257, 317, 322; Jung on 66, 68n15, 78–82; Spielrein on 54, 63, 64, 78–82, 141n20, 160, 162, 165–169, 171–176, 212–216, 220, 224, 229–230, 232, 234, 239, 242, 274–275, 284, 344, 360; Vygotsky and 180
Ur-mother 78, 213, 242

Valsiner, J. 122, 124, 141n16
van der Veer, R. 113, 122, 124, 141n16
Vienna 73, 74, 88–100, 101, 136
Vienna Psychoanalytic Society 73, 88–92, 95, 96–97, 152–153, 170
Vygotsky, L.S. 118–119, 121–124, 128, 156, 161–162, 165, 179–181
Vyrubov, N. A. 115, 265

Wagner, R.: anti-Semitism 99; *The Flying Dutchman* 86–87, 238–239, 245; *Götterdämmerung* 86, 237–238; *Der Ring des Nibelungen* 84; *Tristan und Isolde* 99
we-psyche 167, 168, 173; *see also* collective psyche
Weizman, C. 152
Weltschmerz see world-weariness
Wharton, B. 49, 52, 60, 175, 178
Winnicott, D.W. 41, 65, 80, 175
Wittels, F. 99
Wolff, T. 77, 104n6
world-weariness (*Weltschmerz*) 79, 213
Wulff, M. 116, 184
Wünsche, A. 229, 235–237, 245
Würzburg school of imageless thought 364n30

Yoffe, A. 267
Yuschenko, A. I. 364n23

Zürich 45, 46–47, 74, 115, 136–137
Zürich, University of 37, 42, 73
Zalkind, A.B. 128, 141n18, 265–266

Zeitschrift für Psychoanalyse
 (journal) 96
Zentralblatt für Psychoanalyse
 (journal) 115
Zinzendorf, N. v. 222, 248n27
Zionism 87